CW01466826

THE TIMES

LIVES BEHIND
THE
SILVER SCREEN

Published by Times Books

An imprint of HarperCollins Publishers
1 Robroyston Gate
Glasgow G33 1JN
www.harpercollins.co.uk

HarperCollins Publishers
39/40 Mayor Street Upper
Dublin 1, D01 C9W8
Ireland

First published 2025

ISBN 978-0-00-875296-5

10 9 8 7 6 5 4 3 2 1

The contents of this publication
are believed correct at the time of
printing. Nevertheless the Publisher
can accept no responsibility for errors
or omissions, changes in the detail
given or for any expense or loss
thereby caused.

The Publishers acknowledge that
views around language and sensitivity
in journalism are continually
changing. However the language,
style and format of the obituaries
in this book have been preserved
from when they originally appeared
in the newspaper and should be read
in that context.

A catalogue record for this book is
available from the British Library.

Typeset by Davidson Pre-Press Ltd

Printed in the UK using 100%
Renewable Electricity at CPI Group
(UK) Ltd

Our thanks and acknowledgements
go to Joanne Lovey and Robin Ashton
at News Licensing and, in particular,
at The Times, Ian Brunskill and
Georgia Heneage and, at HarperCollins,
Lauren Murray, Evangeline Sellers,
Kevin Robbins and Rachel Weaver.
With special thanks to News UK
Archives.

If you would like to comment on
any aspect of this book, please contact
us at the above address or online.
E-mail:
times.books@harpercollins.co.uk
www.timesbooks.co.uk

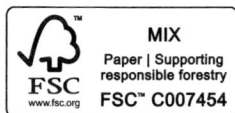

MIX
Paper | Supporting
responsible forestry
FSC
www.fsc.org   **FSC™ C007454**

This book is produced from independently certified FSC™ paper
to ensure responsible forest management.

For more information visit: www.harpercollins.co.uk/green

THE TIMES

LIVES BEHIND
THE
SILVER SCREEN

ERA-DEFINING OBITUARIES
OF ICONIC FILM STARS

EDITED BY NIGEL FARNDALE

TIMES BOOKS

CONTENTS

INTRODUCTION

INTRODUCTION

Nigel Farndale

"Physically he was the antithesis of the conventional film star, very short in build, with an ugly crumpled face (later softened by a beard) and a rasping voice which could really grate on the nerves." This is how The Times described Edward G Robinson in his obituary in 1973.

Our description of Marty Feldman in 1982 wasn't much kinder. "A bizarre appearance – huge, uncoordinated eyes, dishevelled hair and an ear-to-ear grin."

We were, however, almost poetic when it came to James Stewart, describing his "disarming loose-limbed awkwardness, the hesitation and characteristic gulp in his talk, and the persistent air of slightly hurt bemusement."

Our descriptions of actresses (which is still the term preferred by The Times, not "actors") were as casually sexist as you would expect, with much sniggering mention of "assets". During the Korean War, we note in our obituary for Jane Russell, GIs christened a prominent and much fought-over landmark after her. It was of course two pointy hills. Vivien Leigh, according to her Times obituary in 1967, started out "as a girl with nothing to commend her but beauty."

When Betty Grable died in 1973, she was given a single-column obituary which noted her legs were once insured for $1 million. In the adjoining column was an obituary of Dr Abdul Rahman al-Bazzaz, a former Iraqi prime minister. Only one of the two obituary subjects that day got an accompanying photo.

In Elizabeth Taylor's obituary, meanwhile, there are three separate references to her weight, which to a modern sensibility seems rather gratuitous and harsh. To what extent did those views, prevalent at the time, directly affect her career and influence the roles she was offered? Makes you think.

Aside from being ruder about people's appearances than perhaps we would be today, these early obituaries of film stars were also shorter and rather more listy, with no film being too obscure to mention. Today's obits, as you will see from the more recent examples also collected here, tend to be longer, more selective when it comes to filmography and more rounded (or perhaps less euphemistic) when it comes to rackety personal lives. They aspire to examine in depth the real, sometimes flawed person behind the fame mask.

One thing that hasn't changed is that The Times has always tried to give the cause of death, and you notice reading through this collection that a lot of Hollywood film stars died in their 50s from smoking-related cancer.

Sometimes the cause isn't known or hasn't been disclosed. Gene Hackman, for example, died in quite strange circumstances, along with his wife, in 2025. His is a good example of the more modern style, rich in telling detail. Visitors to his home noted the total absence of movie memorabilia. When asked where his Oscar statuettes were, he said he didn't even know. And when he was learning his trade at the Pasadena Playhouse's school of acting, we noted, he was voted one of the two students "least likely" to succeed. He was in good company, for the other would-be thespian given the thumbs down was his lifelong friend Dustin Hoffman.

Errol Flynn's obit, by contrast, is a little frustrating to read. Written in 1959, it is not only quite short, but it simply does not do justice to this most colourful of Hollywood lives. It barely mentions that he was a swordsman off screen and on – hence the expression "in like Flynn". If it was written today, it would include the fact that 1) he had two-way mirrors in his Hollywood mansion to spy on women, something that was reported on when he was still alive, and 2) it was said, not least by him, that he had the largest penis in Hollywood, ergo the quip "Got a match?" "Not since Errol Flynn died." He liked to greet poolside guests wrapped only in a towel and he would then amuse himself by letting it slip, enjoying the reactions of astonishment.

You know those conversations you have when trying to decide the placement for a dinner party? "We can't put Helen next to Phil because she had that affair with Tony who also had a fling with Phil's ex." Well, that's what it was like trying to decide where to put Flynn in the running order for this book. He had flings with everyone and probably broke up quite a few marriages too.

Reading these obits, you realise that Hollywood is a rather small place, where everyone seems to have been married to, or had affairs with, everyone else. The married Spencer Tracey, to give one example, had a not very secret affair with the divorced Katherine Hepburn. And it lasted 26 years.

Among the many women who Jerry Lewis bedded, meanwhile, was Marilyn Monroe. He claimed to have been "crippled for a month" after the experience, which may, according to his Times obit, explain why he turned down an invitation to appear with her in *Some Like It Hot.* The part went to Jack Lemmon, who earned an Oscar nomination and sent Lewis boxes of chocolates every year to thank him.

Monroe herself was no slouch on the promiscuity front, of course, although she was not nearly as prolific as our very own Barbara Windsor.

Sean Connery put it about a bit too, according to his Times obituary from 2020. He lost his virginity in an air raid shelter to a woman in the Auxiliary Territorial Service when he was 14 and never looked back. But in a strong field, Burt Reynolds was probably the most sexually swashbuckling of the "second golden age", giving even Errol Flynn a run for his money.

As you dip in and out of this collection you may feel dizzy trying to keep up with all the "power couple" marriages: Rita Heyworth and Orson Welles, Lauren Bacall and Humphrey Bogart and so on. In the case of Elizabeth Taylor and Richard Burton, they married each other twice.

Given this context it seems surprising when you come across occasional examples of long and happy Hollywood marriages. Sir Alec Guinness was married for 62 years, for example. Charlton Heston 64 years. While Lord (Richard) Attenborough clocked up an impressive 69 years. And James Stewart carried his home-town image into his private life: his long years in the ranks of Hollywood's most eligible bachelors produced no breath of scandal. He was already 41 when he married, in 1949, Gloria McLean, and she came with a ready-made family of two sons.

Tempting as it has been to expand and finesse some of the older obits here – in one, I note, we refer to "the cinemagoer" as "he" – I've kept them more or less as they first appeared, first drafts of history and all that. This makes them more intriguing, in some ways. Bogart's hardly mentions *Casablanca*, for example, because it wasn't considered a classic film at the time he died in 1957, merely a bit of competent wartime propaganda.

Regarding the war, it was a source of great embarrassment to John Wayne, who often played war heroes, that he never enlisted in real life. Many film stars in this collection did though, heroically in the cases of Brigadier-General James Stewart DFC and Major Clark Gable, who both flew in bombers. Lt-Colonel David Niven had a good war too, as did Paul Newman who distinguished himself in torpedo squadrons in the Pacific and took part in the battle for Okinawa.

I hadn't appreciated until reading his obit how political Newman had been, active Democrat that he was. But there were plenty on the right in Hollywood too, notably John Wayne, Charlton Heston, and dear old Jimmy Stewart, whom I seem to keep mentioning. Of the British, Attenborough was a committed lefty while Babs Windsor was a Thatcher supporting rightie.

Apart from being a nostalgic and, for me, slightly indulgent exercise, reminding myself about some of the film stars I was lucky enough to interview over the years – among them Gina Lollobrigida, Charlton Heston, Kirk Douglas, Dickie Attenborough and Glenda Jackson – part of the fun of compiling these obits is that I found myself making lists of all the old black and white films I wanted to see, or see again.

I also quite enjoyed, and I hope you will too, finding much to disagree with. One of my favourite films is *Butch Cassidy and the Sundance Kid* – which The Times obituarist dismissed as a "stylishly genial romp" – and I think my favourite actor of all time is one of its stars, Paul Newman, of whom we wrote: "It was sometimes said of him, even by those who purported to admire him, that his good looks carried him effortlessly through his screen career, without any tangible application of talent. 'Handsome', and therefore 'limited', were the epithets often waspishly applied to diminish his achievement when measuring it against that of other 'serious' actors."

Reading some of the older obits you get the sense that the snobby old Times obituarists who wrote them considered film a rather vulgar art form compared to the theatre. Of Joan Crawford our writer sniffed: "Her most devoted admirers would never have claimed that she was an actress of great range or adaptability." Of Tony Curtis: "He moved from enjoyable hokum, via adventure spectaculars to classic light comedy, with more than the odd flabby costume drama failure in between." And of John Wayne "when cast within his limitations (and he had the shrewdness seldom to overstep them) he could always be relied on to give an authoritative performance."

Some film stars gave as good as they got, though. According to his obit, Robert Mitchum affected to hold a low opinion of his craft, and he once declared that he had only two acting styles – "with and without a horse". Carrie Fisher was even wittier. Asked to lose weight in preparation to wear Princess Leia's famous gold bikini for the *Star Wars* sequel she quipped: "They want to hire about three-fourths of me, so I have to get rid of the fourth. The fourth can't be with me."

There wasn't room to include everyone, of course, and I'm sorry if some of your favourite film stars are missing. I'm sorry too if you feel this collection doesn't exactly hit diversity targets. All I can say is tant pis. The selection of obituaries, as much as the obituaries themselves, convey the attitudes of their time. Where race is explicitly mentioned in the earlier examples, it is done through the lens of a society with views that might be considered offensive today.

This aside, as ever with obits it's the quirky details that fascinate. Carrie Fisher once woke up next to the dead body of a Republican lobbyist. Dennis Hopper was a big *Doctor Who* fan and lobbied his Hollywood agent to be cast in it. Doris Day, we learn, turned down the role of Mrs Robinson in *The Graduate* (1967). And Oliver Reed was once spotted drunk and trouserless on the streets of Toronto. On another occasion, apparently drunk while recording a television programme, he foolishly aimed a punch at the boxer Henry Cooper, connecting instead with the actress Wendy Richard.

My favourite detail, though, is this: Joan Crawford's date of birth was such a secret that her Times obituary stated with splendid vagueness that "When she died of a heart attack on May 10, 1977, she was thought to have been between the ages of 69 and 76".

LIVES BEHIND
THE SILVER SCREEN

SEAN CONNERY

———————— • ————————

Sean Connery was nobody's first choice to play the lead in the inaugural James Bond film, *Dr No*. Cary Grant, Rex Harrison and David Niven declined the part. Other big-name actors including Roger Moore, Michael Redgrave, Patrick McGoohan and Trevor Howard were considered but rejected. In desperation Albert "Cubby" Broccoli and Harry Saltzman, the producers, turned to Connery – a little-known, scarcely trained actor from a Scottish slum who was strikingly handsome and well-built, and had impressed in a few minor roles.

Broccoli had his wife, Dana, watch a clip of Connery in a Walt Disney film called *Darby O'Gill and the Little People* and she was captivated. "That's our Bond!" she cried. The two producers interviewed him in their Mayfair office, liked his confidence ("He looked like he had balls," Broccoli said) and offered him a fee of £5,000. Others were still not convinced. The producers sent clips of Connery to United Artists in Hollywood, who cabled back: "See if you can do better." Ian Fleming, Bond's Eton-educated creator, remarked: "He's not what I envisioned ... I'm looking for Commander Bond and not an overgrown stuntman."

Terence Young, the film's patrician director, had to do a latter-day Henry Higgins, taking the "rough diamond" from an Edinburgh tenement to posh Mayfair restaurants, introducing him to his bespoke tailor, teaching him how to walk, dress, speak and eat.

Yet when *Dr No* was released in 1962 it was a sensation, a cultural hurricane that shook up the film industry just as the Beatles were transforming music, the Pill was triggering a sexual revolution and President Kennedy was rejuvenating America.

With its Jamaican sun, glamorous women, transatlantic jets and fast cars, *Dr No* thrilled austere, joyless postwar Britain, and much of the rest of the world. With the immortal words "Bond ... James Bond", Connery introduced himself not only to the beautiful Sylvia Trench (Eunice Gayson) across a gaming table in a London casino, but to millions of delighted filmgoers. With an unforgettable scene where the erotic Honey Ryder (Ursula Andress) emerges from the azure Caribbean wearing only a white bikini and a diving knife, he began his relationship with the first of many stunning "Bond girls". Suave, languid, witty, oozing charm and sexuality, and with just a hint of menace, Connery became one of the world's biggest film stars almost overnight.

He went on to make four more Bond films over the next five years, wearing a toupee to conceal his receding hairline, before he tired of the role and fell out with the producers. Twice more, in 1971 and 1983, he returned to play Bond but without the verve and success of those first five films.

Out of Bondage, as it were, Connery greatly expanded his repertoire, appearing in some notorious arthouse flops as well as numerous box-office hits but winning praise for the depth and range of his characters. He was the consummate professional, never acting the prima donna and often performing his own stunts. He won the Oscar for best supporting actor in 1988, a lifetime achievement award from the American Film Institute in 2006, and two Baftas.

Connery gave generously to good causes and was knighted in 2000, an award he would probably have received years earlier had he not been such a fervent supporter of Scottish independence. For all that, he will inevitably be remembered as the first James Bond, and as the best of them all. As the film critic Pauline Kael once put it, "Women want to meet him, and men want to be him. I don't know any man since Cary Grant that men have wanted to be so much."

His is a genuine rags-to-riches story. He was born Thomas Sean Connery in Edinburgh in 1930 and known throughout his youth as Tommy. His father, Joseph, a Roman Catholic of Irish descent, worked variously at a rubber mill and as a lorry driver, while his Protestant mother Euphemia "Effie" (née McLean) was a cleaner. He and his younger brother, Neil, were raised in a tenement flat in Fountainbridge with no bathroom or hot water and precious little money; his crib was the bottom drawer of a dresser. "We were poor, but I never knew how poor until a social worker told me," he said to a friend in later life. Even in his sixties a bath was still "something special".

From the age of nine Connery delivered milk before school, and did a shift at a butcher's shop afterwards. He lost his virginity in an air raid shelter to a woman in the Auxiliary Territorial Service when he was 14. Around the same time he left Darroch secondary school and found full-time work delivering milk for the Co-op dairy in a horse and cart. After his rounds were done he indulged his real passion: football. His nickname was "Big Tam" because he was 6ft 2in and hairy-chested. At 17, largely to escape from what he called the "grim no-man's land" of Fountainbridge, he signed up as a Royal Navy volunteer, but was discharged two years later with duodenal ulcers. More menial jobs followed until he trained as a French polisher under a British Legion programme for ex-servicemen. Thereafter he found himself polishing coffins for a living. Sometimes he slept in them to save his bus fare home.

That job did not last long either. He worked as a lifeguard at an outdoor swimming pool, a bouncer and an apprentice machine worker at the *Edinburgh Evening News,* and briefly joined Bonnyrigg Rose as a professional footballer. Having taken up bodybuilding, he posed as a model at Edinburgh College of Art for ready cash, and entered the Mr Universe contest in London. He came only third in the junior section, but then heard that actors were needed for the British run of the American musical *South Pacific.*

Taking his middle name Sean for the stage, Connery got a chorus part on the strength of his physique alone, and signed up for a two-year tour of the UK. The cast formed its own football team and played a Manchester United junior team, where Matt Busby was among the spectators and afterwards Connery was offered a trial. He was dissuaded by Robert Henderson, one of the show's leading American actors, who told him: "If you choose soccer you may have another ten years, but as an actor you could go on till you drop."

Henderson was impressed by Connery's intelligence and ambition, and became his mentor. He encouraged his protégé to lose his broad Scottish accent and to educate himself by reading widely. Connery devoured the works of Tolstoy, Proust, Ibsen, Turgenev and Joyce that Henderson gave him.

He secured Connery a bigger role in *South Pacific*: that of Lieutenant Buzz Adams. Henderson later found him small parts in various London plays until, in 1957, Connery secured his first significant role, playing a fallen boxer in a BBC reworking of *Requiem for a Heavyweight*. It had been made famous in America by the actor Jack Palance. When Palance refused to travel to London, the director's wife suggested Connery. "The ladies will like him," she said. Connery had had no formal training, but his acting career was launched.

He soon found himself playing opposite Lana Turner in *Another Time, Another Place*. He knocked out Turner's gangster boyfriend, Johnny Stompanato, after he had arrived in the studio, pointed a gun at Connery and accused him of having an affair with Turner (he almost certainly was). The film flopped, and one scathing reviewer wrote that young Connery "will not, I guess, grow old in the industry".

Later that year he appeared in Eugene O'Neill's play *Anna Christie* as the lover of a prostitute struggling for redemption played by Diane Cilento, a young Australian actress. He was captivated by her, though she was married with a baby daughter, Gigi. After his first visit to Hollywood to make *Darby O'Gill*, she contracted tuberculosis and he briefly put his career on hold to look after her, turning down the chance to appear with Sophia Loren in *El Cid*.

They married after the premiere of *Dr No* in 1962, by which time she was divorced and seven months pregnant with Connery's child. Jason, born in January 1963, would board at Gordonstoun and eventually follow his father into acting, once playing Bond's creator in an American television production called *The Secret Life of Ian Fleming*. With the proceeds from *Dr No*, Connery, his wife, son and stepdaughter moved into a large house overlooking Acton Park in west London.

In quick succession Connery went on to make *From Russia with Love*, *Goldfinger*, *Thunderball* and *You Only Live Twice*. They earned Connery ever greater fees, as much as $500,000 a film plus a percentage of the profits. However, the quality of the films fell away, his relations with Broccoli and Saltzman soured, and he felt increasingly trapped by the role and the relentless hounding by the media. "It's finished. Bond's been good to me, but I've done my bit. I'm out," he declared after filming *You Only Live Twice*. "After this I will only do things that passionately interest me for the rest of my life."

Anxious to establish himself as a serious actor, he turned to artier films, but they flopped. So did his appearance alongside Brigitte Bardot in *Shalako*, for which he received $1.2 million, and his turn in a Hitchcock film, *Marnie*, though he picked up some valuable tips from the director who encouraged him to speak more slowly and not to listen open-mouthed while others were talking. "The good people of Pocatello," Hitchcock said, "will not be all that interested in your dental work."

I've Seen You Cut Lemons, a play Connery directed with his wife in the lead role, also fell flat with audiences. Finally, in 1971 he agreed to do another Bond film, *Diamonds Are Forever*, tempted by a fee of $1.25 million plus future financing by United Artists for two films of his choice. It was far from the greatest Bond film, but broke box-office records and re-established the Connery brand.

In the following years there were big changes in his private life. He separated from Cilento after having a succession of affairs with models and actresses, including Jill St John, Lana Wood, Carole Mallory and Magda Konopka. He moved from their home in Putney to a flat overlooking the Thames at Chelsea Embankment, and they divorced in 1973. "Our careers were incompatible, not us," he said, insisting the split was amicable.

Cilento, however, alleged in her 2006 autobiography that he had abused her mentally and physically, claims he denied. Connery had been quoted in a 1965 *Playboy* interview as saying, "I don't think there is anything particularly wrong in hitting a woman, though I don't recommend you do it the same way that you hit a man." The remark caused controversy for years, and he refused to apologise when asked in 1987 by the interviewer Barbara Walters if he had changed his views; he maintained he had been quoted out of context.

Connery had learnt to play golf in preparation for a scene in *Goldfinger* and the sport became a passion. He played in pro-am tournaments with a single-figure handicap, and enjoyed rounds with fellow stars Tommy Cooper, Bruce Forsyth and the racing driver James Hunt. He was playing with Rex Harrison in Rome when he heard that Fleming had died, and so the pair played a second round in his honour using the Penfold Heart balls Fleming had prescribed for Bond in *Goldfinger*.

It was during a golf tournament in Morocco that he met Micheline Roquebrune, a French-Moroccan artist with three children. Both had won their respective competitions. They married in 1975 and set up home at Casa Malibu, an estate outside Marbella. Connery had left Britain because of its exorbitant tax rates, speaking of "the need to get out of the umbrella of parasites headed by people like [Denis] Healey [the chancellor of the exchequer]".

Roquebrune helped to push him back towards more commercial films, and some of his better performances. *The Wind and the Lion* was followed by John Huston's version of Rudyard Kipling's *The Man Who Would Be King* in which Connery co-starred with Michael Caine. That was followed by Richard Attenborough's epic *A Bridge Too Far*, but also failures including *The First Great Train Robbery*, *Meteor* and *Cuba*.

Connery's career appeared to be entering another trough, which is one reason why, at 52, he chose to eat his words and make one more Bond film. Another was the $5 million fee. A third was his rivalry with Roger Moore, who had taken over the role. *Never Say Never Again* was to be produced by Jack Schwartzman in direct competition with Broccoli, who failed to stop it in the courts. Connery threw himself into the project but it was unsuccessful, losing out to Moore's *Octopussy*. Roquebrune told a journalist the film had been "a nightmare" and one review concluded: "Let's say never again."

It was advice that Connery accepted, but his feud with Broccoli was not over. The next year, 1984, he sued Broccoli and his production companies. He claimed they had cheated him out of his rightful share of the profits from the first five Bond films and sought $225 million in damages. The action was settled out of court and the terms never publicly disclosed.

For nearly three years Connery retired from view, but in 1986 he bounced back with a masterly performance as a medieval Benedictine monk in *The Name of the Rose*, a film based on Umberto Eco's novel. In the following year came his Oscar-winning role as a streetwise Chicago cop in the gangster movie *The Untouchables*. He received two standing ovations at the awards ceremony in Hollywood.

Connery had finally emerged from Bond's shadow. During the next two decades he delivered some of his finest performances: in Steven Spielberg's *Indiana Jones and the Last Crusade*, as a Soviet submarine commander in *The Hunt for Red October*, as an ageing ethnobiologist searching for a cancer cure in the Amazon in *Medicine Man*, as a reclusive author in *Finding Forrester*, and as a professional thief in *Entrapment*. The only conspicuous failure was a film version of the TV series *The Avengers* that he called "a complete and utter fuck-up".

Meanwhile, his second marriage had survived his well-documented affair in the late 1980s with the singer-songwriter Lynsey de Paul, and Roquebrune remained devoted to him in his last years, which were blighted by dementia.

Immensely wealthy with homes in New York, Los Angeles and the Bahamas, Connery made his last film, *The League of Extraordinary Gentlemen*, in 2003. He announced his retirement in 2005, saying he was "fed up with the idiots" running Hollywood. He resurfaced in 2012 when he and Sir Alex Ferguson, the Manchester United manager and fellow Scot, gatecrashed Andy Murray's press conference after he reached the final of the US Open.

Connery once said he had three great passions in his life outside his family: acting, golf and Scotland, of which Scotland was the greatest. One of his proudest awards was the freedom of Edinburgh, and he named his own Hollywood production company Fountainbridge Films. As a navy cadet he had had "Scotland Forever" tattooed on his arm, and even at the height of his fame he never forgot his roots.

In 1967 he made a documentary about the problems of the Clydeside shipbuilding industry called *The Bowler and the Bunnet* that, in his words, "rose without trace", but it fuelled his appetite for social activism. Enraged by the destruction of Scotland's fishing industry after Britain joined the Common Market in 1973, he began supporting the Scottish National Party (SNP). He used the proceeds from *Diamonds Are Forever* to endow the Scottish International Education Trust, which he had founded to provide bursaries for underprivileged Scots.

In 1992 he formally joined the SNP, having helped it make a party political broadcast for that year's general election. He supported the party financially from 1995 to 2001, campaigning for a "yes" vote in the 1997 devolution referendum and for the SNP in the first Scottish parliamentary elections two years later. Donald Dewar, Labour's Scottish secretary, twice vetoed his nomination for a knighthood because of his support for the SNP, but Connery, wearing Highland dress, was finally knighted by the Queen at Holyrood Palace in 2000.

Although Connery, then 84, did not campaign in the 2014 referendum on Scotland's independence, he issued a statement supporting the Yes campaign. "I am for a Scotland that makes her own decisions, a sovereign state that will be a voice in Europe and around the world," he wrote in *Being a Scot*, a book celebrating Scottish culture and history that he co-authored in 2008.

In that same book Connery recalled how he had returned to Edinburgh for a recent film festival, and had surprised a taxi driver by naming every street he passed. "How come?," the cabbie asked, not recognising his passenger. "As a boy I used to deliver milk around here," Connery replied. "So what do you do now?" the cabbie asked. "That," Connery wrote, "was rather harder to answer."

Sir Sean Connery was born on August 25, 1930. He died in his sleep on October 31, 2020, aged 90

GINA LOLLOBRIGIDA

At the height of her fame as a film star in the 1950s, Gina Lollobrigida was Europe's best-known sex symbol. "She made Marilyn Monroe look like Shirley Temple," said Humphrey Bogart.

Even on her 70th birthday, in 1997, a Rome newspaper saluted her as "opulent, bewitching, carnal, vibrant, earthy, elegant and imperial, with the most celebrated décolletage of the century". But by the end of her life, "La Lollo" was being portrayed as Norma Desmond.

Caught up in an alleged swindle by a much younger lover, she was said to be deluding herself like the faded diva in *Sunset Boulevard* that her toyboys wanted her for her beauty; that the public still knew her name.

Widely accepted though both these characterisations were, they only told part of the story. What Lollobrigida truly was, and remained, was emphatically, archetypically, unrepentantly Italian; that is to say, straight to the point and yet nobody's fool.

Proof of this, and what showed her at her best, were the films that made her name at home but were perhaps less familiar abroad. Chief among these was Luigi Comencini's 1953 comedy *Pane, amore e fantasia*.

Known in English as *Bread, Love and Dreams*, it sent neo-realism in a less searching but more popular direction and made Lollobrigida's reputation. Forever after, Italians identified her with the part she played of "La bersagliera" – the huntress, the headstrong, untamed, barefoot country girl.

The film's portrait of a timeless rural Italy might have been false, given that the postwar economic boom was then transforming the nation. Yet few doubted that Lollobrigida, who had grown up in the hills outside Rome, was doing anything for the camera other than being her pushy, impetuous self.

Certainly, the role showcased her gypsy looks – the narrow waist, the ample bosom, the curls after which "Lollo rosso" lettuce would be named – but these were commonplace in Italy. What singled her out on the screen from other pretty shopgirls and pert housewives, and what made them adore her, was an inner fire.

It was this, together with the perception that she had not forsaken Italy for Hollywood, which let her rival the more abundant glamour, and greater talent, of her contemporary Sophia Loren. The two conducted a long feud. Loren recalled in her memoir that this began when they were in London at the same time as starlets and she was judged by Fleet Street's finest to have the bigger bust.

For her part, Lollobrigida never failed to claim that it was only when she turned down a second sequel to *Pane, amore e fantasia* that Loren got her break. "She plays peasants, I play ladies," said Lollobrigida, untruthfully.

This irrepressible vitality was evident in her best films of the mid-1950s, such as *La provinciale* and *La Romana*, dramas of morals based on stories by Alberto Moravia. Lollobrigida's appeal stemmed from her seeming as if she could be one's, admittedly life-enhancing, neighbour. That quality tended to be lost when Hollywood typecast her as an exotic beauty, which she was not.

American interest in her had begun even before she was a star. In 1950 the tycoon Howard Hughes, who then owned RKO studios, saw some publicity shots of the 22-year-old actress and invited her to Los Angeles. The pretext was a screen test, but Lollobrigida divined his intentions when she arrived at Rome airport with her husband to find tickets waiting just for her. In California, Hughes put her up in a suite, supplied her with an English teacher and gave her a script to rehearse – a divorce scene.

For the next three months she fended off his advances, though she found him fascinating if eccentric company ("More interesting than my husband," she confided to *Vanity Fair* in 2015). In exchange, Hughes taught her English swearwords. He only let her return home after she had signed a contract which in effect made it impossible for her to make a film in America for the next seven years.

But it did not stop her from appearing in those productions which US studios were increasingly making abroad, notably in Italy. Accordingly, in her breakthrough year of 1953, she made her English-speaking debut in John Huston's *Beat the Devil*, albeit her part was dubbed. But then so had been her Italian roles to date, her accent being deemed too provincial. Her co-star Bogart's dialogue was voiced by an unknown Peter Sellers after the American lost his teeth in an accident.

Huston's parody of a hard-boiled thriller proved a curate's egg, but it did not prevent Lollobrigida from catching Hollywood's eye. Thereafter she became definitively a star at home, and as such was cast in leading roles in minor Italian films. These included the biopics *La donna più bella del mondo,* as the soprano Lina Cavalieri, and *Venere imperiale,* as Pauline Bonaparte. She claimed Fellini wanted her for *La Dolce Vita* but that her husband hid the script she had been sent.

On the international stage she was usually seen as a sultry temptress in spectacular hokum such as *The Hunchback of Notre Dame,* where she was Anthony Quinn's Esmerelda, and *Solomon and Sheba,* with Yul Brynner. She rapidly gained a reputation as being difficult, which is to say that she knew what she wanted and spoke her mind.

On the set of *Trapeze,* the director Carol Reed took to shooting the dangerous acrobatic sequences early in the morning, before Lollobrigida and Burt Lancaster were on set. Yet when her stunt double broke her nose, Lollobrigida insisted on doing the aerial scenes herself for the next month.

The best of the slew of American films that she made in the 1960s were those with Rock Hudson ("When we did our love scenes he was quite … normal"). For *Come September* she won a Golden Globe, and lost out on another to Barbra Streisand's *Funny Girl*. The nomination was for her last screen role of note, as a woman who convinces several US soldiers that they are the father of her child in *Buona Sera, Mrs Campbell* (1968). The film later inspired the musical *Mamma Mia!*

Lollobrigida's own love life was no less complex. In 1949 she married Milko Skofic, a Slovenian doctor who was helping refugees housed at Rome's Cinecittà studios. He became her manager, but she attributed some of her failure to land roles that went to Loren to his not being a powerful producer, unlike her rival's husband, Carlo Ponti. She and Skofic had a son, Andrea, but the marriage was not happy. In 1971 Lollobrigida was among the first Italians to obtain a divorce following its legalisation.

Matters had not been helped perhaps by Hughes having continued to pursue her. He would send lawyers to her pink-painted villa on the Appian Way in Rome, where they would play tennis with her husband, accompanied by the screech of her peacocks. Another persistent admirer was Prince Rainier of Monaco, who Lollobrigida claimed would make passes at her even in front of his wife, Grace Kelly. "My God," she reminisced, "at least do it carefully!"

In the 1960s she had an affair with the playboy heart surgeon Christiaan Barnard, and was reputed to have had another with Fidel Castro. When Italian soldiers were sent to Lebanon to keep the peace in 1982, Syria's defence minister ordered that they not be harmed because he held a candle for her.

She also liked to recall how President Mitterrand had looked at her when pinning the Légion d'honneur on her chest: "François understood I was more than just an actress …"

"When you find a love, to refuse it is a crime," she told The Times in 1999. "I am very independent, I have always done my fighting alone, but I do miss someone to protect me. It seems I am too much for one man."

The second of four sisters, she was born Luigia Lollobrigida in 1927 in Subiaco, east of Rome. Her father made furniture but he lost all his stock in an Allied bombardment. Gina herself was much affected by the devastation she witnessed. By the end of the war, the whole family were living in a single room in Rome.

From her earliest years, Gina showed a fiery determination to get what she wanted and she won a place to study at the capital's leading art school. Her sisters worked as usherettes to help pay her fees and she sold caricatures and posed for photo-romance magazines. Only in her final years would she reveal that at the age of 18 she had been raped by a footballer in the Lazio team, and married young partly to try to put the trauma of it behind her.

In 1947 she came third in the Miss Italy competition. This was to become a launching pad for many actresses but when Italian film producers first approached Gina and offered a fee of 1,000 lire, she shrewdly announced that even a million lire would not tempt her into the movies; she got it. Her earliest roles were bit parts, but in 1952 she had her first success in a French swashbuckler, *Fanfan la tulipe*.

She in effect retired only 20 years later, aged 45, after appearing to much acclaim as the Blue Fairy in Comencini's celebrated television adaptation of *Pinocchio*. Thereafter she made very occasional returns to the screen, for instance in the campy American drama *Falcon Crest* in the 1980s, and in a 1988 remake for television of *La Romana*.

This time Lollobrigida played the mother of the protagonist, let everyone know she was unhappy with the casting and at the press conference to publicise the programme had a stand-up row with the leading actress.

Away from the cameras, she concentrated on a career as an artist, mainly of somewhat kitsch sculptures. She also briefly dabbled in politics, standing as a centre-left candidate for the European parliament in 1999. She was an ambassador for Unicef and in 2013 sold her collection of jewellery for £3 million and donated the proceeds for stem-cell research.

Her later years, however, were overshadowed by the acrimonious end of her relationship with one Javier Rigau y Rafols. By his account, which varied at almost every point from hers, they had met in 1984 when she was 57 and he 23 ("I've always had a weakness for young men," she admitted).

In 2006, when she was almost 80, they revealed their love to a surprised world and announced that they were to marry. The ceremony was later cancelled but in 2013 Lollobrigida began a lawsuit against Rigau, alleging that in 2010 he had gone ahead with it in secret in Barcelona and married her by proxy. Lollobrigida claimed that Rigau was trying to get his hands on her fortune. Moreover, she said, they had in fact only known each other for two years, not 22. Rigau made counterclaims of his own, among them that Lollobrigida had known about the marriage and that there had been nothing fake about their romance. "The first phrase she taught me in Italian was 'Let's fuck'," he gallantly revealed.

A Spanish tribunal found that the union was valid and cleared Rigau of fraud. A related application by Lollobrigida's son to take charge of her affairs was rejected by a court. He told the media that he was worried by the influence over the soon-to-be nonagenarian of her new adviser Andrea Piazzolla, 27.

The star, who had a habit of referring to herself in the third person, let everyone know, however, that she had lost none of her forcefulness nor self-regard. She explained that she no longer spoke to her son and praised Piazzolla for giving her the confidence to drive again after she had a crash. "He's got me back in my Ferrari," she said with a wink.

By 2022, however, Piazzolla faced two trials for misappropriating the star's funds, and was accused of having pocketed the proceeds of selling her Jaguar. A court ruled that she should have a guardian appointed to look after her financial affairs.

Later in 2022, she announced that at the age of 95 she would be running in Italy's general election on September 25, representing the Eurosceptic party Italia Sovrana e Popolare (ISP). She was not expected to poll many votes, and in the event won just over 1 per cent of the vote in her constituency, but her place in Italian hearts was never in doubt.

"I am the symbol of Italy, everybody knows me," she reflected. "I've never got used to all the attention, you know ... I am so famous, but no one knows the real me. I am very shy, really. I am just the girl from Subiaco."

Gina Lollobrigida was born on July 4, 1927. She died on January 16, 2023, aged 95

BURT REYNOLDS

Odd as it may seem, Burt Reynolds always felt that he was never taken seriously as an actor. At the peak of his career, films such as *Smokey and the Bandit*, *The Cannonball Run* and *The Best Little Whorehouse in Texas* made Reynolds Hollywood's top-grossing star for an unprecedented five consecutive years.

He was teamed on screen with some of the world's most beautiful women from Raquel Welch and Angie Dickinson to Catherine Deneuve and Lauren Hutton. Despite an ever-present and much-derided $12,000 hairpiece that matched his lush moustache, he defined rugged masculine beauty, and was lusted over by countless women and men. Freddie Mercury reportedly considered Reynolds his dream date, and he became America's first male centrefold when he appeared nude in *Cosmopolitan*. He was also one of the few men to grace the cover of *Playboy*.

With a dazzling smile and an ever-present wink, he strutted on screen and off with a macho swagger. He was not only impossibly virile, improbably good-looking and unfeasibly rich, he was funny, sharp and charismatic, "like Cary Grant crossed with Tom Jones", as one movie critic put it. "Nobody had more fun than I did," he wrote in his 2015 memoir *But Enough About Me*.

And yet it wasn't enough. Racked with surprising self-doubt, he fretted that he was known for movies "they show in airplanes or prisons or anywhere else the people can't get out". He had become the number one box-office star "not because of my movies, but despite them".

"I didn't open myself to new writers or risky parts because I wasn't interested in challenging myself as an actor. I was interested in having a good time," he chided himself. "As a result, I missed a lot of opportunities to show I could play serious roles. By the time I finally woke up and tried to get it right, nobody would give me a chance."

Reynolds branched out into directing, most notably in the 1981 police drama *Sharky's Machine*, but said he returned to acting because he was making too much money to stop. At the height of his box-office success he joked that he "probably could do a film about the sewer system in Moscow and make it commercial".

Yet, in the jargon of the industry, he was guilty of failing to "build his brand" in the long term. From having been Hollywood's highest-paid leading man – Los Angeles bus tours of the homes of the stars would point out six opulent properties owned by Reynolds, including one he bought from George Harrison – he had gone bust by the mid-1990s, and was forced to file for bankruptcy with debts in excess of $10 million.

He blamed a messy divorce – "I'm paying the third highest alimony and child support in the world and the only two ahead of me are sheikhs," he quipped – and a series of investments that went badly wrong. However, his extravagant lifestyle and some poor career decisions were also factors.

In one of his final films, *The Last Movie Star* (2017), in which he played an actor forced to face the fact that his glory days were behind him, it was impossible not to discern an autobiographical thread. "When you're famous, everybody wants to screw ya," Reynolds said as the faded star Vic Edwards. "Bad choices, bad choices," his character went on to lament. "Pacino, De Niro, Brando – they picked the right ones."

Back in his own skin, he remarked that he had made more than 100 movies, but was proud of only "maybe five of them", noting ruefully that younger actors were always asking him "where all of the landmines are because they know I've stepped on them all".

Yet he was being unduly harsh on himself. True, there were rather too many eminently forgettable stuntman action films and the list of far better movies that he turned down suggested his judgment was questionable. George Lazenby, Harrison Ford, Jack Nicholson, Bruce Willis and Richard Gere were all grateful that he refused roles that they made famous in *On Her Majesty's Secret Service, Star Wars, Terms of Endearment, Die Hard* and *Pretty Woman* respectively.

However, his career was bedecked with unforgettable performances, from the intimidating bow-hunting alpha male in *Deliverance* and the rakish Depression-era smuggler in *Lucky Lady*, to a disgraced former pro football player doing time in a Georgia prison in *The Longest Yard* and his memorable 1997 comeback as the pornographer Jack Horner in Paul Thomas Anderson's *Boogie Nights*.

The latter earned him his first Oscar nomination, something that had eluded him during his golden run in the late 1970s and early 1980s when *Smokey and the Bandit* out-grossed *Close Encounters of the Third Kind* and *Saturday Night Fever*, and *The Best Little Whorehouse in Texas*, in which he starred with Dolly Parton, usurped *E.T. The Extra-Terrestrial* at the top of the box-office list.

As one of Hollywood's most eligible men, he acquired a reputation as a hard-drinking playboy and his love life was seldom out of the gossip columns. In the 1960s he was briefly married to the English-born actress Judy Carne, although they had divorced by the time she made her name as the "sock it to me" girl in *Rowan & Martin's Laugh-In*.

When they later found themselves thrown together on the same chat show, Carne told her ex-husband, who by then was living with Dinah Shore, a singer who was 20 years his senior: "I hear you like them a little older these days". "No," he snapped back, "just classier."

A carefree bachelor throughout the 1970s as he ascended to the top, he was dubbed "the cowboy Casanova", jumping the bones of every cocktail waitress or airline stewardess that hove into view. "So often I'd wake up in the morning, look at the girl in bed with me and wonder what her name was," he admitted. "I wasn't interested in their minds, only their bodies."

He even picked up women while appearing on live TV. During a charity phone-in, he gave two women his hotel room number and found them waiting for him when he got back.

There were more serious relationships with the singer Tammy Wynette, the tennis star Chris Evert, the Japanese actress Miko Mayama and numerous Hollywood leading ladies. They included Dyan Cannon; Lorna Luft; Inger Stevens, whom he was still seeing when she took her own life in 1970; and *Charlie's Angels* star Farrah Fawcett, whom he introduced to Lee Majors – her future husband.

One of his longest relationships was with Sally Field, his co-star in *Smokey and The Bandit*, who turned down several marriage proposals from him and for whom he carried a torch for the rest of his life.

In his fifties and desperate to have a child, in 1988 he was married for a second time, to the actress Loni Anderson. They adopted a son, Quinton Anderson Reynolds, who now works as a camera assistant in Hollywood and of whom he was inordinately proud.

"We have a saying in the South: 'No man's a man until his father tells him he is,'" Reynolds recounted. "Well, mine never told me and that was a problem. But my son did."

The gossip columns presented the marriage as a lothario tamed by a blonde bombshell who had finally persuaded an ageing hell-raiser to settle down. However, their relationship was turbulent and they divorced after five difficult years amid considerable public mudslinging. Reynolds went on television to accuse her of being an unfit mother. He complained that she "took five hours to get ready to go to the grocery store" and would disappear for days at a time shopping.

Anderson accused him of beating her and having an affair with the Florida cocktail waitress Pam Seals. Perhaps most woundingly of all, she claimed that Reynolds insisted on buying a new toupee every week. Even by the standards of Hollywood divorces it was spectacularly lurid.

He was born Burton Leon Reynolds in 1936 in Lansing, Michigan, although anxious to be seen as a true southerner, for years he claimed to have been born in Waycross, Georgia. His father Burton Milo Reynolds served in Europe with the US Army in the Second World War, leaving his mother, Fern (née Miller), to bring up him and his sister.

After the war the family moved to Riviera Beach, Florida, where his father, who allegedly had Cherokee ancestry, became chief of police. He was a remote and intimidating presence, whom Reynolds felt he could never please.

"My dad was my hero, but he never acknowledged any of my achievements," he wrote in his memoir. "I always felt that no amount of success would make me a man in his eyes."

Reynolds won a football scholarship to Florida State University and was an outstanding running quarterback, who seemed destined for a professional career. However, a knee injury, aggravated in a car accident, ended his sporting ambitions, and he began training to be a parole officer.

Cast as the lead in a college play, he won a drama award that carried the prize of a summer season at a playhouse in New York and set him on a different path. While sharing rooms with the actor Rip Torn, he landed stage parts on Broadway in *Tea and Sympathy* and a revival of *Mister Roberts* with Charlton Heston. However, he struggled to make a wider impact and there were barren spells spent washing dishes and working as a bouncer.

He crashed into television – quite literally – when he was offered $150 as a stuntman to fall through a glass window, and by the late 1950s he began to appear regularly in shows such as *Riverboat* and *Gunsmoke*, in which he played Quint Asper, a Comanche of mixed heritage.

Reynolds made his film debut in *Angel Baby*, a low-budget 1961 melodrama about the curing of a mute child. However, he was more notable for his striking physique than his acting skills and for a time he was seen as little more than a glorified stuntman, which meant his cinema career was slow to develop.

It was not until the end of the Sixties that he started to establish himself with leading parts in the westerns *Sam Whiskey* and *100 Rifles*.

His transition from journeyman to full-blown star came in 1972 playing Lewis Medlock in John Boorman's *Deliverance*, the riveting tale of four men whose weekend adventure shooting the rapids on a river in the Appalachians turns into a nightmare with its infamous hillbilly male rape scene.

Marlon Brando, Henry Fonda and James Stewart had allegedly turned down the part as physically too dangerous and demanding, and, unusually, Boorman shot every scene in sequence. When Reynolds asked why, the director replied, "In case one of you drowns".

Undeterred, Reynolds relished the physical challenge of the role and when he saw test footage of a dummy in a canoe going over the falls in one scene, he complained that it looked fake.

Always ready to do his own stunts, Reynolds climbed into the canoe, crashed into the rocks below and ended up in hospital. When Boorman visited him, Reynolds asked him how the footage looked. "Like a dummy going over the falls," came the reply.

It was on the back of his success in *Deliverance* that Reynolds was persuaded to pose for *Cosmopolitan*, naked on a bear skin rug, one hand strategically draped across a muscular thigh, a smouldering cigarillo clenched between his teeth in a wry smile. It was an iconic moment in popular culture, but he came to regret it, feeling that he had added to his lack of "seriousness" and fearing that Hollywood disapproval had cost him a best actor Oscar nomination for *Deliverance*.

Nevertheless the shoot helped *Cosmopolitan* to sell an unprecedented 1.5 million copies and establish him as the macho sex symbol of the age. The morning after the magazine came out, he found a group of women outside his home asking him to autograph the picture. He also got lewd fan mail, including a letter from a woman in Nova Scotia containing her pubic hair. The naked image was even merchandised on bedsheets.

Whether it was due to *Deliverance* or *Cosmopolitan*, in 1973 Reynolds appeared for the first time in the list of the ten most popular US film actors. His rise was assisted by some disarmingly candid appearances on late-night television chat shows with hosts such as Merv Griffin and Johnny Carson.

By 1977 Reynolds, an unapologetic "man's man", was the biggest earner in Tinsel Town in a decade when the zeitgeist was starting to throw up a new school of less macho and more thoughtful male stars such as Woody Allen and Dustin Hoffman.

By the mid-1980s, however, Reynolds's fortunes had plummeted as nothing seemed to go right. On the set of *City Heat*, in which he starred with Clint Eastwood, he had his jaw broken when a stuntman hit him with a real bar stool, rather than a fake one, in a fight scene. He suffered year-long complications with his teeth, jaw and inner ear. He also became addicted to painkillers and lost 30lb. His illness was identified incorrectly in tabloid gossip as Aids.

No sooner had Reynolds recovered than his notoriously volcanic temper – rivalled in ferocity, he cheerfully admitted, only by Gene Hackman and Eastwood – got him into a fight while he was filming the 1986 action thriller *Heat*. He hit and seriously injured the film's director, Dick Richards, who sued for assault. It cost Reynolds $500,000.

When a chain of restaurants he had financed collapsed, the actor found himself mired in debt, but refused to curb his lavish lifestyle. This included not only his numerous homes in the Hollywood Hills, but a 160-acre ranch in Florida where he kept 100 horses and had a petting zoo, a helicopter, and a private jet with two pilots – on salaries of $100,000 each – on permanent standby. He also co-owned a professional American football team and a motor-racing franchise.

Substituting quality for quantity, he funded his losses by accepting every script that came his way, no matter how dumb, while British audiences came to know him as the bespectacled face of TV advertisements for Dollond & Aitchison.

In a career in which Reynolds picked up considerably fewer awards than he should have done, he won an Emmy as the small-town football coach in the comedy *Evening Shade* and a Golden Globe for *Boogie Nights*, which also brought the kind of critical kudos that he craved, but which had so often evaded him. "I needed a jump start and so it was a brave choice," he said.

In fact, although Reynolds was proud of his performance, which was one of the finest of his career, he hated the film so much that when he attended its first screening he promptly fired his agent. He felt it "glamorised" the porn industry.

Boogie Nights "just wasn't my kind of film and made me very uncomfortable", Reynolds said. He refused to help to promote the film and suggested he'd like to punch its director in the face.

Nevertheless, he was grateful when the movie's success led to a surfeit of offers, most of which he eagerly accepted, ranging from car-chase romps such as a movie spin-off from the TV series *The Dukes of Hazzard* to the rather unfairly panned *A Bunch of Amateurs*. In this, he appeared alongside Derek Jacobi as a fading star who goes to Britain to play *King Lear* at Stratford, only to find that he has not signed on with the Royal Shakespeare Company in Warwickshire, but with the amateur "Stratford Players" in a Suffolk village of the same name.

Despite a back operation in 2009, necessitated by years of doing his own movie stunts, and quadruple heart bypass surgery the following year, he continued to work. At the time of his death he was due to start shooting in *Once Upon a Time in Hollywood*, Quentin Tarantino's forthcoming film about Charles Manson.

Reynolds once confessed that he may have lacked dignity and class, but hoped he made up for it by having "the heart of a lion". In the final paragraph of his memoir, he wrote: "I always wanted to experience everything and go down swinging." Even his fiercest critics could not deny that he achieved that.

Burt Reynolds was born on February 11, 1936. He died of a heart attack on September 6, 2018, aged 82

BARBARA WINDSOR

For Barbara Windsor, Babs as she was known, acting in the Carry On films involved its own crazed discipline. None had more than a six-week shooting schedule and the director, Gerald Thomas, rarely allowed more than two takes. "Nobody analysed what they were doing," Windsor recalled. "We had to be there early, know the script backwards, cause no aggravations and endure all kinds of awful weather in order to finish on time."

Typical was the shooting of Windsor's famous bra scene in *Carry On Camping* (1969), a film set in midsummer but shot during a cold February and March. The scene required Windsor to lose her bikini top during a keep-fit class, the strap, unable to withstand the physical pressures, snapping with a spectacular twang. The bra was to fly into the face of Kenneth Williams, who was playing the gym instructor.

An elderly prop man had the bra attached to a fishing rod. On the first take, when he started to reel the bra in, the top stayed put and Windsor was dragged unceremoniously through the mud. "Get her up and mop her down. Let's go for another take," Windsor heard as she struggled to her feet.

Of the 31 Carry On films made from the late 1950s to the 1970s, Windsor starred in nine. She came to the series relatively late. Seasoned comedy actors such as Sid James, Charles Hawtrey, Hattie Jacques and Kenneth Williams were already firm favourites of this quaintly un-PC genre, but Windsor slotted perfectly into the saucy, seaside postcard humour.

Originating in the sexually cautious 1950s, the films flourished in the 1960s, a period teetering on the brink of sexual frankness when it was still expected that a coarse joke would be coated in a double entendre. In Windsor, the scriptwriters were handed a comic gift. Brassy and blonde, only 4ft 10½in tall, she had a raucously vulgar laugh and a bosom that Kenneth Williams likened to "a confectionery counter".

Fondness for her Carry On character only partly explained the lasting public affection for Windsor. Like another former sex symbol, Diana Dors, she became something of a national institution in her middle years. When film work dried up she returned to the stage and slogged her way around regional theatres in pantomime and cabaret before unexpectedly reviving her career as Peggy Mitchell, landlady of the Queen Vic in the soap opera *EastEnders*. Her oft-repeated line, "get outta my pub!", amounted to a catchphrase.

The actor Larry Lamb recalled that he was nervous about his first appearance on *EastEnders*, until Windsor put him at ease by pointing out that she had to stand on a beer crate to see over the top of the bar and pull a pint.

Her private life was rarely out of the public eye, partly because of the company she kept. She stuck by her gangland husband, Ronnie Knight, and her old friends the notorious Kray brothers. She described one of the Krays, without irony, as "the most gentlemanly man I've ever met".

Her memoirs recounted failed marriages and five abortions, the first three before the age of 21 and the last when she was 42.

She also breezily admitted to countless affairs, including with Maurice Gibb of the Bee Gees and the footballer George Best at the height of his fame, playing for Manchester United. "There was this vision," she wrote, "this absolute vision. He was so beautiful. He came over to me in the bar and I said, 'Look, don't waste your time with me, darling. You've got all these lovely ladies after you.' And he said, 'Well, when do I ever get to talk to somebody like you?' Well, that did it. That was it. A magic moment."

Perhaps surprisingly, given the usual political preference of those working in the theatrical world, she also revealed that she was a supporter of the Conservative Party.

In 2019, as part of her campaign to raise awareness about Alzheimer's, the disease from which she suffered, she had a meeting with the prime minister, Boris Johnson. At the end of it she turned to him and asked: "Can I have a kiss?"

Barbara Ann Deeks was born in Shoreditch, east London, in 1937. She described her father, John, who sold fruit and vegetables from a barrow, as a "typical Jack-the-lad East Ender". Her mother, Rose, was a dressmaker who aspired to be middle class and hated Shoreditch, where Barbara grew up, because she thought it common. In a BBC documentary in 2006 Windsor traced her mother's side of the family back to John Constable, the painter.

Having passed her 11-plus with exceptional marks she was accepted at Our Lady's Convent in Stamford Hill, but she already had ambitions to act and successfully auditioned for a pantomime. The Reverend Mother disapproved and refused her time off from school. She left soon afterwards and from the age of 13 her education was the Aida Foster theatre school in Golders Green where they tried, with limited success, to detach her from her cockney accent.

At 15 she was in the West End, playing an orphan in the musical *Love From Judy*. With provincial dates as well, she was with the show for two years. As she recalled: "I had gone into the musical with short hair, ankle socks and school uniform. I approached the end of it in 1954 with a bouffant hairdo, stockings and high heels."

She was now known for the size of her bust, although some sources suggested that it was actually several sizes smaller than reported and the illusion was to do with her habit of sticking her chest out whenever she was on stage or screen. When asked about this she would quip: "It's called acting." Either way, for five years or so her career stalled. After a couple of television spots the work dried up and she went on the dole. After a brief spell working in a shoe shop she returned to performing, and found a niche in West End cabaret. In a Soho nightclub she performed a song appropriately titled *My Hair, My Teeth, My Bosom*. She went on tour with Ronnie Scott's jazz band and appeared at another club, Winston's, with Danny La Rue.

In the late 1950s her agent sent her to audition for Joan Littlewood. She met Littlewood backstage and at first mistook this "podgy lady in a woolly hat" for the cleaner. Littlewood immediately warmed to Windsor's sparky personality and offered her the part of an Irish prostitute in Frank Norman's musical about Soho low-life, *Fings Ain't Wot They Used T'Be*. Windsor's song *Where do Little Birds Go in Winter?* stopped the show. When the play moved to the Garrick in February 1960, Windsor became the young toast of the West End.

The East End, however, was still her home, and when Littlewood required a nightclub in which to shoot her film, *Sparrows Can't Sing*, Windsor arranged for the Krays to lend her theirs. Ronnie Knight was an old schoolfriend of the twins. Charlie Kray, their elder brother, had gone out with Windsor while Knight was serving a sentence in Wandsworth Prison. She and Knight were married in 1964.

Windsor's chirpy performance as the sailor's wife in *Sparrows Can't Sing* won her a Bafta nomination, in part, she said, because Littlewood pushed her to do more than "the same old bosomy thing". When in 1965 Littlewood's *Oh What a Lovely War!* transferred to Broadway, Windsor was invited to join the cast. Although it was an ensemble piece, she was nominated for a Tony award. Back in London she suffered the debacle of Littlewood's theatrical swansong, *Twang!*

By now her film career was about to take off. It had begun in 1954 with a tiny part in *The Belles of St Trinian's*. In 1964 she joined Kenneth Williams and Charles Hawtrey in *Carry On Spying*, the eighth in the series that would make her name. On the first day Williams tried to put her down in front of the cast for fluffing her lines: "Ooooh darling, do please get it right," he drawled. She retorted with a quick joke and they became friends.

Three years later she returned to Pinewood to film *Carry On Doctor*. There followed *Carry On Camping* (1969), *Carry On Again*

Doctor (1969), *Carry On Henry* (1971), *Carry On Matron* (1972), *Carry On Abroad* (1972), *Carry On Girls* (1973) and *Carry On Dick* (1974).

Camaraderie kept the team together, and a jovial atmosphere that Bernard Bresslaw likened to "going back to school after the holidays". Kenneth Williams and his mother even accompanied Windsor on her honeymoon. It was not long before she was confronted with an infatuated Sid James. They launched into an affair that became so intense that James warned her he would be dead within the year if she left him. Unhappily, he was right.

The Carry On series was dying, too. Windsor sensibly backed out of the last project, the soft-porn spoof *Carry On Emmannuelle*, and moved on. In the theatre she had a 15-month West End run in the musical *Come Spy With Me*, with Danny La Rue, played the music-hall star Marie Lloyd in *Sing a Rude Song* and diversified into Brecht, appearing with Vanessa Redgrave in *The Threepenny Opera*. In 1976 she tackled her first Shakespeare, playing Maria in *Twelfth Night* at Chichester.

She also toured in her own shows, and there were dozens of personal appearances. By the mid-1970s, approaching her 40th birthday, she could no longer play the sex symbol so she developed as an all-round song-and-dance comedienne, touring with shows such as *Carry On Barbara* and *Calamity Jane*. Though hard work, it was preferable to staying at home and dwelling on her childless, disintegrating marriage.

Windsor claimed to know little about her husband's underworld connections. In 1980 he was charged with the revenge killing of a man held to be responsible for his brother's murder several years earlier. She gave evidence on his behalf and he was acquitted. Four years later he fled to Spain, wanted for questioning by police in connection with a £6-million robbery.

After their divorce in 1985 Windsor was linked with a series of much younger men. First came her marriage to Stephen Hollings, with whom she ran a pub, a project that ran up huge debts for which Windsor became liable. Other youthful lovers included Scott Mitchell, an actor 26 years her junior, who became her third husband in 2000. In the same year she was appointed MBE.

When asked in a TV interview with Piers Morgan in 2010 if she knew how many men she had slept with, she replied: "No, no idea, why? Have you counted them?"

Professional stability returned to her life in 1994 when she was offered the role of Peggy Mitchell, the matriarch in *EastEnders*.

Although she was in the situation comedy, *The Rag Trade*, in the early 1960s, and later played Saucy Nancy, one of the girlfriends of the scarecrow Worzel Gummidge, Windsor had done little television. But as Peggy, landlady of the Queen Vic, she became a feisty and commanding presence behind the beer pumps, capable of reducing her thuggish sons and their crooked pals to quivering youths.

The filming schedule of a soap that went out three times a week and then four could be daunting, but the ever-energetic Windsor took it in her stride and she appeared in more than 1,000 episodes. Even so, she was forced to take a two-year break after being laid low by the debilitating Epstein-Barr virus.

She kept busy standing in for Elaine Paige on BBC Radio 2, and "retired" from *EastEnders* several more times. Every time she came back she continued to prove what a fine straight actress she had become, a long way from the dizzy blonde who stuck out her chest and wiggled her bottom.

In 2016 she was appointed Dame Commander of the Order of the British Empire and that same year she won the outstanding contribution award at the TV Choice awards, and best exit at the Inside Soap awards for her portrayal of Peggy's death. It had been Windsor's decision to have the character killed off, because she said that as long as Peggy was alive, she would always be drawn back to playing her.

Her final appearance on the show came two years after she had been given a diagnosis of Alzheimer's disease. According to her husband, her first words after being given that grim news were: "I'm so sorry."

Dame Barbara Windsor was born on August 6, 1937. She died of complications from Alzheimer's disease on December 10, 2020, aged 83

TONY CURTIS

In a lengthy film career in which his exuberant personality both on and off the screen seemed to thumb its nose at the passage of years, Tony Curtis moved from enjoyable hokum, via adventure spectaculars to classic light comedy, with more than the odd flabby costume drama failure in between.

In the process he made the journey from pretty boy of a certain sultry brand of dark good looks and clean-cut matinee idol sex appeal to unapologetically disgraceful old roué. It was a transformation he always gave the impression of thoroughly enjoying both on screen and in his own life.

It sometimes seemed to his critics that Curtis's career had been largely a matter of being in the right place at the right time. For a long time it was de rigueur to ask how on earth he could ever have been taken seriously. The fact was of course that Curtis was a much better actor than he appeared on a superficial appraisal.

He had learnt his craft under Erwin Piscator in New York after the Second World War, alongside some of the most accomplished actors to emerge in America at that time; men and women such as

Marlon Brando, Elaine Stritch and many more. Curtis also had terrific stamina, and this enabled him in the early part of his career to make film after film in rapid succession, so that the turkeys were soon forgotten but the screen personality inexorably imprinted itself on audiences.

Curtis propelled himself from the ranks of the journeymen to true stardom in three films made during the 1950s. After a number of swashbuckling adventure films in which he thoroughly learnt his trade and acquitted himself with credit (his Bronx accent was never an impediment, whether his screen disguise was a burnous or a stetson), he first came to attention in the tense melodrama of circus jealousies, *Trapeze* (1956).

In this film, which succeeded in bringing vividly to life the claustrophobic emotional atmosphere of the circus, as well as communicating the very smell of the ring, his good looks and vivid personality more than held their own in a cast that starred the maturely accomplished Burt Lancaster and the meltingly pulchritudinous Italian romantic lead, Gina Lollobrigida.

In *Sweet Smell of Success* (1957), again alongside Lancaster, he startled audiences by suddenly appearing in quite another guise, as the exemplar of unprincipled American ambition, a portrayal which was unsparing in its social and psychological criticism of the unacceptable face of the American thirst for success.

With its powerful screenplay written by Clifford Odets, Ernest Lehman and Alexander Mackendrick from the novelette by Lehman, it was a film unlike anything Curtis had appeared in before. At first it startled his fans, who were confronted with his role as an unscrupulous press agent who helps a powerful newspaper columnist to ruin his sister's relationship with a man he considers inappropriate.

Then, in 1959, came the comic tour de force *Some Like It Hot*, which revealed a whole new dimension to his capacities. In this outrageous and side-splittingly funny film Curtis was pitted against Jack Lemmon and a Marilyn Monroe who was acting to the peak of capacity. But Curtis was overtopped by neither. Indeed, in this marvellous concoction of transvestism, role confusion and double entendre he turned in the performance without which, perhaps, the movie could not have staked its claim to the pinnacle of screen comedy. Nothing Curtis did afterwards could ever, perhaps, surpass this. Yet for many years he continued to exercise his flair for light comedy, as well as playing romantic adventurers, and he had a critical success with his most sombre role, as *The Boston Strangler* (1969).

Above all, he gave the impression of enjoying himself both professionally, whatever the fare – he made more than 100 films – and personally. There was something gloriously over the top about his love affairs, his alcoholism, drug addiction, his propensity for marrying and, to the end, a simply unashamed delight in the company of women that really did him credit, and enabled him to grow old gracefully and enjoyably.

Tony Curtis was born Bernard Schwartz in the New York borough of the Bronx in 1925. His parents, Emanuel and Helen Schwartz, were Hungarian immigrants. His father was a tailor who had left his native land for the promise held out by America, and life for Tony and his brothers was lived in the small rooms available to them and their mother at the back of the business premises. Hungarian was in fact Curtis's only language until he was five.

His mother had schizophrenia, a condition which also afflicted his brother Robert and led to his eventually being institutionalised. His other brother Julius was run over by a truck in the street and killed when Curtis was 13. An unstable upbringing and involvement in street gangs was later grist to the cinema publicists.

During the Second World War Curtis joined the US Navy straight from school and served in a submarine tender, USS Proteus, in the Far East. He was wounded in the Pacific campaign and at the end of the war witnessed the Japanese surrender in Tokyo Bay in September 1945.

After being demobilised from the US Navy he studied acting at the dramatic workshop of the New School in New York, with the influential German stage director Erwin Piscator, who had been asked to found the workshop by the New School's president Alvin Johnson.

Here, Curtis found himself among the best of America's burgeoning acting talent, benefiting from the proximity and example of such actors as Marlon Brando, Rod Steiger, Judith Malina, Walter Matthau, Harry Belafonte, Elaine Stritch and Tennessee Williams. He then joined a stock company on the "borscht" circuit. With this he played the lead in a Greenwich Village revival of Clifford Odet's *Golden Boy*.

His journey to Hollywood began when he was noticed by the talent agent and casting director Joyce Selznick. (He was later to claim in a throwaway remark that his discovery was merely down to the fact that he was "the handsomest of the boys".) Nevertheless, this led to a seven-year film contract with Universal.

On arrival he had changed his first name to Anthony and his second name to Curtis (from Kurtz, a surname on his mother's side of the family). He made his first screen appearance (unbilled) in 1948 and acted in several films as James or Anthony Curtis before adopting Tony as his final professional name. His early films were undistinguished, but thanks to effective studio publicity he acquired a huge fan following, not least on account of the quiffed hairstyle that was named after him.

Young men imitated it on both sides of the Atlantic, and girls, in their thousands, wrote in to the studio to request locks of his hair. Among these early titles were such films as *Across the River* (1949), *Kansas Raiders* (1950) and *Winchester 73* (1950).

In 1951 he married the actress Janet Leigh and they made several films together, including a biopic of the escape artist, *Houdini* (1953), which gave him his first significant role. Other titles from the early 1950s were *Son of Ali Baba* (1953) and *The Black Shield of Falworth* (1954). In neither the oriental nor the medieval European setting was the protagonist's strong Bronx accent any impediment. Indeed, he made the "Bronx medieval" diction hugely enjoyable.

Trapeze (1956), directed by Carol Reed, took Curtis well beyond this and established him as an actor of substance. And in *The Sweet Smell of Success*, under another British director, Alexander Mackendrick, he gave a fine performance as the slimy acolyte of Lancaster's vicious gossip columnist.

The Vikings (1958), in which Curtis fought a stirring duel with Kirk Douglas, was perhaps the best of his many costume pictures, and he followed it with another effective dramatic part in *The Defiant Ones* (1958). He and Sidney Poitier played convicts who escape from a chain gang but are still handcuffed together in an ironic denial of their freedom. Curtis was nominated for an Oscar.

In Billy Wilder's *Some Like It Hot* (1959), an exuberant comedy of the Prohibition era, Curtis and Lemmon played musicians who dress up as women to escape pursuing gangsters. As well as relishing the chance to play in drag, Curtis also did a wickedly funny impersonation of Cary Grant as an English millionaire trying to seduce Marilyn Monroe.

In a much-quoted remark, Curtis apparently said that "kissing Monroe was like kissing Hitler". He was (sometime later) to deny ever having said anything so ungallant; gallantry was the very essence of his persona by that time: "The studio made it up... We had an affair for a couple of months. We were very close," he protested.

Curtis played opposite Grant in *Operation Petticoat* (1959), a comedy which was to be the forerunner of many during the 1960s: *Captain Newman, MD* (1963); *Sex and the Single Girl* (1964); *The Great Race* (1965); and *Boeing Boeing* (1965). He also appeared in Stanley Kubrick's *Spartacus* (1960).

In 1968, with his box-office appeal somewhat on the wane and needing to find a strong part, Curtis departed from type to play the criminal protagonist of *The Boston Strangler*, a sex killer who terrorised the eastern United States in the early 1960s. Curtis turned in a skilful, low-key performance, which stood out in a cast that included Henry Fonda and George Kennedy, and was very much in harmony with the quasi-documentary style of the film which was directed by Richard Fleischer.

In 1971 and 1972 Curtis starred with Roger Moore in *The Persuaders*, a light-hearted adventure series for British television. As his film career tended to wind down he turned increasingly to television, playing the villain in *The Count of Monte Cristo* and the film mogul David O Selznick in *The Scarlett O'Hara Wars*, the story of the making of *Gone with the Wind*.

Among the more notable of his later cinema parts was the Senator Joseph McCarthy figure in Nicolas Roeg's *Insignificance* (1985). He continued to make films regularly well into the 1990s, but titles such as *Lobster Man from Mars* (1989) were an indication of a certain decline in seriousness.

Curtis published a novel, *Kid Andrew Cody and Julie Sparrow*, in 1977. He was also an artist of some accomplishment, whose paintings, in particular his portraits of Monroe, proved popular in the salerooms. In 2007 his painting *The Red Table* was on display in the Metropolitan Museum in New York.

In October 2008 he published a volume of memoirs, *American Prince: A Memoir* (written with Peter Golenbock). Although disappointed at not being awarded an Oscar, Curtis received a Sony Ericsson Empire Lifetime Achievement Award and in 1995 received the Ordre des Arts et des Lettres from France.

Curtis's marriage to Janet Leigh was dissolved in 1962. He was married a further five times: to Christine Kaufmann, 1963–67; Leslie Allen, 1968–82; Andrea Savio, 1984–92; Lisa Deutsch, 1993–94; and Jill Vandenberg, 1998. The first four of these marriages were dissolved.

Curtis is survived by his wife, Jill. One of his sons predeceased him and his surviving children include the actress Jamie Lee Curtis, one of two daughters from his marriage to Janet Leigh, who has such pictures as *Halloween, Trading Places* and *A Fish Called Wanda* to her credit.

Tony Curtis was born on June 3, 1925. He died of a heart attack on September 29, 2010, aged 85

GENE HACKMAN

When Gene Hackman was learning his trade at the Pasadena Playhouse's school of acting, he was voted one of the two students "least likely" to succeed. He was in good company, for the other would-be thespian given the thumbs down was his lifelong friend Dustin Hoffman.

Within months Hackman had flunked out with the lowest grade the theatre had ever given any student. He headed for New York, where for a while it seemed that his tutors and classmates might be right, as stage work eluded him.

He worked as a shoe salesman and as a furniture removal man. When he was employed as a doorman, one of his former officers from his time in the marines recognised him and told him: "Hackman, you're a sorry son of a bitch." He even stood in Times Square dressed as the American War of Independence hero Paul Revere and wearing an advertising sandwich board. "That was acting!" he later joked.

Yet perhaps it was his training as a marine that meant he refused to accept defeat. "It was psychological warfare," he said. "I wasn't going to let those fuckers get me down. If you're really interested in acting there is a part of you that relishes the struggle. It's a narcotic in the way that you are trained to do this work and nobody will let you do it, so you're a little bit nuts. You lie, you cheat, you do whatever it takes to get an audition."

On the surface, Hackman was unlikely star material, and when he managed to get an audition it was easy enough to understand the rejections. Tall and muscular, he was, in his own words, a "big lummox kind of person" with the face of "your everyday mine worker".

His stubbornness slowly began to pay off. After failing an audition for a speaking part in a production of Arthur Miller's *A View from the Bridge,* he was told by the director that there was an opening as an extra, playing a strong, silent Italian workman. He gratefully seized the opportunity and his foot was in the stage door. More off-Broadway roles followed, although he was 37 before he landed his first major film role when he played Buck Barrow, the older brother of Warren Beatty's titular role in 1967's *Bonnie and Clyde.* It won him his first Oscar nomination as best supporting actor.

The casting was fortuitous. He only got the role because with Hoffman's help he had been cast as Mrs Robinson's husband in *The Graduate,* only to be sacked a few days into rehearsals. Had he lasted even a day or two longer before getting fired, he would not have been available when Arthur Penn was casting *Bonnie and Clyde.* Another Oscar nomination followed for 1970's *I Never Sang for My Father,* starring opposite Melvyn Douglas.

Yet at 40 his cinematic life was only just beginning and the following year came the performance of a lifetime as the hard-bitten New York drug cop "Popeye" Doyle in *The French Connection.* It won him an Oscar as best actor and secured his place on Hollywood's A-list of leading men.

Hackman claimed that he was "at least seventh choice" for the part and was so troubled by the violence of the role – the script required him to shoot a suspect in the back and accidentally kill a fellow agent – that at one point he told the director, William Friedkin, that he should consider replacing him.

His squeamishness was somewhat surprising, for in real life he had a history of getting into fights in bars, and his volatile bust-ups with directors earned him the nickname "Vesuvius". Yet his temper tantrums were almost always forgiven. "There's something very charismatic in him, even when he's being his worst," said Wes Anderson, who directed Hackman in *The Royal Tenenbaums*.

Throughout the 1970s he was so in demand that he was able to pick and choose his parts at will. He turned down lead roles in *Jaws*, *Close Encounters of the Third Kind* and *Raiders of the Lost Ark* but said yes to *Superman: The Movie* (1978), in which he made a splendidly villainous Lex Luthor. He proved he could play comedic roles as well as tough guys in Mel Brooks's *Young Frankenstein* (1974).

His performance in Francis Ford Coppola's *The Conversation* (1974) was another career highlight. That he had been second choice to Marlon Brando, one of his early heroes, inspired him to a bravura performance as the secretive, introverted private detective Harry Caul. Hackman called it "the pinnacle of my acting career in terms of character development", while Roger Ebert, the influential American film critic, praised his portrayal as "one of the most affecting and tragic characters in the history of movies".

The performance deserved an Academy Award but Coppola had two films out simultaneously and it was his *The Godfather Part II* that got the Oscar glory. Audiences were also confused by the film's themes of illegal bugging at a time when the Watergate scandal was front-page news, although the movie had been completed before the story broke. Ironically, two years earlier Hackman had appeared on Nixon's infamous "list of enemies". The reasons why were not apparent, for Hackman was nothing more than a middle-of-the-road Democrat and later expressed an admiration for Ronald Reagan.

A healthy disregard for celebrity meant he steered clear of the Hollywood party circuit, which he found "shallow", but he enjoyed the wealth that went with stardom and by the 1980s had blown much of his fortune on private planes, racing cars and bad investments.

That he hadn't kept up to date with his tax liabilities further exacerbated his financial problems and once the IRS had caught up with him he was reduced to borrowing his daughter's "piece of shit" car to drive around Hollywood.

He worked furiously, making 20 films over the course of the next decade, some of them more forgettable than others. "I was just barely hanging in, taking pretty much anything that was offered to me and trying to make it work," he said.

However, a dramatic career revival came with 1988's *Mississippi Burning*, in which he played an FBI agent investigating racist murders in the Deep South in the 1960s against the hostility of the local police and the Ku Klux Klan.

The director, Alan Parker, decided to cast Hackman at the outset and discussed the project with him as the script was being written. "It felt right to do something of historical import," Hackman said. "It was an extremely intense experience, both the content of the film and the making of it in Mississippi."

The film earned seven Academy Awards nominations, including one for best actor for Hackman's masterfully wry and self-deprecating performance. On the night, he missed out to his old friend Hoffman, who won the Oscar for *Rain Man*.

Another 30 films followed before his retirement in 2004, including *The Firm* (1993), *Get Shorty* (1995), *Enemy of the State* (1998) and *The Royal Tenenbaums* (2001).

Among the best of his later films was Clint Eastwood's 1992 western *Unforgiven*, in which he played a sadistic sheriff who brutally beat a gunslinger played by Richard Harris, a task he seemed to undertake with some relish. He later revealed the reason. The two had appeared together before in the 1966 film *Hawaii* and Hackman was insulted that Harris did not remember him. "I remember thinking: 'Oh, I can use this,' so I took that disappointment and did this kind of transference," he noted. His fired-up performance won him an Oscar and a Golden Globe.

Another Nineties classic was *Crimson Tide*, a Cold War action thriller in which Hackman plays a combat-hardened submarine captain who spars with a new officer he signs, played by Denzel Washington. It featured one of the most memorable dressing-downs in cinematic history ("You repeat this order, or I'll find somebody who will!" he yells to a stunned Washington, before requesting he be removed from the control room and arrested on the charge of mutiny).

Perhaps because he came to acting late, he had a broader hinterland than many in Hollywood. He flew stunt planes, went deep-sea diving and drove in Sports Car Club of America races.

There were more cerebral pastimes, too and he painted and wrote several novels. "I like the loneliness of writing," he said. "It's similar in some ways to acting, but it's more private and I feel like I have more control over what I'm trying to say and do."

When he retired he declared he was no longer willing to make "the compromises that you have to make in films". The only way he could be tempted to make another movie, he said, would be if they filmed it in his house in Santa Fe, where he lived quietly with his second wife, Betsy Arakawa, a former classical pianist 32 years his junior, who was found dead alongside her husband.

Visitors to his home noted the total absence of movie memorabilia, apart from a framed poster of the actor Errol Flynn. When asked where his Oscar statuettes were, he claimed he didn't even know. "Maybe they're packed somewhere," he told the LA Times.

His first marriage, to Faye Maltese, a bank secretary whom he met at a YMCA dance in 1956, ended in divorce in 1986. He is survived by their three children, Christopher, Elizabeth and Leslie.

Eugene Alden Hackman was born in San Bernardino, California, in 1930, the younger son of Anna (née Gray) and Eugene Hackman. His father, who ran a printing press, walked out when he was 13 and the desertion scarred him for life. He never forgot his father's last wave from his car as he left: "It was like he was saying: 'OK, it's all yours. You're on your own now, kiddo.'"

The family went to live with his maternal grandmother in Illinois and the teenage Hackman went off the rails. There was a night spent in jail after stealing from a sweet shop and a fight with his basketball coach, which led to him leaving school at 16. He joined the US Marines by lying about his age but the uniform did not tame him. He managed a promotion to corporal but was immediately demoted again for brawling.

Based in Japan, his battalion was about to be shipped to fight in the Korean War in 1952 when a motorcycle crash left him with a broken leg and shoulder, which resulted in his discharge.

Back home, he spent six months studying journalism at the University of Illinois before dropping out. He drifted to New York and did a succession of dead-end jobs until his new wife persuaded him to move to Los Angeles to "follow the dream" of acting, which had been seeded as a boy when his mother took him to the cinema to see the films of Flynn and James Cagney.

Within months he was back in New York with another failure to his name and a family to feed. It was then that the famous Hackman stubbornness kicked in and he obsessively set about improving the acting skills which drama school had dismissed as non-existent. In the end he learnt to act from the school of life, wandering around the streets of New York, endlessly watching people and absorbing their mannerisms, like a "seminar in humanity".

It made him a character actor with few peers. According to the script's requirements, he could be "sad and gentle" in one scene and then in the next "scary as hell at the drop of a hat", said an admiring Wes Anderson. "That's the way he attacked every scene, with everything he's got."

Gene Hackman, was born on January 30, 1930. He was found dead at home on February 26, 2025, aged 95

SIDNEY POITIER

It is hard today to comprehend fully the hurdles that faced Sidney Poitier at the start of his acting career. Resistance came not just from some sections of American society – when he emerged into the public eye, segregation was still prevalent in the southern states – and from a Hollywood establishment that had hidebound ideas about the kind of role that an African American could play. He also encountered a backlash from some sections of the Black community, which criticised him for being insufficiently radical and for habitually favouring roles that were non-threatening to a White audience.

Poitier nevertheless became the first bona fide African American movie star, and not only that but the first Black performer to win an Oscar for best actor in a leading role. He paved the way for a whole generation of actors, directors and writers of African American descent and other minority groups.

Poitier's career travails were only the latest battle in a life that, from the very beginning, was a struggle. When he was born in 1927 in Miami, during a visit by his Bahamian parents to the US, he was two months premature and weighed just 3lb. He wasn't expected to survive. Resigned, his father found a shoebox in which to bury his tiny, fragile son. Yet against the odds, the child pulled through and spent the first years of his life in extreme poverty, his father eking a dirt-poor existence on the family farm on Cat Island in the Bahamas. His mother supplemented the meagre living they made from growing tomatoes by breaking rocks into gravel for the construction industry.

When Sidney was ten he moved with his family to Nassau; at 15 he was sent to live with his brother in Miami. Two years later he found himself sleeping rough in New York. He was briefly jailed for vagrancy and later recalled getting shot in the leg during a race riot – he avoided arrest by eschewing the hospital and treating the wound himself. He bore the scar throughout his long life.

With little formal schooling, Poitier drifted between menial jobs in construction, cleaning and working as a dishwasher. He improved his reading with the help of a waiter who sat with him after hours in the diner where they both worked. Having been thrown out of his first acting audition by a director who took issue with his accent, Poitier purchased a cheap radio and shed his Bahamian lilt by mimicking the announcers' precise diction while he toiled over the washing-up in a restaurant kitchen.

His introduction to acting came in 1945 at the American Negro Theatre in Harlem. The limitations in Poitier's abilities – he was tone deaf – worked in his favour. Rather than follow the song and dance entertainer route, he concentrated on his acting. His efforts were rewarded with a starring role in a Broadway production of *Lysistrata*. His first film role, playing a doctor in Darryl F Zanuck's *No Way Out*, came in 1950. That year Poitier married his first wife, the former dancer Juanita Hardy.

Poitier's breakout role came in 1955, playing a rebellious but promising student in Richard Brooks's searing social commentary picture *Blackboard Jungle*. Capitalising on the profile that the film brought him, Poitier relocated with his family to Los Angeles. Notable roles included *Edge of the City* (1957), in which he played a stevedore opposite John Cassavetes, and *The Defiant Ones* (1958), co-starring with Tony Curtis in the story of two escaped convicts chained together. This latter picture earned Poitier his first Academy Award nomination, the first nomination for any African American male actor. Five years later he won the Oscar for best actor for *Lilies of the Field* (1963), a rather saccharine drama that was notable for the fact that it was the first film in which his race was incidental, but not much else.

The year 1967 was pivotal, with Poitier starring in three of its most commercially successful films: *To Sir, with Love; Guess Who's Coming to Dinner* and *In the Heat of the Night*. Of the three, it is the latter, a crime drama in which Poitier played the detective Virgil Tibbs and Rod Steiger co-starred as a racist police chief, that is now considered to be a classic. The film spawned two sequels, *They Call Me Mr Tibbs!* (1970) and *The Organization* (1971). Steiger said of it at the time: "The races, in cinema as much as in real life, didn't mix. *In the Heat of the Night* wasn't just risky cinema: it was a revolution. Suddenly police brutality, government crackdowns, the civil rights movement – they were all thrown into the American consciousness. Hell, the south hated the film so much, it was banned there."

Although the film was set in Mississippi, Poitier had been threatened by the Ku Klux Klan there during a previous visit, and insisted that it was filmed in the north. Illinois doubled for the south in all but a few scenes. However, the production was forced to shoot in Tennessee briefly. Poitier slept with a gun under his pillow throughout, and the location shoot was cut short after local racists made death threats.

The quiet poise and restraint that Poitier exhibited in front of the camera was matched by his behaviour on set. The calm and level-headed actor very rarely lost his temper. If he did, there was usually a good reason. He apparently became enraged on the set of *The Wilby Conspiracy* when the script was changed so that his character blew off a pair of handcuffs with a shotgun. He felt that rewrite was frivolous and lowered the dignity of the character.

From the outset Poitier was careful about the kind of roles he accepted. The filmmaker Robert Townsend recalled: "If he had played just one pimp, there would have been no *In the Heat of the Night*." As the only African American lead actor he felt that it was his responsibility to challenge the orthodoxy and to stand up against the stereotypes that cinema perpetrated. At times the responsibility of being the lone Black actor weighed heavily. "The pressure of that circumstance was excruciating," he later recalled. "When you are carrying everybody's dream, all the minority people."

With the advent of the civil rights movement Poitier and his morally unimpeachable "whiter than white" on-screen persona increasingly became the target of criticism from the Black community. He was described as an "Uncle Tom", a damning indictment that cut deeply and contributed to Poitier moving away from acting and focusing on directing, with his notable films including the 1980 comedy *Stir Crazy* starring Gene Wilder and Richard Pryor. The screenwriter Al Young recalled that Poitier's Oscar statuette was permanently displayed on the floor, toppled over on its side, reflecting his ambivalence about an industry and an audience that never seemed satisfied.

Pressure from the backlash against him and guilt over the break-up of his first marriage led to Poitier spending most of his Hollywood years in therapy. His marriage to Juanita, who later became a mosaic artist, unravelled in 1965 over his affair with the actress Diahann Carroll.

He met Carroll on the set of *Porgy and Bess* (1959), and later said, "We had not been on the set … more than a few days when I realised that she was unique. She had fantastic cheekbones, perfect teeth and dark, mysterious eyes. She was confident, inviting, sensuous, and she moved with a rhythm that absolutely tantalised me … I acted very, very gentlemanly for weeks, but halfway through the picture we fell in love." He told Juanita about the affair straight away, but it took a further six years before the marriage ended.

Coming, as he did, from an era that celebrated gentlemanly propriety ("My father had thoroughly indoctrinated me when I was young," he later recalled), Poitier found the failure of his marriage particularly hard to reconcile. His relationships with his four daughters were tested. "I think there was a time when they were as mad as hell at me because of the threat to their own security. Although I never severed links with them, I was a villain of sorts in their eyes."

Poitier rebuilt bridges between himself and his children, and at least two of them, Pamela and Sherri, followed their father into the family business. Pamela acted in *The Jackal* and *Stir Crazy*. Sherri appeared in her father's film, *A Piece of the Action* (1977). Of the other two daughters, Beverly is a jewellery designer and Gina predeceased him in 2018.

Poitier's next marriage, to the Canadian actress Joanna Shimkus, came in 1976. They met when they co-starred in *The Lost Man* (1969). They had two daughters, Anika, who dabbled in acting before choosing to direct, and Sydney Tamiia, an actress who has worked with Quentin Tarantino and Clint Eastwood. His daughters described him as a strict father, but recalled his playful side: they used to dress him up in lipstick and hair decorations then make him call room service in hotels.

In addition to his film career Poitier also worked in the diplomatic service. In 1997 he was appointed ambassador of the Bahamas to Japan, a position he held for ten years. He also concurrently served as the ambassador of the Bahamas to Unesco.

Although Poitier was vocal about his reservations regarding the film industry and the dip in quality of the films produced, his contribution was acknowledged through numerous awards and accolades including an honorary knighthood in 1974 and an honorary Oscar in 2002, awarded "for his extraordinary performances and unique presence on the screen and for representing the industry with dignity, style and intelligence". In 2009 he was awarded a Presidential Medal of Freedom by Barack Obama.

His contributions to cinema and to racial politics were gratefully acknowledged by the generation that followed him. The film-maker Spike Lee is just one industry figure who credits Poitier as an influence on his own career. "He was the only strong Black figure I saw in the movies when I was growing up," he said in 1989. "I am able to do what I am today because of the hell he went through."

Sidney Poitier KBE was born on February 20, 1927. He died of heart failure on January 6, 2022, aged 94

MARILYN MONROE

Marilyn Monroe's career was not so much *a* Hollywood legend as *the* Hollywood legend: the poor orphan who became one of the most sought-after (and highly paid) women in the world; the hopeful Hollywood unknown who became the most potent star-attraction in the American cinema; the uneducated beauty who married one of America's leading intellectuals.

The story thus dramatically outlined was in all essentials true. Marilyn Monroe began life as Norma Jean Baker in Los Angeles, where she was born in 1926. She was brought up in an orphanage and a series of foster homes, married first at the age of 15, obtained a divorce four years later and began a career as a photographer's model. From this, in a few months, she graduated to a screen test with Twentieth Century-Fox, a contract and the name which she was to make famous. Nothing came of this contract immediately, however, and her first appearance in a film was for another studio in 1948, when she played second lead in a not-very-successful B picture called *Ladies of the Chorus*. There followed a number of small roles in films such as *Love Happy* (with the Marx Brothers);

The Asphalt Jungle, directed by John Huston in which she was first seriously noticed; Joseph Mankiewicz's *All About Eve*; Fritz Lang's *Clash by Night* and others, until in 1952 she was given her first starring role in a minor thriller, *Don't Bother to Knock*, in which she played (improbably) a homicidal baby-sitter.

This was where she began in earnest to become a legend: during the shooting of the film it came to light that some years before she had posed nude for a calendar picture, and her career, hanging in the balance, was saved by the simple avowal that she had needed the money for the rent and was not ashamed. From then on her name was constantly before the public, even if the parts she played were not always large or important, and the advertising for her next major role, in *Niagara*, which showed her reclining splendidly the length of the Niagara Falls, established the image once and for all.

At about this time she married the baseball star Joe di Maggio – the marriage was dissolved in 1954 – and began to show signs that she had talent as well as a dazzling physical presence. In *Gentlemen Prefer Blondes* and *How to Marry a Millionaire* startled critics noticed a real gift for comedy and by the arrival of *The Seven Year Itch* there was no doubt about it: she gave a performance in which personality and sheer acting ability (notably an infallible sense of comic timing) played as important a part as mere good looks. From then on she appeared in an unbroken string of personal successes: *Bus Stop*, of which as severe a judge as Jose Ferrer has said: "I challenge any actress that ever lived to give a better performance in that role"; *The Prince and the Showgirl* in which many critics felt she outshone her director and co-star Sir Laurence Olivier; *Some Like It Hot* and *Let's Make Love*.

In 1956 Marilyn Monroe was married again – to the playwright Arthur Miller (they were divorced in 1960) and his next work, the original screenplay of *The Misfits*, was written for her. This was, in the event, her last film (the most recent, *Something's Got to Give*, being shelved after her failure to fulfil the terms of the contract) and in it under John Huston's direction she gave a performance which provoked its reviewer in The Times to a comment which might stand for her work as a whole: "Considerations of whether she can really act seem as irrelevant as they were with Garbo; it is her rare gift just to be in front of the camera, and, to paraphrase the comment of her apologetic employer in an earlier, more frivolous film, 'Well, anyone can act'."

Marilyn Monroe was born on June 1, 1926. She died of an overdose of barbiturates on August 4, 1962, aged 36

GENE WILDER

Gene Wilder never thought he was funny in real life. "People say, 'What a comic, what a funny guy' and I'm not. I'm really not," he insisted. "I make my wife laugh once or twice in the house. But nothing special."

On screen it was a different story. Curly-haired and chubby-cheeked with melancholic blue eyes and the bemused smile of a neurotic cherub, Wilder was a comic master, specialising in playing eccentrically loveable oddballs nervously struggling to make sense of an uncertain world.

From the antsy accountant with a security blanket in *The Producers* to the burnt-out gunslinger in *Blazing Saddles*, and the lead role in *Young Frankenstein* to the zany but faintly menacing title role in *Willy Wonka and the Chocolate Factory*, Wilder's comic gifts were complex, subtle and endearing.

Much of his inspiration was derived from Charlie Chaplin and his ability to be "funny, then sad, then both at the same time".

Mel Brooks, who directed him in several of his most acclaimed roles, joked that he made the perfect on-screen victim, which "the wolves are waiting to devour". It was perhaps no coincidence that in five different movies Wilder played a man wrongly accused of committing a crime.

Woody Allen cast him as the doctor who falls in love with a sheep in *Everything You Always Wanted to Know About Sex (But Were Afraid to Ask)*, because he said that Wilder was the only person who could convince by playing it straight.

However, after making some of the wittiest, smartest comedies of the 1970s and 1980s, Wilder fell out of love with Hollywood. "I like show but not the business," he said. He moved to Connecticut, claiming that to have stayed in Los Angeles would have "taken my soul". By the mid-1990s he had virtually disappeared from the screen and turned to writing. He produced three novels, short stories and a well-received autobiography.

He spiced his performances with the pain, trauma, guilt and sexual repression he had suffered and which led him to spend years in therapy. "I'd be insane to lose my insanity. That's probably why people pay money to see me," quipped Wilder, who once said that choosing his favourite book would be an agonising choice between Jean Renoir's *The Notebooks of Captain Georges* and the complete works of Sigmund Freud.

Jerome Silberman was born in Milwaukee, Wisconsin, in 1933. His Russian-Jewish émigré father, William, traded in novelty whisky miniatures, while his mother, Jeanne, who came from a Polish family, suffered from a heart condition.

Wilder remembered a doctor telling him never to argue with his mother because it might kill her, but he could help her by making her laugh. From the age of eight, comedy had literally become a matter of life and death. He began acting out little comic sketches for her in Yiddish accents and scenes from Danny Kaye films.

He took drama lessons but at the age of 13 he was sent to a military institute. Carrying puppy fat and being the only Jew in the school, he became a target for bullying and sexual assault. He returned home after one term. His teenage years were scarred by self-doubt. "I was a milksop as a kid," he said. "I had no confidence, no guts. I felt I was going to be someone else someday – someone who didn't have my weaknesses."

Any sort of happiness led to excruciating guilt, which he sought to assuage by praying out loud for hours. "My mother was suffering every day of her life and what right did I have to be happy?" he said. "Whenever I got happy about something, I felt the need to cut it off, and the only way to cut it off was to pray, 'Forgive me Lord'. For what, I didn't know."

This obsession and self-loathing only passed after his mother's death when he was 24. "About a month after, I bought my first condom," he noted.

By then he had graduated in drama from the University of Iowa and enrolled at the Old Vic Theatre School in Bristol because he thought that studying in Britain would improve his speaking voice. He became an anglophile, later choosing "a huge can of Twinings Earl Grey tea" as his luxury item on *Desert Island Discs*.

Called up to the US Army he served as an aide in a psychiatric ward administering electric shock treatment to patients. Given his own neurotic tendencies, it was perhaps not the ideal assignment but it was at his own request: "I imagined the things I would see there might relate more to acting than any of the other choices. I wasn't wrong."

On his discharge he studied method acting, latterly at Lee Strasberg's Actors Studio. He changed his name because he couldn't envisage "Jerry Silberman in Macbeth" up in lights on Broadway. He chose his new surname after the playwright Thornton Wilder. The first name came from a combination of Eugene Gant in Tom Wolfe's novel *Look Homeward, Angel* and a distant relative named Gene who had been an air force navigator during the war: "He was handsome and looked great in his leather flight jacket, and I liked that."

While appearing in Brecht's *Mother Courage and Her Children* in 1963, his co-star, Anne Bancroft, introduced him to her boyfriend and future husband, Mel Brooks. "He was complaining that they were laughing at his serious performance," Brooks recalled. "He couldn't understand it. 'Because you're funny!' I told him. 'Get used to it. Go with what works!'"

Brooks was trying to get his debut film off the ground and considered Wilder perfect for a starring role. It became *The Producers*, in which Wilder played the nervous accountant, Leo Bloom, who with his partner, Zero Mostel, stages a tasteless musical called *Springtime for Hitler*, which becomes a surprise hit.

By the time the film appeared in 1968 Wilder had already made his screen debut in *Bonnie and Clyde*. He played the terrified undertaker, Eugene Grizzard, who was kidnapped by Faye Dunaway and Warren Beatty and taken on a dizzying joyride before being dumped at the side of the road when they discover his gloomy profession. "Instead of being conventionally frightened, I put on an act of trying not to be afraid, which was, I guess, amusing," he said.

The Producers earned Brooks an Oscar for Best Original Screenplay and Wilder a nomination for Best Supporting Actor. Recalling the ceremony, Wilder said: "Mel and I went to a tuxedo rental shop and he said 'I'm not paying $18 to rent a dress shirt. I'll wear my button down.' All I could think was, 'Please God don't make us win'. When Brooks got up to accept the Oscar, he said: "I would like to thank Gene Wilder, Gene Wilder and Gene Wilder."

They teamed up twice more when Wilder played a brain surgeon descended from Mary Shelley's famous character in the horror spoof *Young Frankenstein*, and the Waco Kid in *Blazing Saddles*, in which he reassures the Black sheriff, who is not getting on with the locals: "You've got to remember that these are just simple farmers. These are people of the land. The common clay of the new West. You know … morons."

Wilder's other great partnership was with Richard Pryor, with whom he made four movies – *Silver Streak; Stir Crazy; See No Evil, Hear No Evil* and *Another You*. "On the first day of rehearsing with him we started improvising," Wilder recalled. "It was just a magical chemical thing."

Their friendship soured as Pryor fell into drug addiction and started turning up late on set. Wilder knew their working relationship was coming to an end when at one point between shoots Pryor set himself on fire while lighting his crack pipe.

Wilder appeared in a number of box-office flops. Surprisingly they included *Willie Wonka and The Chocolate Factory*. The film came

54th in the list of box-office returns in 1971 and was only hailed as a children's classic several years later after being shown on television. Fred Astaire and Joel Grey had both been touted for the role of Wonka in the adaptation of Roald Dahl's novel. The director, Mel Stuart, knew he had his man as soon as Wilder read for the part.

Wilder suggested that in Wonka's first appearance he should pretend to be crippled and feign the need for a walking cane. It became one of the film's most memorable moments as Wilder faltered and tumbled before leaping to his feet with a winning smile. "I spent three weeks rehearsing that flip with a gymnastics coach," Wilder said. "But I knew that from then on the audience wouldn't know if I was lying or telling the truth."

The scene encapsulated the morality play at the heart of the film as Wonka invites a group of children to tour his factory and tests their mettle with a series of temptations before the question of his veracity is answered at the end.

As his career flourished, Wilder's private life grew more complicated. He married the British actress and playwright Mary Mercier in 1960. They divorced after five years. In 1967 he married Mary Joan Schutz, a friend of his sister, who had a daughter, Katharine, from a previous marriage, and whom he adopted. After writing *Young Frankenstein*, he asked Katharine to read the script and draw a smiling face where she laughed and a frown if she found a passage she did not like.

Schutz and Wilder separated amid rumours of his infidelity. He became permanently estranged from his adopted daughter and had no other children.

In 1984 he married the actress and comedian Gilda Radner after meeting her on the set of *The Woman in Red*. The couple longed to have children, but in the course of having IVF treatment Radner discovered that she had ovarian cancer. She died five years later. After her death he founded Gilda's Club, a support group to raise awareness of the illness. He met his fourth wife, Karen Webb, a speech therapist, when she coached him in how to play a deaf man in the film *See No Evil, Hear No Evil*. They married in 1991. She survives him.

Wilder was diagnosed with non-Hodgkin's lymphoma in 1999 but was in full remission after chemotherapy and a stem-cell transplant. He subsequently developed Alzheimer's disease.

He spent his final years in domestic contentment in the 18th-century colonial home in Stamford, Connecticut, which had belonged to Radner, writing, painting watercolours and rejecting every script the studios sent him. His curly mane, now grey, was thinner and wispier, though no less chaotic.

Wilder's withdrawal was echoed in the advice he offered to aspiring actors dreaming of a career in Hollywood: "There's nothing but rejection and rejection and rejection. If you can't take that, give it up. I was lucky. I got Mel Brooks and from then on, everything was okay."

Gene Wilder was born on June 11, 1933. He died on August 29, 2016, aged 83

REX HARRISON

Rex Harrison was an actor whose career on the stage and in films continues, it seemed agelessly, for more than 50 years. He was, at first, a lively, debonair and charming juvenile lead; he graduated, through a series of more mature parts which allowed him to temper charm with eccentricity, into roles like that of Shaw's Professor Higgins, playing them with a naturalism which totally concealed art and authority which comes from precision of judgment and certainty of effect.

He was born Reginald Harrison in Huyton, near Liverpool, in 1908 and educated at Liverpool College. He joined the Liverpool Repertory Company in 1924, making his first appearance on the stage as the Husband in Beatrice Mayor's *Thirty Minutes in a Street*, and remained in Liverpool for three years. Three years in touring companies – in *Charley's Aunt*, *Potiphar's Wife*, *The Chinese Bungalow* and *A Cup of Kindness*, by Ben Travers – passed before he reached London, where he was first seen at the Everyman Theatre in *Getting George Married*. In 1936 he made his first appearance in New York, as Tubs Barrow in *Bitter Aloes*.

The success of Terence Rattigan's *French Without Tears* at the Criterion in 1936 gave Harrison a personal success in the role of Alan Howard, which asked not only elegance and charm of him but proved him capable of a certain quality of creative wit. He played the part for more than a year. After that came Leo, in Coward's *Design for Living*, and Gaylord Esterbrook, in SN Behrman's *No Time for Comedy*.

Among the films he made in the 1930s and 1940s were some no less demanding than the comedies of Coward and Behrman. As Adolphus Cusins in the film of Shaw's *Major Barbara*, he showed himself well capable of giving personality to the author's didactic high spirits, and as Charles Condamine, in the screen version of Coward's *Blithe Spirit*, the speed, ease and elegance of his playing were equally impressive. Those films which simply exploited his personality like *The Rake's Progress*, in which he displayed a more than Raffles-like criminality redeemed by wartime sufferings, always showed him capable of more effects than the original work seemed to contain.

At the end of the war, in which he had served in the RAF Volunteer Reserve, he became one of the essential English gentlemen of Hollywood films, an expert in pointed understatement and exactitude of timing. But on the New York stage, as Henry VIII in *Anne of the Thousand Days*, Sir Henry Harcourt-Reilly in Eliot's *The Cocktail Party*, Hereward in Christopher Fry's *Venus Observed* and the Man of Ustinov's *Love of Four Colonels*, he was given work of greater importance and more challenging quality than he had normally played in England.

His mature style in film comedy, as in pleasant trifles such as *The Reluctant Debutante* (1958), became an object lesson in effective simplicity, and though parts like that of the Pope in *The Agony and the Ecstasy* (1965), patronising Michelangelo in both senses of the verb, seemed not by nature designed to match his personality, he played against the grain of his own style with results that were never less than interesting.

The authority of his account of Professor Higgins, in *My Fair Lady*, the musical version of Shaw's *Pygmalion*, both in New York in 1956 and later when the work reached London, had a driving force, an intellectual energy and a swiftness of response which were the first opportunity English audiences were given to see a popular idol at his most effective. The charm which he might have exploited for his own ends was harnessed to the role in a way which illuminated its rampageous egotism and thoughtless rudeness. Incapable of singing, he convinced the world that Lerner's lyrics and Loewe's score lost nothing when he simply declaimed the words in rhythmic speech, refusing to notice their melodies. He later played Higgins in the film of *My Fair Lady*, and his performance won the Oscar for best actor.

Harrison was made, and very well made, out of the stuff which once had been used to construct "Matinee Idols". He could delight any audience, even the most conscientiously intellectual, by his ease, insouciance and elegant light-heartedness. But these were qualities which he harnessed to the plays in which he appeared, often, it seemed, adding them as his own contribution to an author's blueprint. In the film of Charles Dyer's *Staircase* (1968), with Richard Burton, he demonstrated that they had as sure a place in the world of problematic and problem-setting modern comedy as in that of Rattigan's sunny prewar comedy.

If his later films were mainly undistinguished, he was able to demonstrate his considerable stagecraft in Pirandello's *Henry IV*, William Douglas-Home's *The Kingfisher* (which he played in New York and on British television), as Captain Shotover in Shaw's *Heartbreak House*, and in the Frederick Lonsdale comedy, *Aren't We All?* His autobiography, *Rex*, was published in 1974. The Higgins of Lerner and Loewe marked the apex of the Harrison career. He took on some of the personality of the irascible professor in private life.

When booking seats at the theatre or making a restaurant reservation he tended to use the alias of Higgins. After the Broadway production, the London one at Drury Lane and the film, he was the obvious first-choice Higgins for any major revival of the musical which captivated the world. But Harrison began to worry that the character was taking him over.

He sought, very carefully, in his 70s other characters to play on stage. He had never had much time for contemporary drama after

Rattigan. Unlike his old rival, Laurence Olivier, in the days when matinee idols were matinee idols on screen and on stage, he would never have considered a part such as Archie Rice in *The Entertainer*. He preferred roles in which the character was urbane, polished and properly dressed, although earlier he had impressed as Platonov in Chekhov's play of the same name at the Royal Court.

There was no shortage of scripts arriving through the Harrison letterbox. He frequently declared himself a theatrical conservative and complained that he had no taste for wrestling with new words. But there was another reason: his eyesight, which had never been strong, was failing, and difficulty in reading meant difficulty in learning. He turned, understandably, to the tried and trusted after much discussion with friends: Shaw's *Heartbreak House*, JM Barrie's *The Admirable Crichton*. Typically, just before his death he was in Somerset Maugham's *The Circle* in New York. This was due to come to the West End shortly at The Haymarket, which was the theatre most associated with him. It is a house where the star system still reigns, as do polish, style and well-dressed productions. He was happy there.

His marriage in 1978 to Mercia Tinker was his sixth. His previous wives were Colette Thomas, Elizabeth, daughter of Lord Ogmore, and the actresses, Lilli Palmer, Kay Kendall and Rachel Roberts. He had two sons.

Sir Rex Harrison was born on March 5, 1908. He died of cancer on June 2, 1990, aged 82

JERRY LEWIS

Jerry Lewis was candid about his gifts as a comedian. "I get paid for what most kids get punished for," he said of his on-screen persona. His stock-in-trade was a geeky and brattish overgrown man-child whose only defences against an uncomprehending and unsympathetic world were pathos and to resort to mayhem.

It was a style rooted in the pratfall traditions of Stan Laurel and Charlie Chaplin, both of whom were friends as well as role models, and it made him one of the richest men in Hollywood.

During the 1950s, his double act with Dean Martin, which started in nightclubs and moved into theatre, television and films, took the pair to the top of the list of America's biggest box-office earners. Between 1949 and 1956 they made 16 films together and by the time their partnership came to an end – amid some acrimony – it was said that only Frank Sinatra and Elvis Presley rivalled their fame among American entertainers.

Lewis's celebrity was such that DC Comics – home of Superman, Batman and The Flash – even gave him his own comic book series, *The Adventures of Jerry Lewis*.

After his break with Martin, he signed a $10-million contract with Paramount Studios – at the time said to be the biggest in Hollywood history – and became a comic auteur, directing, producing and starring in films such as *The Nutty Professor* and *The Bellboy*, which have become bona fide classics.

Martin Scorsese, Quentin Tarantino and Steven Spielberg all confessed to being influenced by his work. "He doesn't censor himself as a performer, a film-maker or a public figure, which is difficult to accept for many people," Scorsese said. "I think Americans are still coming to terms with his astonishing artistry. It's as if they had to invent a new place for it, a new category."

Yet like so many comedians cast in the mode of Leoncavallo's Pagliacci, Lewis was an enigma who possessed a troubled dark side in stark contrast to the zany screen antics that led the French to dub him "Le Roi du Crazy".

He once put a revolver in his mouth with the intention of ending it all, but thought better of it. "If you add up everything that makes the totality of the comic, there's a lot of shit there and you can't ignore it," he said.

Pain and laughter marched hand in hand and he was sometimes called the "Dark Prince" of American comedy. Peter Bogdanovich, the actor and director who knew Lewis for more than 50 years, described "a secret desire to resort to some form of infantilism in order to survive the hard knocks of life". It came as no surprise to learn that his favourite novel was *The Catcher in the Rye* and that he strongly identified with the book's angst-ridden adolescent protagonist, Holden Caulfield. He planned to direct a film version but its author, JD Salinger, refused to sell him the rights.

He once visited a psychiatrist only for the doctor to tell him that it would be a mistake for him to undergo analysis. "If we peel away the emotional and psychological difficulties your pain may leave, but it's also quite possible that you won't have a reason to be funny any more," the shrink told him.

He attempted to marry his dark and comic sides by making a movie titled *The Day the Clown Cried*, about a circus clown in Auschwitz forced by the Nazis to lead children into the gas chambers. The select few who saw an unfinished version reported the film to be baffling, bizarre and unsettling. Because of the adverse reaction it was never released.

When he succumbed to depression his cure was to seek a tonic by flying to France, a country that he loved and where the feeling was reciprocated. When he was awarded the Légion d'honneur in 2006, the citation called him the "French people's favourite clown".

He earned an unenviable reputation as a vain, narcissistic and ill-tempered egomaniac. It was a judgment with which he was not prepared to argue. "I'm a multifaceted, talented, wealthy, internationally famous genius," he said with his tongue barely in his cheek. "People don't like that. But my answer to all my critics is simple: I like me."

He was also prone to homophobic and misogynistic statements, although it was sometimes hard to tell whether he was joking or not. "I don't like any female comedians. Seeing a woman in comedy sets me back. I think of her as a producing machine that brings babies into the world," he said in 1998.

He lost his virginity at the age of 12 to a stripper named Trudine who lured the boy into her dressing room. "I remember it took only a minute," he said. "She was a piece of work. She danced with a snake."

It was later said that he slept with all his leading ladies and he admitted that when he was directing a film, he would often get to the set early for "a little hump", to get the day started right.

Among those he bedded was Marilyn Monroe. He claimed to have been "crippled for a month" after the experience, which may explain why he turned down an invitation to appear with her in *Some Like It Hot*. The part went to Jack Lemmon, who earned an Oscar nomination and sent Lewis boxes of chocolates every year to thank him.

He married his first wife, Patti, a singer with Jimmy Dorsey's band, when he was 19. Despite his innumerable infidelities – "I banged anyone I could meet," he confessed – they remained married for 36 years until divorcing in 1980. They had five sons: Gary, the lead singer with the 1960s pop group Gary Lewis & the Playboys;

Scott, who works in the film industry; Christopher, who acted as his father's archivist; Anthony, a film-maker and cinematographer; and Joseph, who died in 2009. They also adopted a sixth son, Ronnie.

He married for a second time in 1983 to SanDee Pitnick, a dancer in Las Vegas who was 25 years his junior. They had one daughter, Danielle, whom they adopted in 1992, when Lewis was 66.

Suzan Lewis claims to be his daughter from his relationship with the model Lynn Dixon. In 2014 she wrote a memoir called *Jerry Lewis, My Father, Is Always in My Mirror*.

By his own admission Lewis craved applause and the need never left him. Late in life when asked how he would like to be remembered, he replied that he had no interest in what people would think after he had gone: "I want to hear all the good stuff while I'm here."

His behaviour frequently exhibited symptoms of obsessive-compulsive disorder. He refused to wear a pair of socks more than once and changed them several times per day. He gave away his suits rather than have them cleaned and refused to carry "dirty money", insisting on only immaculate dollar bills. He kept them in his pocket in a wad of hundreds and fifties, folded once, wrapped in a rubber band and arranged by his bookkeeper, consecutively, by serial number.

For many years he was addicted to painkillers, which he took to counter the knocks that came with doing all his own stunts. In 1965, while performing in Las Vegas, he threw himself off a piano, landed on the base of his spine and spent four months in hospital. It led to him becoming a walking medicine cabinet and by the 1970s he was taking fistfuls of Percodan, Quaaludes and Nembutal every day. He described most of the decade as a "complete blackout" and after averaging two pictures a year throughout the 1950s and 1960s, he released only one film in the 1970s.

He attributed many of his struggles to a difficult childhood. Born Joseph Levitch in Newark, New Jersey, in 1926, his father, Daniel, and mother, Rae, were Jewish vaudeville entertainers who used the stage name Lewis. From the age of five their only son was joining them on stage singing *Brother Can You Spare a Dime?*

For much of his childhood he was passed from one relative to another and his early memories of his parents were "an occasional phone call or penny postcard". They missed his bar mitzvah. He felt, he wrote in a memoir, like "a dummy, a misfit, the sorriest kid alive".

Bogdanovich had no hesitation in suggesting that his desire for applause and attention as a comic was driven by neglect as a child.

By the age of 15 he had dropped out of school and developed his own comedy routine in burlesque houses where comics took the stage between strippers, performing for "guys in the front with the newspapers in their laps and the trench coats".

He was exempted from military service because of a heart murmur and in 1946 he joined forces in a nightclub act with Martin, who was almost a decade older. Three years later they were signed to Paramount and made their film debut in *My Friend Irma*. There followed a string of formulaic films that lacked subtlety and were savaged by the critics but which were huge box-office draws. Their double act reached Britain in 1953 when they broke house records at the London Palladium.

Yet such success could still not buy the affection of his father. When Jerry bought him a custom-made Cadillac and had it delivered with a huge bow tied around it, the only response was said to be: "How come it's not a convertible?"

Lewis and Martin dissolved their partnership in 1956 on the tenth anniversary of their first performance. By then they were both multimillionaires but were barely on speaking terms. Lewis's version of their falling out was that Martin was sick of hearing everyone talk about his sidekick's wacky brilliance. He reported that when he tried to talk about the depth of their friendship, Martin told him: "To me, you're nothing but a fucking dollar sign."

It was 20 years before they spoke again, although when Martin died in 1995 Lewis described himself as "completely shattered and grief-stricken".

The dollar signs continued to flash without Martin and his solo pictures such as *The Ladies Man*, *The Bell Boy*, *The Nutty Professor*, *The Patsy* and *The Family Jewels* were superior to anything they had done together.

After a long gap he returned to the screen in the 1980s and enjoyed a notable artistic rehabilitation when Scorsese cast him in *The King of Comedy* as a chat show host who is stalked and kidnapped by Robert De Niro's obsessive fan. As late as 1995 he was breaking records when he was said to have become the highest-paid performer in Broadway history for his role as the Devil in *Damn Yankees*.

For more than 40 years he presented an annual "telethon" on American TV in aid of children with muscular dystrophy. Yet even in his charitable work, controversy was never far away as children in wheelchairs and their parents staged a picket line, questioning the destination of the money and objecting to his use of the word "cripple".

In later years he endured prostate cancer, two heart attacks, viral meningitis, diabetes and pulmonary fibrosis. Yet he remained incorrigible and insisted that he was going to live to 101 in order to win a bet with George Burns. "Whatever your last year is, I'm going a year after you," he had told his fellow comedian. Burns, who would die aged 100 in 1996, told him, "If that's what your dream is, sonny, go for it."

Jerry Lewis was born on March 16, 1926. He died on August 20, 2017, aged 91

JOHN WAYNE

———————•———————

John "Duke" Wayne, with his strong masculine presence, had played fliers, soldiers and hard men of all kinds on the screen, but in the public memory he remains the archetypal westerner, tough, resilient, but not without a certain kind of sensibility; he was, in fact, John Ford's conception of the embodiment of the true, American pioneering spirit.

He was born at Winterset, Iowa, in 1907; his real name was Marion Robert Morrison. He entered films more or less by chance; while studying at the University of South California he took vacation work at Twentieth Century-Fox studios and attracted the attention of Raoul Walsh. His first film was a western, *The Big Trail* (1930), and during the next few years he appeared in any number of cheaply made westerns and action dramas, as well as playing smaller parts in a few major films. One of these was directed by John Ford, who determined to give him an important role when the opportunity arose. In 1939 Ford offered him the lead in his famous western *Stagecoach*, which at once established him as leading star in open-air drama, and incidentally was the beginning of a lasting friendship and film partnership between him and Ford, in many of whose subsequent films he appeared.

During the war he appeared in westerns such as *Tall in the Saddle* and war films such as *Back to Bataan*, as well as de Mille's *Reap the Wild Wind* and the sometimes underrated *The Long Voyage Home*. His first postwar film was Ford's naval drama, *They Were Expendable*, which was followed by a series of notable westerns, including *Three Godfathers*, *Ford Apache*, *She Wore a Yellow Ribbon*, *Rio Grande* and *The Searchers*, all directed by Ford, and Howard Hawk's *Red River*. He also played in Sternberg's eccentric *Jet Pilot* and Ford's spectacularly popular Irish comedy *The Quiet Man*.

In 1952 he formed an independent production company with Robert Fellows and showed his sound business instinct by producing a series of successful vehicles for himself, such as *Island in the Sky*, *Hondo* and *The High and the Mighty*, as well as films in which he did not appear like *Goodbye My Lady* and *Track of the Cat*. His later films also included an improbable appearance as Genghis Khan in *The Conqueror* and two biographical roles, the flier Frank "Spig" Wead in Ford's *The Wings of Eagles* and Townsend Harris in Huston's *The Barbarian and the Geisha*, as well as further westerns by Ford (*The Horse Soldiers*) and Hawks (*Rio Bravo*).

In 1960 he took a new step in his career by directing a film for the first time, *The Alamo*, in which he also starred. It was very much a personal statement, both of his views on the American way of life and code of honour and of his right-wing political position. During the next few years he was to become ever more active in politics, but without letting up at all in his film-making: the 1960s brought some of his most notable films, such as Hawk's *Hatari!* and *El Dorado* and Ford's *The Man Who Shot Liberty Valance* and *Donovan's Reef*, as well as Darryl Zanuck's spectacular *The Longest Day*. *The Green Berets* (1968), his second film as director, had something of the character of a personal political statement, with its unfashionable defence of United States policy in Vietnam. In 1970 his career received its ultimate consecration when he received an Oscar for his performance as an ageing gunman in *True Grit*.

He never truly retired but continued to make films of varying quality: *The Shootist*, the story of an ageing gunfighter dying of cancer was seen in Britain in 1976.

John Wayne was always a personality player who made no claims to any great acting ability and generally gave a slightly varied version of the same performance: the drawling, hawk-eyed man of action who, even if gnawed by a slow-burning fanaticism (as in *The Searchers*), allows little sign of it to appear on the surface. But when cast within his limitations (and he had the shrewdness seldom to overstep them) he could always be relied on to give an authoritative performance. As a western hero his manner and physique gave him every advantage, and he appeared in almost every really good western made in Hollywood during the Forties and Fifties; whatever the critics might say of his performances, for this public he was one of America's best-loved stars, and for many years he was never out of the Top Ten stars in terms of money made at the box office.

He was three times married and had three sons and four daughters.

John Wayne was born on May 26, 1907. He died of cancer on June 11, 1979, aged 72

GRACE KELLY

Princess Grace of Monaco, the former American film actress Grace Kelly, was a cool and elegant blonde who took naturally to the cinema screen. She had a brief but spectacular career in Hollywood during which, in 1955, she was voted the second most popular box-office draw in the country. A year later came her engagement and marriage to Prince Rainier III and in spite of several attempts to woo her back, she renounced the cinema to become a full-time first lady of Monaco.

She was born in Philadelphia in 1929. Her father, John Kelly, the son of an Irish farm boy from Co Mayo, in the Republic of Ireland, was a wealthy self-made businessman who had twice, in 1920 and 1924, been an Olympic sculling champion. Her interest in acting, however, may have come from an uncle, George Kelly, who was a popular playwright. She studied at the American Academy of Dramatic Art and was soon offered a film contract, which she turned down, preferring to concentrate on television and modelling.

After good parts in television plays and on Broadway, where she played in Strindberg's *The Father*, opposite Raymond Massey, she was again approached by Hollywood and made her film debut in 1951 in *Fourteen House*. It was a small role of a woman who tries to mend her marriage after seeing a man threatening to throw himself off an apartment block.

The following year she played Gary Cooper's Quaker wife in the celebrated western, *High Noon*, although she benefited little from the film's critical and box-office success and had to wait some time for her next part. It came in John Ford's African melodrama, *Mogambo*, as a reserved Englishwoman who entices Clark Gable away from the more animal attractions of Ava Gardner. Her performance brought an Oscar nomination for best supporting actress and her career had taken off.

Its subsequent development owed much to Alfred Hitchcock, who starred her in three of his films in succession. She probably best realised his idea of the woman who could radiate enormous sex appeal from a prim exterior.

A smaller part in *The Bridges at Toko-Ri*, with William Holden, failed to add to her reputation but after a battle between MGM, who was making the film, and Paramount, who had her under contract, she landed more promising material in Clifford Odet's *The Country Girl*. In fact, her performance as the wife of a man (Bing Crosby) fighting alcoholism won her the 1954 Oscar for best actress and confirmed her standing as one of Hollywood's most sought-after stars.

Difficulty finding a suitable film to follow it led to temporary suspension by the studio but Hitchcock came to the rescue with an engaging comedy thriller set on the Riviera, *To Catch a Thief*. She played an aloof American girl who gradually succumbs to the charms of Cary Grant, signalling her conversion by planting a huge kiss on him. It was during the location shooting that she met Prince Rainier. Their engagement was announced in January 1956 and it was made clear that she would retire from the screen after their marriage.

Grace Kelly's wedding took place at Monte Carlo in April 1956, attracting more than 1,500 journalists and the world's television cameras. Not surprisingly, the bride seemed slightly overawed by such attention. In 1969 she said in an interview that she intended to return to acting, probably in theatre, once her children had grown up. She did appear on radio and television from time to time to reminisce about her Hollywood days and former colleagues such as Cooper, Gable and Crosby. In 1976 she took part in poetry readings at the Edinburgh Festival to mark the American bicentenary and she continued to appear on stage to read poetry and prose, most recently in Britain last March at Chichester to mark the Festival Theatre's twenty-first anniversary.

In Monaco Princess Grace founded the Garden Club, and she instituted an annual flower festival, which was extremely popular, as well as writing an attractive book about flower arranging. She also took a warm and personal interest in the Ballet School, and while preferring a private life could always be persuaded to extend her patronage to a charitable cause.

The public clamour over the unfortunate marriage of her elder daughter, Princess Caroline, greatly distressed her and the prince. To bring up a family in the full and relentless glare of international publicity was a difficult feat, even for someone who had been accustomed to fame, first as a film star, then as a royal princess. She accomplished it with grace and charm, and her death will leave the people of Monaco quite stunned with grief and shock.

There were three children of the marriage: Princess Caroline, born 1957, Prince Albert, heir to the throne, born 1958, and Princess Stephanie, born in 1965.

Grace Kelly was born on November 12, 1929. She died in a car crash on September 14, 1982, aged 52

DONALD SUTHERLAND

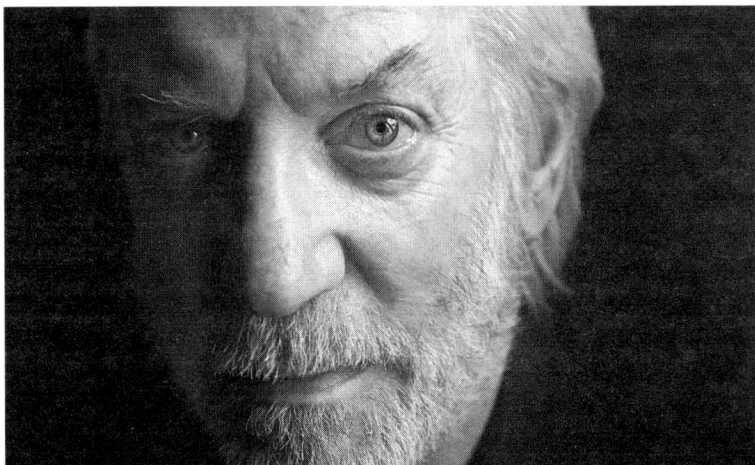

Donald Sutherland enjoyed the irony of appearing in one of cinema's steamiest scenes – up to that point he had often been described as gangling, slouching, droopy-eyed and big-eared. While filming the 1973 thriller *Don't Look Now*, the director Nicolas Roeg instructed him and his co-star, Julie Christie, to walk into the bedroom naked.

"I didn't take my clothes off very often," he said. "Holy cow. Julie and I walked in like Adam and Eve and we didn't really know each other. We laid on the bed and the director said, 'All right Julie pull your knees up to your shoulder. Donald take your mouth and slide it down the inside of her left thigh.' It went on like this for 12 hours. Neither of us could speak afterwards."

The resulting scene was one of the first to depict sex realistically in a mainstream film, although Sutherland – unlike Christie – always denied rumours that the sex had been real. It made the off-beat actor into a sex symbol, but then he quickly learnt that his life in film was nothing if not random.

He had risen to prominence in the 1967 war film *The Dirty Dozen*. His role was a small one until the day he was sitting around a table with Lee Marvin, Charles Bronson, John Cassavetes and other members of the cast who were arguing about which of them was going to impersonate a German general. "Aldrich [the director Robert Aldrich], who made decisions faster than you can imagine, looked down the table, saw my shaved head, but didn't know my name. He said, 'You with the big ears, you do it.' That changed everything."

He still did not have many lines, but the scene, which comes towards the climax of the movie, gave him the chance to employ various physical tics as the suspense of the mission builds and he is forced to hang around outside the mansion where Marvin has infiltrated a meeting of German top brass.

Sutherland's naturally laid-back demeanour was complemented by a warm chuckle and distinctive little whistle, spectacles and what looked like an angler's hat when he played an army surgeon in the original 1970 film version of *M*A*S*H*. Shooting was reported to have been chaotic, the film was episodic in structure, the acting was naturalistic with Robert Altman pioneering his famous "overlapping dialogue" and the end result contained more blood than a Peckinpah western. Nevertheless it was one of the biggest hits of the year.

It was followed by Clint Eastwood's war film *Kelly's Heroes*, in which Sutherland presented a vision of detached cool as a hippy tank commander while the craziness of war rages around him.

Although his three early hits were all set during either the Second World War or the Korean War, Sutherland was very much a part of the zeitgeist and became a countercultural figure both on screen and off. He had a three-year affair with Jane Fonda, his co-star in *Klute* (1971), in which he played the titular private detective, while Fonda played a prostitute mixed up in his case. The couple became prominent campaigners against the Vietnam War.

Sutherland was described as one of the finest actors never to win an Oscar, although many thought he was "robbed" when he was not even nominated for a brilliant 15-minute cameo as the Pentagon whistleblower Colonel X in Oliver Stone's *JFK*.

Offbeat and relaxed, Sutherland was never overly reverential about his craft, once saying: "When I'm acting I'm just the director's concubine. I just do what he wants as perfectly as I can."

Donald McNichol Sutherland was born in Saint John, New Brunswick, in 1935, to Frederick, a salesman, and Dorothy (née McNichol). As the name suggests, the family were originally from Scotland, though they also had English and German ancestry. He grew up largely in Nova Scotia, where he attended Bridgewater High School and in his teens worked as a reporter and disc jockey for a local radio station. At Toronto University he opted for the unusual combination of engineering and drama. Thinking about a career in acting, he once asked his mother if he was good-looking. She replied: "No, but your face has a lot of character."

Intent on becoming an actor, he headed for England in 1957 and enrolled at the London Academy of Music and Dramatic Art, but dropped out after a year. In 1959 he married Lois Hardwick, an actress whom he had met in Canada, and they found work at the Perth Repertory Theatre in central Scotland, appearing in several plays there in the early 1960s, including *Inherit the Wind.*

Back in London in the mid-1960s he was in several episodes of *The Saint, The Avengers* and *Man in a Suitcase*. He also began securing film roles and played an American doctor who discovers his wife is a vampire in one of the segments of Freddie Francis's *Dr Terror's House of Horrors* (1965), the film that inspired Steve Coogan's comedy series *Dr Terrible's House of Horrible* (2001).

The Dirty Dozen was his first major break. It featured a team of psychopathic military prisoners who are given the chance to redeem themselves on a dangerous operation behind enemy lines. Lee Marvin played the officer in charge, while the prisoners themselves were divided into a group of stars, including Charles Bronson and Telly Savalas, and – as Sutherland put it – "the bottom six", who were there to make up the numbers.

One of his more interesting roles from the period was in Dalton Trumbo's *Johnny Got His Gun* (1971), in which Timothy Bottoms plays a soldier who has lost his limbs, eyes, ears and mouth, and Sutherland is Christ, to whom he appeals for help. But it was not a commercial success.

Sutherland subsequently turned his back on Hollywood and made several films in Europe, playing the title role in Federico

Fellini's *Casanova* (1976). He later described Fellini as his favourite director because "he has even made my face into something I like". He appeared as a child-rapist and fascist killer in Bernardo Bertolucci's period epic *1900* (1976) and was impressive as the man who realises the awful truth in the 1978 remake of *Invasion of the Body Snatchers*. He was a dope-smoking college professor in John Landis's cult comedy *Animal House* (1978) and the father in Robert Redford's earnest Oscar-winning family drama *Ordinary People* (1980).

By the end of the 1970s his brief period as a leading man was virtually over and he was moving towards character roles, playing a sadistic British sergeant-major in the British-financed historical flop *Revolution* (1985) and a liberal South African schoolteacher in *A Dry White Season* (1989), with Marlon Brando.

His second marriage, to Shirley Douglas, lasted from 1966 to 1971. Douglas was involved in the Black Panther movement. While filming *Kelly's Heroes*, his co-star Clint Eastwood approached Sutherland and said: "I've got some bad news for you. Your wife has been arrested. It seems she tried to buy some hand grenades from the CIA." He is survived by their twins, Kiefer, who became a successful Hollywood actor in his own right, and Rachel.

The marriage ended in divorce and soon afterwards Sutherland became involved with Jane Fonda. With opposition to American involvement in the Vietnam War growing, Sutherland and Fonda put together a revue called *FTA (Free The Army)* and staged it in venues near military bases. He described their affair as "very bright, hot and terrific and then it ended". The break-up, he said, was "very painful, but it was terrific to be upset. It was very invigorating".

He eventually settled down with the Canadian actress Francine Racette, whom he married and with whom he had three more children: Roeg, Rossif and Angus.

His career picked up again in the Nineties. Roles included a New York art dealer forced to reconsider his values by the arrival of a stranger, played by Will Smith, in the drama *Six Degrees of Separation* (1993) and one of Clint Eastwood's team of veteran astronauts in *Space Cowboys* (2000).

The John Grisham adaptation *A Time to Kill* (1996) enabled him to realise his ambition of appearing on screen with his son Kiefer. He was Nicole Kidman's minister father in *Cold Mountain* (2003) and even for a generation that had never seen *M*A*S*H* and *Kelly's Heroes*, he was a familiar face. He had reached a stage where he could pick and choose his roles, and do nothing, if he wanted.

In later years Sutherland took on character roles in a wide range of films and television series, proving equally adept at fatherly figures and villains. He could be enormously charming, though his wolfish grin could hide, or hint at, sinister intent. He was a curious but inspired choice as Mr Bennet, the long-suffering husband and father, in the 2005 version of *Pride and Prejudice*, and he made a memorably Machiavellian senator in the TV series *Commander in Chief*.

He continued to make films into his eighties. His best-known role in recent years was President Snow in *The Hunger Games*. If there was one lesson he had learnt from Hollywood it was that anyone who promises a sure-fire hit is lying. "Al Pacino and I sat on the top of a hill once when we were doing *Revolution* and he said, 'I've never said it before in my life, but this one really I believe will be great.' And it wasn't. It's impossible to tell."

Donald Sutherland was born on July 17, 1935. He died after a long illness on June 20, 2024, aged 88

ERROL FLYNN

The early life of Mr Errol Flynn sounds more like something out of one of his films than sober fact. Born in 1909 in Tasmania, the son of a biologist, he went to school in London and Paris before embarking on a period of wandering which included, as well as a brief appearance in repertory at Northampton and writing (an activity he kept up throughout his career, writing a novel among other works), diving for pearls in Tahiti and hunting gold and headhunters in New Guinea. His introduction to films was quite by chance; a company working on a short film about the mutiny on the Bounty in the South Pacific hired his schooner, some of the material in which he appeared fell into the hands of a talent scout, and in 1935 he was offered a contract with a Hollywood company, his first professional appearance being in *Don't Bet on Blondes*.

It must be admitted (he admitted it often enough himself) that his early films showed little sign of acting ability, but fortunately he seldom appeared in a role which required much acting: his great popularity was based on a series of swashbuckling adventure stories, such as *Captain Blood, The Charge of the Light Brigade, The Adventures of Robin Hood* and *The Sea Hawk*. If these parts did not require any very remarkable acting ability, however, they did call for other qualities – a colourful personality, a striking presence, considerable grace and agility and the ability to look well in period costumes – all of which he possessed in abundance. He also began to show signs of acting ability after five years or so, for he was not so overshadowed as might have been expected in *The Private Lives of Elizabeth and Essex*, in which he played opposite Miss Bette Davis as Elizabeth.

The war years produced few films of any great interest for him, except perhaps *Objective Burma*, which has never been forgotten in this country as "the film in which Errol Flynn took Burma single-handed". After the war he made a group of emotional dramas in which he seemed rather less at home, such as *Never Say Goodbye*, *Need for Each Other* and *Escape Me Never*, but was soon back in the action roles which he played best, with films like *Gentleman Jim*, *Against All Flags*, *The Master of Ballantrae* and *Crossed Swords*. He also appeared, rather improbably, as Soames in *The Forsyte Saga*, though plans for him to appear on the London stage in *Jane Eyre* never materialised.

During the early 1950s his career seemed to be taking several wrong turnings while the amount of personal publicity he received only increased. A film he was producing and starring in based on the life of William Tell foundered for lack of funds, and the two films he made in this country with Anna Neagle, *Lilacs in the Spring* and *King's Rhapsody*, were not really suited to his talents. He had already almost been written off by the film industry when he was offered a leading role in *The Sun Also Rises*, based on Hemingway's novel.

His performance as the cheerily dissolute Englishman in this film was a revelation of hitherto unsuspected talents (he maintained that this was the first opportunity he had ever had to play himself on the screen) and made him a leading star again. It was followed by an excellent portrayal of John Barrymore, whom he had known well, in *Too Much, Too Soon*, and the leading role in Huston's *The Roots of Heaven*. In the Cuban revolution he fought on the side of Castro, and shortly before his death he had completed his autobiography.

Errol Flynn's career provides the perfect example of the old actor's adage that short of a couple of years in a repertory company there is nothing like 20 years of top stardom for teaching a performer how to act.

Errol Flynn was born on June 20, 1909. He died after collapsing on October 14, 1959, aged 50

CARRIE FISHER

Carrie Fisher was fresh out of drama school when she was auditioned by George Lucas for the part of Princess Leia in an obscure sci-fi film called *Star Wars*. Almost 40 years later she reprised her role for one of the franchise's many films, *The Force Awakens*, in which once again she was fighting intergalactic foes.

Between those two milestones Fisher, born into "Hollywood royalty" and once described as "too eccentric for Tinseltown", starred in only a handful of major films, including *The Blues Brothers* (1980) and *When Harry Met Sally* (1989), in which she played Marie, keeping a card-index system of men she tries to set up with Sally. She also wrote a series of books such as *Postcards from the Edge* (1987) about an actress called Suzanne trying to restore her life after taking a drug overdose; *Wishful Drinking* (2008), a memoir about her addictions; and *The Princess Diarist* (2016), in which she disclosed that during the filming of the original *Star Wars* she had an affair with Harrison Ford, who was married at the time to Mary Marquardt.

While the force may have been with her, it was never very clear in which direction forces were pulling her. At times her whole life seemed like one big drama. There was a drug-induced psychotic breakdown; her father ran off with the actress Elizabeth Taylor; the father of her only child left her for a man; on one occasion she woke up next to the dead body of a Republican lobbyist (whose ghost she later feared haunted her house); and just before Christmas she suffered a cardiac arrest on a flight from London to Los Angeles.

Some said that despite the well-publicised addictions, which did no harm to her book sales, Fisher's real addiction was to shocking other people. She spent Michael Jackson's last Christmas with him (they shared the same dentist, Evan Chandler, who accused Jackson of molesting his son); was asked by Senator Ted Kennedy at a dinner party in 1985 whether she would have sex in a hot tub ("I'm no good in water," was her reply); and arranged deliveries of marijuana and prostitutes to ease her dying father's pain when he was wheelchair-bound.

Fisher made no secret of her bipolar disorder, attracting praise for talking candidly about her condition at the American Psychiatric Association's annual meeting in May 2004 in New York City, and discussing it in detail with Stephen Fry, a fellow sufferer, in a BBC programme in 2006. She was also an advocate for electroconvulsive therapy, which helped her with depression but shredded her memory.

Yet it is as Princess Leia, with her hairdo clamped like two bagels to either side of her head, that Fisher will forever remain in the public memory. "In the street, they call out, 'Hey, Princess!', which makes me feel like a poodle," she once complained, adding with resignation: "I'll go to my grave as Princess Leia."

Carrie Frances Fisher was born in 1956. Her father was the Fifties crooner Eddie Fisher, of Russian-Jewish descent, and her mother is the actress Debbie Reynolds, a Nazarene of British ancestry who starred in *Singin' in the Rain*. Family legend was that her mother was so anaesthetised at the birth that when her father fainted as Carrie's head emerged, the doctors and nurses devoted all their attention to him and Carrie arrived "virtually unattended". "And I have been trying to make up for that fact ever since," she once said. A photograph taken of her at two hours old appeared in *Life* magazine, the start of a lifetime in the public eye. Almost 18 months later her brother Todd, who became a film director, was born.

Her parents divorced when she was two and soon afterwards Fisher became the fourth of Taylor's eight husbands. As a child Carrie immersed herself in books and writing poetry, but by 13 she was smoking pot. She was a pupil at Beverly Hills High School, dropping out to be a chorus girl in the show *Irene*, starring her mother, and to appear in a nightclub act in Las Vegas, again arranged by Reynolds. "Chorus work is more valuable to a child than any education could ever be," Fisher wrote in *Wishful Drinking*.

Her 18 months in London at the Central School of Speech and Drama were the nearest thing she had to normality, but they were barely finished when she made her screen debut in the comedy *Shampoo* (1975), starring Warren Beatty, Julie Christie and Goldie Hawn, about a hairdresser who massages more than just the hair of his female clients. Her moment of screen glory came when she propositioned Beatty with the words: "Wanna fuck?"

She gave up marijuana while filming *Star Wars* (1977; later retitled *Star Wars Episode IV: A New Hope*). By the time she reprised her role in *The Empire Strikes Back* three years later she was a celebrity in her own right, featuring on the cover of *Rolling Stone* magazine. She returned to its cover in 1983 to promote *Return of the Jedi*, this time in a metal bikini. Yet even more serious addictions – to cocaine and prescription medication – were round the corner and in 1985 she had to have her stomach pumped after a drug overdose.

As befits the daughter of two celebrities, her private life – if indeed it ever was private – was colourful. In 1983 she married Paul Simon after a seven-year romance, later claiming that his songs *She Moves On* and *Hearts and Bones* were about their relationship. She once explained the attraction: "Paul is a short, Jewish singer. My father Eddie is a short, Jewish singer. Short. Jewish. Singer. Any questions?" Their courtship was interrupted by her brief engagement in 1980 to Dan Aykroyd, the Canadian actor and comedian, who once used the Heimlich manoeuvre on her when she choked on a brussels sprout. The marriage to Simon ended after less than a year, but they continued dating for several more years ("We had make-up sex all the time, we broke up so often," she said).

From 1991 to 1994 she was in a relationship with Bryan Lourd, her agent, with whom she had a daughter Billie Lourd, who had a minor role in *The Force Awakens* in 2015. When asked how she didn't realise that Lourd was gay she replied: "He must have forgotten to tell me." Thereafter, she said, she was single. "I don't have a boyfriend," she told The Times in 2011. "Maybe there's a website I can start for over-the-hill celebrities?"

Although *Postcards from the Edge*, which appeared in 1987, soon became a film starring Meryl Streep and Shirley MacLaine, she now dipped somewhat out of view, often busy with appointments at rehab clinics and the like. Drugs and celebrity aside, when not appearing in front of the camera Fisher was a hardworking, sharp and incisive rewriter of Hollywood scripts (among them *The River Wild, The Wedding Singer* and *Sister Act*), on many of which she went uncredited. In 2014 she spoke at the Hay Festival, demonstrating again her sharp mind and quick wit.

Meanwhile, books such as *Wishful Drinking* (2008), which was also a play, and *Shockaholic* (2011) brought her back into the public conscience with a jolt before the *Star Wars* franchise flew back into her orbit. She claimed that the directors of *The Force Awakens* ordered her to lose 35lb before shooting started. "They don't want to hire all of me – only about three quarters," she quipped.

For those who thought her on-screen relationship with Han Solo, played by Ford, some 14 years her senior, in the original *Star Wars* was intense, the reason was revealed with the publication of *The Princess Diarist*, her final memoir. "It was Han and Leia during the week and Carrie and Harrison during the weekend," she told *People* magazine of their secret affair.

In later years Fisher's constant companion and friend was her French bulldog, Gary. He accompanied her on the endless round of TV talk shows where she was a popular guest, and even went with her to the White House Correspondents' Dinner in May this year. On one occasion she tried to deliver a petition containing 11 million signatures objecting to a dog-meat festival in southwest China to the Chinese embassy in London, but it was refused.

Chrissy Iley, who interviewed Fisher for The Times magazine in 2011, described her home, which once belonged to Bette Davis, as "like the witch's house in Hansel and Gretel" with its secret room for storing drink that dated from the Prohibition era. In truth it was more like a commune, with a rotating cast of lodgers, visitors and hangers-on, among them James Blunt, who wrote songs in her bathroom, and the screenwriter Bruce Wagner, in whose film *Maps to the Stars* Fisher played herself.

There was certainly little sign of Fisher growing old gracefully, nor was she interested in doing so. "With age comes wisdom," she once said, "and a whole bunch of other bad shit."

Carrie Fisher was born on October 21, 1956. She died on December 27, 2016, after a heart attack, aged 60

HUMPHREY BOGART

Cinema audiences first encountered Mr Humphrey Bogart's seamed, sardonic cast of countenance and mordant tongue in *The Petrified Forest*, which won him much praise when it was released in 1936.

Bogart was born in New York in 1899, the son of Dr Belmont Bogart, a physician, and his wife, who as Maud Humphrey had made a name for herself as a watercolour artist and commercial illustrator. He was educated at Trinity School, New York, and at Phillips Academy, Andover, Massachusetts, whence he was destined to go to Yale, but this intention was not fulfilled. The United States had entered the First World War and Bogart joined the Navy. He had always been attracted to the theatre and as soon as the war ended he joined the staff of a promoter of theatrical ventures as manager of a travelling company. But he was determined to act and made his way to New York, where he made his first appearance in 1922 in *Drifting*.

Thereafter he appeared regularly in plays and it was not until 1930 that he went to Hollywood. Of his first efforts he himself later said they were "a flop". He returned to the stage and it was only after the success of the play *The Petrified Forest* that he again turned to the screen, to make an immediate impact with the film of the play with Leslie Howard and Miss Bette Davis. Bogart played a Dillinger-like gangster.

There followed many other films, and notable among his earlier successes was *Dead End*, in which Bogart again played the part of a gangster; and a gangster on the screen he often was, but a gangster with a difference. If Mr Clark Gable may be said to stand in the parts he plays for the uninhibited American male, the happy extrovert whom every college boy would wish to be, the lad for the girls and the lad for the liquor, Bogart represented a contrasting, yet allied, type of American hero. He dwelt in the shadows and was on the other side, so far as the police and the law were concerned, but that was because the police and the law were themselves often shown as corrupt. He was the masculine counterpart of the girl of easy virtue who has a heart of gold.

Typical was the role he played in *The Big Shot*. Here he was, of course, the "big shot", the head of a gang which took beatings-up and murder in its stride, and yet at the end he gave himself up rather than see an innocent man, a man he did not even know, electrocuted. It is, of course, wildly improbable that the "big shot" would do any such thing and, to make the climax convincing, some powerful acting would seem necessary. But that was not Bogart's way. "He has charm and he doesn't waste energy pretending to act," wrote James Agate. "He has a sinister-rueful countenance which acts for him. He has an exciting personality and lets it do the work."

Certainly Bogart seemed to do little more than project his film personality on to the screen and leave it at that, but it was astonishing how much he could convey with a suggestion of pathos in that husky voice of his, with a shadow of a smile wryly turned against himself, and in films which gave him a chance, a film, for instance, such as John Huston's *The Treasure of the Sierre Madre*, he showed that his acting could be positive even though it never moved far away from the essential Bogart. Bogart appeared in a great number of films, among them *High Sierra*, *The Maltese Falcon*, *Across the Pacific*, *The African Queen*, *To Have and Have Not*, *Casablanca*, and *The Caine Mutiny*, and, while other reputations waxed and waned, he went on unchanged and unchangeable in calm, complete command of himself, the situation and the screen. He had what Kent found in Lear – authority.

Humphrey Bogart was born on December 25, 1899. He died of cancer on January 14, 1957, aged 57

OLIVER REED

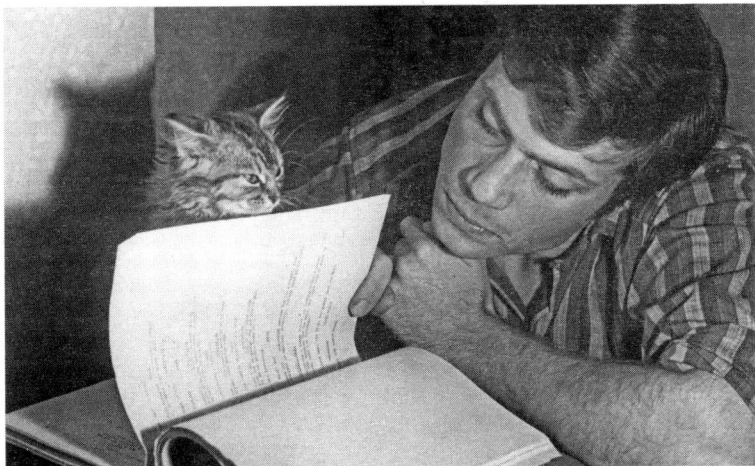

Oliver Reed was better known as a hell-raiser than an actor. Indeed acting came a poor third to his main pursuits: arm wrestling and consuming prodigious quantities of alcohol. The two were often combined in any convenient hostelry, where he would cause the drink to flow and then challenge anyone in the house to take him on.

Yet his undoubtedly powerful screen presence never flagged and he remained in demand by producers and directors throughout a switchback career in which he starred in more than 50 films. The majority of them were forgettable, and were soon forgotten by a man who could never take his talent seriously, but there were a few of which he could be justly proud.

His nude wrestling scene with Alan Bates in Ken Russell's 1969 film of Lawrence's *Women in Love* was a daring first which electrified audiences. The two actors were to confess later that they were able to do the scene with the necessary conviction only after comparing the size of their respective manhoods (they decided they were both on the small side) and then getting gloriously drunk. This last was no hardship for Reed.

The year before, Reed had starred as the wicked Bill Sykes to wonderfully chilling effect in his uncle Carol Reed's film adaptation of Lionel Bart's *Oliver!* Reed's dour demeanour was ideal for the role in a musical which, alongside the jollity, retained something of Dickens's message about the iniquities of child labour, pimping, abduction, prostitution and murder. Ron Moody, as Fagin, came close to having his scenes with Reed stolen from under his twitching nose.

Reed made his mark, too, in director Nicolas Roeg's *Castaway* (1987), based on a true account of a publisher who advertised for a woman to spend a year with him on a desert island. Reed played the publisher and Amanda Donohoe the woman adventure-seeker. Once again he was near-naked, as was she, and their rompings, fierce quarrels and imminent starvation amid splendid scenery all went to show that tropical islands are not necessarily paradise getaways.

Robert Oliver Reed was born in Wimbledon in 1938, the son of a novelist and racing journalist. A chequered education included attending Ewell Castle in Surrey, although he later said it was just one of his 15 schools. He was in fact dyslexic. "I was taken out of boarding school because my father thought I was ill-disciplined," he said.

Leaving school he took a job briefly as a nightclub bouncer and then worked as a medical orderly before joining the Medical Corps for his National Service. He decided he wanted to be an actor and found work as a film extra. He also by-passed all recognised acting tuition, since he reckoned that his army experience was better than anything he could learn at a drama school.

His first fleeting appearance on screen was in the teenage trifle *Beat Girl* (1959), playing a young lout. His next was more promising, a factory worker in *The Angry Silence* (1960), a significant film of its day in which Richard Attenborough is sent to Coventry by his workmates for refusing to join a union. In that same year came an obvious casting against type when he played a ballet dancer in *The League of Gentlemen*, a crime caper in which ex-Service misfits led by Jack Hawkins carry out a military-style robbery.

His first screen credit was in a dull comedy, *His and Hers*, in which he played a poet, followed by another in the brighter Tony Hancock vehicle *The Rebel*, where he was cast as a fellow painter. Reed's grimacing dynamism on the screen stood out, and a big break was inevitable.

Star billing came with the title role in the Hammer horror film *The Curse of the Werewolf* (1961). The bloodletting was excessive even for Hammer, but Reed was off and running and his ability to switch from menacing charm to sullen-eyed rage made him a Hammer favourite for a series of films.

Among them was the science-fiction thriller *The Damned* (1963), directed by Joseph Losey, in which Reed led a motorcycle gang. He led another kind of gang, described as "Chelsea beatniks", in Guy Hamilton's *The Party's Over*. There was a row when the British censor demanded cuts, and the film was not released until 1965.

Reed put in an impressive performance alongside Rita Tushingham in *The Trap*, in which he played a brutal and callous fur trapper, although the film itself was not a success. A couple of comedies followed – *The Jokers* with Michael Crawford, and *I'll Never Forget What's'isname* with Orson Welles, before Reed's success in *Oliver!* and *Women in Love*.

Through the 1970s Reed churned out film after film, including Ken Russell's *Tommy* (1975). Most were unremarkable, yet his confidence never wavered. He told one American reporter: "Destroy me and you destroy the British film industry. Keep me going and I'm the biggest star you've got. I'm Mr England." And this was not just exaggeration. He was perhaps the first actor to break the mould of the typically bland English matinee-idol screen star since the scowling James Mason back in the 1940s in films such as *The Wicked Lady*.

In Britain and in Hollywood, Reed contributed toughly and sinisterly to numerous routine dramas and thrillers; he proved a gutsy Athos in robust costume romps such as *The Three* (and later *The Four*) *Musketeers*.

Meanwhile his dedicated boozing and bingeing around the globe – he was once spotted drunk and trouserless on the streets of Toronto in December – attracted countless column inches in the press. It occasionally resulted in a punch-up, police arrest, and even a few hours in jail.

At one time he saw himself as Britain's answer to Errol Flynn, and he liked to boast occasionally of his sexual prowess. He claimed membership of the Mile High Club – sex in an aircraft – and his name was linked with a number of his co-stars, including Jill St John, Faye Dunaway, Susan George, Carol White, Carol Lynley and Sarah Miles. As a symbol of his sexual flamboyance he even had a small emblem (a pair of cockerel's claws) painfully tattooed on his manly pride. Womanising, however, was of less interest to the roistering Reed than his alcoholic exploits, whether abroad, in his favourite Surrey pubs, or at his tax-exile mansion home in Guernsey; at home he favoured champagne and good wines by the case.

Reed was married twice. His first wife was the Irish model Kathleen Byrne, whom he married in 1960. The marriage lasted ten years and produced a son. He also had a daughter by the ballet dancer Jacquie Daryl. His second marriage created yet more headlines in 1985 when he married Josephine Burge, who was 27 years his junior and whom he had first courted when she was 16. She vowed at the time to wean him off the drink, and succeeded – but only briefly. Two years later Reed stopped again for six months when one of his kidneys played up and doctors warned him that he had only two years to live if he continued.

But once more he fell off the wagon when, as he put it, "I realised what a bore I was becoming." The uncharitable said that they could see no difference. He appeared seemingly drunk on Michael Aspel's television show (although he later said it was a put-up job to give the viewers what they anticipated). On another occasion, apparently drunk while recording a television programme, he foolishly aimed a punch at the boxer Henry Cooper, connecting instead with the actress Wendy Richard.

Reed's second marriage to the tall, beautiful, country-bred Josephine was largely happy though they remained childless. She was totally devoted to him and headed off any marital difficulties by leaving him to do what he wanted. He was rarely out of work because the power of his screen personality remained unscathed to the end.

He was a better actor than he gave himself credit for. He might have achieved more if he had chosen roles carefully, instead of doing whatever came along for the money and the kicks. He made at least three films last year, of which *Gladiator* has yet to be seen here.

Oliver Reed was born on February 13, 1938. He died after being taken ill in a bar on May 2, 1999, aged 61

DORIS DAY

———————— • ————————

Que Sera, Sera (Whatever Will Be, Will Be) was not only Doris Day's most popular song, but also the theme tune to her life. She was cinema's most enduring innocent, bubbly as soda, wholesome as apple pie; blonde, blue-eyed and fair skinned. For six years from 1959 she was one of the top box-office draws in American cinemas. Only Frank Sinatra or Bing Crosby could sell a song as well as she.

Day began her career as a wartime band singer, graduated to Hollywood musicals and later appeared in a run of comedies with Rock Hudson, who called her Zelda or Eunice (she called him Murgatroyd). She had hit records, became a pin-up for the troops, and starred in *Romance on the High Seas* (1948) and the enjoyable musical *Tea for Two* (1950). The success of *Love Me or Leave Me* (1955) – a biopic of Ruth Etting, a singer who had found fame in the 1920s as a torch singer – showed Day in a more beguiling light. Singing blues songs such as *Ten Cents a Dance*, she was a revelation.

Alfred Hitchcock offered her the lead in his thriller *The Man Who Knew Too Much* (1956) with its song *Que Sera, Sera*, which seemed to best sum up her fatalistic philosophy. For behind this relentlessly sunny screen image lived an emotional woman who suffered much bad luck in her personal life. She was a serial bride: beaten by her first husband, abandoned by her second, swindled and widowed by her third, and bored by her fourth. She claimed never to have known that Hudson, to whom she was particularly close and who died in 1985, had AIDS. The death of her son in 2004 was a further blow.

Those who knew Day spoke of a woman who, despite being the blonde sweetheart of the silver screen, was refreshingly straightforward. "In the case of Doris Day, there is no artifice. She's not turning on a new face for the public. She is sunny and likeable," reported AE Hotchner, her biographer. "At the same time there is a woman who is depressed, full of doubts, has sleepless nights and needs constant reassurance."

She worked hard as a dancer and proved surprisingly versatile as an actress, although not for her the Method school; as Spencer Tracy advised, she aimed to know her lines and not bump into the furniture. This made her perfect material when the producer Ross Hunter had an idea for *Pillow Talk* (1959), a sophisticated sex comedy without the sex. Day plays a New York interior designer; Hudson, her neighbour, is a playboy and she heartily disapproves of him chatting up girlfriends on their shared telephone line. The film includes the famous split-screen scene with Hudson and Day in bubble-filled baths in adjoining bathrooms with their feet appearing to touch through the wall. Predictably she ends up marrying him.

Pillow Talk was followed by two more comedies with Hudson, as well as comedies with David Niven, Cary Grant and James Garner. There was a thriller with Rex Harrison as a would-be wife murderer in *Midnight Lace* (1960), when the new Doris Day heroine had a job, an apartment, a couture wardrobe and a lacquered hairstyle. She used her chastity as a weapon in the battle of the sexes and invariably won. Yet she disputed suggestions that she was a prude. "I think my pictures are sexy," she said. "But there's a difference between good, clean, farcical sex and dwelling on sordid themes."

She was now America's No 1 box-office attraction, the first woman to hit that spot since Shirley Temple, and she did so by embodying an image that gave rise to that well-worn line, variously ascribed to Oscar Levant and Groucho Marx: "I'm so old I knew Doris Day before she was a virgin."

She was born Doris Mary Ann von Kappelhoff in Cincinnati, Ohio, of German-Catholic stock, in 1922, although she was prone to shaving a couple of years off her age when it suited. Her father, William, was a piano teacher and organist at St Mark's Church, Cincinnati. Her mother, Alma (née Welz), was from a family who ran a bakery. She was named after Alma's heroine Doris Kenyon, the early film star who appeared opposite Rudolph Valentino. One neighbour recalled that "she would put on a show, using the front porch as her stage ... the lawn was full of little kids ... we were her audience".

As a child she always had pets, although her father did not take kindly to a Manchester terrier puppy. "[He] said, 'The puppy has to be in the basement,' and I never forgave him for that," she recalled in 2008. "I realised he didn't like animals. But I put up such a fuss that that little dog wound up in my bed."

There were two elder brothers: Richard, who died before Doris was born, and Paul, who died in his thirties. William and Alma divorced when Doris was 12 and Alma now took in sewing to help to pay the bills. "At ten years of age, I discovered that my father was having an affair with the mother of my best friend," Day recalled of discovering him in the act. Her father later caused a scandal by marrying an African American barwoman; his daughter did not acknowledge the telegram informing her of the nuptials.

Young Doris began dancing lessons with the Hessler Studio of Dancing at an early age and by 12 was appearing in a Fanchon and Marco stage show; she formed a dance act with a local boy called Jerry Doherty, winning $500 in a talent contest. On the back of this her mother was preparing to move the family to Hollywood, but the night before they were due to leave, Doris, who was 15 years old, was on a double date with a friend, Marion Bonekamp, when a freight train hit the side of their car while it was on an ill-marked crossing. She was dragged from the wreckage with her legs shattered and spent 18 months recuperating under the care of the Sisters of Mercy. "I would visit Doris while she was still on crutches and she would still entertain us, singing," Bonekamp recalled in 2008.

During her convalescence she listened to the radio. Ella Fitzgerald was a favourite and Doris sang along, trying "to catch the casual yet clean way she sang the words". To ease the boredom she had vocal training from Grace Raine, a coach with useful radio connections. Before she was off her crutches, Doris had her first engagements, with three of the best big bandmasters in the US: Barney Rapp, Bob Crosby and Les Brown. She took the name Day from one of her hits, *Day after Day*, after Rapp insisted that he could not put the name Kappelhoff on billboards and advertisements, although she preferred to be known among close friends as Clara Bixby.

Unlike her wholesome, innocent on-screen image, Day's off-screen life was frequently sexy, vapid, tragic, bedevilled and pitiful, as she confirmed to Hotchner between bike rides around Beverly Hills.

She was 18 years old when she married Al Jorden, a trombonist from Rapp's band with a penchant for violence, especially when she was pregnant. She stayed just long enough to have a son, Terry, then escaped (Jorden once threatened her with a gun and years later turned the weapon on himself with fatal consequences). In 1946 she married George Weidler, a saxophonist who left after eight months, unhappy about becoming Mr Doris Day. Years later, during a brief reconciliation, he introduced her to Christian Science.

In wartime America, under the paternal care of Brown, Day chalked up several hit records. Although she had little confidence in her acting, she was persuaded to audition for *Romance on the High Seas*, a musical directed by Michael Curtiz. He was expecting another Betty Hutton and wanted Day to sway her hips to the music. "I don't bounce around. I just sing," snapped Day, who spent much of the screen test in tears. Nevertheless, she got the lead role, the film was a hit and Day followed it with *Tea for Two*.

She also enjoyed singing for films. Unlike on radio or on stage, she could repeat a song until it came out right. She had suffered badly from nerves as a band singer, but in Hollywood that kind of pressure was off. As an actress she began to show her range, starting by stealing the show with her pert smile and sugar-cane voice in *Romance on the High Seas* with Jack Carson, who became one of her many lovers. *Storm Warning* (1950), in which she played the wife of a

Ku Klux Klansman, was her first non-singing role. Also good was the infelicitously titled *Young Man with a Horn* (1950), a biopic of Bix Beiderbecke, the jazz cornetist, starring Kirk Douglas and Lauren Bacall.

Warner perceived Day as the girl next door with a freckled face and a golden smile who was virginal and eager to please (the two not being mutually exclusive in those days), and that is how the studio cast her. Despite the mediocrity of her material, she was well on the way to becoming a big draw when she made *Calamity Jane* (1953), a character with whom she could identify. "I was such a tomboy growing up, and she was such a fun character to play," she told *The Hollywood Reporter*. "Of course, the music was wonderful too." Here was a vehicle worthy of her talent – a delightful musical that includes the daffodil-filled scene where she sings *Secret Love*. Women loved Day's films because she seemed so ordinary, men liked her for being unthreateningly sexy, and directors appreciated her professionalism.

Management of her career was taken over by her third husband, Marty Melcher, a former road manager for the Andrews Sisters; she married him on her 29th birthday after briefly dating Ronald Reagan ("How Ron loved to talk and dance," she recalled wistfully). Melcher was not popular – Sinatra, who starred with Day in *Young at Heart* (1954), had him banned from the set. Yet Melcher knew how to negotiate a deal, dragging her name into business investments, including a hotel chain, oil wells in Oklahoma and property holdings in Hollywood, as well as a cattle ranch. Before long she had suffered a breakdown and told friends that she was dying of tuberculosis and heart trouble, although exhaustion and nervousness were the real causes.

By the start of the 1960s she was the hottest property in Hollywood, making a fortune for the movie moguls while never remotely offending the wholesome values of middle America. "She's the No 1 money-maker for 1963," trumpeted the *Los Angeles Times*. "The experts claim Hollywood needs more sex and less dishwater, but the most daring thing Doris has done on screen is to go through a car wash – without a car."

Her last film with Hudson was *Send Me No Flowers* (1964). It showed healthy returns, but nothing like those for *Pillow Talk*, for which she had been nominated for an Oscar. Yet by the middle of the decade, films, and the women in them, were changing. Day's trademark look of wide-eyed horror at any man who made a pass at her now seemed old-fashioned and *The Glass Bottom Boat* (1967) was her last hit. Day turned down the role of Mrs Robinson in Dustin Hoffman's classic *The Graduate* (1967), which might have set her on a new path, although in her memoir Day recalled refusing it on "moral grounds".

A standing joke in Los Angeles is that parking spaces immediately outside a shop or restaurant that a driver wants to visit are known as Doris Day spaces, because that was what always seemed to happen in her movies: she would magically pull up right outside. No hunting around for a space for her.

Although she also signed a record deal worth $1 million with Columbia Records, which included an album called *Duet* with André Previn, she rarely saw the money. When she asked where it had gone, Melcher talked mysteriously of "tax shelters". After his death from a stroke in 1968, Day was horrified to discover that he had signed her up for a television series. Worse, Melcher had apparently embezzled millions of dollars of her money. "What I really wanted to do with my money was to buy paintings and antiques and some land in the San Fernando Valley," she said.

She went ahead with six series of *The Doris Day Show*, but did so under the strain of a new crisis. Her son, Terry Melcher, who had taken his stepfather's name, was by then a successful record producer. After the murder of Sharon Tate it emerged that Melcher had once refused Charles Manson a recording contract. The murder took place at Melcher's old address, which was now rented by Tate and Roman Polanski. Day hired bodyguards.

Day would insist that she had never had any great ambitions. "My desire as a girl was to get married and live happily ever after, have children, take care of my husband, cook and do all those things," she said at the time of her 50th birthday. "I have no drive in me. I turn down one thing after another. I'm not bragging, but I'm really not happy accepting showbusiness offers."

As if to prove her point, Day finished the television work in 1973 and retired. The next year a Californian judge awarded her $22 million in damages from Jerry Rosenthal, Melcher's lawyer, who had helped with his deception. From 1975 to 1981 she was married to Barry Comden, who was ten years her junior and the maître d' at the Old World Eatery, one of her favourite restaurants. Critics suggested that she had adopted him, like one of the many stray animals she now took in. Thereafter she concentrated on the Doris Day Pet Foundation, at one time sharing her home in Beverly Hills with 17 dogs. "I've never met an animal I didn't like, and I can't say the same thing about people," she quipped. After Hurricane Katrina struck Florida and Louisiana in August 2005, her group was instrumental in airlifting stranded and abandoned animals to safety. "The hard part is that I want them all," she added.

Later she retired to a remote spot in Carmel, California, where she was a co-owner of the boutique Cypress Inn.

During the 1980s, film festivals, retrospectives and seminars were held in her honour. Day declined to attend them, although she did make the odd appearance in documentaries. She became reclusive, yet was far from disappearing from the public eye. In 1994 she released *The Love Album*, which had been recorded in 1967, but never issued. Then, in 2011, she released *My Heart*, which included previously unreleased recordings by her son Terry, made before his death from melanoma in 2004. It entered the UK chart at No 9.

There was much excitement when a rumour circulated in 1988 that she would attend the Oscars. The producers had even procured a dog sitter, so she could have no excuse for backing out. Contrary to the words of her most popular song, however, it was not to be, to be.

Doris Day was born on April 3, 1922. She died from pneumonia on May 13, 2019, aged 97

MARTY FELDMAN

Feldman, who was born in Canning Town, East London, of a poor Jewish family, was an individual talent who will be much missed. A bizarre appearance – huge, uncoordinated eyes, dishevelled hair and an ear-to-ear grin – gave him a natural advantage as a comic though he went through several false starts before emerging as one of the most original performers on television in the late 1960s.

As a youngster he played jazz in London clubs and was later a trumpeter in a variety act called Maurice, Marty and Mitch. It was during his tour of the music halls, then in their death throes, that he met another aspiring comic, Barry Took, and eventually the two got together as scriptwriters for such shows as *The Frost Report* and the *Round the Horne* series, starring Kenneth Horne. Feldman did not come to prominence as a performer, however, until he joined John Cleese, Tim Brooke-Taylor and Graham Chapman in *At Last the 1948 Show*.

In 1968 Feldman starred in his own comedy series, *Marty*, on BBC2, with Barry Took again as his writing colleague. It was one of the best shows of its time, revealing a splendidly creative and anarchic talent, with an ability to breathe fresh life into familiar routines. It also had a strong visual sense and naturally led Feldman into films.

In 1974, after further series of *Marty*, Feldman left Britain for Hollywood where he found a kindred spirit in the director Mel Brooks. Their first venture together was *Young Frankenstein*, a splendid spoof on the monster legend, and they also worked on *Silent Movie*. Feldman appeared under Gene Wilder's direction in another tilt at a classic, *The Adventures of Sherlock Holmes' Smarter Brother*.

After that Feldman turned director himself, with *The Last Re-Make of Beau Geste*, though, in spite of some inspired moments, the whole was less than the sum of the parts and raised doubts whether Feldman could sustain his comic invention over feature film length. His last film as director and star, *In God We Trust*, which appeared last year, was also something of a disappointment.

At the time of his death he was acting in *Yellow Beard*, a pirates comedy written by Graham Chapman, and he had been considering a return to British television from which he had been too long away.

Marty Feldman was born on July 8, 1934. He died of a heart attack on December 2, 1982, aged 49

CHARLTON HESTON

Charlton Heston played epic heroes. Moses, John the Baptist, El Cid, General Gordon and Michelangelo all sprang to life on screen via this muscular, lantern-jawed actor. He made his name by playing Ben-Hur, a role for which he won the best actor Oscar in 1959. He deserved it, if only for that astonishing re-creation of a chariot race at the Circus of Antioch.

Laurence Olivier once paid Heston a high compliment. At Olivier's invitation, the two had starred together in a Broadway play, *The Tumbler* (1959). The show flopped, but Olivier was sufficiently impressed to say that Heston had the "equipment" to be the greatest American actor of his day. That promise was never quite fulfilled before the camera. The dignity which served him so well in theatrical roles such as Antony and Sir Thomas More made Heston appear a little unapproachable on film – not quite as interestingly flawed as Henry Fonda or Gary Cooper.

What Heston could convey, however, through a twitch of those patrician cheekbones, was authority. In roles where many actors would have been lost in a crowd of angry, spear-brandishing slaves, Heston stood tall. As the director James Cameron explained, when casting him in *True Lies* (1994), "I need you because you can plausibly intimidate Arnold Schwarzenegger". Not many 70-year-olds could pull that off.

Politically, Heston was a rare creature in Hollywood, a town of often unthinking Democrats. He walked behind Martin Luther King in the march on Washington of 1963, and was president of the Screen Actors Guild for six terms during the Sixties.

But in the Eighties Heston switched his allegiance from the Democrats to the Republicans and in later years he became prominent for his ardent defence of Americans' right to bear arms. From 1998 to 2003 he served as president and spokesman for the National Rifle Association (NRA), becoming the rugged public face of rigid opposition to gun control and, more broadly, of a distinctively American spirit of defiant self-reliance.

Two days before being elected president of the NRA, he launched his term with a stinging attack on President Clinton: "America doesn't trust you with our 21-year-old daughters, and we sure, Lord, don't trust you with our guns." And in a rousing speech at the NRA's convention in 2000 he spoke out against the Democratic presidential hopeful Al Gore, who, he said – while waving a musket above his head – would have to take his gun "from my cold, dead hands".

In earlier years he had visited the troops in Vietnam and campaigned for his old friend Ronald Reagan during the 1984 election. He was asked to run for Senate in 1970 for the Republicans, but declined the offer.

Political correctitude was not his style, nor the modern American tendency to, as he put it, "extol the ordinary, enshrine the victim". On screen he played enough eccentrics and prophets to believe in greatness. "Thomas Jefferson and Andrew Jackson, Thomas More and Richelieu, Mark Antony and Michelangelo, Moses and John the Baptist are not like everyone. They are extraordinary and they have shaped the world."

Heston played countless saints and geniuses, but he had advantages: at 6ft 3in he dominated other actors. His broken nose, acquired in a school game of American football, gave him a profile. It made him, in William Wyler's words, "the best imitation Jew in Hollywood".

There was a particular resemblance to Michelangelo's statue of Moses in Rome – a likeness which was pointed out to Cecil B DeMille when he was casting the part. More biblical parts followed, and after a number of these a certain saintliness began to rub off on the actor. Like James Stewart or Gregory Peck, Charlton Heston came to represent certain qualities – courage, moderation, responsibility, justice – which Americans claimed as their own.

Heston had no truck with hyphenated ethnic labels. Had he been forced to apply one to himself, it would have been "Scots-English American", from his mother's side of the family, a branch of the Fraser clan, but to everyone he was the archetypal American, and proud of it.

Charles Carter – known as "Chuck" – was born in No Man's Land, a small settlement in the woods around Lake Michigan, in 1923 (some sources say 1924). Self-sufficiency was essential in this rural community, and he was a proficient shot with a rifle at an age when most boys were playing with wooden swords.

After divorce, his mother married a businessman, Chet Heston. Growing up in the Depression gave the young Heston a lasting admiration for hard graft. Later he was to be the most conscientious of stars, and strove to get films finished on time, on budget. As the producer Walter Mirisch once told him: "We sure lost a great first assistant director when you took up acting."

Heston attended the local New Trier high school, which had a good drama course. He took part in all the school plays and worked at weekends with a local drama group. At Northwestern University, to which he won a scholarship, he met a fellow drama student, Lydia Clarke, whom he married in 1944. He had an uneventful war in the Army Air Corps, when he was based in the Aleutian Islands. Afterwards he and his wife moved to New York to begin their acting careers in earnest.

In 1947 Heston heard that Katharine Cornell, First Lady of American Theatre, was casting for *Antony and Cleopatra* and bluffed his way into an audition. Though he won only the tiny part of Proculeius, the cachet of having worked with Cornell on Broadway got Heston into the new world of television.

Television drama was in its infancy, and snubbed by the Hollywood directors. It was left to a group of youths to mould the new art form. The Cornell card landed Heston a role in the CBS production of *Julius Caesar* and this led to more major roles in television dramas. Heston acted in five Shakespearean productions in two years, invaluable experience for a young actor. The early days of television were, he recalled, "like the beginning of Hollywood – Griffith and Chaplin and DeMille bouncing around in touring cars with the camera on the end of a board".

On the East Coast the septuagenarian Cecil B DeMille was still directing films. One day he spotted young Heston driving around the Paramount lot. Heston was visiting Hollywood for an audition and waved cheerily at the grand old man of film. DeMille, it is recorded, decided instantly to offer Heston the part of the circus manager in *The Greatest Show on Earth*.

DeMille's homage to circus life included stars such as Dorothy Lamour and James Stewart, but Heston held his own. After the film's successful release, one enchanted cinemagoer wrote to DeMille to compliment the cast. "And I was amazed," the correspondent concluded, "at how well the circus manager did in there with the real actors."

Heston made ten films in the next three years. *Ruby Gentry* (1953), directed by King Vidor, was a hit, and showed that he could play a romantic lead. There were westerns and the first of his biographical films, as Andrew Jackson in *The President's Lady* (1953).

But Heston was being prepared for loftier things by his mentor: the role of Moses in DeMille's next biblical extravaganza, *The Ten Commandments* (1956).

He parted the Red Sea with panache and it confirmed him as a top name. As he remarked of his good fortune when he got the part: "If you can't make a career out of two DeMilles, you'll never make it." As with all his historical roles, Heston came to the role having read everything available on the subject: for Moses, he read Freud, the historian James Henry Breasted, and the King James Bible. Like Olivier, he was also keen to get the make-up and costume just right. Few stars have sported such an array of beards as Heston.

By the mid-Fifties, the top Hollywood directors were sending Heston scripts. Orson Welles cast him in the minor classic, *Touch of*

Evil (1957). William Wyler directed him opposite Gregory Peck in *The Big Country* (1958), a pairing which produced one of the best bare-knuckle fist fights in cinema.

Heston made a good impression on Wyler, particularly in his sporting acceptance of second billing to Peck. Soon afterwards MGM asked Wyler to direct an expensive remake of the silent classic *Ben-Hur*. It was a gamble to save the studio's ailing finances.

Wyler's instinct to cast Heston as brawny, kindly Ben-Hur proved right. Heston was not only excellent in the quiet family scenes but had trained himself to be a competent charioteer and oarsman. *Ben-Hur* won nine Oscars, including Heston's.

Although *Ben-Hur* was the best of Heston's spectaculars, there were several good ones to come: *El Cid* (1961), *The Greatest Story Ever Told* (1965), in which Heston played John the Baptist, and *Khartoum* (1966). For the last he was kitted out by the London costumiers Bermans, which made a replica of General Gordon's tunic to fit his hulkier frame. He congratulated the tailor on his skill at re-creating the costume. "Oh, it wasn't difficult, sir," came the reply. "We made the original, you see. We still have the patterns."

These big-budget films made Heston rich. But he interspersed them with films by new talents like Sam Peckinpah (*Major Dundee*, 1965) and Tom Cries (*Will Penny*, 1967). For Carol Reed's *Agony and the Ecstasy* (1965) Heston played Michelangelo. He spent several months balanced on flimsy Sistine Chapel scaffolding, staring up at the ceiling with paint in his eyes. Despite his memorable performance, the film did not prosper at the box office. Heston's crusty agent complained: "Whaddya expect, kid? Another picture with no dames about some guy painting a ceiling."

Briefly his career seemed to decline, but he came back with *Planet of the Apes* (1968), a superior science-fiction film about a group of astronauts who travel into the future, when Earth is run by apes. There was more than a little Adam in Heston's commander, just as there was a good deal of Christ in his character in *The Omega Man* (1970), another sci-fi classic.

In the Seventies Heston, along with many middle-aged Hollywood stars, made several well-paid disaster movies. In the

1980s he succumbed to the lure of soap opera and starred in *The Colbys*. He also acted in several films scripted by his son Fraser.

Now unencumbered by financial worries, Heston returned to theatre. He was a regular at the Ahmanson in Los Angeles and in the early Eighties toured Britain – a country he always regarded with fondness – with a production of *The Caine Mutiny Court-Martial*.

In the early Nineties he visited Israel to film *Charlton Heston Presents the Bible* for television. His popularity in America was sufficient that no one detected hubris in the title. In his seventies he published an excellent autobiography, *In the Arena* (1995), and his collected film journals.

Heston made a cameo in the 2001 remake of *Planet of the Apes*, but in his latter years his association with the National Rifle Association threatened to overshadow his acting career. One of his final moments on screen was in Michael Moore's documentary, *Bowling for Columbine* (2002). Heston walks out of the interview when asked by Moore about the insensitive timing and location of an NRA meeting held in Denver in the aftermath of the massacre at the nearby Columbine High School.

In 2003 Heston was presented with the Presidential Medal of Freedom, the nation's highest civilian honour, by President Bush. That year he stepped down as the president of the NRA, a year after revealing symptoms of Alzheimer's disease, although he continued to be an honorary life member.

Most of Heston's friends were not in the business and he remained happily married to his first love, Lydia, who gave up her own career to raise their children. In semi-retirement he had more time to spend in the house he had built in the 1950s, on a ridge above Hollywood. He surrounded himself with dogs, a vintage gun collection and a library full of history books and Patrick O'Brian novels. The scholarly streak which had served him so well in his film career also made him eccentric by Hollywood standards.

Charlton Heston was born on October 4, 1923. He died of pneumonia on April 5, 2008, aged 84

GLENDA JACKSON

Glenda Jackson was filming in England when the 1971 Academy Awards ceremony took place in Los Angeles. An exuberant early-morning telephone call from Bette Davis, her friend, brought word of her best actress Oscar for playing the sexually curious Gudrun Brangwen in Ken Russell's DH Lawrence adaptation *Women in Love* (1969).

"You've won, you've won," Davis hollered, herself a prewar two-time Oscar winner. "Thank you very much," replied Jackson in her low-key manner before hanging up the receiver and returning to bed.

Three years later she received another best actress Oscar for her performance as the flirtatiously funny Vickie Allessio, a divorced mother of two who has an affair with George Segal's Steve Blackburn, a married man, in the romantic comedy *A Touch of Class* (1973).

Again, she did not attend the ceremony and for many years the two statuettes served as bookends for her mother's shelves, before ending up in a storage box at her sister's house.

She was filming until very recently, having recently completed *The Great Escaper* alongside Michael Caine, about a D-Day veteran who escapes his care home to attend a 70th anniversary ceremony for the landings. The film, in which Jackson plays Caine's wife, is due to be released later this year.

Jackson, an occasionally abrasive figure who considered acting to be "artificial and strained" and no more than work, never understood the glitz and glamour. She eschewed celebrity, had an unbridled contempt for sentimentality and made films because they interested her rather than for the money. Likewise, she sometimes expressed exasperation that her audience, "mostly want what they have liked before".

Her aim was never to be adored but simply to be a master of her craft. "I thought Hollywood was going to be different somehow, some special magic," she said after a brief foray into Tinseltown. "But a camera is a camera is a camera, wherever you are." Despite many awards, she often said that her most fulfilling role was stooging as Cleopatra on Morecambe and Wise's 1971 Christmas show. Arguably this gave Jackson her entrée into Hollywood to play comic roles.

Jackson was a pioneer, becoming known as the actress who made nudity respectable on the big screen. This was perhaps most notable in her frenzied naked writhing in a swaying railway carriage in Ken Russell's *The Music Lovers* (1970). She played the sex-starved wife of the homosexual Russian composer Pyotr Tchaikovsky (Richard Chamberlain). A measure of how shocking it seemed at the time can be gleaned from the way Auberon Waugh berated in print the exposure of her "Mohican pubic tufts".

She later found fulfilment on the political stage, serving as an MP for 23 years and rising to junior transport minister in Tony Blair's new Labour government. Yet many found her Commons performances to be stiff and expressionless, a stark contrast to her commanding appearances on stage and screen. Sir Tim Bell, the Tory PR guru, suggested running a picture of her as a mischievous campaign ad under the words "New Labour: less style, more substance." She seemed to be overcompensating for her ephemeral image as an actress by becoming Labour's answer to that gloriously uncompromised Conservative, Ann Widdecombe.

Jackson was no different as an actress. Oliver Reed once said: "Working with Glenda was like being run over by a Bedford truck." Her voice could seem quite deep and flat-vowelled and critics would sometimes comment on how "unconventional" her looks seemed for a film star. She had strong cheekbones and mousy-auburn hair that was cut in a severe Bauhaus style, "while something about the arrangement of her teeth made her smile look like a snarl". Had the critic known she had a phobia about dentists, he might have been kinder.

Glenda May Jackson was born at her grandmother's house in Birkenhead in 1936, the eldest of four daughters of Harry Jackson, a labourer and bricklayer who during the war served on a Royal Navy minesweeper, and his wife Joan (née Pearce), who supplemented the family's meagre income with cleaning and bar work. Her sisters were Gill, Lynne and Liz.

In 1939 she moved with her family to Hoylake, later recalling the smarter seaside town's close-knit community. "We were related to two thirds of the town," she explained. Here she forged a work ethic that became her personal creed. "I come from a family where if you didn't work you didn't eat," she said. "That was the class structure."

Her education at West Kirby Grammar School was an unhappy experience, though she was entranced by seeing Donald Wolfit playing Shylock in a rare school outing to the Liverpool theatre. Lacking self-esteem – she described herself as "fat, shy and acne'd" – she felt bored with her schoolwork, grew increasingly mutinous and left at 15 to work as an assistant in Boots, selling laxatives because she was too young for the contraceptive counter. "My ambition then was to get over to the other counter which sold make-up, scent, bath salts and pretty things," she said.

She did, however, have a thirst for books, ballet classes and the theatre. A friend suggested she join Hoylake YMCA Players and three shows later she was awarded a place at the Royal Academy of Dramatic Art in London. To make ends meet she worked in British Home Stores, while living in unheated bedsits. Yet her prospects were not great and her graduation diploma in 1956 was accompanied by the warning: "Don't expect regular work until you're 40, dear."

Her first big outing was as Eliza Doolittle in *Pygmalion* at St Pancras Town Hall in November 1956. That was followed by six years of honourable obscurity in repertory theatre interspersed with spells working at Butlin's holiday camps. In 1958 she married Roy Hodges, a similarly struggling actor whom she had met the previous year when appearing together in Crewe. Her guts and determination were perhaps encapsulated in his oft-quoted remark: "If Glenda went into politics she'd be prime minister. If she went into crime she would be Jack the Ripper."

Jackson's fortunes changed at the age of 26 when her performance as Charlotte Corday in Peter Brook's erotically charged staging of *Marat/Sade* at the Aldwych Theatre was hailed by the critics. This was part of Brook's pioneering Theatre of Cruelty season and Jackson's mixture of incipient sexual hysteria, soporific melancholia and horrifying and horrified political resolve was so electrifying that, as Charles Marowitz, one of her earliest mentors, exclaimed, it was as if she was an explosion waiting to happen. The play transferred to Broadway and Paris, and she also appeared in the 1967 film, again directed by Brook.

This rigorous and austere concept of drama suited her forthright approach and she was promptly offered a contract by the Royal Shakespeare Company.

Although *Women in Love* became infamous for the nude wrestling bout between Oliver Reed and Alan Bates, there was an equally ground-breaking love scene between Jackson and Reed in which she became one of the first serious British actresses to bare her breasts on screen. Meanwhile, *A Touch of Class* was a rare venture into comedy for an actress not known for her sense of humour. Television came calling, most notably in 1971 when she gave an Emmy award-winning performance as Elizabeth I in the six-part series *Elizabeth R*, shaving her head and perfecting the art of chillingly narrowing her eyes and curling her lip.

She repeated the role in *Mary, Queen of Scots* (1971) with Vanessa Redgrave as Mary, though a better film in many respects was John Schlesinger's *Sunday Bloody Sunday* (also 1971) in which Jackson's Alex competes with Peter Finch's Daniel for the favours of Bob

(Murray Head), a young bisexual artist. Finch, Schlesinger and Jackson were nominated for Oscars and all three were among the film's five Bafta winners.

Her marriage was dissolved in 1976 after she began a relationship with Andy Phillips, the lighting designer on a stage production of *Hedda Gabler* with Timothy West as Judge Brack. That lasted for about five years and thereafter she was single, declaring herself happy to be so – "Men are awfully hard work for very little reward". She is survived by her son Dan Hodges, a columnist with The Mail on Sunday. Latterly she lived in a basement flat of his home in Blackheath, southeast London, going upstairs every evening to eat dinner with the family, argue politics and complete The Times crossword.

Work began to dry up in the mid-1980s as she reached the time when "significant unemployment starts among my age group". She took up lecturing on drama at Oxford and in Pennsylvania before returning to the London stage in 1986 with a witheringly autocratic performance in Nuria Espert's acclaimed production of Lorca's *The House of Bernarda Alba* at the Globe. She knew her limits and drew the line at writing for the stage. "I have difficulty writing a postcard, I could never write a play," she said.

She had been a member of the Labour Party since 16, campaigned for Oxfam and spoke out on causes such as homelessness, human rights and women's rights. In 1983 she considered an offer to stand for the Welsh Labour Party in the marginal seat of Bridgend, but demurred.

Yet during the 1980s she grew increasingly political, especially after Margaret Thatcher's "no such thing as society" speech in 1987. "It made me so angry that I walked into my closed French windows and almost broke my nose," Jackson recalled. "In the light of that I felt I was prepared to do anything I could to help create a Labour government."

In 1992 she retired from acting and at that year's election beat Oliver Letwin to take Hampstead & Highgate for Labour, joining Tony Blair's shadow cabinet when he succeeded John Smith as party leader. After the party's victory at the 1997 election she put her feminist principles aside to take part in the famous group photograph of what the tabloids called "Blair's babes". Recalling her move into politics, Jackson said: "I was told I was replacing one form of theatre with another. I said if that was the case then the Commons is remarkably under-rehearsed, the lighting is appalling and the acoustic is even worse."

As a junior minister Jackson instructed civil servants to call her Glenda and arrived at her office in tracksuit and running shoes. Despite such informality she approached politics with the same sense of purpose as she had done with acting, displaying a seriousness that bordered on the obsessional and ridiculing any suggestion that life should be about pursuing happiness. Her chief pleasure, Jackson said, was reading Hansard in bed. Her pet hate was untidiness. She was said to have turned down a damehood.

She resigned as a transport minister to seek the party's nomination as candidate for the newly created London mayoralty in 1999, but lost to Frank Dobson. He in turn lost the election to Ken Livingstone, the maverick former Labour leader of the Greater London Council who had turned independent. Boundary changes in 2010 left her with a majority of 42 in the newly named Hampstead & Kilburn seat, while her remarks on the death of Thatcher in 2013 and the "heinous social, economic and spiritual damage" caused by the former prime minister were seen as ungracious and she stepped down in 2015.

Her return to the stage at the age of 80 was marked by a fearless and extraordinarily powerful appearance in the title role of Deborah Warner's staging of *King Lear* at the Old Vic, receiving an Olivier award nomination for a performance that Ann Treneman in The Times described as "hard as nails, furious, capricious but also frail and vulnerable". She continued to deliver powerful roles and in 2019 won a Bafta for best actress as Maud, a woman suffering from dementia, in the BBC One drama *Elizabeth Is Missing.*

To keep fit, Jackson regularly joined a group of older women for a 7.30am swimming class. "But I'm still smoking between eight and ten cigarettes a day," she told The Times conspiratorially. Her biographer, Ian Woodward, subtitled his account of her life "A study in fire and ice", though she struggled with that perception, adding: "People think I'm scary. I'll never understand why."

This year she completed filming *The Great Escaper* with Michael Caine, the true story of Bernard Jordan, an octogenarian who in 2014 "escaped" from his care home.

However, her attitude to the profession remained unchanged. "It's always surprised me that my career is taken so seriously," she once said. "I don't think it that important... If my acting career ended tomorrow, then that would be that. There would be no tears. I'd become a social worker."

Glenda Jackson CBE was born on May 9, 1936. She died after a brief illness on June 15, 2023, aged 87

KIRK DOUGLAS

———————•———————

"I'm probably the most disliked actor in Hollywood," Kirk Douglas noted proudly at the height of his success and fame. "And I feel pretty good about it because that's me. I'm a pretty unlikeable character."

If Douglas enjoyed cultivating a real-life image of a ruthless tough guy driven by egomania, it served only to enhance his screen charisma in a series of memorable and sometimes monstrous roles that he summed up succinctly as "tough sons of bitches".

With his barrel chest, chiselled jaw and dimpled chin, he was made to play virile, if not always likeable, all-action characters. The robust template was forged from the moment he slugged his way to stardom in the 1949 film *Champion* as a prizefighter trampling all-comers in his pursuit of success.

The role won him his first of three Oscar nominations and he went on to stride his way grittily across the Wild West in assorted cowboy movies – most notably playing "Doc" Holliday alongside Burt Lancaster's Wyatt Earp in *Gunfight at the O.K. Corral*. He also bared his chest as a 9th-century marauder in *The Vikings*, grew a beard to play Van Gogh in *Lust for Life* and plundered Rome as he escaped from enslavement in the title role of the film for which he is best known, *Spartacus*.

He seemed to excel, even to revel, in portraying characters with a cynical amorality, from the callous newspaper reporter exploiting a mining disaster for his own ends in Billy Wilder's *Ace in the Hole* to the hard-heartedly ambitious film producer in Vincente Minnelli's *The Bad and the Beautiful*. "A shit, but such an interesting guy," Douglas recalled of the latter part many years later, clearly intending the epithet as a compliment.

Off screen his seeming enjoyment of confrontation led to broken studio contracts and falling-outs with directors. "I don't think I'd be much of an actor without vanity. I'm not interested in being modest," he admitted.

As he was often the first to point out, there were also affairs with some of the most desirable women of the day, including Rita Hayworth, Marlene Dietrich and Ava Gardner. "I was in an environment with incredibly beautiful women," he said. "I was surrounded by beauty, so I was like a kid in a candy store, not knowing which one to reach for."

He claimed once to have slept with 29 women in as many days and then told his therapist that he was worried he might be impotent because on the 30th night he couldn't manage a repeat performance. His therapist reputedly told him that even God gave himself a day of rest.

His philandering meant he was a mostly absentee father to his elder sons, the actor Michael Douglas and the film producer Joel Douglas, from his first marriage to the actress Diana Dill, whom he met as a student before the Second World War. While Douglas was serving in the US Navy he showed his shipmates an issue of Life magazine with Dill on the cover and told them that he would marry her. They mocked him, but she became his wife in 1943. They divorced eight years later and in her subsequent memoir she not only described him as a "sexually voracious bird of prey" but made mention of his partiality to orgies and hallucinogenic drugs.

He was married again in 1954 to the German-born producer Anne Buydens, whom he met on the set of *Lust for Life*, in which he played Vincent van Gogh, widely acclaimed as one of his best roles. Their relationship was complex but enduring. He said that he had been true to her "in my fashion" but that "fidelity was overemphasised". They renewed their vows in a ceremony at the Greystone Mansion in Beverly Hills in 2004. "The first marriage, we were in Las Vegas and got married in cowboy hats and Sinatra held up his show so he could come," he recalled. "But Anne got the vows wrong. She said, 'I take thee, Kirk, as my awful wedded husband.' So I thought 50 years later we should have another stab at it."

They had two sons, the producer Peter Douglas, who was given the middle name Vincent in honour of the film that had brought his parents together, and Eric Douglas, who became an actor, but whose career was eclipsed by addictions and run-ins with the law. His father disowned him at one stage but was devastated when he died of an accidental drug overdose in 2004.

It was one of several traumatic experiences that had a profound impact on Douglas's later life. In 1991 he was injured in a collision between a helicopter in which he was travelling and a small aircraft. Considering that two died in the crash he got off relatively lightly, with a compressed spine that left him three inches shorter. Even so, this was a cruel fate for a man who had always been sensitive about his stature. As a young man he had stood at around the 5ft 8in mark, and when filming he would wear stacked shoes, ones that Lancaster (6ft 1in), a regular co-star of his, used to hide in a spirit of mischief. What he lacked in height he made up for with a muscular physique of which he was inordinately proud, always claiming that he never needed to use stuntmen, which caused some ill feeling among the stuntmen.

His helicopter crash was to have one positive impact: it led him to re-embrace the Jewish faith in which he had been brought up. He documented his spiritual reawakening in *Climbing the Mountain: My Search for Meaning.*

Five years later, while undergoing a manicure, he suffered a stroke that impaired his ability to speak. Told he would never talk again, he thought about killing himself, even though in his younger years he had described depression as a form of narcissism.

At one point he even put a loaded gun in his mouth, but hesitated when the barrel hit his teeth: "The thought that I would never make another movie echoed in my brain. I just wanted to lie in bed and do nothing, but my wife would say, 'Get your ass out of bed and work on your speech therapy.'"

Weeks after the stroke he determinedly faced the public at the 1996 Academy Awards ceremony, where he was presented with a lifetime achievement award by Steven Spielberg. He had spent long hours relearning how to say the words "thank you". His strength of character also enabled him to return to acting in 2003 with *It Runs in the Family*, a comedy-drama that was stacked with other members of the Douglas tribe, including his son Michael, grandson Cameron and his first wife, Diana.

Douglas came to enjoy playing the patriarch to a theatrical dynasty, although he had initially discouraged Michael's desire to act and urged him to become a lawyer or a doctor. Once parental guidance had been ignored, his father declared him to be "one of my favourite actors".

Kirk gave Michael the film rights to *One Flew Over the Cuckoo's Nest*, which he had bought in 1963 after appearing in the Broadway stage adaptation of Ken Kesey's book. As producer, but not actor, Michael went on to turn it into an Oscar-winning film but passed over his father for the lead role in favour of the younger Jack Nicholson. When the movie won nine Oscars Kirk was genuinely proud of Michael's achievement but still struggled to conceal his rivalry. "I sure as hell don't want to go down in history as Michael Douglas's father," he quipped, while he told Nicholson: "Jack, I wanted you to be lousy."

There was a further blow to familial pride when his grandson Cameron – Michael's elder son – was given a five-year prison sentence for possession of heroin and dealing cocaine. It led Kirk to speculate publicly on the handicaps of wealth and fame. "I told my sons that they had not had my advantages in life because I had the advantage of being born poor and not having enough to eat," he noted ruefully.

In later life Douglas tried to become a better husband and father and also one of Hollywood's most generous philanthropists.

Through the Douglas Foundation he gave an estimated £35 million to a variety of non-profit organisations, including an Alzheimer's unit at a home for retired film industry workers, a shelter for homeless women and a university scholarship programme for ethnic-minority students.

He also took a close interest in the Kirk Douglas Continuation High School in Northridge, California, which helped troubled teenagers to resume and complete their education. Each pupil who graduated received a $500 cheque from him, which he insisted on presenting in person. He funded his foundation partly by the sale of some of the choicest pictures in his substantial art collection, including works by Chagall, Picasso and Miró. He shrugged off any praise by saying: "I think being generous is selfish because it makes you feel so good."

Politically he leant towards the left and in the early days of his career was a forthright opponent of the McCarthyite blacklisting of actors and screenwriters suspected of communist sympathies. When he made *Spartacus* – for which he was executive producer as well as starring alongside Laurence Olivier and Tony Curtis – he employed the writer Dalton Trumbo, one of the so-called Hollywood Ten who had been jailed for refusing to testify before the House Un-American Activities Committee.

The Hollywood hierarchy had signed an agreement to bar them from the studios but Douglas ignored the edict and ordered security to admit Trumbo. John Wayne was among those who attacked him for breaking the ban and Douglas later admitted that if he had been less of a hothead he "might have said to myself, 'Wait a minute, Kirk, why not let someone else take the heat? This is going to ruin your career.'"

Instead his action ended the blacklist and Douglas remained proud of his stand. "Spartacus was important for me because that was the picture with which I broke the blacklist. I think that it is the most important thing I've done in my career," he said.

He remained a lifelong Democrat, but placed patriotism above party affiliation, acting as a goodwill ambassador for the US Information Agency, travelling the world to preach the principles of American freedom and democracy. "If you're a Democrat or a

Republican, always do what's good for your country," he said. "As the product of immigrants, I realise what this country has done for me."

He was born Issur Danielovitch in 1916, in Amsterdam, New York state. His parents, Herschel and Bryna, were illiterate Russian-Jewish immigrants. His hard-drinking father derived a meagre income as a rag-and-bone man. "He was the toughest guy in town. He was always fighting and I became a fighter too," Douglas recalled. "Became a wrestler in college." Yet there was little affection between father and son: "I think what I missed most was the pat on the back."

The family spoke Yiddish at home and Douglas attended a Jewish school. In his autobiography he described getting beaten up regularly as part of the casual anti-Semitism prevalent in America at the time, long before the rise of Nazi Germany in Europe.

As an only son, he found living with six sisters a stifling experience. "I was dying to get out. In a sense it lit a fire under me," he said.

He began his womanising at the age of 15 when he lost his virginity to his English teacher. "I realise she could have gone to jail for it, but she got me interested in poetry," he remarked, a little incongruously.

At high school he discovered a love of acting but had to work odd jobs as a gardener and janitor. He lobbied university deans and drama school bosses for scholarships and loans to fund his further studies, first at St Lawrence University and then at the American Academy of Dramatic Arts, where one of his classmates was Betty Joan Perske, who became a lifelong friend and was soon to find fame as Lauren Bacall.

For a while he used the stage name Demsky, borrowed from a Russian uncle, but by the time his Broadway debut came in a minor supporting role in 1941, he had opted for Kirk Douglas. Shortly afterwards he enlisted in the US Navy.

After his discharge he landed his first film part when Bacall recommended him to the producer Hal B Wallis, who cast him as Barbara Stanwyck's insecure and alcoholic husband in *The Strange Love of Martha Ivers*. It was the first and last time he played a weakling, although off screen he flexed his muscles when Wallis told him to have the make-up department fill in the famous cleft on his chin. "I said, 'Listen, this is what you get.' I didn't cave," Douglas later said. Not only are his handprints outside Grauman's Chinese Theatre in Hollywood, but also a print of the dimple in his chin.

His rise to Hollywood royalty was rapid. By 1951, two years after his first Oscar nomination, he became one of the first actors in postwar Hollywood to establish his own production company. To do so he broke his contract with Warner Brothers and announced that he objected to being treated as "a studio poodle". He named the company Bryna after his mother.

Douglas began producing his own films, one of the most striking of which was the 1957 drama *Paths of Glory*, in which he played a French First World War officer and on which he employed the director Stanley Kubrick, then little known. Typically, Douglas soon let his director know who was boss after Kubrick rewrote the screenplay. He summoned him to a meeting and threw the rewritten screenplay across the room, telling him: "We're going back to the original script or we're not making the picture." Douglas was not one to hold a grudge: three years later he invited Kubrick back to direct *Spartacus*.

Douglas continued to work prolifically and had clocked up 87 significant feature films by the time he made his last in 2004, *Illusion*, in which he poignantly played a dying film director looking back on his life's work.

In later years he divided his time between philanthropic work for his foundation, playing solitaire on his computer and indulging his two labradors. Into his nineties he was a regular swimmer and enjoyed taking part in races against his housekeeper's seven-year-old daughter. "She always gives me a head start, and she always beats me," he said. He also enthusiastically embraced the digital age, joining MySpace and becoming an avid blogger.

Even in his twilight years, he never lost his appreciation of the opposite sex. "I still love to look at beautiful women," he said. "You never grow out of recognising that a woman looks sexy. No one will ever get that old."

Kirk Douglas was born on December 9, 1916. He died on February 5, 2020, aged 103

LEE MARVIN

Lee Marvin was helped on his way to international stardom by his gravelly voice and rugged features. He was one of the screen's most effective tough guys, specialising in cynical, cold-blooded killers, of which the best known was probably his convict-turned-commando in *The Dirty Dozen*. His life off the film set was equally colourful, and he revelled in his hard-drinking, hell-raising reputation.

He won an Oscar for his drunken gunfighter in the comedy western *Cat Ballou*, while his throaty and unorthodox rendering of *I Was Born Under a Wandering Star* from the musical *Paint Your Wagon* became a hit record.

In 1979 he was at the centre of a famous legal battle when his former mistress, Michelle Triola, sued him under a new Californian law for half the $3.5 million she said he had earned during the years they lived together. But the judge awarded her only $104,000 and ruled that there had been no contract between the couple.

Lee Marvin was born into a long-established Anglo-American family in New York in 1924. His father was an advertising executive and his mother a fashion writer.

After an unsettled childhood, during which he was expelled from several schools, he enlisted in the United States Marines, and served in the South Pacific, as a scout sniper during the Second World War. In one of the many Pacific island landings in which he participated, he was hit by a Japanese bullet, which severed a nerve in his spine. He was in hospital for 13 months, after which he was invalided out of the service.

Returning to New York, he worked as a plumber's mate and took other jobs before starting his acting career in summer stock. He joined a theatre school in New York and in 1951 appeared in the Broadway production of *Billy Budd*.

In the same year he made his film debut in *You're in the Navy Now* and during the 1950s made a steady reputation playing villains in westerns and gangster films, often being cast as a hired assassin.

Of his early parts, the most notable was in *The Big Heat* where he threw boiling coffee into the face of Gloria Grahame. He was Marlon Brando's gang rival in *The Wild One* and one of Spencer Tracy's adversaries in *Bad Day at Black Rock*. In the late 1950s he concentrated on television, starring as a Chicago detective in more than 100 episodes of the series *M Squad*, and he also played Ira Hayes, the hero of Iwo Jima.

He made three successive films with John Wayne, including John Ford's ironic western, *The Man Who Shot Liberty Valance*, and he was chillingly effective as another assassin in *The Killers*. But it was *Cat Ballou* (1965), not itself a particularly distinguished picture, that finally enabled him to make the transition from character player to star.

The Dirty Dozen soon followed and he went on to give two excellent and contrasting performances for the British director, John Boorman. In the hard-edged thriller *Point Blank* he was a gangster avenging himself on the organisation that had betrayed him, while in *Hell in the Pacific* he and Toshiro Mifune played two Second World War survivors stranded on a remote island.

In *Paint Your Wagon* he and Clint Eastwood were cast as gold prospectors sharing the same wife, and his unashamedly hammed-up performance helped to redeem an otherwise overlong and tedious film. He was paid $1 million for the role, a sum which reflected his status as one of Hollywood's most potent box-office attractions.

By now Marvin's screen persona was mellowing. Though he was still essentially tough and unsentimental, he tended to be seen more often as hero than villain. During the 1970s he played yet another hired killer in *Prime Cut*, a hobo in *The Emperor of the North Pole* and a Second World War foot soldier in *The Big Red One*. More ambitiously, he was Hickey in Eugene O'Neill's *The Ice Man Cometh*.

But none of his later work, which also included the 1983 thriller, *Gorky Park*, added substantially to his reputation. Had he retired fifteen years ago, he would still be assured of a place in cinema history. He was a striking embodiment of American masculinity, often, in the early years, spilling over into brutality and sadism, but also capable of a softer and more appealing side and a rough integrity.

He was three times married; his third wife, Pamela, survives him.

Lee Marvin was born on February 19, 1924. He died of a heart attack on August 29, 1987, aged 63

INGRID BERGMAN

———————•———————

Miss Ingrid Bergman was a screen personality who managed remarkably to bridge the gap between film star and actress: though as a classic Hollywood star her face and personality were her principal fortune, she demonstrated at difficult stages in her career considerable gifts as an actress which carried her through one major reversal in her career and brought her back with her standing enhanced, if anything, by the setback.

She was born in Sweden in 1915, and after some experience on stage and screen scored a major success in Sweden and Europe generally with her performance in Gustav Molander's *Intermezzo* (1936), in which she played a young music teacher involved in a hopeless affair with the violinist father of a pupil.

In all she made ten films in Sweden before going to Hollywood in 1938 under contract to David O Selznick, who had discovered her in *Intermezzo*. She began her American career with a remake of it in which she starred opposite Leslie Howard.

Despite attempts to change her name, and regroom her (Selznick was worried when she proved to be 69 inches tall), she emerged in the American *Intermezzo* (also called *Escape to Happiness*) with very much the natural, well-scrubbed, fresh look which at once rendered her distinctive and was to remain her particular quality throughout her career. Graham Greene noted in his review of the film that she made her first appearance on the international screen with "a highlight gleaming on her nose-tip", and added, "That gleam is typical of a performance which doesn't give the effect of acting at all, but of living without make-up."

In most of her subsequent American films she was remarkable, even if the films frequently were not. In *Dr Jekyll and Mr Hyde* (1941) she played the good girl and would have preferred to play the bad girl. In *Gaslight* (1944) she was reduced to a nervous wreck with improbable rapidity by her husband's machinations, and won an Academy Award for it. For the role of the heroine in *For Whom the Bell Tolls* (1943) she was Hemingway's own choice, but the film was gutless.

Her most famous film of this era, *Casablanca* (1942) was little more than a timely soap opera which by a happy combination of casting and the moment at which it was made assumed a sort of mythic status as a quintessential movie-like-they-don't-make-them-any-more, but probably did more for her than she did for it. And much the same could be said of *The Bells of St Mary's* (1945), in which at least her crisp, no-nonsense manner helped to take the curse off a saccharine tale of whimsical religious life in a benevolent world.

In 1945, back again under the rule of Selznick, to whom she was still under contract, she began one of the most fruitful collaborations of her career, that with Hitchcock, for whom she played the lead in three films. The first of them, *Spellbound*, had her cast as a psychiatrist who falls in love with her unofficial patient, Gregory Peck. In *Notorious* (1946) she was involved with Cary Grant in some complex espionage activities in Brazil, not to mention some of the most sustained love scenes filmed up to that time. The third Hitchcock film, *Under Capricorn* (1949), though much admired by French critics, seems by comparison heavy and turgid, and suffers from some signs of preoccupation on its star's part: she had already embarked on the affair with the Italian director Roberto Rossellini which was to make her an outcast for some years from a still-on-the-surface prudish and moralistic Hollywood.

This began when Rossellini approached her with the idea of starring in a film to be made in the Neo-Realist fashion without studio work, without a formal script, working directly out of the location and the real life of its inhabitants. The location selected was a small Mediterranean island, and the story of *Stromboli* (1950) was in the event a somewhat flimsy and even novelettish affair of illicit love and psychological retribution.

Rossellini was in fact moving away from the directly social preoccupations of his earlier films, and the presence of Ingrid Bergman as his regular star and collaborator helped to turn him in four subsequent features more in the direction of inward, psychological drama and even a semi-mystical view of human nature, guilt, expiation and the importance of the word, of confession. *Europa 51, Journey to Italy* and *Fear* (this last made in Germany) were only very patchily distributed, and *Joan at the Stake*, a film version of the spectacular stage production of Honegger's opera-oratorio with which Rossellini and Bergman toured Europe, not even that.

It seemed as though the liaison (turned into marriage as soon as both were free) was disastrous for both parties, professionally at least – though recent years have brought about a re-evaluation of the films Rossellini made at this time, now seeable without the preconceptions inescapable in the heyday of Neo-Realism. The fact remains that at the time Ingrid Bergman's career seemed to have slipped into total obscurity. After the break-up of her marriage with Rossellini she began to rebuild it in various ways: she starred in the Paris stage production of *Tea and Sympathy*, and made a film in France with Jean Renoir, *Eléna et les hommes*. And then in 1956 she achieved a triumphant return to the American cinema with *Anastasia*, an effectively fictionalised account of the main claimant to the Romanoff succession, for which she won the Academy Award of that year, her second.

No more conclusive sign of Hollywood's "forgiveness" could be given, and from then on she remained in a privileged position as a star who remained almost ageless, could work when she liked on what she liked, and established the hard way her right to be independent of Hollywood, and made Hollywood come to her.

Not all the films she made subsequently were altogether wise choices. Stanley Donen's *Indiscreet* (1958), in which she was teamed again with Cary Grant, was a comedy of considerable charm and polish, though in parts it suggested that light comedy was not perhaps her forte. *The Inn of the Sixth Happiness* (1958), in which she played the missionary in China, Gladys Aylward, was one of her biggest popular successes, and *The Visit* (1964), Bernhard Wicki's ambitious version of Duerrenmatt's play, saw her doing her best with a role which, in its rooted malevolence, was far remote from her normal screen persona.

In 1967 she made a brief return to Sweden for an episode in the composite film *Stimulantia* which brought her together again with the veteran director Gustav Molander in a polished adaptation of Maupassant. Of the other latter-day films, *Cactus Flower* (1969) is probably the most effective, showing that even if comedy did not come very naturally to her on screen, she could, when she chose, be very funny indeed, letting her hair down in broad farce.

In the 1970s, unexpectedly, she moved on to new triumphs in the cinema. In 1974 she won another Oscar, this time for a supporting role in the all-star *Murder on the Orient Express* (not that her role was any more supporting than anyone else's), appeared interestingly, cast against type, as the mysterious, mad old woman in Vincente Minnelli's *A Matter of Time* (1976), and gave one of her finest, most unsparing performances back in Sweden, in Swedish, for her namesake Ingmar Bergman's *Autumn Sonata*. She claimed that this would be her last, crowning film role, but promptly changed her mind to play the even more unlikely role of Golda Meir in a screen biography.

Throughout this time she had also continued to act on stage, scoring major successes in London in a distinguished revival of *A Month in the Country* with Michael Redgrave, and in New York in the first production of Eugene O'Neill's posthumous *More Stately Mansions*; in the 1970s she appeared in *Captain Brassbound's Conversion* and *The Constant Wife* in both Britain and America, and played with Wendy Hiller in a revival of NC Hunter's *Waters of the Moon.*

In all these performances, varied though they were, the keynote, as in her screenwork, was naturalness. It was difficult sometimes, such was her skill in suggesting that she was not acting but just living in front of the camera, to recognise her real skills as an actress, which tended (at least up to *Autumn Sonata*) to be underestimated. But there was a whole range of roles which were from the beginning unmistakenly, unarguably "Ingrid Bergman roles", and that was that.

Ingrid Bergman was born on August 29, 2015. She died of cancer on her 67th birthday, August 29, 1982

SPENCER TRACY

───────────── ● ─────────────

"When I go," said Spencer Tracy once, "a whole epoch will have ended." The comment was made dispassionately, without conceit, for his attitude to life was far too philosophical and objective for any indulgence in the self-adulation which characterised so many of his contemporaries. A difficult man in the studios in many ways, he was temperamental through perversity rather than self-esteem. He disliked on principle anyone who tried to push him about.

When he spoke of an epoch, he was thinking of the film star era that dominated Hollywood in the Thirties and which was itself dominated by the MGM studios, who carried the star system to its ultimate peak. Greta Garbo, Clark Gable, Robert Taylor, Norma Shearer, Myrna Loy, William Powell, Jean Harlow, Jeanette MacDonald, Mickey Rooney and Judy Garland were but a few of the names which Louis B Mayer created. And when Mayer died in 1957, it was Spencer Tracy who read the funeral oration. That, too, marked the end of an epoch.

When Tracy spoke of an epoch, he was also thinking of the qualities which made a star in those days. Personality allied to an expert technique was the answer. The star system called for no outstanding histrionic ability, and Spencer Tracy never thought of himself as a great actor. He looked upon himself as a professional who thoroughly understood his trade.

Tough, honest and indomitable, a man of sober authority and rugged good sense, he became a symbol on the screen of all those qualities which represented the pioneering spirit of America. There was nothing fancy about Tracy. He was never seen as the great lover or the debonair seducer. Throughout his career he was at his best when he represented the plain and solid citizen who spoke up for what he believed to be right. A man of the people.

He was born in Milwaukee, Wisconsin, in 1900, and was educated at the Wisconsin University. He then studied for the stage at the American Academy of Dramatic Art. His New York debut was made at the Garrick Theatre in October 1922, and for the next eight years he appeared in the theatre with reasonable frequency and success.

In 1930 he played a ruthless gangster in the Broadway production *The Last Mile*. Hollywood, at that time, was just beginning to interest itself in the melodramatic possibilities of the gangster film, and so Tracy was summoned to the Coast by the Fox Film Company to play in tough parts. He did not like these parts, and became troublesome to his new employers, who were happy enough to let him go to MGM. But here again he was required at first to play only tough-guy parts – in *Riffraff*, opposite Jean Harlow, and *Whipsaw*, with Myrna Loy.

His first real opportunity came with the production of one of Mayer's most ambitious pictures – *San Francisco*, with Jeanette MacDonald and Clark Gable. Tracy, to the surprise of everyone, including himself, was cast as a priest. This was in 1936, and the same year saw the release of another unusual picture in which he played the leading part. In *Fury*, directed by Fritz Lang, Tracy was seen as an innocent man who is almost lynched by a mob who suspect him of kidnapping. It was one of the best pictures ever to come out of the MGM studios, and it firmly established Tracy as a star. The following year saw him appear as the Portuguese fisherman in the Kipling story *Captains Courageous*, and although he was apprehensive about taking the part, which was very different from anything he had done previously, he achieved another success and won his first Academy Award. His second came within a year, for his performance as Father Flanagan in *Boys Town*.

Tracy worked for 21 years for MGM, but his contract was cancelled by mutual agreement in 1955 – a year after the cancellation of that between MGM and Clark Gable. The star epoch was already dying, and the old brigade at MGM were drifting away. Tracy, like Gable, was unmoved. He knew that there were still many good years of acting in him and he was not sorry to be parted from Mayer. In spite of the oration at Mayer's funeral, he had never had much regard for the man; for Tracy was far less gullible than some.

"As Tracy gets older, he acts less and less," wrote a critic of him in his later days. He might have added that his technique became ever more skilful and mature. To this later period belong such notable films as *Bad Day at Black Rock, The Mountain, The Old Man and the Sea, Devil at Four O'clock, Inherit the Wind*, in which another old-timer, Fredric March, put up a tremendous performance against him, and *Judgment at Nuremburg*, in which he played a judge at the Nuremburg trial.

By now he was something of a grand old man of the cinema – a little tetchy, a bit cynical, and as stubborn as of old, but still philosophical, and with a sense of humour. "I hear that you're quite impossible now on the set," a friend once said to him in these later days. "That," said Tracy indignantly, "is only about 98 per cent true."

He missed his old associates greatly – Gable, Cooper, Bogart, and all the others of the golden epoch of stardom. But he never went to see his old films. The epoch was dying, and he had no wish to be reminded of its past glories. He will be remembered as one of the best examples of it.

Tracy had been a sick man for several years, and he knew that his days were numbered, but he continued to appear in films because idleness was anathema to him. Wherever possible he sought out another of the old brigade to play opposite him. Katharine Hepburn was his favourite, a sparring partner of many epics, and another experienced veteran of the MGM team. A resolute and independent thinker like himself, who had never submitted weakly to the Mayer regime. A professional, too, to the fingertips, as he was himself. His death came shortly after they had completed *Guess Who's Coming to Dinner* in which they were directed by Stanley Kramer.

During his life he never sought publicity and never wished for his private life to be described. He was married in 1923 to Louise Treadwell and had one son born in 1932. By the end of his apprenticeship with MGM he and Gary Cooper were together the most skilled and highly professional film actors in business – players who had ceased to act consciously in the studio because they did the right thing by instinct. They understood the camera and the camera understood them. An epoch has ended with his death as he forecast. And the opening words of his speech at Mayer's funeral return to the memory: "It is the Book of Genesis which says: there were giants in those days ..."

Spencer Tracy was born on April 5, 1900. He died of a heart attack on June 10, 1967, aged 67

RITA HAYWORTH

———————●———————

Rita Hayworth's career reached its peak in the years during and just after the Second World War when with Betty Grable (a less talented performer) she was the serviceman's favourite pin-up and starred in a series of films that deftly exploited her particular brand of erotic glamour.

Her screen persona was probably best realised in the 1946 film *Gilda*: a seductress in black satin. She was also a graceful and talented dancer, appearing twice with Fred Astaire and inviting favourable comparisons with his previous partner, Ginger Rogers (who was, in fact, her cousin).

At the height of her fame, and to the consternation of her employer, Columbia Pictures, she gave up films to marry the Prince Aly Khan – he was the third of five husbands and though she returned to the screen she never recaptured her former allure.

In later years her career was increasingly overshadowed by personal problems. In 1977 it was announced that she had been confined, a chronic alcoholic, to the psychiatric ward of a California hospital and a court was asked to put her affairs in the hands of a public guardian.

She was born Margarita Cansino in New York in October 1918. Her father came from a family of Spanish dancers and her mother was a Ziegfeld girl. After they moved to Los Angeles in 1927 she danced with her father in night clubs and made her professional stage debut at the age of 14.

She entered films in 1935 under her own name but was soon dropped by her first studio, Fox, and it was mainly due to her first husband, an oilman, that she managed to get a contract with Columbia. Soon afterwards, having shortened her first name to Rita, she adopted her mother's maiden name of Hayworth.

Her appearances were mainly in B pictures until she was given the second female lead in Howard Hawks' aviation drama, *Only Angels Have Wings*, in 1939. After more good films, including George Cukor's *Susan and God* and *Strawberry Blonde*, with James Cagney, she was acclaimed as the new Hollywood "love goddess" and lived up to the billing with a splendid performance in the Latin American swashbuckler *Blood and Sand*.

For the next few years she was Columbia's biggest female star. Though she had frequent disputes with the studio and was one of several actresses to fight the "slavery" of the seven-year contract, most of her best films were made during this time. Reviewers tended to dismiss them as Rita Hayworth vehicles but this was to underestimate the skill of the Hollywood dream factory: certainly they can still be watched with pleasure.

She danced with Astaire in *You'll Never Get Rich* and *You Were Never Lovelier* and with Gene Kelly in a successful "backstage" musical, *Cover Girl*, with a score by Jerome Kern. (She sang as well but her voice was usually dubbed.)

She was in *My Girl Sal*, with Victor Mature, and a Hollywood tribute to the London Windmill theatre called *Tonight and Every Night*. But all of these are eclipsed, at least in retrospect, by *Gilda*, which was made by the director of *Cover Girl*, Charles Divor.

It was a steamy melodrama of murder, jealousy and corruption set in Buenos Aires and an outstanding example of the 1940s film noir. Hayworth was the female part of a triangle which also comprised George Macready and Glenn Ford and is particularly remembered for her provocative dance in a night club, tossing back her long hair and peeling off elbow-length gloves.

Another notable film of the period was *The Lady from Shanghai*, directed by, and co-starring, her second husband, Orson Welles. She was another femme fatale, but more vulnerable and meeting a bizarre death in a hall of mirrors.

By this time her marriage to Orson Welles was breaking up. After one more film, an unsuccessful version of *Carmen* with the *Gilda* team of Ford and Vidor, she eloped to Europe with Aly Khan and they were married, in a blaze of publicity, in 1949. But within two years she was seeking a divorce and planning a screen comeback.

She added to her gallery of predatory women in two tailor-made pictures, *Salome* and *Miss Sadie Thompson* (from Somerset Maugham's *Rain*) but the old magic was missing and after her fourth marriage, to the singer Dick Haymes, she went into retirement again.

She returned to films in *Fire Down Below*, a Caribbean adventure with Robert Mitchum, in *Pal Joey*, with Frank Sinatra, and in Rattigan's *Separate Tables*, and had an effectively unglamorous part in *They Came to Cordura*.

In 1958 she married the producer, James Hill, but they were divorced three years later.

The rest of her screen career, which ended with *The Wrath of God* in 1972, was an anticlimax marked by unworthy character parts in mostly undistinguished films.

She had two daughters: Rebecca, by Orson Welles, and Princess Yasmin from her marriage to Aly Khan.

Rita Hayworth was born on October 17, 1918. She died of Alzheimer's disease on May 14, 1987, aged 68

STAN LAUREL

---•---

Mr Stan Laurel will always be remembered as a partner in the comedy team of Laurel and Hardy, and he would not have had it otherwise. The two worked as a team, and their success was indivisible.

Separately they did not amount to very much. Together they seemed despite their differences in appearance and possibly because of it to become a single unit, an expression of well-intentioned muddle-headedness in a harsh and practical world.

Stan Laurel was small and thin. Oliver Hardy was very fat. Hardy was expansive, bland and self-assured. Laurel was anxious, frail and perplexed. When Hardy attempted anything it went wrong in the end. When Laurel put his hand to it, it went wrong immediately.

Arthur Stanley Jefferson (Laurel's real name) was an Englishman, born in Ulverston, Lancashire in 1890. He was educated at King James Grammar School in Bishop Auckland and learnt the profession of a comedian the hard way – in the circus, the music hall and the theatre. Like Chaplin, he first saw America as a member of Fred Karno's touring company when he was still in his teens (they played together in a sketch called *Mumming Birds*), and – like Chaplin – he stayed in the United States to play in the early silent films. Hal Roach gave him his first film part in 1917, and he made some 50 short comedies for the Hal Roach Company, and also tried his hand both as a producer and a director.

The partnership with Oliver Hardy started in 1926, when the silent film was at its zenith, and competition among screen comedians was acute. This was in many ways the golden age of screen comedy, which was so ideally suited to the silent films, and the competition to be faced included such great names as Chaplin, Harold Lloyd and Buster Keaton. When sound came it was in no way a handicap to them, for their voices exactly matched their appearance Hardy's benign and soft, Laurel's plaintive and often a little squeaky, especially in moments of anguish – and their comedies were introduced by a catchy little signature tune that became almost as well-known as they themselves. The second major hurdle in their career – the full-length film – was less easily surmounted. Their first long picture was *Jailbirds*, made in 1931, but although their long films were frequently very funny there is no doubt that it was within the framework of their short comedies that they were seen at their best.

Hardy died in 1957, but before that their star was on the wane.

Stan Laurel was born on June 16, 1890. He died of a heart attack on February 23, 1965, aged 74

IRRFAN KHAN

Irrfan Khan was proud of his status as one of the most respected stars in Hindi cinema, but he hated the term Bollywood. "It shows the inferiority complex of our film industry, which has nothing to do with aping Hollywood," he complained. "So why did they lose their identity by calling it Bollywood?"

Khan understood better than most the differences and the similarities that characterise the world's two most prolific film industries, for he was also one of the few Indian actors to become a box-office draw in America.

As what one critic called "Hollywood's go-to Indian", he played a doctor in *The Amazing Spider-Man*, appeared alongside Tom Hanks in *Inferno*, was the owner of the dinosaur theme park in *Jurassic World* and was chosen by Ang Lee to play the adult narrator in the film adaptation of Yann Martel's novel *Life of Pi*.

Other leading directors to cast him included Wes Anderson in *The Darjeeling Limited*, Michael Winterbottom in *A Mighty Heart* and, perhaps most notably of all, Danny Boyle, in whose Oscar-winning *Slumdog Millionaire* Khan gave a riveting performance as the police inspector who interrogates the young pauper from the back streets of Mumbai suspected of cheating in a TV game show.

There were also invitations from the directors Steven Spielberg, Christopher Nolan and Ridley Scott, all of which he turned down because their production schedules clashed with his commitments to the Indian film industry. "I didn't decide I was going to work in Hollywood," he said. "When I tried to cultivate it, it never worked, but when I left it alone, it happened organically."

If his list of appearances in English-language films was impressive, it was noticeable that they all came in supporting roles. "Hollywood isn't ready for an Indian leading man," he said. "It will take time before they feel free to write a story about an Indian guy, unless it's about the dark side, like *Slumdog*. They don't want to see a normal India – that's not the shock value they have to have."

The comment was made without rancour and offered as an objective observation. What's more, it was almost certainly true. On the release of *Life of Pi*, Ang Lee was asked if Khan could become the first Indian actor to land the lead in a mainstream American movie. "Probably not as a romantic lead, because he's not White," Lee answered candidly. "But maybe he can break through. He's definitely rare and very special."

In any case, Khan's prime loyalty remained to Indian cinemagoers. "Our audiences feel proud when they see me working with Tom Hanks," he said. "They have a sense of identity in the international market. It makes them feel, 'We exist.'"

That he put his Indian audience first was evident when he turned down the chance to appear in Nolan's 2014 sci-fi epic *Interstellar* because he refused to spend four months filming in America. "They expected a huge commitment from my end. It wouldn't have been possible for me to be there for that long," he said. The film went on to gross more than $650 million and he admitted that rejecting the invitation was "one of the most difficult decisions" he ever made.

Known to Indian film fans as "The Great Khan", he featured in more than 50 domestic films, often playing memorably villainous roles. His first big lead in a Bollywood blockbuster came in *Rog* in 2005.

His international success further fed his standing as one of India's biggest box-office names, culminating with *Hindi Medium*, which became one of the highest-grossing films in the history of Indian cinema and won him best actor at the Filmfare Awards, Bollywood's equivalent of the Oscars.

His success was hard won and at the start of his career Khan spent long and unsatisfying years appearing in Indian TV soaps "chasing middle-class housewives", as he put it. "Once, they didn't even pay me because they thought my acting was so bad."

By the late 1990s he was on the point of quitting until the London-based director Asif Kapadia gave him the lead in *The Warrior*, released in 2001. Filmed in Rajasthan, in Hindi, it won the Alexander Korda Award for best British film at the Baftas.

Khan's career was cut short in 2018 when he had a neuroendocrine tumour diagnosed. Khan's 95-year-old mother died four days before him and he was unable to attend her funeral, but was said to have participated via videolink.

Throughout his illness Khan was supported by his wife, Sutapa Sikdar, a screenwriter he met at India's National School of Drama, where they were both students in the 1980s. "If I get to live, I want to live for her," he said. "She is the reason for me to keep at it."

She spoke of his dedication to acting, reading at least one new script a week and staying up until 3am, making notes about how to play his character. When they worked together on an Indian TV soap in the 1990s, she recalled that he had demanded endless rewrites from her. She survives him, along with their two young sons, Babil and Ayan, whose disappointment when he initially turned down the role in *The Amazing Spider-Man* persuaded him to change his mind.

Sahabzade Irfan Ali Khan was born in 1967 into a Muslim family in Jaipur, Rajasthan. The extra "r" in Irrfan was added in 2012. Asked why, he replied that he "liked the sound of it".

His mother, Begum, claimed royal lineage and his father, Jagirdar Khan, owned a tyre shop and was a game hunter. As the eldest of two sons, there was strong pressure for Khan to work in the family's tyre business, which intensified when his father died.

Instead he plotted his escape, initially hoping to be a professional cricketer. He was selected to play for his state side in an under-23 tournament but lacked the money to take up his place.

He turned his dreams instead to acting and with the help of his sister raised enough money to enrol at drama school. "No one could have imagined I would be an actor, I was so shy and so thin," he recalled. "But the desire was so intense, I thought I'd suffocate if I didn't get admission."

After graduating, his struggles included working as an air-conditioning repair man. One of his first clients was the Bollywood superstar Rajesh Khanna, who encouraged him not to give up.

Khan was endlessly ambitious for Indian cinema to broaden its horizons and believed that films such as *Slumdog Millionaire* and *Life of Pi* played a significant part in the emergence of a new breed of Indian directors and cinemagoers. "They are younger and more aware of international cinema," he said. "They want a fresh approach and haunting films that stay in your psyche. That's the magic and magnetism of cinema."

Irrfan Khan was born on January 7, 1967. He died of a colon infection on April 29, 2020, aged 53

JEAN HARLOW

Our New York Correspondent telegraphs that Miss Jean Harlow, the "platinum blonde" of the screen, died yesterday at the age of 26.

She was taken ill only 10 days ago with internal inflammation, but insisted on working as long as she could as she did not want to delay the picture *Saratoga*, in which she was acting with Clark Gable. Three days ago she was stated to have virtually recovered, but yesterday she took a sudden turn for the worse and was removed from her Beverley Hills home to hospital. She was given two blood transfusions and intravenous injections and placed in an oxygen tent, but she lapsed into a coma and did not regain consciousness. Her mother, Mrs Jean Bello, and Mr William Powell, the actor, were at her bedside.

Born in 1911, at Kansas City, she belonged to a family of good position. She first showed her talent for acting at her exclusive school at Lake Forest, Illinois. Determined to try her luck in Hollywood, she was given a contract to feature in comedies, but her grandfather and guardian strongly disapproved, and she reluctantly withdrew from the studios. At last, after many months, with the aid of her mother, she obtained her grandfather's consent. Beginning over again, she was playing as an extra in a film starring Clara Bow when Howard Hughes selected her for leading lady in the sound version of his air-war spectacle, *Hell's Angels*. Miss Harlow gave a brilliant performance and became a film star overnight. Howard Hughes immediately gave her a long-term contract with the Caddo Company. Other film producers were quick to recognise a new star, and she became one of the busiest actresses on the screen.

Later she made a striking success in *China Seas*. Last year Miss Harlow startled the film fans by becoming a brunette. Among her other principal films were *Dinner at Eight, Blonde Bombshell, Suzy, Reckless, Wife versus Secretary, Libelled Lady,* and *The Man in Possession,* the last a film in which she struck a more sophisticated note and which is not yet released in this country.

Miss Harlow's first husband was Paul Bern, the film director. They married in July 1932, but two months later Bern took his own life. A year later she was married to Harold Rosson, a Hollywood cameraman. This marriage ended in divorce in March 1935. Jean Harlow had steadily become known to film audiences for much more than her striking "platinum blonde" colouring and other abundant physical gifts. She used an intensely vital and robust personality with imagination to portray a character of unfailing appeal to most playgoers – the girl of humble origin and proud of it, steeped in knowledge of the world and particularly of men, with an incredible command of vituperation and rapid, "wisecracking" speech, and beneath it all a heart of pure gold. When Jean "sailed in" to trounce the man who had "done her wrong", or to apply a spur to the diffident husband for whom she had ambitions, the house sat back in delighted anticipation.

Jean Harlow was born on March 3, 1911. She died of uremic poisoning on June 7, 1937, aged 26

DENNIS HOPPER

A screen actor who first came to notice while still a teenager for his performance alongside James Dean, Natalie Wood and Sal Mineo in the 1950s movie classic *Rebel Without a Cause* (1955), Dennis Hopper was triumphantly to capture the spirit of the youth revolution of the following decade in the film that became iconic of the spirit of Sixties counterculture, *Easy Rider* (1969).

As scriptwriter (with Peter Fonda and Terry Southern), actor (with Peter Fonda) and director of *Easy Rider*, Hopper was the controlling genius of a film that could so easily have degenerated into chaos as it pursued him and Fonda as a couple of dropouts on Harley-Davidson motorcycles on a ragged odyssey across America (on the way giving Jack Nicholson his big screen break). Hopper did more than any other film-maker to encapsulate the often woolly-headed aspirations of the alternative culture without, however, over-sentimentalising it.

And *Easy Rider* graphically depicted aspects of the sheer nastiness in US society ranging from intolerance of long hair to murderous homophobia, to which the hippy culture was opposed.

Against expectation, *Easy Rider* exerted a fascination well outside what might have been considered as its target audience, becoming a runaway box-office phenomenon not only in the US but throughout the world.

It had been made on a modest budget of $350,000, but was to go on to gross more than $50 million throughout the world. Queues for it included those of an age for which it represented a completely alien way of looking at society and for whom its subject was no more nor less than the subversion of right-thinking civilisation.

Given Hollywood's proven tendency to exploit a successful formula, it was not surprising that *Easy Rider* had many imitations. But none could touch the sheer (and what appeared unforced) authenticity of the original, and some even went unreleased. The moment so effectively captured by Hopper had passed.

For Hopper, the moment of triumph which effectively gave him carte blanche to make whatever films he liked, was also a creative disaster. Simply, *Easy Rider* was a hard act to follow, and he never was able to follow it. It was succeeded by the self-indulgent *The Last Movie* (1971), a largely autobiographical project shot in Peru. This featured plenty of artistic flourishes but lacked the unifying sense of purpose and truth to reality that had characterised *Easy Rider*.

Edited down from 40 hours of footage, a task that took Hopper a year, the film was too muddled and pretentious to please the critics or find an audience. Although it was praised at the Venice Film Festival, *The Last Movie* proved a box-office disaster. Ironically, having made his name as a director it was now as an actor that Hopper, with his combative, neurotic style, continued to be in demand.

However, his problems were compounded by the drinking and drug-taking that now took over his life. That and a succession of failed marriages often claimed more attention in the media than his work in the cinema.

Interviewed in his sixties he ruefully admitted: "Creatively I should have contributed a lot more. I was a very talented person and I did not fulfil that talent."

Dennis Hopper was born in Dodge City, Kansas, in 1936. His father was a post office manager who was also in the Office of

Strategic Services (OSS, precursor to the CIA). His mother, a swimmer of near-Olympic standard, worked as a lifeguard instructor after the family moved to California when he was 13. He attended high school in San Diego and started acting as a teenager in local theatres. He later appeared in repertory at the Pasadena Playhouse.

Put under contract by Warner Brothers after being spotted on television, after an uncredited film debut in *Johnny Guitar* (1954), he had his first big movie role in *Rebel Without a Cause*. He played opposite Dean again in *Giant* (1956) and was strongly influenced by Dean's brooding style. He always regarded Dean as the most talented and original actor he worked with. They became close friends, and Dean's death in a car crash in 1955 at the age of 24 affected him deeply.

Much of Hopper's subsequent work was in westerns, from *Gunfight at the OK Corral* (1957) to *The Sons of Katie Elder* (1965), *Cool Hand Luke* (1967) *Hang 'em High* (1968) and *True Grit* (1969). But after a falling-out with the director Henry Hathaway he was branded as a difficult actor and for a time he was blacklisted. He used the enforced sabbatical to move to New York and study at the Actors Studio.

Easy Rider was not his first excursion into alternative culture. That had come a couple of years earlier with Roger Corman's opt-out movie *The Trip* (1967) and though widely banned because of its drug theme, it was a significant departure from the Hollywood mainstream and it teamed Hopper for the first time with Peter Fonda, who later became his co-star in *The Last Movie*.

After that disastrous reception from audiences, it was nearly a decade before Hopper directed again, and his acting also went into a decline. For much of the 1970s he turned his back on Hollywood, retreating to New Mexico where drink and drugs took over. For five years, he claimed, his daily intake was 20 to 30 beers, half a gallon of rum and three grams of cocaine. Looking back in 2001 he reflected: "I should have been dead ten times over. I believe in miracles. It's an absolute miracle that I'm still around."

He lived for a time in Paris and London and his acting was mainly in obscure European films. The exception was *The American Friend* (1977) directed by Wim Wenders, in which he played Patricia

Highsmith's psychotic hero, Tom Ripley. He did not return to Hollywood until Francis Ford Coppola cast him as the unhinged photojournalist in the Vietnam film, *Apocalypse Now* (1979). Hopper largely improvised his lines.

He finally returned to directing with *Out of the Blue* (1980), a Canadian film about a dysfunctional family in which he played the abusive father. The decade of the 1980s, by which time he had made a huge effort to give up drinking, were fruitful on the acting front. He had a strong supporting part in Coppola's *Rumble Fish* (1983) and played the deranged drug dealer in *River's Edge* (1986). But his most memorable role, and one of the finest of his career, was the psychopath Frank Booth in David Lynch's unnerving portrayal of middle America, *Blue Velvet* (1986), while his alcoholic basketball coach in *Hoosiers* (1986, *Best Shot* in the UK) brought him an Oscar nomination.

Hopper also won praise for his direction of *Colors* (1988), a quasi-documentary treatment of street gangs in Los Angeles with Sean Penn and Robert Duvall as the cops. He was less fortunate with the thriller *Catchfire* (1989). After its release was held up for two years because of disputes with the producers Hopper insisted on taking his name off the directing credits.

His most notable acting roles during the 1990s came in *Paris Trout* (1991), as a racist storekeeper, *True Romance* (1993), a scene-stealing cameo as a security guard in a violent chase thriller from a Quentin Tarantino script, and *Speed* (1994), as a mad bomber trying to hold a city to ransom. He played another psychotic in the epic *Waterworld* (1995), almost stealing the picture from its star, Kevin Costner, while in *Carried Away* (1996, *Acts of Love* in the UK) a quieter Hopper was a middle-aged schoolteacher seduced by a girl pupil. Hopper continued to work busily in the cinema well into the 21st century, often appearing in several films a year. In 2008 he supported Ben Kingsley and Penélope Cruz in *Elegy*, from the Philip Roth novella, and played a presidential candidate in the political comedy, *Swing Vote* (2008).

Hopper married his fifth wife, Victoria Duffy, in 1996. His previous wives were Brooke Hayward, daughter of the actress

Margaret Sullavan; Michelle Phillips, singer with the Mamas and the Papas, who left him after eight days; Daria Halprin; and Katherine LaNasa. He had three daughters and a son from different marriages.

He returned, with some success, to television, playing the villain Victor Drazen, in the first season of *24*, and a drug-addicted record producer in *Crash*, a series based on the Oscar-winning film. He also, intriguingly, came close to being cast in *Doctor Who*.

During 2007 Hopper contacted the producers of the BBC show, saying he was interested in taking part, but other commitments got in the way. Away from films Hopper was a talented photographer, who had several shows devoted to his work, as well as a painter and sculptor. He also amassed a fine collection of modern American art. Given his longtime rebellion against the established order, he emerged as a surprising supporter of the Republican Party, backing Ronald Reagan and casting his vote for both George Bushes. But in 2008 he switched to Barack Obama.

Dennis Hopper was born on May 17, 1936. He died of cancer on May 29, 2010, aged 74

ELIZABETH TAYLOR

From the age of ten, Elizabeth Taylor was a superstar, perhaps one of the biggest Hollywood ever made. Her career, its rise and decline, was inextricably linked to the story of that town, to the glory days of the studio system and to the advent of the modern age of film-making.

But her talents as an actress went only a small way to explaining her rumbustious, headline-making appeal. Married eight times to seven different husbands, she conducted her affairs like a Beverly Hills Wife of Bath. Plagued by accidents as she was, she was also blessed with apparent indestructibility. She bounced back after divorce, bereavement, alcohol and drug addiction, career droughts and the venom of the world's press.

In her youth she was often described as the brunette counterpart to Marilyn Monroe. But there was nothing remotely vulnerable about Taylor. She proved to be tougher than any of her husbands, and she claimed, after a lifetime's hard work, the right to enjoy her money and celebrity.

Her greatest gift as an actress was her face. She was incomparably photogenic, with jet-black hair, so dark it seemed almost blue on screen, and eyes the deep purple colour of an aubergine skin. Her figure presented more problems for cameramen. Small, curvaceous and top-heavy, she had the bust of a much taller woman.

Beauty aside, she could strike those who met her, particularly when she was sober, as rather ordinary, happiest talking about her children and dogs. It was that streak of normality which saved her. Her acting talents were peculiarly limited to the big screen. Both Paul Newman and Richard Burton, when they first rehearsed with her, complained to their directors that Taylor was wooden and gave them nothing to act against. Both had to agree, when they saw what the camera had picked up – her instinctive, understated gestures, the flicker of her eyes – that she knew what she was doing. Even so, there were some critics who made a living out of lambasting Taylor, those who could never look past the awfulness of some of her early work, or who could not admit that such a pretty girl could act.

While they conceded that she had been excellent in *National Velvet* and *Who's Afraid of Virginia Woolf?*, they complained that these roles were merely aspects of Taylor's own character, and therefore required no effort.

They were right, to the extent that Taylor could be lazy as an actress. She never attempted to improve her worst faults, which were her high-pitched voice and weight problem, and she was at her best when the plot revolved around sex. But it was her misfortune to be hitting her stride as an actress just as she reached middle age, and the plum roles began to dry up.

Elizabeth Rosemond Taylor was born in London, near Hampstead Heath in 1932. Though Hollywood fan magazines later liked to stress her upper-class English background, she was, in fact, the daughter of two Americans. Her mother, Sara, was a promising actress who had given up her career to bring up the children, and her father was Francis Taylor, a handsome art dealer, whose job in London was to ship Constables home for the American market.

The family's entrée onto the bottom rungs of British high society was guaranteed by their friendship with the Cazalet family. Victor Cazalet, the gregarious Conservative MP, acted as unofficial godfather to the young Elizabeth. In truth, he was also her father's lover for several years – one reason, perhaps, why Elizabeth, as she grew up, seemed happiest in the company of homosexual men.

On the outbreak of the Second World War, Francis Taylor left England with crates of drawings by his friend Augustus John and set up an art boutique in the Beverly Hills Hotel. The Cazalets' family friend Hedda Hopper gave the boutique a good notice, and also announced in her column "a new find – eight-year-old Elizabeth Taylor".

In the beauty-obsessed culture of Beverly Hills, Elizabeth enjoyed being at the centre of attention. She was a compliant child who danced for guests and allowed herself to be fussily dressed and ringletted. Having watched Shirley Temple, she also harboured ambitions to act, ambitions which her mother eagerly encouraged.

A year's contract at Universal gave her her first screen outing, *There's One Born Every Minute* (1942). It was a flop.

But her father, who had got to know a producer at MGM, persuaded him to take a look at his little girl. Sam Marx was then casting for *Lassie Come Home*. He already had six children lined up in his office when in walked his friend's daughter, Elizabeth.

"It was like an eclipse of the sun," said Marx. "The child, dressed in blue velvet with white trim and matching hat, was breathtaking. She looked so splendid that we opted to forgo a screen test. I walked her to the casting office and we drew up a contract."

For the next two decades, Louis B Mayer's MGM was Taylor's teacher, surrogate parent and eventually, in her eyes, her jailer. After *Lassie Come Home* (1943), in which she was cast opposite Roddy McDowall, her career stalled momentarily. The next year she played the consumptive Helen Burns in *Jane Eyre*, such a tiny part that she did not even receive a screen credit.

However, backed by her resourceful mother, she accosted Clarence Brown, who was to direct *National Velvet*, and, legend has it, talked him into giving her the lead. The film was about a little girl who rides her horse to victory at the Grand National, disguised as a boy.

Taylor was very short, with a high-pitched voice that tended to screech. But the real problem was that Velvet Brown was an adolescent with breasts.

"Don't worry," Taylor is supposed to have said. "You'll have your breasts." Three months later, as if by willpower, she had grown three inches and graduated to a B-cup bra.

Her performance put her in the top rank of child stars. But considering that she was still a child, Elizabeth was blossoming into a surprisingly adult-looking creature, with the face – slightly oversized for her short body – of a much older woman.

Even at this age, she had a disconcertingly sexual effect on men around the MGM block, an effect of which she seemed fully aware.

Studying during her afternoons at MGM's Little Red Schoolhouse, she made a film a year steadily through her adolescence: with another dog in *Courage of Lassie* (1946); in Victorian costume in *Life with Father* (1947); and in a blonde wig for *Little Women* (1949).

When she moved on to adult roles, Vincente Minnelli drew a charming performance from her in *Father of the Bride* (1950), opposite Spencer Tracy, as the eager young virgin, ready for marriage but tearful at the prospect of leaving her still-beloved father.

A Place in the Sun (1951) showed what she was capable of with another good director, when George Stevens cast her as the spoilt rich girl who proves to be Montgomery Clift's nemesis.

In real life, with two broken engagements behind her and an enamoured Howard Hughes in pursuit, Taylor's love life was worryingly out of control. Her parents persuaded her to marry, and in 1950, disastrously, she chose Nicky Hilton Jr, heir to the Hilton hotel chain.

After a spectacular MGM stage-managed wedding, the marriage barely outlasted the honeymoon in Europe. Taylor returned to Hollywood covered in bruises and determined on divorce. While she enjoyed a little plate-smashing with her men, she would not stand for being beaten.

In 1952, seemingly as a reaction to Hilton's temper, she married the much older, kindly British actor Michael Wilding, by whom she had two sons. But Wilding proved too mild-mannered for Taylor.

Not content with having destroyed his career by transplanting him to Hollywood, she proceeded to humiliate him with her affairs with Victor Mature and Frank Sinatra, much as she was later publicly to emasculate the gentle Eddie Fisher.

Eventually she left Wilding for the producer Mike Todd. They were married in 1957, when he was in the middle of a publicity drive for *Around the World in 80 Days*, and she bore him a daughter. Having declared twice before that all she wanted was to settle down to a happy marriage, Taylor now seemed genuinely to have met her match in Todd.

Professionally, too, she was riding high after several years of drubbings from the critics. One, who had watched her performance as Rebecca the Jewess in *Ivanhoe* (1952), wrote that he would never forget her being led to the stake with the expression of a girl who has just been stood up on a date. *Giant* (1956), in which she played the wife of a Texan cattle rancher, gave her a chance to change their minds. The Times talked of "a long-sustained achievement by Elizabeth Taylor which is an astonishing revelation of unsuspected gifts". The film was aided at the box office by the untimely death of its co-star, James Dean.

By the mid-1950s Taylor was a role model. A new hairstyle or strapless dress worn by her could change fashions. As a sex symbol, she was in the same league as her slightly older blonde equivalent, Monroe.

Oscar nominations followed for *Raintree County* (1957), in which she played a southern belle, and *Cat on a Hot Tin Roof* (1958), in which she was the frustrated wife of a homosexual man (played by Paul Newman). During filming of the latter Todd was killed in a plane crash, and production ground to a halt as Taylor grieved. *Suddenly, Last Summer* (1959) brought a third nomination, despite the ludicrous nature of her role – an unstable woman who has witnessed her homosexual cousin being eaten by cannibals, and who is being threatened with a lobotomy.

In the interim Taylor had flouted public opinion after her bereavement by almost immediately being seen out on the town with her dead husband's best friend, the crooner Eddie Fisher, who was then married to Debbie Reynolds. Hedda Hopper, when she heard the rumours, rang Taylor to find out what was happening. "Mike's dead and I'm alive," Taylor snapped down the telephone. "What do you expect me to do – sleep alone?" Taylor never expected an old family friend to publish her ill-judged words, but Hopper did and the column fanned Taylor's growing notoriety as a man-eater.

It seemed ironic, therefore, that the last film which MGM wrung out of her contract was *BUtterfield 8* (1960), in which she played a prostitute. She had wanted to go straight on to film *Cleopatra*, for a reported $1 million. (In due course it was to pay her several times that much.) Incensed to be forced to make the film before her old studio would release her, she behaved badly on set. It was the last film she made as a contract player. From then on, like other stars of her generation, she became independent, and started making real money.

However, *BUtterfield 8* did bring her her first Oscar, though she called it a sympathy vote. Filming on *Cleopatra* was held up when she was stricken with pneumonia. Her health had never been robust. She had suffered from chronic back pain since a fall in 1956 on Lord Beaverbrook's yacht, and despite surgery she took handfuls of painkillers daily for the rest of her life. This time the pneumonia had the benefit of restoring public affection.

That affection was tested again when the cast of *Cleopatra* continued filming in Rome, where Taylor, her new husband Fisher and their entourage took a villa. The former Shakespearean actor Richard Burton, playing Mark Antony, lived in a villa nearby. He first met Taylor on the set when he was suffering from a hangover. She was solicitous and their friendship rapidly became a passionate and not very discreet love affair.

The director Joseph Mankiewicz did not have time to contain "le scandale" as Burton jokingly called it, as he was battling with budgetary problems of his own. *Cleopatra* eventually cost about $40 million to make, and to pay for it Twentieth Century-Fox had to sell many acres of its backlots. No studio could bear that kind of expense, and the fallout from *Cleopatra* changed irrevocably the way Hollywood did business.

Once the critics had seen the laboured product, they agreed unanimously that its cost and the Taylor-Burton affair were the only aspects of *Cleopatra* worth remembering – "The mountain of notoriety has produced a mouse," wrote Judith Crist in The Herald Tribune.

After filming ended, Burton wavered for a while between Taylor and his wife Sybil, before eventually getting a divorce and marrying Taylor in 1964. Her fifth marriage introduced Taylor to a more normal life than she had ever known. Burton took her to rugby matches, to his Welsh home town and taught her to drink beer and eat fish and chips. The daughter she had intended to adopt with Fisher became instead her adopted daughter with Burton.

Just as after Todd's death she had converted to Judaism in his memory, so now she took up British citizenship in honour of Burton. Even as respectably married tax exiles living in Switzerland, the Burtons were still big news, and they cashed in by making a run of films together. Films such as *The VIPs* (1963) and *The Sandpiper* (1965) were good as well as lucrative. *The Taming of the Shrew* (1967), for which Burton threw out two fifths of Shakespeare's lines and concentrated on gorgeous pictures, was rewarded with excellent box-office takings.

Who's Afraid of Virginia Woolf? (1966), in which Taylor played the frowsy, academic wife, Martha, was the high point of their collaboration, and won Taylor her second Oscar. It was one of her most brilliant performances, vulgar yet truly passionate. Taylor yelled her "screw-yous" and "God-damn-yous" at top volume, daring to abandon glamour to show life's underbelly.

The pendulum began to swing the other way at the end of 1967 with *Reflections in a Golden Eye* and *The Comedians*, followed the next year by *Boom!* – all of them flops. Audiences were staying at home, perhaps out of boredom with the Burton-Taylor double act, perhaps because Taylor, despite giving good performances, was looking out of date. Modern bare-faced actresses such as Vanessa Redgrave were casually stripping for the camera, where Taylor was still clinging to low-cut gowns.

Having bordered on chubby since the late 1950s, she was now becoming uncontrollably fat. In the film of *Under Milk Wood* (1971) her personal photographer, according to one observer, "kept flinging himself to the ground to photograph her from below so that her double chins wouldn't show".

But if Taylor was not such good box office, her personal life was still as big news as ever. As the Burtons had become richer, so their lifestyle had become more ostentatious and imperial. Her habit of arriving late on set, which had been a minor annoyance to directors in MGM days, seriously threatened to undermine some of the independent productions in which she now appeared. Directors would be alerted to her arrival by a stately procession of secretaries and hairdressers.

It was during the 1960s that Taylor became the owner of some of the world's costliest diamonds. Princess Margaret asked to try on one of them, the 33.19 carat Krupp, when she met Taylor at a wedding.

"How very vulgar," she said when it was on her finger. "Yeah, ain't it great?" was Taylor's response. Besides the Krupp, she also owned the 69.42 carat pear-shaped Taylor-Burton diamond, a gift from the actor. A book, *My Love Affair with Jewellery*, appeared in 2002.

It was Burton's yearning for a more normal life, as much as his wife's professional slump, which led to their divorce in 1974. To a noisy fanfare they were remarried in Botswana in 1975, but the second marriage was upset almost immediately by Burton's womanising and drinking. He went on to marry Suzy Hunt, the former wife of the racing driver James Hunt, and Taylor, in 1976, wed the Republican Senator John Warner.

In 1981 she leapt at the chance to act in a stage play, *The Little Foxes*, and, meeting Burton in London, she agreed to do another with him, Noël Coward's *Private Lives*. The plot about two middle-aged divorcees who still love each other would guarantee good box office.

Taylor divorced Warner in 1982. But any hopes that the old Burton-Taylor magic would be renewed on the American tour of *Private Lives* in 1983 were soon dashed. In rehearsal they were quarrelsome; in performance they were unexciting (and, in Taylor's case, not always audible). Taylor had other problems too. Although not at her heaviest, she was 12 stone, and no amount of whalebone could conceal it. The show limped on to Los Angeles where it closed in November.

The next month Taylor was persuaded to book herself into the Betty Ford Center in California to tackle her addiction to painkilling drugs and alcohol. Though the cure appeared to work, she readmitted herself in 1988, and it was then that she met her eighth husband, a recovering alcoholic builder named Larry Fortensky. Not many gave the Fortensky marriage more than six months. But Taylor, who had always enjoyed thumbing her nose at Hollywood, seemed genuinely happy with her young husband – until their divorce in 1996.

Her feature film career never recovered after the 1970s. There was an ill-fated attempt at a comeback as an ageing diva in *Young Toscanini* (1988). And there were also unworthy television movies, mini-series and cameo roles. She hardly needed the money. Apart from her fortune invested in jewels and Impressionist paintings, she was making a tidy sum from the launch in 1987 of a new scent, Passion.

But a shortage of good roles hardly affected her popularity. As she weathered the 1980s, in particular the deaths of Burton and her friend Rock Hudson, she was as newsworthy as ever. Her friendship with the singer Michael Jackson made her visible to a younger generation; and her charity work for an Aids foundation used up much of her formidable energy.

In 1987 France bestowed on her the Legion of Honour (she was also a Commander of Arts and Letters); in 2001 President Clinton awarded her the Presidential Citizens Medal in recognition of her philanthropic works. In 2000 she had been appointed DBE, and in 2005 she received the Britannia Award for Artistic Excellence in International Entertainment.

She had two sons from her marriage to Michael Wilding, and a daughter with Mike Todd. She and Burton adopted a daughter.

When she became 60 Taylor appeared on Oprah Winfrey's talk show, and, for a moment, became introspective: "I worked all during my childhood, except for riding horses. My peers were all grown-ups. The child in me was really suppressed. I worked, and was paid. And it was on the screen, but it wasn't me." Typically, the introspection did not last long. A moment later she raised her fist, triumphantly and said: "I feel great. I am happy. My life is wonderful. I never think about growing old. I barely think about growing up."

That vulgar joie de vivre was the key to Taylor's longevity in the business. At home she looked at ease with herself, a plump, suburban grandmother in a tracksuit. And, at Hollywood parties, garishly dressed and pasted in diamonds, she showed that she could still play the grande dame.

Dame Elizabeth Taylor DBE was born on February 27, 1932. She died on March 23, 2011, aged 79

STEVE MCQUEEN

———————•———————

Entering films just as the traditional star system appeared to be crumbling, Steve McQueen became a worthy successor to the John Waynes and the Gary Coopers, and in a nervous and contracting industry his was one of the handful of names that held out a promise of box-office success. He did not pretend to be a versatile actor but like all stars he had his peculiar screen magnetism. It stemmed, in part, from a strong physical presence: he was tanned, trim and athletic, with a thatch of fair hair, large blue eyes and a quizzical mouth.

McQueen in films and to an extent in real life was Superman reincarnated for his times: tough, capable, rebellious, never fooled and always his own man. He was perfectly at home with the technology of his age, a private passion for motorcycles – of which he had a large collection – and fast cars frequently spilling over into his work.

Though apt to be embellished by Hollywood publicists, McQueen's early years were nothing if not colourful. He was born Terrence Steven McQueen in Beech Grove, Indiana in 1930. His father deserted the family soon afterwards and the boy was brought up on a farm by his mother and a great-uncle.

Family tensions helped produce an unsettled childhood and at the age of 13, after being caught by the police for petty stealing, McQueen was sent to a reform school for problem boys at Chino in California, where he stayed for 18 months. After this he drifted from job to job – merchant seaman, lumberjack in Canada, selling ballpoint pens – before joining the United States Marines shortly after his 17th birthday.

He served for three years, and on being discharged went to live in New York where, after a further succession of casual jobs, he was given an introduction to an acting school, the Neighborhood Playhouse. For someone who had shown few inclinations in this direction he took to acting very quickly, going on to win a scholarship to the Uta Hagen-Herbert Boerghof Dramatic School in Manhattan.

In 1952 he made his professional stage debut with a small part in *Peg O' My Heart*, which starred Margaret O'Brien. He was one of five young actors out of 5,000 accepted for Lee Strasberg's Actors Studio, though the Method seemed to have little influence on his acting style. He started to get parts on Broadway and had his first big break when he replaced Ben Gazzara in *A Hatful of Rain*.

Television work followed, and this led McQueen to Hollywood where he made his first screen appearance as an extra in 1956. The following year, appearing in the credits as Steven McQueen, he made his first film as a featured player, a Harold Robbins story called *Never Love a Stranger*.

His early films, however, made little impact, and his screen career was really launched by television when he starred in a popular western series *Wanted – Dead or Alive*. On the strength of this he landed a good part in a war film, *Never so Few*, with Frank Sinatra, and the director, John Sturges, liked McQueen's performance enough to give him third billing in his next picture which became one of the most successful westerns ever made. Taking its plot from a Japanese film, *The Seven Samurai*, *The Magnificent Seven* told how a group of mercenaries rescue a village threatened by bandits. McQueen played second-in-command to the mercenary leader, Yul Brynner, and it was the beginning of stardom.

For a while after this he seemed to mark time – though he gave a fine performance as a psychopathic GI in *Hell Is for Heroes* – until John Sturges again came up with a plum part in what turned out to be an enormously popular film. *The Great Escape*, based on the true story of a mass break-out from a German prison camp, is probably best remembered for the sequences in which McQueen tries to gain his freedom on a motorcycle, finally attempting to leap a barbed wire barrier between Germany and Switzerland. McQueen, who had started motorcycle racing some years before, did much of the riding himself, though a stuntman was brought in for the most dangerous parts.

Able to name his price and choose his projects, McQueen settled for two quieter films with the director Robert Mulligan. *Love With the Proper Stranger* had him as a musician helping a pregnant shopgirl (Natalie Wood) in New York's East Side, while in *Baby the Rain Must Fall* he was a man on parole trying to pick up his family life. *The Cincinatti Kid* was notable for its poker games between McQueen and the veteran Edward G Robinson.

By now McQueen had formed his own production company and the next few films saw him at the height of his box-office power – *The Sand Pebbles*, a gunboat adventure for which he gained an Oscar nomination; a glossy thriller, *The Thomas Crown Affair*, and, above all, *Bullitt*, in which he played a laconic San Francisco cop and became involved in one of cinema's most celebrated car chases. This time he did all the stunt work himself.

His popularity was unassailable, though *Le Mans*, a pet project designed to exploit his motor-racing skills, did poorly. He went on to make two films for Sam Peckinpah. In *Junior Bonner* he had one of his best parts as a rodeo rider whose day has gone; in *The Getaway* he and Ali MacGraw played husband-and-wife bank robbers. In 1973 Ali MacGraw became the real Mrs McQueen – he had been previously married to a former Broadway dancer, Neile Adams.

Then, after two more pictures, *Papillon* and *The Towering Inferno*, he suddenly withdrew from filming and became a virtual recluse. He had apparently found the burden of success too much to bear and decided to take a rest. It was an unhappy time. His marriage foundered and eventually broke up.

In five years he made only one film, hiding behind a vast beard in an Ibsen adaptation, *An Enemy of the People*. Fans who remembered his trim figure were alarmed to discover that he had put on several stones and was almost unrecognisable.

Eventually he slimmed down again and in 1979 made a film comeback as an enigmatic western hero, Tom Horn, but amid rumours of serious illness his future seemed uncertain. The rumours proved to be all too true.

Steve McQueen was born on March 24, 1930. He died of cancer on November 7, 1980, aged 50

OMAR SHARIF

Many would say that Omar Sharif owed his international film career to the British director David Lean. While preparing his epic biography *Lawrence of Arabia*, Lean was alerted to a handsome young actor little known outside Arab cinema and cast him as the chieftain, Sherif Ali, who befriends Lawrence in the desert. Yet there was another figure who arguably played a more crucial role in Sharif's success: his mother.

"She was determined that I would be the most handsome and most successful man in the world," he said. "At 11, I was becoming incredibly fat, so she thought, 'Where is the worst food in the world?' and she sent me to an English boarding school. After a year I was skinny and I spoke perfect English – without which my career would never have taken off."

Despite competition from his fellow supporting actors – Alec Guinness, Jack Hawkins and Claude Rains – Sharif's engaging performance alongside Peter O'Toole in *Lawrence of Arabia* was widely noticed and earned him an Oscar nomination. With one, comparatively modest, part a new career was launched and Sharif was suddenly in demand, playing everybody from Ingrid Bergman's lover in *The Yellow Rolls-Royce* to the Mongolian warlord Genghis Khan.

Lean re-emerged in 1965 to offer Sharif the title role in Boris Pasternak's *Doctor Zhivago*. The actor's daily routine, as he played a physician caught up in the violence of the Russian Revolution, consisted of hair-straightening and skin-waxing to disguise his Middle Eastern heritage.

Despite being a big, and largely unexpected, commercial success, the film failed to impress the critics, who were particularly underwhelmed by what they saw as Sharif's dull and wooden performance. Even he agreed with them. "I found the part diabolically hard and I thought I was no good. I was on set every day, with a tight elastic band around my head to make my eyes look less Arabic. I remember phoning Lean in the middle of the night and saying, 'You've made a mistake'. Even now, I hate that melodramatic performance, with my big, wet, cows' eyes."

Such carping failed to damage Sharif's career and he continued to be in demand for Hollywood and international films for another 20 years, winning three Golden Globes. His striking presence and dashing looks – his sleek black hair, thick moustache and gleaming teeth – could not disguise his limitations as a performer, however, and for one French magazine his appearance in the 1969 film *The Appointment* confirmed him as "the worst actor in the entire history of the cinema".

He was by no means that, though there were too many forgettable performances in undistinguished films. Interviewed on the set of *Mayerling*, in which he played the troubled Crown Prince Rudolf of Austria, he said: "If a director wants Omar Sharif to play a part he gets Omar Sharif, not some nutty prince. I play Rudolf like I play all my parts. Prince Rudolf is me. I don't give a damn how his mind works. All I care about is getting to the studio on time and remembering my lines."

Away from the screen Sharif became almost as well-known as one of the world's leading bridge players. He was a familiar figure at tournaments and ensured that his film contracts gave him time off to take part in them. He wrote books on the game, contributed bridge columns to the *Sunday Express* and *Observer* newspapers, and found a mentor in *The Sunday Times* bridge correspondent Boris Schapiro, whom he first met at the Hamilton Club in London. They became close acquaintances and always found time for a game whenever the actor was visiting. In his later years Sharif enjoyed explaining the fundamentals to his grandson, mischievously telling him that playing bridge was like making love: "You need a good partner or a good hand."

Sharif, whose real name was Michael Demitri Chalhoub, was born in 1932 in Alexandria into a family of Lebanese and Syrian descent. His father was a wealthy timber merchant and cosmopolitan enough to bring up his son as a French speaker. Only when he went into films did Sharif learn Arabic. He was sent to Victoria College, an English-style boarding school in Alexandria that was modelled on Eton, and earned a degree in mathematics and physics from Cairo University. After working briefly as a timber salesman in his father's business, he decided to focus on acting and applied to study at RADA in London.

He made his first film, *The Blazing Sun*, in 1954, by which time he had changed his name to Omar El-Cherif. He later claimed – though he liked to tease interviewers – that the "Omar" came from the American general Omar Bradley, and the Cherif/Sharif from the sheriff in western films. Peter O'Toole, who became a fast friend, considered the name ridiculous and insisted on calling him "Fred" when they were on the set of *Lawrence of Arabia*.

Sharif's co-star in *The Blazing Sun* was Faten Hamama, one of Egypt's leading actresses, and they fell in love. He converted from Catholicism to Islam in order to marry her in 1955.

There followed a busy apprenticeship in Egyptian films, of which he made more than 20 in five years, and he also appeared in a couple of French co-productions. Only the latter were seen in Europe and he seemed destined to remain a star of the Arab cinema until Lean discovered him for *Lawrence of Arabia*. The first time he set foot in Hollywood was for the film's opening. "There was a party afterwards and people like Gregory Peck and Ava Gardner came to shake my hand. I was completely starstruck."

Of his films post-Lean, *Funny Girl*, where he played the husband of Barbra Streisand's showgirl Fanny Brice, was one of the better ones and reports of a real affair between Sharif and his co-star caused a stir. It was not the first time, or the last, that Sharif was to be linked romantically to his leading ladies, who included Catherine Deneuve, Anouk Aimée and Sophia Loren. Undoubtedly he enjoyed the company of beautiful women, but he insisted he was "the stud of nothing" – "I wish I'd lived the life that they say I did."

If his love life, real or imagined, occupied many of the column inches devoted to him once his film career was no longer able to excite, much of the rest was devoted to his gambling habits. His mother had been a famous gambler, in the company of the former Egyptian king, Farouk. Sharif said he made so many bad films because he needed the money to pay off his debts. In 1991 he lost £750,000 at roulette in one evening; two years later, with film work drying up, he claimed he was broke and could no longer afford an opulent lifestyle.

In between films Sharif made forays into television and the theatre. In 1984 he appeared in *The Far Pavilions*, an ITV mini-series based on MM Kaye's novel of India under the British Raj, and in 1996 he was the sorcerer in *Gulliver's Travels* for Channel 4. His marriage to Faten Hamama produced a son, Tarek, but their filming commitments meant they spent months apart. In 1974 they divorced. Tarek, now a restaurant proprietor, dabbled in acting when he was younger and even appeared in *Zhivago* playing an eight-year-old version of Sharif's character.

Despite periodic reports to the contrary, Sharif did not remarry. He said he married only once because he loved only once, though he claimed that at the height of his popularity he received 3,000 proposals a week. He also had an illegitimate son, Ruben, from a brief relationship with Paola de Luca, an Italian journalist. The boy grew up in Rome and his father rarely saw him.

For decades he chose to live in hotels rather than a permanent home, and had most recently been staying in the tourist resort of El Gouna.

He remained an avid supporter of Hull City football club having been introduced to the Tigers by Sir Tom Courtenay. "On a

Saturday afternoon, if I was in the desert and could not reach a television, I would telephone the club and say: 'Can you tell me the score, please?'"

Earlier this year he was diagnosed with Alzheimer's disease. A perennial gentleman, he accepted life with a good grace. "Sometimes you make mistakes, but I never feel regret because that would make me unhappy. Given the circumstances, I'd probably do exactly the same things again."

Omar Sharif was born on April 10, 1932. He died of a heart attack on July 10, 2015, aged 83

SHIRLEY TEMPLE

"When the spirit of the people is lower than at any other time during this Depression," said President Franklin D Roosevelt in the 1930s, "it is a splendid thing that for just 15 cents an American can go to a movie and look at the smiling face of a baby and forget his troubles."

Shirley Temple in her prime was a bit bigger than a baby and considerably more than a smiling face. With her dimples, golden curls and winning smile she was undeniably cute, but with a knowingness that cut across the sentimentality of her films, and she had a precocious natural talent as actor, singer and dancer that could make seasoned professionals look awkward beside her.

For millions of American cinemagoers during a bleak period in their history, she offered optimism and reassurance. Not for nothing did the plots of her most successful films cast her as a saviour and a healer, softening the hearts of grouchy grandpas, comforting the luckless and persuading divided families to set aside their feuds. For four years running during the 1930s she was the most popular film star in America. Temple's time at the top was brief. She did not have the same appeal as a teenager that she had had as a toddler and was finished with films by the age of 21. However, she made a happy second marriage and spent contented years bringing up her children before returning to public life in Republican politics. Although her attempt to win a seat in Congress failed, she was given important diplomatic jobs by Presidents Nixon, Ford and Bush, culminating in three years as US Ambassador to Czechoslovakia during the post-Cold War turmoil in Eastern Europe.

She was born in Santa Monica, California in 1928, and like many young stars she owed her early start to a fiercely ambitious mother. The motive was not financial. Temple's father, George, was a banker, and although he had to take a pay cut during the Depression the family was comfortably off, with its own house and car.

Her mother, Gertrude, had been frustrated in her own ambition to become a dancer and was determined that her daughter should not miss out. Her sons showed neither the talent nor the inclination to become performers, but Shirley, who was born when her brothers were 13 and nine, did.

She was enrolled for dancing classes at the age of two, and at three was spotted by a scout for the Educational Film Corporation, which was about to launch a series called Baby Burlesks to rival the Our Gang comedy shorts. The Baby Burlesks were ten-minute films in which children parodied the film stars of the day – Temple took easily to the idea, not least with a character called Morelegs Sweet Trick, alias Marlene Dietrich. When any of the children starring in the Baby Burlesks misbehaved, they were locked in a windowless sound box with only a block of ice on which to sit. "So far as I can tell, the black box did no lasting damage to my psyche," Temple wrote in her 1988 autobiography *Child Star*.

The Baby Burlesks were a start but it took the persistence of her mother to ensure that she made the transition to feature films. Gertrude Temple became her daughter's coach, teaching her how to project herself physically and through her voice, as well as her agent, scouring casting offices to find her work. She would always instruct her daughter to "Sparkle, Shirley!" before she appeared before an audience.

After a series of small parts Shirley was recommended to the Fox studio, which put her in *Stand Up and Cheer* (1934), a film designed to counter the Depression blues. Temple sang a song, *Baby Take a Bow*, and although she was well down the cast list she impressed Fox enough to put her under contract. Her first starring role came in *Little Miss Marker*, a Damon Runyon story in which she did the first of many celluloid good deeds by reforming Adolphe Menjou's renegade gambler. She proved so intimidating, with her 56 perfect blonde ringlets, unshakeable optimism and boundless self-confidence, that Menjou said that Temple was "making a stooge out of me".

After supporting Gary Cooper and Carole Lombard in *Now and Forever* she confirmed her stardom on *Bright Eyes*, in which she performed her most famous song, *On the Good Ship Lollipop*, which sold half a million copies in sheet music. During 1934 she made nine films and the year's work brought her a special miniature Oscar.

By the end of 1935 she was America's most popular star, thanks to well-chosen vehicles such as *The Little Colonel*, which saw the first of several appearances with the Black dancer, Bill "Bojangles" Robinson, and *The Littlest Rebel*, in which she sat on President Lincoln's knee to plead for her imprisoned father.

In 1935 she was taken by her parents to Washington to meet President Roosevelt and his wife, Eleanor. The president invited the Temples to a barbecue at the Roosevelt home in Hyde Park, New York, where Eleanor, bending over a grill, proved too much of a temptation for the impish child star. Temple unleashed a pebble from the catapult she carried in her lace purse, it was reported, and hit the First Lady smartly on the rear.

Temple herself proved such a money-maker that her mother and studio officials colluded to shave a year off her age to maintain her child image. At her peak she earned huge sums and an industry grew up around her, of dolls, toys, clothes, books and soap. As a result of her father's banking expertise her money was sensibly handled and led to none of the acrimony which blighted the adult lives of other child actors. The price of wealth and fame, however, was vulnerability to kidnap and the studio was forced to provide Temple with a bodyguard.

While films such as *Curly Top* and *Dimples* were created around Temple's natural assets, others were specially tailored versions of well-known children's stories. *Wee Willie Winkie* (1937), her most expensive picture and the first with a frontline Hollywood director, John Ford, came from a Kipling story in which the child who becomes a mascot to a British regiment in India was a boy.

Wee Willie Winkie sparked a famous London court case in 1938 in which Temple and Twentieth Century-Fox sued Graham Greene, then a leading film critic, for libel. In his review in the magazine *Night and Day*, Greene suggested that Temple was an adult masquerading as a child and wrote of her "dimpled depravity" and "dubious coquetry". Greene lost, and *Night and Day* was closed down. Temple was awarded £2,000 in damages – later used to build a youth centre in England – and the film companies were awarded £1,500 for the "beastly libel".

Johanna Spyri's *Heidi* was another children's classic accorded the Temple treatment; yet another was Frances Hodgson Burnett's *The Little Princess* (1939), her first Technicolor feature. By now Temple's popularity was slipping fast. She was a candidate to play Dorothy in *The Wizard of Oz* but a scheduling clash meant the part went to Judy Garland, and at the age of 11 Temple's career as a child star was over.

Her contract with Fox was cancelled and she moved to MGM – which let her go after one film. From then on she made her way in character parts, and apart from John Ford's *Fort Apache* her later films were undistinguished. Ford, though, still thought enough of Temple's pulling power in his 1948 western to pay her the same as his lead actors, John Wayne and Henry Fonda. In *Fort Apache* Temple played opposite her husband, John Agar, the former Army Air Corps sergeant turned actor, whom she had married in 1945 when she was 17. The marriage, which produced a daughter, Linda, was short-lived: Temple filed for divorce in 1949.

In January 1950, at a cocktail party in Hawaii, where she was taking a holiday after her divorce, she met the man who was to become her second husband, Charles Alden Black, a decorated war veteran and businessman from a wealthy Californian family. "We were introduced," Temple later recalled, "and he said 'What do you do, are you a secretary?' I said, 'I can't even type. I make films.' He wasn't too sure what I did. It was very refreshing to me – a handsome guy who wasn't interested in Hollywood or anything about it."

After a whirlwind romance – Black wooed her with a Tahitian love song and proposed after 12 days – they were married in December of that year, and she announced her retirement from films. The couple subsequently had a son, Charles Jr, and a daughter, Lori, and Black adopted Linda, Temple's daughter with Agar.

In the late 1950s, having given up her acting career to be a mother and housewife, she made a comeback on television. *Shirley Temple's Storybook* was a series of dramatised fairytales which she introduced and appeared in, along with star names including Charlton Heston, Claire Bloom and Elsa Lanchester. *Shirley Temple Theater*, a similar concept, followed two years later, but the show lasted only one season and her screen career fizzled out.

The Temple family had always been Republicans and in 1966 Shirley worked for a fellow screen actor, Ronald Reagan, during his successful campaign for Governor of California. When a congressional seat became vacant the next year, Temple declared herself a candidate. Her political inexperience showed, however, and she failed to get beyond the primary. It probably did not help that *On the Good Ship Lollipop* was repeatedly played at rallies during her campaign.

There was compensation when President Nixon appointed her as a US delegate to the United Nations in 1969. She performed well in the role, speaking out about the problems of the aged, the plight of refugees and, especially, environmental problems.

When President Ford made her Ambassador to Ghana in 1974, it caused an outcry in some quarters. She said after her appointment: "I have no trouble being taken seriously as a woman and a diplomat here [in Ghana]. My only problems have been with Americans who, in the beginning, refused to believe I had grown up since my movies."

She later became the first woman to hold the post of Chief of Protocol of the United States, responsible for organising President Carter's inauguration in January 1977. One of her duties was leading a one-week training programme for new government envoys; she said: "We teach them how to get used to being called Ambassador and having Marines saluting. Then, on Day 3, we tell them what to do if they're taken hostage."

Although no worthwhile job resulted from the Reagan Presidency, George Bush chose her to run the US Embassy in Prague when he succeeded Reagan in 1989; her time in office thus coincided with the fall of communism in Eastern Europe. The post would normally have been expected to have been awarded to a career diplomat, but Temple served for nearly four years in the post, earning widespread admiration in the process – Henry Kissinger, for one, called her "very intelligent, very tough-minded, very disciplined". While in Prague she also learnt that there had been a Shirley Temple fan club in the city 50 years previously; people with long memories brought old "Shirleyka" membership cards for her to autograph.

She was disappointed that her political appointments did not lead to bigger things. Her film career, however, was recognised: in 1985 the Academy of Motion Picture Arts and Sciences presented her with a full-size Oscar to replace the miniature one given 50 years earlier.

In 1972 she had breast cancer diagnosed and underwent a radical modified mastectomy. In going public about it, she was one of the first Hollywood stars to highlight the disease, which brought her 50,000 letters of support. She held a news conference from her hospital bed to urge women who found lumps not to "sit home and be afraid".

When her second husband died of bone marrow disease in 2005, she kept his voice on their answering machine, saying: "I don't ever want to erase it." As he lay dying she sang him the same Tahitian love song that he had sung to her during their courtship.

She is survived by her three children: Lori played bass guitar for various bands before becoming a photographer, Charles Jr became a businessman and Linda a high school librarian.

Shirley Temple was born on April 23, 1928. She died of chronic obstructive pulmonary disease on February 10, 2014, aged 85

DANNY KAYE

After a few false starts, Danny Kaye shot to fame in the early 1940s and soon became one of the highest-paid and best-known variety artists in the world. He later combined his showbusiness career with a practical interest in underprivileged children, and travelled to developing countries to see the problems at first hand.

He came to Britain in February 1948, at the height of his fame, and his season at the London Palladium was a sensation, breaking all attendance records and attracting the sort of hysterical fan worship that was later to be given to pop stars.

He was such a tonic to a country recovering painfully from war that the cartoonist Vicky depicted leading members of the government trying to boost their popularity by adopting Danny Kaye's effervescent style.

He was a tall, thin man, with a mop of reddish hair, twinkling blue eyes set in a rubbery face, and a gangling body which he could apparently twist into whatever shape he wanted. He was a superb mimic and a dancer of extraordinary energy but his speciality was an ability to pour out comic nonsense at a furious speed.

His act (which he often sustained, alone, for up to an hour and a half) was so fresh and spontaneous that it often appeared to be made up as he went along. Certainly no two performances were exactly the same: but behind the flair for improvisation and the comedian's gift of being able to manipulate an audience lay a solid professionalism acquired over many years.

His work with children was a logical extension of his career, demonstrating afresh how he could achieve perfect rapport with human beings who might not understand a word of the English language.

Danny Kaye was born David Daniel Karminsky in Brooklyn, New York, in 1911. His parents were Jewish immigrants from Russia. His gifts for comedy were apparent early on, though his first ambition was to be a doctor and he maintained an interest in medicine throughout his life.

On leaving school he did a variety of jobs, until he was invited to join a touring vaudeville troupe. Eventually this took him to the Far East where he learned that his nonsense doggerel could be a sure laughter-raiser among audiences who would not otherwise understand what he was saying.

In 1938 he came to London to appear in cabaret at the Dorchester Hotel: in view of his later fame, the engagement created remarkably little impression.

It was in the 1930s, too, that he started his film career in a series of two-reeler comedies which again made little impact at the time.

His career had begun to stagnate when, in 1939, he met and married a pianist and songwriter, Sylvia Fine. She dedicated herself to providing songs for Kaye and was an important element in his sudden rise to the top.

One of the first songs she wrote for him was a satire on the Stanislavsky school of acting which allowed Kaye to demonstrate his facility for accents: it was to stay in his repertoire for many years. Two successful Broadway musicals led Sam Goldwyn to take him off to Hollywood where he was given the sort of build-up that fortunately his talent could match.

His film career proper began with *Up in Arms* in 1944: it was followed by *The Secret Life of Walter Mitty* – possibly the best vehicle ever devised for him – *The Inspector General, Hans Christian Andersen* (which spawned two hit songs, *The Ugly Duckling* and *Wonderful Copenhagen*), *Knock on Wood* and *White Christmas*.

Kaye was paid handsomely for his films and his employers almost invariably got their money back many times over; but somehow his talents were never fully exploited on the screen, as if he found a script and the need to work with other actors constricting. In 1954 he was awarded a special Oscar.

Kaye continued to make films regularly throughout the 1950s – they include *The Court Jester, Me and the Colonel,* and *The Five Pennies* and in the early 1960s he started his own television show. But his appearances on the variety stage were getting rarer and more of his time was spent travelling the world as ambassador-at-large for the United Nations International Children's Emergency Fund (Unicef).

One of his first trips took in the Far East and was the subject of a film called *Assignment Children*. Kaye travelled many thousands of miles for Unicef and regularly gave concerts in aid of the fund.

Kaye had never emphasised his Jewishness in his showbusiness work but the crisis in the Middle East found him an outspoken champion of Israel. This led to his films being banned in Arab countries, and to a controversial visit to Israel after the Six-Day War in 1967 which meant breaking a contract with the Chichester Festival Theatre, where he was to have taken the leading role in Goldoni's comedy, *The Servant of Two Masters*.

It would have been Kaye's first appearance in a classic play and as such it was sold out weeks ahead. The production had to be cancelled and another play put on at very short notice. Kaye was widely criticised for his action.

The India–Pakistan conflict found him once more in Asia, concerned about Unicef's latest burden.

In November 1970 he returned to the Broadway stage for the first time in nearly 30 years to play Noah in a Richard Rodgers musical, *Two by Two*. During the run of the show he injured an ankle but instead of taking a rest, he insisted that he should carry on with the help of crutches and a wheelchair.

He continued to work for Unicef and other charities but he virtually retired from the stage and cinema.

Danny Kaye was born on January 18, 1911. He died of heart failure on March 3, 1987, aged 76

ALEC GUINNESS

———————●———————

Alec Guinness lacked many of the advantages of his theatrical peers. He could not claim Olivier's outstanding good looks and pure animal magnetism: he was bald by the time he reached 32, which emphasised his pointy, puckish ears. Unlike Gielgud he was not steeped in theatrical tradition: his childhood was disrupted and unhappy and his most vivid memory was of Nellie Wallace in music hall at the Coliseum. He lacked Richardson's ability to be a "card", and he certainly did not have the Richardson ruthlessness, which ensured that Ralph was never upstaged: late in his life Guinness remarked, a little ruefully, "I'm not a very confident person, never have been."

But he had one great gift denied the others: anonymity. On stage or on screen Olivier was always Olivier, Gielgud always Gielgud and Richardson always Richardson. Guinness had the ability to obliterate himself completely within each character he played.

He was a master of disguise, and some of his critics claimed that he achieved this by building around himself a carapace of privacy and mystery. Such an explanation is too superficial. Guinness achieved much of his distinction by sheer graft, aided by high intelligence and a gift for acute observation.

His beginnings in the theatre before the war were uncertain. It took him two years to get a commission in the Royal Navy during the war, and his command of a rickety landing craft in the Mediterranean had its inglorious moments, as he recounted with some irony in his autobiography *Blessings in Disguise*.

In the cinema his great mentor was David Lean, who gave Guinness his first major role in *Great Expectations* and later established him as a truly international star in films such as *The Bridge on the River Kwai* and *Lawrence of Arabia*. Director and star had several well publicised rows. But the two men needed one another.

Guinness was rare among actors in being a master of self-deprecation. He once said: "Essentially I'm a small-part actor who's been lucky enough to play leading roles for most of his life." For luck read good judgment. Guinness knew what was beyond his reach. After the early days his excursions into Shakespeare were comparatively rare and on the whole not very successful. He attempted Lear only on radio when he was well on in life. He shied away from the avant-garde, getting no closer to it than Ionesco's *Exit the King* at the Royal Court. Alec Guinness believed in the art of the possible.

Offstage Guinness usually tried to be just a face in the well-behaved crowd and generally succeeded. No breath of scandal touched his marriage of over sixty years, and he was rarely stalked by the gossip columnists. He liked good restaurants, especially the Connaught, but there again he blended into the background. He was fond of telling the story of how he handed in his coat at a hotel cloakroom and, offering to give his name, was quite pleased to be told that it would not be necessary. The coat was later handed back with the ticket still attached and on it the inscription "Bald with glasses".

Alec Guinness was illegitimate and no father's name appeared on his birth certificate. There have been suggestions that the man in question was a middle-aged banker called Geddes. His mother, Agnes de Cuffe, a temporary barmaid, did not admit to her son for several years that Guinness was not his real name.

She was married briefly to a self-styled "Captain" David Stiven, who treated his stepson brutally. Agnes was little better, leaving behind her a trail of unpaid bills at cheap London hotels. Guinness had as little affection for her as John Osborne had for his monstrous mother Nellie Beatrice, although unlike Osborne he was too polite to vent his dislike in public. School was little better than home, as he moved through a succession of undistinguished South Coast establishments. By 18 he had found a modest job in a London advertising agency and cut off all relations with his mother.

He got a little training at the Fay Compton School of Dramatic Art, and plucked up the courage to write to John Gielgud, ten years older than Guinness and already an idol. Gielgud, who had been a judge at the Fay Compton end-of-term performance, engaged him as Osric and Third Player for the *Hamlet* he was preparing for the

New Theatre in 1934 and stuffed a few much-needed shillings in Guinness's pocket. Guinness always claimed that it was Gielgud who launched him on his career, but an equal influence was the flamboyant Martita Hunt. She regularly told him that he had little talent, but encouraged him nonetheless and her coaching helped to get him his drama school scholarship. The two were to meet again twenty years later when Hunt played Miss Havisham in *Great Expectations*.

Guinness had a season with the Old Vic company in 1936–37, playing a number of small roles and one quite large one, Sir Andrew Aguecheek in Tyrone Guthrie's production of *Twelfth Night*. He worked there with Michael St Denis, but Guthrie himself was to be far the greater influence.

Guthrie took him on tour with *Hamlet* to Elsinore to play before the royalty of Denmark and Sweden. His parting words before the first night were: "Be polite to Kings and Queens if they get in your way, Alec." Guinness, fortified by some schnapps to keep the Danish cold out, duly laid his sword on the King of Sweden's lap. Despite such indiscretions Guthrie thought his protégé good enough to play the title role, which he did under Guthrie's direction in 1938. This was reasonably well received and even drew some encouraging words from Gielgud, but it did not greatly stir the public.

By this time Alec Guinness had married Merula Salaman, a young actress whom he had met while they were appearing in Andre Obey's *Noah*, a St Denis production. She took him into a different world, that of cultivated and affluent Jewish society with wide connections in the arts. Guinness profited from it as he was to profit from her support for the rest of his life.

In the early days of the war Guinness tried his hand at adaptation, turning to *Great Expectations* and casting himself as Herbert Pockett. He had formed the Actors Company with George Devine and *Expectations* was staged at the Rudolph Steiner Hall in December 1939.

Guinness then appeared in a couple of contemporary plays before enlisting in the Navy. Eventually he was hauled off the lower deck and put on an officers' training course, ending up by commanding a landing craft in the Mediterranean. In between times Terence Rattigan persuaded the Admiralty to give him temporary release to play in *Flare Path* on Broadway, which was reckoned to be good wartime propaganda.

After being demobbed Guinness found himself back in London with a decent reputation from before the war but no longer of an age or with the looks to play juvenile leads. He turned his hand again to adaptation, this time *The Brothers Karamazov*, directed by Peter Brook, who was just beginning to make a name for himself as an enfant terrible.

At this point enter David Lean, who was planning a film of *Great Expectations*. He remembered Guinness's prewar performance on stage as Herbert Pockett and engaged him for the same role, although the actor's screen experience had been confined to a walk-on part in a 1933 movie called *Evensong*. Pockett led to Fagin in Lean's next Dickens picture, *Oliver Twist*, and this was the part which established Guinness as a screen actor of the highest quality. He was so good that there were calls in America to ban the film on grounds of anti-Semitism.

Guinness went on to work with Lean on four other films, three of which were international successes: *Kwai*, *Lawrence of Arabia* and *Dr Zhivago*. Finally came *A Passage to India*, Lean's last film, in 1984. Guinness knew how much he owed to Lean, especially at the beginning, but there was a price to pay. He put it delicately, as always: "We made six films and on three we had our differences."

Guinness also made a substantial career with Michael Balcon's Ealing Studios. *Kind Hearts and Coronets* was the first of four films there with the brilliant but undependable Robert Hamer – and by far the best. Guinness, at his own suggestion, played all eight members, male and female, of the D'Ascoyne family who are killed by Dennis Price, and so delivered eight virtuoso performances. He was later to dismiss the film as "pretty cardboard", but *Kind Hearts* established him as a comedian of exceptional polish. Ealing quickly capitalised on this and had him working with its best directors, Charles Crichton (*The Lavender Hill Mob*) and Sandy Mackendrick (*The Man in the White Suit* and *The Ladykillers*).

This screen success began to tug him away from the classical theatre in which he had spent much of his acting life. He had played the Fool to Olivier's Lear at the New in 1947 and had not been forgiven for upstaging the master. Richardson directed him as Richard II at the same theatre the next year, but with only modest success. And Guinness tried his own hand at direction with *Twelfth Night*, also at the New. But he was slowly deciding that he was not really a company man and did not want to be in thrall of his more famous contemporaries.

His next major role took him back to the commercial theatre, albeit the classier end of it, as the Unidentified Guest in TS Eliot's *Cocktail Party*, which he played both at the Edinburgh Festival and in New York. His second *Hamlet* in 1951, which he co-directed with Frank Hauser, was not a success, despite the presence of Kenneth Tynan and other luminaries in the cast. Tynan was later to write an early and not very good study of Guinness.

Tyrone Guthrie invited him over to the newly opened Shakespeare Playhouse in Stratford, Ontario, as the first British actor to lead the company, which he did with success, Irene Worth standing at his side. After that there was little more Shakespeare on stage, apart from a Shylock at Chichester when he had just turned 70. There was a weird *Macbeth* at the Royal Court in 1966, given the full Brechtian treatment by Bill Gaskill and with a disastrous Lady Macbeth from an improbably cast Simone Signoret.

Once or twice during his life Alec Guinness had considered converting to Roman Catholicism and his resolve was strengthened while playing the Cardinal at the Globe in Bridget Boland's *The Prisoner*. The play, much admired in its time (1954), was a complex debate between spiritual qualities and materialism. Shortly afterwards Guinness was received into the Catholic Church, followed, independently, by his wife.

After appearing as Boniface in *Hotel Paradiso*, marvellously directed by one of his regular collaborators, Peter Glenville, Guinness left the stage for six years. The films flowed regularly – impressive ones such as *Tunes of Glory* and one or two best forgotten – and he developed a good line in little men enmeshed in political intrigue in thrillers such as *The Quiller Memorandum* and Graham Greene's *Our Man in Havana* and *The Comedians*.

Guinness was always attracted by people with secrets, and few had deeper secrets than Mrs Artminster in Simon Gray's early transvestite comedy *Wise Child* at Wyndham's in 1967. Guinness alternated between skirts and a frightening red crew-cut wig. The play shocked some of his more staid admirers, but delighted a new generation learning to live with Ortonesque humour. Alan Bennett also provided Guinness with a mischievous character in *Habeas Corpus*, and then capitalised on his ability to play spies by writing the part of Hilary (based on Kim Philby) for him in *The Old Country*. Actor and author became good friends.

Two very different roles brought Guinness huge popular acclaim when he was in his mid-sixties. The first was that of George Smiley in *Tinker, Tailor, Soldier, Spy*, which kept the nation glued to its television sets in 1979 as people tried to follow the intricacies of John le Carre's plotting. This was followed by *Smiley's People* a couple of years later. The other very different role was that of Ben Obi-Wan Kenobi in George Lucas's hugely successful *Star Wars*, which also spawned a couple of sequels.

Guinness's last appearance on the stage was in *A Walk in the Woods* at the Comedy Theatre in 1988, a highly serious debate about arms control. He left the West End commenting that he had no wish to go on playing before the "blank faces" of uncomprehending tourists. He made occasional forays into television, but they were rare; Guinness had none of the compulsion to go on appearing in cameo parts that seemed to drive Gielgud and John Mills.

He was content to live in semi-retirement near Petersfield, guarding his privacy and safe in the knowledge that within the profession he would be remembered as a great actor and, always ready to help others, the most generous of men. His memoirs, *Blessings in Disguise*, appeared in 1985; a second volume, in 1996, bore the appropriate title *My Name Escapes Me: The Diary of a Retiring Actor*.

Sir Alec Guinness was born on April 2, 1914. He died of cancer on August 5, 2000, aged 86

EDWARD G ROBINSON

Edward G Robinson was originally a stage actor and did not make his first film until he was 30; and it was some years after that when his brilliant portrayal of the vicious gang leader in *Little Caesar* made him a world star almost overnight. But after this late start he remained in constant demand for another 40 years and it is a measure of his quality as a screen actor that he was able to survive the typecasting which inevitably followed the success of *Little Caesar*.

As his career developed he revealed himself as a very polished comedy actor and when, later on, he took to character parts rather than leads, he often upstaged the nominal stars.

Physically he was the antithesis of the conventional film star – very short in build, with an ugly crumpled face (later softened by a beard) and a rasping voice which could really grate on the nerves. He naturally exploited these attributes to the full in his early gangster roles but his professionalism and natural screen presence was able to sustain his career long after the initial fame had evaporated.

He was born in Bucharest, Romania, in December 1893; the family emigrated to the United States when he was nine. He was educated at public schools in New York and, briefly, at Columbia University, before deciding to train for the stage when he changed his name from Emmanuel G Goldenberg to Edward G Robinson. After some years in the theatre, playing a variety of modern and classical parts, he got his first star role in a play called *The Racket* in 1927. Significantly he was cast as a gangster and it was from this time on that his film career started to develop, with one gangster part after another until *Little Caesar* in 1930 made him a star.

One of the first (and still one of the best) talking gangster pictures, *Little Caesar* tells the archetypal story of the rise and fall of the hoodlum, starting in the gutter and ending in the gutter. Robinson's dying words, as he lies riddled with bullets, have become part of cinema lore: "Mother of mercy, is this the end of Rico?"

For the same director, Mervyn LeRoy, Robinson played a ruthless newspaper editor in *Five Star Final*, and there followed a string of generally less distinguished films in the same mould. Evidence that Robinson was capable of more came in 1935 when he played two parts in John Ford's comedy, *The Whole Town's Talking*: one was the now familiar gang leader, but the other (slightly sending up his screen persona) was a timid little clerk who gets mistaken for the villain. Robinson completed his change of image, as it were, the following year when for the first time he sided with the law against Humphrey Bogart in *Bullets or Ballots*.

He was awarded a special Oscar to mark his outstanding contribution to the cinema.

The 1940s were a particularly rich period, embracing the biopic, *Dr Ehrlich's Magic Bullet* another biographical film in which he played Reuter (of news agency fame), and the famous Billy Wilder thriller, *Double Indemnity*. Robinson also played with great effect opposite Joan Bennett in the Fritz Lang films noir, *The Woman in the Window* and *Scarlet Street*. He was the war crimes commissioner tracking Orson Welles in *The Stranger*, the head of the family in Arthur Miller's *All My Sons*, and yet another memorable gang leader in John Huston's *Key Largo*.

In the Fifties, after a brush with the Un-American Activities Committee about alleged communist leanings, his career had a temporary lapse and he spent some time in rather unworthy B pictures. After an absence of 20 years, he returned to the stage in Koestler's *Darkness At Noon,* and Paddy Chayefsky's *The Middle of the Night.* At the end of the decade he made a triumphant return to the cinema in Henry Hathaway's *Seven Thieves,* a comedy-thriller about a robbery of the casino at Monte Carlo. In 1963 he was a diamond smuggler in the British film, *Sammy Going South,* and two years later played his last substantial role as an old poker player with too many tricks for the younger Steve McQueen in *The Cincinnati Kid.*

Robinson, who was married twice, was in private life a man of refinement and taste. He put together a magnificent collection of Impressionist paintings which fetched more than £1 million when it was sold in 1957.

Edward G Robinson was born on December 12, 1893. He died of cancer on January 26, 1973, aged 79

AUDREY HEPBURN

———————•———————

When she burst on an unsuspecting world in *Roman Holiday* in 1953, Audrey Hepburn seemed, and was, a totally original creation. It was just the time that the whole film world seemed to be swarming, understandably, in the direction of Marilyn Monroe, the other late flower of the Hollywood system. Monroe inspired dozens of imitators, but one could hardly imagine Hepburn inspiring any. Monroe was the busty blonde in excelsis, easy to ape superficially, if impossible to equal; Hepburn was tall, dark, gawky, strange-looking, a star who had, perforce, to create her own style. And so, indeed, she did.

Her figure was a dress designer's dream (she had been briefly a fashion model) and she worked out for herself that the ideal designer for her was Givenchy, with his uncompromising simplicity. She was a lady, in a cinema which was emphatically reacting against any such notion of womanhood. She was elfin, ethereal, with a touching, almost waif-like quality about her which fitted her particularly for the romantic fairy story. And above all, she had charm and a sparkling sense of humour which made the whole world fall in love with her at first sight. Well, not, perhaps, quite at first sight.

Before she was picked by William Wyler to play the errant princess in *Roman Holiday*, she had made brief appearances in several European-made films. She was a cigarette girl in the opening scene of *The Lavender Hill Mob* in 1951 and played a substantial role in Thorold Dickinson's serious but flawed *The Secret People*, before being spotted by Colette in a hotel lobby while making a film called *Nous Irons a Monte Carlo*. At Colette's suggestion she was auditioned by Gilbert Miller for the title role in a Broadway adaptation of Colette's novel *Gigi*. She got the role, and achieved a great personal success in it, but Paramount were still tentative enough about her screen possibilities to sign her up for only one film in the first instance.

So she was not quite an overnight sensation, though it looked very much like it when she went on to win the New York Critics'

Award and the best actress Oscar for *Roman Holiday*. Paramount wanted, too late, to put her on an exclusive long-term contract, but discovered that instead they had to hire her services from Associated British, which had already signed her as a starlet during her brief period in British films.

She was the daughter of an English banker working in Brussels, Joseph Anthony Hepburn-Ruston, and his wife, the Dutch Baroness Ella van Heemstra. Audrey (originally Edda) was the only child of this marriage, though she had two half-brothers from one of her mother's previous marriages. She seems to have been a solitary and withdrawn child, brought up bilingual and, after the break-up of her parents' marriage in 1935, commuting awkwardly between their respective homes in England and Holland. She was also, amazingly for those who remember her spare elegance as an adult, inclined to be plump and considered rather plain.

When war broke out her mother brought her back quickly from England, thinking that Holland would be safer. She was in Arnhem when the Germans invaded, already studying dance with the hope of becoming a ballerina. On several occasions during the occupation she and her family were close to starvation, but she survived, took up her dance studies again, and in 1947 emigrated with her mother to London, where chances seemed to be better for making dancing her profession.

She returned briefly to Holland for a small part in an obscure film, but did not take the possibility of becoming an actress seriously. She continued her dance studies with the Ballet Rambert, and danced in the chorus of *High Button Shoes* and in the revues *Sauce Tartare* and *Sauce Piquante* in the West End before playing a bit in the film *Laughter in Paradise*. This led to the Associated British contract and further small parts before the encounter with Colette.

Once she was launched in America she was unstoppable: major film-makers fell over themselves to give her major roles. If *Roman Holiday* was a Cinderella story in reverse, Billy Wilder's *Sabrina* was the classic article, and for the first time on screen she was allowed to become glamorous and sophisticated.

Back on Broadway she played in Giraudoux's *Ondine,* co-starring with Mel Ferrer, whom she subsequently married and appeared with in King Vidor's version of *War and Peace,* in which she was a dazzling Natasha. Throughout the 1950s she went from triumph to triumph, singing and dancing with Fred Astaire in *Funny Face,* having another May/December affair with Gary Cooper in *Love in the Afternoon,* and rounding out the decade with the enormous success of Fred Zinnemann's *The Nun's Story.*

Her first real failure was Mel Ferrer's unconvincing version of WH Hudson's *Green Mansions,* a fantasy about a girl who lives with the birds.

Memory of this was soon wiped out by another of her classic roles, as Holly Golightly in *Breakfast at Tiffany's,* a film the original author Truman Capote heartily disliked, but everyone else adored. Wyler's second version of Lillian Hellman's *The Children's Hour* (called *The Loudest Whisper* in Britain), with Hepburn and Shirley MacLaine as the teachers whose lives are ruined by scandal, was less successful, but her teaming with Cary Grant in Stanley Donen's decorative comedy-thriller *Charade* worked perfectly. Another peak in her career came in 1964 with her casting as Eliza Doolittle in George Cukor's version of *My Fair Lady,* inspired casting which yet caused some resentment in that it involved passing over the claims of Julie Andrews, who had played the role on Broadway. It also required the dubbing of Hepburn's singing voice (by Marni Nixon).

This phase of her career continued with two more big successes, Stanley Donen's *Two for the Road,* in which she was coupled with Albert Finney in an intricately structured anatomy of a marriage, and an all-out thriller, *Wait Until Dark,* in which she could pull out all the stops as a threatened blind girl.

By this time the external circumstances of her life had changed. In 1968 her marriage to Mel Ferrer broke up, and soon after she married an Italian psychologist called Andrea Dotti. Living with him and her son by her first marriage, Sean, in Rome, she did not feel particularly drawn to moviemaking, and she had had another son, Luca, before she returned to the screen in 1976 with Sean Connery in Richard Lester's bittersweet Sherwood Forest tale *Robin and Marian.* People were pleased that she was back, though the film was only a moderate success. And from there her films were few and far between. At least she played a full-blooded leading role (rather than a mature star's cameo) in *Bloodline*, a thriller of considerable foolishness, but one made close to home. On the other hand, her next film, Peter Bogdanovich's *They All Laughed*, took her back to America and signalled her separation from Dotti, though not, for several years, their divorce.

At various times in the 1980s she was announced for films she did not make, and certainly was offered many roles that she refused. She was rich, she was living with a rich man, Robert Wolders, widower of Merle Oberon, and she did not need to work unless she wanted to.

Instead she devoted herself to working for Unicef on behalf of starving and endangered children, focusing public attention on their plight by her visits to areas of devastation and famine. She was spurred on in this activity by her memories of her own childhood in Nazi-occupied Holland. In 1990, however, she suddenly reappeared on screen, looking as gorgeous as ever, playing the custodian of the fantasy heaven in Stephen Spielberg's *Always*.

Last September, after a visit to Somalia, she appeared before the press and television cameras in London to recall, vividly, the horrific conditions she had witnessed. Two months later she underwent treatment for cancer of the colon and was too ill to visit Los Angeles, three weeks ago, to receive the Screen Actors Guild award for lifetime achievement.

Audrey Hepburn was born on May 4, 1929. She died of cancer on January 20, 1993, aged 63

GREGORY PECK

Gregory Peck was the romantic swoon of his day and one of Hollywood's indestructibles. From the moment he arrived there in the middle of the Second World War, he was talked about as the next big leading man. He more than lived up to that early promise.

Peck was helped by certain indisputable assets. He was an almost indecently handsome man. He had the dark eyes and hair, the height and the strong bone structure which showed to advantage on film. His voice, once he had dropped the theatrical delivery of his early-stage career, was perfect for the medium, and instantly identifiable. Men seemed to like him as much as women did.

He came across just as effectively in action films, leading a team of saboteurs in *The Guns of Navarone* (1961), as in love stories. There was an air of moral strength about Peck (rarely did he play a villain). He was the Good American, a stranger to weakness and self-doubt. James Agee described it as an "unusual ability to communicate sincerity".

His finest performance, the one which silenced all those critics who had accused him of being wooden, came in middle age, when he played the southern lawyer Atticus Finch in *To Kill a Mockingbird*. It was a perfect piece of casting. Peck described the experience as "like putting on a comfortable, well-worn suit of clothes". Earlier this month an American Film Institute listing of the cinema's top heroes ranked Peck's Finch as number one.

Peck was one of the first actors to take on the studio system in Hollywood and win. He refused to sign away his career to any one studio, instead choosing his roles with care. He was right to do so. A good script and good director were essentials for him to give a good performance. If he found himself on a sinking ship, he was quite capable of drowning with the rest of the cast. Fortunately he had an instinct for a good script. The one film he regretted turning down was *High Noon*.

That independence of character was rooted in a difficult childhood. Eldred Gregory Peck was born in 1916 in the seaside town of La Jolla, California, the son of a businessman. His parents were divorced when he was three and he was shuttled between them before being sent, at the age of ten, to St John's Military Academy in Los Angeles (where, perhaps, the seeds of his dislike for the Establishment were sown). He looked set to make a career in medicine, but he was also athletic and rowed for the University of California, Berkeley. A back injury in a college rowing race put paid to his sporting career and he took up amateur college theatricals instead.

Encouraged by positive reviews he went to New York and studied acting at the Neighborhood Playhouse. His movement teacher there was Martha Graham, who took the view that actors should, in the name of mobility, be made to practise impossible contortions, such as putting their head beneath their knees while crouching. He was not, in his own estimation, a particularly good stage actor, but he carried on during the war after he had been refused for service in the army because of his back.

David O Selznick saw him in a Broadway run of *Morning Star* in 1942, and screen-tested him, though that came to nothing. Nor did a couple of film offers. But the director Casey Robinson eventually lured him to Hollywood in the unlikely role of a Russian guerrilla named Vladimir in *Days of Glory* (1944), playing opposite Robinson's fiancée, the ballerina Tamara Toumanova. Toumanova had such a thick Russian accent herself that the only way to make any sense of the dialogue was to have the entire cast speak in a similar manner. Peck made a strong impression and in due course received many offers from the studios.

The studio system, which had so manacled previous generations of Hollywood stars, was then starting to crack. Peck was taken to the office of Louis B Mayer to be flattered into signing a contract. Mayer reminded him what he had done for Mickey Rooney and Judy Garland. Peck stood firm, and told him he had no intention of signing an exclusive contract for anyone. As Mayer went on, Peck remembered, a strong note of emotion entered his voice: "He pulled out a handkerchief and began to weep to think I wouldn't allow him to make me the greatest star of all time. My refusal to sign was portrayed as an offence to American motherhood, patriotism and family decency. It was an extraordinary performance."

Armed with a bright agent, Peck began making films at the rate of three a year. The result was a variety of roles, initially all quite different. Some, like the sardonic Lewt in King Vidor's *Duel in the Sun* (1946), had a dark edge which Peck hoped would prevent any permanent halo from forming around his head, which was also the reason for his later refusal of *High Noon*. He played an aged priest in *The Keys of The Kingdom* (1944), which was a commercial hit; and the wealthy mill owner who courts Greer Garson (a maid) in *The Valley of Decision* (1944). He thought Garson a lovely actress to work with ("all woman") and was equally complimentary towards Ingrid Bergman in *Spellbound* the following year ("she was like a rose in bloom"). Almost immediately Peck had been cast opposite the best of Hollywood's actresses. Carole Lombard had warned him that it would take at least ten films to make him a star. He had done it in half that number.

But the luminous support he received did not necessarily help his own performances, however popular he was becoming. He knew that he had been disappointing in *Spellbound* and blamed Hitchcock for not giving him the sort of help he needed with his character. Two years later Hitchcock gave him a second chance in *The Paradine Case*. But this again was not a success for Peck, and was arguably Hitchcock's worst film.

In the late 1940s Peck signed a lucrative, non-exclusive four-film contract with Twentieth Century-Fox. Two of the films, for Henry King, enhanced his reputation. In *Twelve O'clock High* (1949), thought to be the best war film since fighting stopped, Peck gave a fine performance as the commander of a bombing mission. In *The Gunfighter* (1950) he was almost unrecognisable behind a heavy moustache, but again excelled.

His biggest commercial hit of the early 1950s was *The Snows of Kilimanjaro* (1952), again with King, starring alongside his old friend Ava Gardner. For tax reasons he decided to spend the next year or so abroad, and filmed William Wyler's delightful romantic comedy, *Roman Holiday* (1953), in Italy. Peck, playing an American journalist, towered handsomely over the tiny Audrey Hepburn in their scenes together. But despite the heat generated on screen, his thoughts during filming were elsewhere. His first marriage, to a Finnish hairdresser Greta Konen, had broken up, and his wife returned to America with their three sons. Peck was despondent, but he was not alone for long. A 19-year-old reporter for France Soir, Veronique Passani, interviewed him during a break from shooting. They were married after his divorce came through in 1955 and became a model, thereafter, for a successful Hollywood marriage.

Peck was an expensive addition to Rank's stable in Britain during the 1950s (*The Million Pound Note*, *The Purple Plain*). Back in America he starred in *The Man in the Gray Flannel Suit* (1956), as Ahab in *Moby Dick* (1956), and *The Big Country* (1958), also co-producing the latter with William Wyler. *On the Beach* (1959), based on Nevil Shute's novel, won him some brutal reviews; as did *Beloved Infidel* (1959), for which, in a spectacular piece of miscasting, he played F Scott Fitzgerald.

It was from such professional doldrums that *The Guns of Navarone* (1961) rescued him. Co-starring Anthony Quinn, David Niven and Richard Harris, *The Guns of Navarone* was a classic war film. It was full of *Boys Own* heroics and explosions, as Peck described it, "a parody of a war film, like a comedy. The Germans like cops would always run around the wrong corner".

The original *Cape Fear* was followed by *To Kill a Mockingbird* (both 1962), in which Peck played the bespectacled southern smalltown lawyer, defending a Black man unjustly accused of rape. He won the Oscar for best actor for the performance, and the right to answer critics about his acting abilities thereafter.

Strangely, Peck's acting career slumped for the remainder of the 1960s. There was a long hiatus during which nothing was released, followed by a spate of dreary westerns. A new generation of leading men had taken his place and wisely Peck decided to concentrate on politics and production. He released *The Trial of the Catonsville Nine* in 1972 as a protest against the Vietnam War. He was proud to have made and released it at a time when Nixon was still in the White House, and when Peck himself was on a White House blacklist.

Peck had been active in Democratic politics for years. He had first campaigned against Nixon in the 1950s. During the 1960s he became a favourite of Lyndon B Johnson, and served on his Council on the Arts. There was even talk in 1966, when Ronald Reagan was elected to the California Governorship, that Peck might stand for the Democrats.

Peck bounced back to top commercial form in 1976 with *The Omen*, playing the American ambassador in Britain who finds that his child is diabolically inspired. He inherited the role from Charlton Heston, who had turned it down: *The Omen* brought Peck back to a creative and lucrative period as an actor in the autumn of his career. Now in his sixties he continued to take top billing over younger men such as Roger Moore in *The Sea Wolves* (1980, a waterlogged version of *The Guns of Navarone*). He played a Nazi in *The Boys from Brazil* (1978), but, more typically, was Lincoln in a television mini-series *The Blue and the Gray* (1983) and a sympathetic MacArthur in a biopic of the general in 1977. He had reached that level of superstardom, like Marlon Brando, where his briefest appearance in a film could adorn the whole production. In 1998 his performance in a television mini-series of *Moby Dick* won him a Golden Globe.

As a man Peck liked to keep his public at a distance. He spoke eloquently, but in a slow, deliberate manner. He was not extrovert and interviewers were frustrated when they found how adept he was at fielding personal questions. That lack of flamboyance, a refusal to put himself on the line, was probably what stopped him wanting to direct films, or to take a more active role in politics. It was also what limited his undoubted talents as an actor, even if it never damaged his career as a star. He recorded his own version of events in an autobiography, *An Actor's Life* (1978).

Despite the breakdown of his first marriage, he remained close to his three sons, and was hit hard when his eldest son took his own life in 1975. He also had a son and daughter from his second marriage.

Gregory Peck was born on April 5, 1916. He died of pneumonia on June 12, 2003, aged 87

GENE KELLY

The career of Gene Kelly, which spanned four decades, was a classic American success story, with virtually no setbacks. Almost at once he established himself as a dancer without rival on screen apart from the perennial Fred Astaire, and his later work extended itself to choreography and film direction with equal success. Two, at least, of the films he starred in, choreographed and directed, *On the Town* (1949) and *Singin' in the Rain* (1952), are among the unquestioned classics of the cinema.

Yet, in spite of these triumphs it often seemed that Kelly was not a natural dancer in the way Astaire was. There was always an awareness of the pains he was taking, the sheer hard work of brain and body which went into his performances. But this sense of physicality, of constant struggle, was an important and perhaps the most personal element of his style. It was all of a piece with the extrovert, insistently masculine quality of his dancing. It is not coincidental that one of his later television specials was called *Dancing: A Man's Game*. It was possible to find Kelly's screen personality antipathetic, but not to deny him the major credit for some of the American cinema's finest films and some of its most exciting musical moments.

Gene Curran Kelly was born of Irish parents. Sent by his mother to dance school from the age of seven, he graduated early from being taught to teaching himself, and by his early twenties was running two dance schools. In 1938 he decided to try his luck on Broadway, and soon got a part as a speciality dancer in the Cole Porter musical *Leave It to Me*. From that he went on to ever bigger roles in various musical shows, and worked as dance director on several.

He first made a big impression in 1939 playing the role of Harry the Hoofer in the first production of Saroyan's *The Time of Your Life*, and the following year became unmistakably a star when he played the title role in the Rodgers and Hart musical *Pal Joey*, in which he was required to sing, dance and act as the unscrupulous gigolo and would-be owner of a nightclub. It was his enormous success in this show which got him noticed by Hollywood, though curiously enough he was never called upon in Hollywood to play anything so tough and cynical. There his screen persona was to develop into something more wholesome, athletic and unmistakably all-American.

He went out to Hollywood under contract to David O Selznick, but Selznick had no suitable role for him, and his first film was a loan-out to MGM. It was a musical, *For Me and My Gal* (1942), and in it he had a starring role, opposite Judy Garland. The teaming (repeated on subsequent occasions) was a success, the film was a success, and MGM liked their new star so much they bought up his contract. The connection was to be a long and happy one, since Kelly stayed at the same studio for the next 15 years and made 27 films for it during that time, including nearly all of his classics.

Though through the years Gene Kelly did from time to time play non-singing, non-dancing roles in straight dramas, he and everybody else felt that his special talents lay in the musical area. He began as a dancer, but already on stage he had had experience as a director and choreographer, and before long he began to fulfil these functions in the cinema too.

He began to choreograph his own numbers with *Thousands Cheer* (1943), the most memorable part of which was a dance in which he used a mop as his partner. In *Cover Girl*, made the next year on loan to Columbia, he starred opposite Rita Hayworth and had the opportunity to develop more fully his qualities as a performer and choreographer. The film contains one of his first anthology-pieces, the "alter ego" dance in which he dances with himself in double-exposure.

Experimentation of this kind with the actual materials of the medium was to remain a continuing preoccupation with Kelly. The form to which he was to return most frequently first appears in *Anchors Aweigh* (1945), which features a sequence in which he dances in a cartoon framework, matching his actions with those of animated characters. He was to return to this not, finally, very satisfactory procedure in *Invitation to the Dance* (1956) and his later television version of *Jack and the Beanstalk*.

Other films of these years which remain memorable include *Ziegfeld Follies* (1946), in which for the first time he danced with Fred Astaire; *The Pirate* (1948), a musical by Cole Porter in which he was happily reunited with Judy Garland; and *Living in a Big Way* (1947), a curious comedy-drama by Gregory La Cava into which were interpolated a couple of excellent numbers devised by Kelly and his regular collaborator Stanley Donen.

These two evidently wanted even more overall control over the films they worked on, and in *Take Me Out to the Ball Game* (1949) they were given it when they originated the story and collaborated on the direction, under the practised eye of Busby Berkeley. This breezy musical of life in a baseball team, with Gene Kelly, Frank Sinatra and Jules Munshin as the three male principals, was obviously a sort of sketch for the following year's *On the Town*, in which Kelly and Donen for the first time received full directorial credit; it was perhaps the most innovatory single film in the history of the musical.

What was really original about *On the Town* was its complete freedom of form, with song, dance and dramatic action merging almost imperceptibly into one another, each used according to the best interests of the moment. Its refreshing use of actual locations let fresh air into the studio conventions usual at that time for the musical. If anything, the formula was improved upon in the next Kelly-Donen collaboration, *Singin' in the Rain*, a loving recreation of Hollywood in a period of transition with the coming of sound, which permitted Kelly himself to give one of his most charming performances and create one of his most magical moments in his solo version of the title number.

A third Kelly-Donen collaboration, *It's Always Fair Weather*, followed, less successfully, in 1955, but meanwhile Kelly had branched out on his own to make *Invitation to the Dance* (1956), a feature film consisting entirely of dance episodes. This was his most cherished and personal concept but unfortunately for the most part it showed up rather cruelly the limitations of his range as a choreographer. This had been much better served in *An American in Paris* (1951), one of the most popular among his films, in which he worked as star and choreographer with Vincente Minnelli as director. It climaxed in the famous ballet sequence which remains one of the screen's most ambitious attempts to come to terms directly with the dance.

After the end of his contract with MGM in *Les Girls* (1957) Kelly turned increasingly to straight acting, in films such as *Inherit the Wind* (1960), in which he played a cynical journalist based on HL Mencken, and to directing films in which he himself did not appear, most spectacularly *Hello Dolly!* in 1969. He also returned to the theatre, staging among other shows the Rodgers and Hammerstein *Flower Drum Song* and the spectacular, ill-fated *Clownaround*.

In 1974 he returned to his old home, MGM, as co-narrator of *That's Entertainment*, a compilation of great numbers from old MGM musicals. There was a sequel, directed by Kelly, *That's Entertainment, Part II* in 1976, introduced by him and Fred Astaire. Kelly also participated in a third dose of the same medicine, *That's Entertainment, Part III* (1994), directed by Bud Friedgen and Michael J Sheridan. Cyd Charisse, Lena Horne, Debbie Reynolds and Mickey Rooney were among the stars of Hollywood's past featured on that occasion, but not Fred Astaire, who had died in 1987.

Gene Kelly was three times married. His first marriage, in 1940, to the actress Betsy Blair ended in divorce in 1957. His second wife, a dance assistant, Jeanne Coyne, died in 1973. After her death Kelly raised their children. In 1990 he married the writer Patricia Ward and is survived by her and by the daughter of his first marriage and the son and daughter of his second.

Gene Kelly was born on August 23, 1912. He died following a stroke on February 2, 1996, aged 83

VIVIEN LEIGH

At the age of 21 Vivien Leigh had been a beautiful girl, and literally, an overnight celebrity; for a number of years she was the wife and stage partner of Sir Laurence Olivier. She died when still in mid-career; until the other day she was studying a role in the forthcoming production of a play by Mr Edward Albee; and on the night of her death all theatres in the West End extinguished their exterior lights for an hour as a sign of mourning.

As a beginner she won success in London as a girl with nothing to commend her but beauty, whom a jealous woman in Ashley Dukes' *The Mask of Virtue* made use of to entrap and ridicule her own unfaithful lover. As a young woman she became an international star with her film portrayal of Scarlett O'Hara, southern belle and world famous heroine of the bestselling novel *Gone with the Wind*; somewhat later she starred as Blanche Du Bois in *A Streetcar Named Desire*, a woman whose wits do not survive the fading of her beauty, and later still in her last two Hollywood films, as women who obviously were beautiful and who now are obviously not young, she proved herself one of those actresses who, always themselves, are always different, always learning, always turning their looks and personality to new, scrupulously prepared dramatic account.

Vivian Mary Hartley was born in India under the British Raj, at Darjeeling in 1913, the daughter of Mr and Mrs Ernest Hartley, her father being junior partner in a firm of stockbrokers. She was brought to England in 1920, went to school at the Convent of the Sacred Heart at Roehampton, and entered RADA. First her marriage at the age of 18 to Mr Vincent Leigh Holman, barrister-at-law, then the birth of their daughter Suzanne in 1933, caused her to break off her training, but she began to act professionally in 1934, and within a few months she was now known as Vivien Leigh – her spectacular appearance in Ashley Dukes' costume-play brought her a five-year contract with Alexander Korda of London Films.

For a time she made little progress, but her ambition, sustained by post-graduate work on her voice under Elsie Fogerty, was reinforced by encouragement from the actor who had played opposite to her in her first film for Korda, Laurence Olivier. In 1938 she found on visiting Hollywood, where Olivier was making *Wuthering Heights* – the idea of Cathy's being played by her had been dropped – that Scarlett O'Hara was still not cast, though *Gone With the Wind* was in production. The untried English girl made tests, and the most coveted part in the world was offered to her on condition that she signed a seven-year contract with David O Selznick. On the film's being shown in Atlanta and soon afterwards in New York, the south and the north as one man capitulated — and Hollywood awarded her the first Oscar of her career.

But when Olivier and she appeared in his production of *Romeo and Juliet* in New York in 1940, it was a failure; when she hoped to join the Old Vic company on her return to England, the director was of the opinion that her new celebrity would make it impossible for her to fit in; and when Olivier wanted her for the Princess in his film of *Henry V*, Selznick restrained her from appearing. He attempted to do the same, but in the end gave way, when she proposed playing Sabina the maid in Thornton Wilder's *The Skin of Our Teeth*, the part originally played by Tallulah Bankhead in America, under Olivier's direction. Vivien Leigh had married Olivier in California in 1940, after her marriage to Mr Holman and Olivier's marriage to Miss Jill Esmond Moore, the actress, had been dissolved.

Olivier was knighted in 1947. In the following year the Oliviers led an Old Vic company on a tour of Australia and New Zealand in *Richard III*, *The School for Scandal* and *The Skin of Our Teeth*, and in 1949 brought the company back to the New Theatre, London, where Vivien Leigh's most notable performance was as Antigone in the play by Jean Anouilh. She went on to make a two-fold success as Tennessee Williams's Blanche Du Bois, first under Olivier's direction on the London stage, and again in the film directed by Elia Kazan, in which her performance gained an Oscar for her for the second time in 13 years.

At the St James's in London, where her husband had established himself, she played Cleopatra to his Caesar in Shaw's play and to his Antony in Shakespeare's during the 1951 Festival of Britain, and when this theatre was about to be demolished six years later, she led a vigorous if unsuccessful movement to save it, interrupting a debate in the House of Lords in order to protest. She was then appearing with Olivier in London, after a tour of Europe, in *Titus Andronicus*, one of the three plays, the others being *Twelfth Night* and *Macbeth*, in which they had been seen together at Stratford-on-Avon in 1955.

Both husband and wife were in Terence Rattigan's comedy *The Sleeping Prince*, but Marilyn Monroe took over the showgirl's role in the film version, which Olivier made later, and Vivien Leigh appeared without him and under other directors in Noël Coward's *South Sea Bubble*, in an adaptation by Coward of Feydeau, and in Jean Giraudoux's last play *Duel of Angels*.

While Vivien Leigh was in Giraudoux's play in New York, her intention to appeal for divorce was announced, and the divorce was made absolute in 1961. During that year and the following year she had an Old Vic company on a tour of Australia, New Zealand and South America in *Twelfth Night*, *Duel of Angels* and *The Lady of the Camelias*, and, in 1963, made her debut in a musical, on Broadway, in *Tovarich*, playing, singing and Charlestoning the role of a former Grand Duchess which in the prewar production in London had been played straight by Eugenie Leontovitch.

A comedy in which she toured the English provinces in 1965 did not reach London, nor did London see her as the neglected Jewish wife of Ivanov in Chekhov's play of that name, for she took over the role for the American run, following the run in England, of this production, in both of which Sir John Gielgud took the title part. It had been announced that she would play opposite Sir Michael Redgrave in Albee's *A Delicate Balance* in London, when she was ordered to rest a month ago and rehearsals were postponed until September. This was the third occasion since 1945 on which she had been obliged to give up work on account of illness.

She received the Knight's Cross of the Legion of Honour in 1957 and a French award for her performance as a divorced American woman in her last Hollywood film, Stanley Kramer's *Ship of Fools*. Somerset Maugham had hoped to see her play his favourite feminine character, the charming, promiscuous and kind-hearted Rosie Driffield of his own *Cakes and Ale*, and had encouraged her to play Bathsheba Everdene, the innocently vain and unstable heroine of Hardy's *Far from the Madding Crowd*, but in fact neither of those promising projects for films was carried out. It might almost be said that the roles she did not play and the opportunities that now lay behind her gathered about her lately to form an aura peculiarly her own; but if so, it was an aura surrounding a beautiful woman whose strong character, humour and wit, love of works of art and delight in their collection, had all been proved and were well-known.

Vivien Leigh was born on November 5, 1913. She died of tuberculosis on July 8, 1967, aged 53

CLARK GABLE

Mr Clark Gable, for many years one of Hollywood's most consistently successful actors was born at Cadiz, Ohio in 1901, and came to the cinema in the mid-1920s after a period of theatrical touring, playing mostly bit parts. His rise in the film world was by no means meteoric; for some years he took only small parts in westerns, until his first major role came in *The Painted Desert* in 1931.

In a number of subsequent films he became typed as a brooding villain or an aggressive lover, but Gable's first real chance came through one of those ironies which often intervene in Hollywood. His company, believing his popularity to be fading, lent him to a small company for an inexpensive film. That film was *It Happened One Night*, which started a whole cycle of crazy comedies, brought Academy Awards to Clark Gable, his co-star Claudette Colbert, and the director, Frank Capra, and established Gable as the masculine ideal of his generation (so much so that, we are told, when he revealed in *It Happened One Night* that he did not wear a vest, there was at once a disastrous slump in the sales of vests throughout America).

The character of the good-natured, extrovert man of action which he established in this film recurred, with variations, throughout the next decade in such films as *Red Dust* and *China Seas* (both with Jean Harlow), *Mutiny on the Bounty*, *Boom Town* and *San Francisco*. In 1939 he played the most famous of all his roles, that of Rhett Butler in the film version of *Gone with the Wind*, which confirmed once and for all his right to his Hollywood nickname "the King".

During the Second World War he rose to the rank of major in the US Army Air Force and was awarded the Air Medal for his part in bombing missions over Europe. His postwar films successfully maintained his popularity, if they made few demands on his acting ability; most notable, perhaps, was Mogambo, a remake of his prewar success Red Dust. In 1954, after 23 years under contract, he left MGM to work independently on such films as Soldier of Fortune, *The Tall Men*, and a very happy return to comedy – *Teacher's* Pet. Recently Gable continued his success, playing opposite Sophia Loren in It Started in Naples, and had just completed a new film with Miss Marilyn Monroe, The Misfits, immediately before his death. Gable had little ambition to be regarded as a great actor: his parts seldom required much subtlety or penetration, and indeed differed very little through the years. What they did require was a dynamic personality and a virile physique, qualities which he possessed in abundance. To give him the coveted part of Rhett Butler was obviously a classic piece of typecasting, but it is difficult to think of any other actor who could have assembled all the qualities required and used them to such advantage. Neither should Gable's real skill as a comic actor go unpraised; his timing was perfect – a legacy, no doubt, of his stage training – and his face remarkably expressive. In his younger days the model American he-man, Gable was touched little by the passing years, and gradually matured into the perfect Claudius for some eventual Hollywood Hamlet. Not a great actor but a great personality and a great star, he will be hard to replace.

His marriages to Josephine Dillon, his dramatic coach; to Rhea Langham, and Sylvia Lady Stanley of Alderley were all dissolved by divorce. His third wife, Carole Lombard, the film actress, was killed in an air crash in 1942. He is survived by his widow, Kay Williams Spreckles, whom he married in 1955.

Clark Gable was born on February 1, 1901. He died of a heart attack on November 16, 1960, aged 59

FRED ASTAIRE

———————•———————

For several generations of play and filmgoers the word "musical", especially if accompanied by some reference to dancing or top hat, white tie and tails meant Fred Astaire. From the 1920s to the 1970s his name was synonymous with all that was most graceful and elegant in popular dancing.

Frederick Austerlitz was born at Omaha, Nebraska, in 1899. He began his long career at the age of eight when he formed a dancing partnership with his sister, Adele, and in 1908 they were touring together in vaudeville. By the early 1920s they had become top stars on the American stage and subsequently repeated their triumphs in London and elsewhere.

Their first notable Broadway appearances were in *Over the Top* and *The Passing Show* (1918), but their most spectacular early success was in the Gershwin musical *Lady Be Good* (1924), specially written for them. Other famous musical comedies in which they appeared during the next decade included another Gershwin, *Funny Face*, *The Gay Divorcee* and *Band Wagon*.

In 1932 Adele married and the dancing partnership was dissolved.

At this point in his career Astaire decided to try his luck in Hollywood where, since the introduction of talking pictures, musicals had become very popular.

His international fame on the stage made little impression in Hollywood, and he first appeared briefly as dancing partner in a Joan Crawford vehicle, *Dancing Lady* (1933). In the same year he appeared in *Flying Down to Rio*, in which he performed two or three dance numbers with a relatively obscure dancer called Ginger Rogers.

This time the public was impressed, and a new partnership resulted, which lasted for another eight films, starting with a film version of his former stage success, *The Gay Divorcee*.

The films in which he appeared with Ginger Rogers have become a legend: the very names have an almost unbearably nostalgic quality for anyone who lived through the 1930s – *Roberta,*

Top Hat, Shall We Dance?, Follow the Fleet, Swing Time, Carefree ... – while their frequent revivals have captivated many younger generations of admirers.

The secret resided, as much as anything, in the perfect partnership of the principals, ideally suited in appearance and temperament, and of course in the lightness and grace of the dance routines, devised together by Astaire and Rogers on the set and rehearsed from the beginning with the camera-movements in mind to achieve real film-dancing instead of just dancing recorded on film.

During the 1930s Astaire made only one film with another partner, *Damsel in Distress*, with Joan Fontaine (1937), and when his partnership with Ginger Rogers broke up in 1939 after *The Story of Vernon and Irene Castle*, a period of uncertainty followed.

During these years he appeared in a number of films, the best remembered perhaps being *You Were Never Lovelier*, in which he was teamed with Rita Hayworth, and *Holiday Inn*. But it was not until 1945 that he again hit his stride with a director worthy of his talents, Vincente Minnelli, and a new partner, Lucille Bremer, in *Yolanda and the Thief* and *Ziegfeld Follies* (with the songs *This Heart of Mine* and the splendid *Limehouse Blues*).

Shortly afterwards he announced his retirement, and was persuaded to change his mind only when Gene Kelly was unable to play in *Easter Parade*, and he took over the lead opposite Judy Garland. Following this success he continued to be kept busy in a series of films, of which the most interesting were *The Barklays of Broadway*, which reunited him with Ginger Rogers, and *Band Wagon*, in which he appeared with Jack Buchanan.

He announced his retirement again after one of his biggest successes, *Daddy Long Legs*, with Leslie Caron, and did not make a film for two years. But in 1957 he returned with two of his finest films, *Funny Face* and *Silk Stockings*, saying that he had retired for the last time and would go on making films as long as he could.

This he did to such effect that nearly twenty years later, in 1975, he was still hard at work and found himself, for the first time, nominated for an Oscar for his performance as a straight actor in *The Towering Inferno*.

Meanwhile he had played a number of non-singing, non-dancing roles, starting with *On the Beach* in 1959; had made three landmark television spectaculars featuring his own singing and dancing with a new partner, Barrie Chase; and in 1968 had appeared in his last musical, Francis Ford Coppola's *Finian's Rainbow*.

In 1960 he published his autobiography, *Steps in Time*, and continued to be seen regularly on television as an actor and, sometimes, as a living monument to the nostalgic delights of the screen musical's heyday. It was in very much this capacity that he took part in introducing MGM's tributes to their own glorious past *That's Entertainment* (1974) and *That's Entertainment, Part II* (1976).

He also received many honours and awards, starting in 1949 with a special honorary Oscar "for his unique artistry and his contribution to the techniques of motion pictures".

His first wife Phyllis died in 1954, the marriage producing two sons and a daughter. In 1980 he married Robyn Smith, who survives him.

Fred Astaire was touched more lightly by the passing of the years than almost any other star; never conventionally good looking, he retained his puckish charm and was hardly a shade less agile in his sixties than in his twenties, dancing as ever with an exquisite sense of style and grace of movement.

He was always an accomplished light comedian and though he had no real singing voice he possessed an inimitable way of putting over a song and made many of the most famous songs of Gershwin, Kern and others peculiarly his own.

Perhaps the most poignant moment in all his films comes in *Band Wagon*, when he and Jack Buchanan sing *I Guess I'll have to Change my Plan* dressed in top hat, white tie and tails: it summed up in a brief number all that was most elegant and stylish in the 1920s and 1930s; precisely those qualities which Fred Astaire always exemplified in his person and his work, even into an age in which they were otherwise often sadly lacking.

Fred Astaire was born on May 10, 1899. He died of pneumonia on June 22, 1987, aged 88

LESLIE NIELSEN

Tall and rugged, in the traditional mould of American outdoor heroes, Leslie Nielsen had a decent if unspectacular early career as a straight actor and occasional leading man. But in his middle years it was as the delightfully deadpan star of a string of movie spoofs that he really distinguished himself, dominating the genre for several decades.

His early credits include the commander in the 1956 sci-fi classic *Forbidden Planet* and the captain of the ship in the original 1972 version of *The Poseidon Adventure*. His career took a dramatic change of direction in 1980 when he played Dr Rumack, the hopelessly logical, but rather dim doctor who takes control in an airborne crisis in *Airplane!* "This woman has to be gotten to a hospital," he says. "A hospital! What is it?" says the stewardess. "It's a big building with patients," Nielsen replies with a deadpan face.

Although it looks likely that the plane is about to crash and everyone is going to die, his character's greatest concern seems to be about being misnamed. "Surely you can't be serious." "I am serious – and don't call me Shirley." The film was a belated send-up of

Airport (1970) and other more recent disaster movies and it cleverly used Nielsen and his co-stars Robert Stack, Lloyd Bridges and Peter Graves to undermine their established heroic, rather po-faced screen personae in a jamboree of sheer silliness, visual gags and crazy non sequiturs. It cost around $3.5 million, grossed $83.5 million in North America alone and prompted a spate of spoof movies.

Many of the most notable and most successful starred Nielsen, including *The Naked Gun* series (1988–94), *Dracula: Dead and Loving It* (1995) and *Spy Hard* (1996). The distinguished American critic Roger Ebert called Nielsen "the Olivier of spoofs", though most critics would agree they suffered from the law of diminishing returns. Such was Nielsen's iconic status within the genre that he was called in to play the president in later instalments in the *Scary Movie* series of films in the 2000s.

The son of a Mountie, Leslie William Nielsen was born in Regina, Sastakchewan in 1926. His father's family was Danish; his mother's Welsh. His uncle was the actor Jean Hersholt, after whom the Academy of Motion Picture Arts and Sciences named a humanitarian award. His elder brother Erik Nielsen became a prominent Canadian politician and served as deputy prime minister in the 1980s.

Towards the end of the Second World War Nielsen joined the Royal Canadian Air Force. Subsequently he worked as a disc jockey and presenter on Canadian radio and won a scholarship to study at the Neighborhood Playhouse drama school in New York. By 1950 he was appearing in television plays, including several Actors Studio productions.

He figured in hundreds of television programmes from the early 1950s onwards and reportedly appeared in almost 50 live shows in 1950 alone, for which he recalled he got around $75–$100 a show. His distinctive, authoritative voice also brought him work as a narrator on documentaries and a voice-over artist on commercials.

In the mid-1950s he moved to Hollywood and made his film debut in the 1956 thriller *Ransom!*, which was remade 40 years later with Mel Gibson. That same year he starred in *Forbidden Planet*, which imaginatively transferred the plot of Shakespeare's

The Tempest to outer space in the 23rd century. Its concept of a "monster from the id" was to prove very influential.

He co-starred with Debbie Reynolds in *Tammy* (1957) and with Glenn Ford and Shirley MacLaine in *The Sheepman* (1958). He auditioned for the role of Messala in *Ben-Hur* (1959), but lost out to Stephen Boyd. The screen test survives and was later included on a video release. He returned to television, starring as the American revolutionary war hero Francis Marion in *The Swamp Fox* stories on the Disneyland TV show (1959–61).

He starred as the Los Angeles Police Department's Lieutenant Adams in the crime series *The New Breed* (1961–62) and made guest appearances in numerous hit series, including *Rawhide* (1959), *The Fugitive* (1963–64), *Dr Kildare* (1965), *Bonanza* (1967), *The Man from U.N.C.L.E.* (1968) and *M*A*S*H* (1973).

In some series he played several different roles over the years, working steadily but unremarkably before a brief appearance in the low-budget comedy sketch film *The Kentucky Fried Movie* (1977) signalled a new direction. It was a surprise international hit and when the writers Jim Abrahams, David Zucker and Jerry Zucker moved on to directing with *Airplane!* they gave Nielsen a starring role.

Abrahams and the Zucker brothers attempted to export the formula to television with *Police Squad!* (1982), with Nielsen as the silver-haired police detective Frank Drebin. It was cancelled after only a handful of episodes. Nielsen continued to work regularly in television and had a supporting role in the 1987 Barbra Streisand drama *Nuts*.

But Abrahams and the Zuckers still believed that their dopey police detective Frank Drebin had the potential to be a hit and they reworked their ideas into a feature film, with Nielsen reprising the role in *The Naked Gun* (1988). The story revolved around a plot to kill the Queen. In Drebin's attempts to blend in at a baseball match, he takes on the role of umpire and starts a furore with his exhibitionist behaviour, always remaining oblivious to the mayhem around him.

It was a major hit and Nielsen starred in the sequels *Naked Gun 2½: The Smell of Fear* (1991) and *Naked Gun 33 ⅓: The Final Insult* (1994).

Later films include *Repossessed* (1990), which parodied *The Exorcist* (1973); *Wrongfully Accused* (1998), a spoof of *The Fugitive* TV series (1963–67); and *2001: A Space Travesty* (2001). But few of his later films compared with the sustained brilliance of *Airplane!* and *The Naked Gun*.

He also made several humorous golf instructional videos, beginning with *Bad Golf Made Easier* (1993), wrote a fictionalised autobiography called *The Naked Truth* (1993) and played the title role in a live-action version of *Mr Magoo* (1997), which proved a commercial and critical disappointment. Nielsen is survived by his fourth wife, Barbaree, and two daughters from his second marriage.

Leslie Nielsen was born on February 11, 1926. He died of pneumonia on November 28, 2010, aged 84

AVA GARDNER

———•———

Ava Gardner, who justified throughout her career her reputation as one of the screen's most notable beauties, became an original personality, who hinted at greater potential as an actress than she was ever actually permitted to show.

She was born in North Carolina in 1922. Her family were farmers, but during the Depression they moved into the city, where her mother kept a boarding house for teachers. On leaving school she trained to be a secretary, but her brother-in-law, a professional photographer, sent some photographs of her to the offices of film companies, and in consequence she was offered a contract with MGM at the age of 17.

In Hollywood, however, no one seemed to know quite what to do with her (apart from giving her voice lessons to reduce her Deep South accent), and for six years she was given merely walk-on parts and very brief roles in a series of minor films. In 1946 her chance finally came when she was lent to another studio to play the female lead in Robert Siodmak's *The Killers*, an effective thriller elaborated from a Hemingway short story. From this she went on to play one of her best roles in *The Hucksters,* which exploited her talents as a comedienne in a wisecracking "other woman" characterisation.

Though this film finally made her a star, it did not immediately guarantee her more interesting roles. Among the better films that she made at this period were *One Touch of Venus,* an adaptation of the Broadway musical by Kurt Weill, and *The Great Sinner,* Robert Siodmak's version of Dostoevsky's *The Gambler.* In 1951 she came to Europe and visited Spain, where she was later to make her home, to star in *Pandora and the Flying Dutchman,* a bizarre symbolic drama by Albert Lewin which established her definitively as one of the cinema's most beautiful women with obvious star presence, even if it hardly made any great calls on her acting abilities. These were better demonstrated by *Show Boat,* in which she played the role created by Helen Morgan, and *The Snows of Kilimanjaro,* another film remotely based on Hemingway. In *Mogambo* (1953), directed by John Ford, she again had some opportunity to demonstrate her comic talents in a role originally played by Jean Harlow. The following year she gave another of her best performances in Joseph Mankiewicz's *The Barefoot Contessa,* a behind-the-scenes story of film-making life which, among other things, got her labelled by the publicity men as "the world's most beautiful animal".

After that she made fewer films, but in general better ones, either in themselves, like George Cukor's *Bhowani Junction,* or as roles for her, like *The Naked Maja* (1959), a film about Goya in which she played the Duchess of Alba. In Stanley Kramer's film version of *On the Beach* she gave a subdued and effective performance as an alcoholic waiting for the extinction of humanity, and had rarely looked more beautiful on the screen than as the Russian countess in Nicholas Ray's *55 Days at Peking.* John Frankenheimer's *Seven Days in May* gave her only a brief, incidental role, but in 1964 she had, and made the most of, another comic opportunity in John Huston's version of Tennessee's Williams's *Night of the Iguana.* She worked again with Huston in his ambitious film *The Bible,* in which she played Sarah from youth to extreme old age.

After making her home in Spain for several years in 1968 she moved to London, where she lived quietly in semi-retirement. Her later films included *Mayerling* in which she played the Austrian Empress; *The Life and Times of Judge Roy Bean*, another John Huston picture; and *Earthquake*.

On television she was seen in the American soap opera, *Knots Landing*; in the mini-series, *AD* (as the tyrannical Empress Agrippina); and *Harem*. Ava Gardner's career was a perfect demonstration of the ability a real film star must possess to impose himself or herself in some mysterious way, regardless of the varying quality of roles on offer. She was certainly one of the most striking and genuine star personalities of her time, and yet she made relatively few films of more than passing interest, and was given worthwhile roles in even fewer. What worked a spell for her on the public, in fact, was her great beauty and, even more, the sheer personality shining through even the most indifferent vehicles.

She was married three times: to Mickey Rooney, Artie Shaw and Frank Sinatra.

Ava Gardner was born on December 24, 1922. She died of pneumonia of January 25, 1990, aged 67

WILLIAM HURT

In the zoo of monstrous egos that is Hollywood, William Hurt took an almost Zen-like attitude to his profession. "I am not an actor. I am nobody. I don't exist," he insisted. "But the work exists. The work is more than the actor."

Never one to under-theorise, he likened his craft to the building of an iceberg. "You build what isn't seen and then just play the tip of it. That's sometimes hard to do in American movies, where the philosophy is to show the whole berg," he said.

It was an approach which in the 1980s garnered him the rare phenomenon of three consecutive nominations for the Academy Award for best actor – in 1986 for *Kiss of the Spider Woman*, the following year for *Children of a Lesser God* and in 1988 for *Broadcast News*.

He won the Oscar for his bruising portrayal of a fluttery, sensitive transvestite incarcerated in a South American prison in *Kiss of the Spider Woman*. It was a hard and well-earned prize. While filming on location in Brazil he was kidnapped and held hostage at gunpoint before being released without ransom. He also waived his salary so that the film could be made within budget. "There was no angling for gratuitous reward. This was just a glorious opportunity to do the right thing," he said.

On the night he cut an oddly reluctant winner. "I thought I was going to put on my penguin suit and have a couple of drinks and look at the other salivating guys in the penguin suits like you study a character," he recalled. "When they called my name out I really thought, 'Oh no, no, don't put that target on my chest.'"

When Sally Field presented him with his statuette he looked at her suspiciously and asked "What the hell do I do with this?" "You live with it," she told him.

A mesmerising presence on camera, his "iceberg" theory enabled him to inhabit his roles with an almost preternatural immersion, which he likened to "walking through a mirror and it's not you any more".

In *Broadcast News* he played a shallow self-absorbed television news anchor but as if by stealth brought a compelling empathy to the role which as one critic put it, conveyed "surprising depths to his vapidity".

Other 1980s box-office hits included *Body Heat*, in which he played a lawyer manipulated by Kathleen Turner's femme fatale into murdering her wealthy husband; *The Big Chill*, in which he excelled as an impotent, stoned Vietnam vet; and *Gorky Park*, in which he played an enigmatic Soviet detective trying to solve a triple murder.

His patrician good looks and the physique of an athlete coupled with the way he explored the sensitivity, compassion and intelligence of his characters led to him he becoming known as "the thinking person's hunk".

At 6ft 2in and with a dramatic cleft in the chin and intense blue eyes, Hurt was reckoned by *The Hollywood Reporter* to have "picked up a mantle that had belonged to Robert Redford through the previous decade, the all-American blond Adonis who was neither jock nor jerk".

Hurt himself suggested he was "a character actor in a leading man's body" who brought a different "mask" to each role he played. "The more complete your mask, whether it's in flagrante delicto or subtle, the more complete its psychology, the more you see the soul of your own being," he philosophised.

His exacting approach gave him a reputation for being difficult, although his integrity meant that directors came back for more. "Hurt promises you a bad time and he delivers. How he made me suffer," said Héctor Babenco, the director of *Kiss of the Spider Woman*. "Would I work with him again? Tomorrow." Yet "the innate art" of acting, Hurt believed, resided not in movies but in live theatre. He was 30 when he landed his first film role in Ken Russell's *Altered States*. By then he had appeared in 60 stage productions and had played what David Mamet called the best Hamlet he had ever seen. "If all the cinemas in the world burnt down today, you'd still have acting," Hurt said.

He remained a company member of New York's Circle Repertory throughout the 1980s and was nominated for a Tony award for his role in the Broadway production of *Hurlyburly* in the same year that he was collecting an Oscar as best actor for *Kiss of the Spider Woman*.

He disliked the Hollywood notion of action heroes and preferred to concentrate on his characters' inner lives. "What's wrong with heroism being a man who has travelled two inches?" he wondered gnomically. "Why is it that in the movies we have to spend so much time escaping rather than being freed by accepting?"

Yet the stillness that became his trademark on screen was somewhat in contrast to a manic personality off. He suffered from logorrhoea, which he treated with lithium, and interviews with him sometimes read like a script from one of Dr Anthony Clare's *In the Psychiatrist's Chair* programmes.

One interviewer reported that when asked how shooting on his latest film was going, he answered with "a thesis on the interconnectedness of quantum mechanics, Tibetan Buddhism, infected blood, the Gulf War, chaos theory and Third World population growth". Another question prompted references to William Blake and Spinoza. It wasn't pomposity, simply the way that his overactive mind worked.

Another interviewer compared a typically unruly Hurt sentence to "a balloon being folded into a matchbox", while his first wife noted with evident frustration that "most people will just eat a hamburger, he will want to know where the cow was born".

For a long period he was a heavy drinker until he woke up one morning in 1986 and had an epiphany. Concluding that it was a myth that "living life on the edge is conducive to great acting", he decided to check into a Betty Ford clinic.

His private life was also complicated. He was married and divorced twice, first to the actress Mary Beth Hurt between 1971 and 1982 and then between 1989 and 1993 to Heidi Henderson, whom he met in rehab.

He also lived at different times with Sandra Jennings, a dancer with the New York City Ballet, Marlee Matlin and the French actress Sandrine Bonnaire, whom he met on a set in 1992.

After he had ended his relationship with Jennings she sued to have their common-law marriage legally recognised and accused him in court of violence, having religious hallucinations and urinating on the sofa, among other offences.

The hearing was followed daily on television by millions and became one of the most notorious "palimony" cases in American legal history. Hurt won but compared the experience to having his skin steamed off in public.

Matlin in her 2009 autobiography *I'll Scream Later* also accused him of subjecting her to physical abuse. He subsequently issued a public apology "for any pain I caused".

He is survived by four children, Alex from his relationship with Jennings, Samuel and William Hurt Jr from his second marriage, and daughter Jeanne Bonnaire-Hurt, who was born in 1994 after he had moved to Paris.

William McChord Hurt was born in 1950 in Washington DC, one of three sons to Claire (née McGill), a secretary at Time magazine, and Alfred Hurt, an official in the US Agency for International Development. His father's job meant his earliest years were spent peripatetically in Pakistan, Somalia, Sudan and Guam but his parents divorced when he was six. Three years later his mother married her boss, Henry Luce III, the son of the publishing magnate who founded Time and Life magazines, and he found himself living in a 22-room apartment on New York's Upper East Side.

Educated expensively at the Middlesex School in Concord, Massachusetts, Hurt took the lead in school plays and on graduating in 1968 his school yearbook predicted "you might even see him on Broadway".

Instead, under the influence of his strict Presbyterian stepfather, he opted to study theology at Tufts University. He later dropped out and by 1972 had enrolled in the drama department at the Juilliard School, where fellow students included Robin Williams and Christopher Reeve.

Although his greatest success came in the 1980s, he continued to work steadily in supporting roles. Later successes included his compelling portrayal of a glowering mob boss in David Cronenberg's 2005 action thriller *A History of Violence*. Despite being on screen for less than ten minutes, it earned him his fourth Oscar nomination as best supporting actor.

He also became familiar to a younger generation of moviegoers as General Thaddeus Ross in 2008's *The Incredible Hulk*. He reprised the role in four further superhero movies.

Fame he saw as "a vacuum" which brought him little pleasure. Instead his enjoyment came from fly-fishing, playing chess and flying his six-seater private plane.

Asked what he might have done if he hadn't been an actor, he suggested that "being in a monastery would be a good way of life". In some ways a life of monastic contemplation might have suited him, but given his reputation for restless intelligence and hyperactive curiosity, he was probably being ironic.

William Hurt was born on March 20, 1950. He died of prostate cancer on March 13, 2022, aged 71

RICHARD ATTENBOROUGH

───────●───────

Richard Attenborough was the personification of British cinema. As actor or director – he liked to call himself "actor-manager" – he was a star for well over half a century. He was also the fiercest political champion of British cinema, defending it throughout the many economic and artistic crises that his long career witnessed.

Because he served on so many committees and organisations, he was often seen as an Establishment figure – but he was no stooge. Whenever he felt that the government was wrong – particularly where the cinema was concerned – he was its most implacable critic. When Channel 4, of which he was then chairman, was ordered to disclose its informants in a programme impugning the Royal Ulster Constabulary, he personally defied the court, convinced that to expose these people would be to condemn them to death by terrorism.

He was a committed, lifelong socialist – though he attracted the ire of one former Labour leader, Neil Kinnock, for his habit of turning up in his Rolls-Royce for the party's photocalls during the

1987 election campaign. Despite the cuddling and caressing and the "darling" that was his catchword, he was far more than a quintessential "luvvie". Underneath he was an inveterate mover and a shaker, a networker known for his forceful charm, to which no one, however high or low, appeared to be immune, from Nelson Mandela to Diana, Princess of Wales.

He became friends with the princess after Prince Charles wrote to him in 1985, explaining "that making speeches was causing his young wife a great deal of anxiety. Could I recommend someone discreet who would be willing to give her some tuition? ... Although there was an age gap of 38 years between us, I became her friend, sounding board, cheerleader and, on occasion, her admonitory Dutch uncle. She would refer to herself jokingly, in deference to my wife Sheila, as 'the other lady in your life'."

His greatest cinematic achievement was his biography of Mahatma Gandhi, not least for the quixotic persistence with which he battled for 20 years to make it possible. His efforts to raise finance for the picture were repeatedly thwarted, leading him to sell his shares in *The Mousetrap*, in which he had appeared in the original cast with his wife, the actress Sheila Sim. Along the way he rejected all sorts of inappropriate studio suggestions, such as financial backing if he agreed to cast Richard Burton in the title role "because he was sexy – an idea so idiotic it was not worth further thought".

The seeds of the idea had been sown in 1962, when an Indian devotee of Gandhi, Motilal Kothari, approached Attenborough with an idea for a film biography of the Mahatma. Reading Louis Fischer's biography fired him. "The truth is that I don't really want to be a director at all," Attenborough explained. "I just want to direct that film."

Gandhi brought him Oscars for best picture and best director and a place in the *Guinness Book of Records* for the funeral scene, in which he directed 300,000 extras. It was the most people ever gathered together specifically for a scene in a feature film. One of the reasons that Attenborough was so determined to make the film was that his father held Gandhi in high esteem. He wrote in his memoirs: "The Governor, as my brothers and I always called my father, had always wanted me to follow in his footsteps and become an academic. Even as an adult, I still desperately wanted to prove myself to him. If I could make a film with something important to say, perhaps he would take real pride in what I was doing."

Attenborough's beaming figure was affectionately recognised all over the world, though he hated being called "Dickie"; the name came about when he enrolled at RADA in 1940 and was told that they already had a Richard and a Dick. "I hated it then and I hate it now," he later said. "My wife, family and close friends call me Dick, except after I've done something absolutely dreadful, when Sheila calls me Richard."

He was justly proud of his accomplishment as an actor, but consistently underrated his achievement as director, frequently speaking of himself as a "boring" director. "I don't use film in the way that the great auteurs do. I use film, the camera, to record as effectively and as perceptively as I am able what I want to say through the actors."

Because he believed passionately in the themes of his films, and in the importance of heroes, he always wanted to reach the biggest audience. "I'm not interested in appealing to two men and a dog in a barn. In some quarters 'popularise' is a dirty word. But it is a banner under which I will gladly sail."

In truth he may well have underestimated his qualities as a director. On the set he had an astonishing ability to inspire loyalty. Units would work far longer hours, without complaint, for him than for the other director. Moreover he had a true sense of mise-en-scène, even though this could often be obscured by the technical conventions of the blockbuster productions in which he was mostly involved.

He loved big family Christmases, but they became hugely painful for him after his daughter Jane and granddaughter Lucy died in Thailand in the Boxing Day tsunami in 2004, which he described as "the worst day of my life". After that he and his wife would head for the isolation of their remote farmhouse on the island of Bute.

He said in an interview in 2007: "We have six grandchildren, but we used to have seven. We have two children, Michael and Lottie, and we used to have three... I can't bear to see the empty spaces at the table. Sheila and I will be spending Christmas in Scotland where we can talk about Jane and Lucy, talk about our feelings and weep."

The ideal of service to others was bred into the Attenborough boys (Richard had two younger brothers, John, a former executive at Alfa Romeo who died in 2012, and David, the famous naturalist and broadcaster) from infancy. His parents, he later recalled, "felt unquestionably that to enjoy life to the full you simply had to be conscious of others and their quality of life. It followed that you should be prepared to make some sort of sacrifice – and I don't mean that in an over-moral sense – wherever it was possible to help." The family always took deprived children with them on their summer holidays. During the 1930s the Attenborough parents worked tirelessly in the cause of refugee children, in turn from the Spanish Civil War and from Nazi Germany. For eight years the family gave a home to two orphaned Jewish girls from Germany.

Richard Samuel Attenborough was born in Cambridge in 1923, the son of May Clegg, a founding member of the Marriage Guidance Council, and Frederick Levi Attenborough, a scholar. When he was nine the family moved to Leicester, where his father was appointed principal of University College (now the University of Leicester). Both parents passed on their passion for music and the arts, though Frederick Attenborough also infected his sons with his enthusiasm for football. (Richard was to become a director of Chelsea FC).

As a child he became accustomed to meeting celebrities. He remembered his parents' lunch guests including such distinguished visitors to Leicester as Jan Masaryk, Sir Hugh Roberton, Sir Thomas Beecham, Sir Stafford Cripps, Matheson Lang, Eric Gill, Reynolds Stone and Dilys Powell. He attended Wyggeston Grammar School, Leicester, and it was assumed that he would go on to university. From infancy though he had loved performing, and the taste had been sharpened by teenage roles with the Leicester Little Theatre, a progressive amateur group of which his mother was president. His father suppressed his disappointment, and agreed that he might go to RADA on condition that he could earn a scholarship. Richard obliged by winning the 1941 Leverhulme Scholarship, but to the end of his life he seemed to carry a sense of guilt at disappointing parental expectations. Years later he rejected a proposal to direct the National Theatre on the grounds that he was "not intellectually up to it", which was patently not so.

With equally unjustified modesty he attributed his extraordinary success in the RADA period to lack of competition: the war had removed most eligible young actors from London. At the end of his first year he won the Bancroft Medal. During his first summer vacation in 1941 he appeared in *Ah, Wilderness!* at the Intimate Theatre, Palmers Green, where he was spotted and taken on by the formidable agent Al Parker. Still a student, he played at the Arts Theatre in *Awake and Sing* (which transferred to the Cambridge Theatre for his West End debut in 1942), *Holy Isle*, *Twelfth Night*, *The Little Foxes* and a Christmas entertainment, *Maria Marten, or the Murder in the Red Barn*, in which he did a musical number which got his photograph in *Picture Post* as "the hit of the show".

Parker also found him his notable first film role, as the frightened stoker in Noël Coward and David Lean's *In Which We Serve* (1942). The role was small, but Attenborough won notices for it. His electrifying performance as the little gangster Pinkie in *Brighton Rock*, which opened at the Garrick Theatre on March 11, 1943, established him as a star overnight. The doyen and terror of theatre critics, James Agate, stormed backstage and announced, "Young man, I never make a practice of coming round to actors' dressing rooms. I consider you are in danger of becoming a great actor. I therefore never wish to see you again." Attenborough was now launched to the top of the acting profession, where he was to remain for the rest of his career.

The run of *Brighton Rock* was cut short when Attenborough was called up into the RAF. He began to train as a pilot but was soon seconded to the RAF Film Unit. For the unit he played in a propaganda feature film, *Journey Together*, directed by John Boulting. The opportunity to work opposite Edward G Robinson made a lasting impression. Another fellow artist in the film, whose part ended on the cutting room floor, was Sheila Sim, whom he had first met at RADA. They were married in January 1945; his wife survives him as does a son, Michael, former artistic director of the Almeida Theatre in London, and a daughter, Charlotte, who is an actress.

On demobilisation Attenborough found no shortage of work. On stage he played in *The Way Back* at the Westminster (1949), *To Dorothy a Son* (Savoy, 1950; transferred to Garrick, 1951) and *Sweet Madness* (Vaudeville, 1952). He and his wife were the original stars of *The Mousetrap* (Ambassadors, 1952), destined to become the longest-running play in history. Subsequent stage appearances were in *Double Image* (Savoy, 1956; transferred to St James, 1957) and *The Rape of the Belt* (Piccadilly, 1957–58). At this period too he was a pioneer and immensely popular disc jockey with his own programme, *Record Rendezvous*.

On the screen he repeated his stage success in the film version of *Brighton Rock* (1947). However, he quickly began to recognise a danger of being typecast as a young delinquent or cowardly serviceman. His baby face was becoming a handicap. In *The Guinea Pig*, already 25 and with his hair thinning, he played a 15-year-old schoolboy (with Sheila Sim as his housemistress). In those militaristic days of British cinema, he was too often put back into uniform. More rewarding parts began to offer with the Boulting Brothers' satires, *Private's Progress* (1956), *Brothers in Law* (1957) and *I'm All Right Jack* (1959). Such roles, along with a current sense of revolution and renewal in British theatre and films, made Attenborough look for greater independence.

With the actor and writer Bryan Forbes, he formed Beaver Films, whose first production, *The Angry Silence* (1960), made for under £100,000, starred Attenborough as a workman unfairly victimised as a result of corruption in trade unions. Beaver's subsequent films – all with Attenborough as producer or co-producer – were *Whistle Down the Wind* (1961), *All Night Long* (1961) and *Seance on a Wet Afternoon* (1964). This last film gave him an outstanding acting role as the asthmatic husband of a disturbed woman, memorably played by Kim Stanley. With Forbes and a group of other British film artists he was involved in the formation of Allied Film Makers, for whom he played in *The League of Gentlemen*.

The Sixties brought Attenborough some of his best parts: opposite Steve McQueen in *The Great Escape* (1963) and *The Sand*

Pebbles (1967); and as a martinet RSM in *Guns at Batasi* (1964), which won him one of his several British Film Academy Awards. While working on *The Sand Pebbles* he was cast at short notice to play the singing-dancing Albert Blossom in *Dr Dolittle* (1967). He won Golden Globe Awards for both roles. One of his most chilling appearances was as the murderer John Reginald Christie in *10 Rillington Place* (1970). Distasteful as he found the role, he felt it worthwhile for the contribution the film made to marshalling opinion against capital punishment.

His debut as a director came after an old friend, the actor John Mills, approached him with a proposal to direct a film version of the Theatre Workshop production *Oh! What a Lovely War*. Mills delivered the script by hand to Attenborough's home at 10am. An hour and a half later, Attenborough rang Mills in great excitement, saying that if he didn't make the film he would die. In this he was echoing the advice of David Lean, who years before had told him not to direct any film "unless you feel that you would die if you didn't make it".

Attenborough raised the funding for *Oh! What a Lovely War* largely as a result of his one-man performance of the script for the head of Paramount Pictures, and set about finding his cast. Few British films were ever more star-studded: from Dirk Bogarde, Laurence Olivier and John Gielgud to Vanessa Redgrave. Boldly innovative in style, the film, released in 1969, was a success and led to an invitation to direct *Young Winston* (1972).

Next he undertook two projects produced by the old-style mogul Joseph Levine. The first, *A Bridge Too Far* (1977), recreated the heroic fiasco of Arnhem. William Goldman's script failed to contain the sprawling action and multitude of characters, but Attenborough showed his skill for mass spectacle. In contrast *Magic* (1978) was an effective small-scale thriller. Badly received at the time (Goldman's story of the ventriloquist possessed by his dummy was considered hackneyed) the film, with Anthony Hopkins's frightening performance, now has a cult status.

Thanks to the collaboration of the Indian government and the financial skills of Jake Eberts of Goldcrest Films, Attenborough was finally able to embark on *Gandhi*, which was completed in 1982. The outcome justified all his faith. Attenborough dedicated its eight Oscars to Gandhi. He derived greater satisfaction, though, when the film inspired the launch of a series of Gandhi foundations to undertake social work around the world.

As a complete change of style, Attenborough next undertook to film the stage musical *A Chorus Line*. The essence of the piece was its location in a live theatre, and other directors had rejected it as impossible. Attenborough's attempt, though brave, was generally badly received, though he always insisted that it was his best film.

Cry Freedom (1987) was adapted from the writings of a South African journalist and friend of Steve Biko, Donald Woods. The film was again disappointing financially, but its attack on apartheid was undoubtedly effective. The film was a difficult undertaking, though. Attenborough went to South Africa to research it, met Biko's widow and Winnie Mandela, and was determined to see it through despite being followed by agents of the South African government and repeated attempts to intimidate him. He told Winnie Mandela: "If all goes according to plan shooting will start in October." This innocent comment was apparently recorded and supplied to a South African TV station, which edited it into a piece alleging that Attenborough was being financed by Moscow to initiate an armed insurrection, and it was pencilled in to kick off that autumn.

He met Nelson Mandela several times after the latter's release from prison. In his memoirs, *Entirely Up to You, Darling* Attenborough recalled his first meeting with him. "He said, 'Your film had more impact on the White population than any speech I ever made in my life.' I was completely overwhelmed by his generosity. Was it true? Of course not. But I like to think *Cry Freedom* did help the struggle."

Committed to the spectacular screen biography, Attenborough battled in vain to interest the studios in a film of the life of Thomas Paine, which he always regarded as his great unfinished project. Instead he made a biography of Charlie Chaplin, at a cost nearing $40 million. While still working on *Chaplin*, Attenborough was tempted to return to acting, after a break of 13 years, playing an eccentric billionaire in Steven Spielberg's *Jurassic Park* (1993). The work proved unexpectedly hazardous, since he was caught with the rest of the unit in the disastrous typhoon that hit Hawaii in September 1992.

Attenborough served on numerous film, media and arts bodies. He was deputy chairman in the lead-up to the launch of Channel 4 in 1982 and subsequently chairman, and as such was involved in Channel 4's determination to pump money into the British film industry, which at the time was on its knees. The new broadcaster financed a series of films, including *My Beautiful Laundrette* (1985), which made a star of Daniel Day-Lewis. Attenborough was, moreover, closely involved with Bafta and was president from 2001 to 2010, when he was succeeded by Prince William. He was also the recipient of numerous honorary degrees and awards, was appointed CBE in 1956, knighted in 1976 and made a life peer in 1993.

After suffering a stroke in 2008 he was confined to a wheelchair and subsequently sold his estate on Bute and his house in Richmond, southwest London (fittingly, the property had a cinema in its garden), as well as his art collection, which included works by LS Lowry and Graham Sutherland. Latterly he had been living with his wife in Denville Hall, a home in west London for senior citizens from the theatrical profession, for which he and his wife had helped to fundraise.

His public image was that of a passionate, impetuous, concerned, generous man who was utterly free of cynicism. Remarkably, the real man was little different. With his twinkling eyes, white beard and saintly smile, he looked just like Father Christmas – a role he played with glee in his seventies in *Miracle on 34th Street*. In the film he appears in court to prove that he is the real Santa Claus. In many ways, he was.

Lord Attenborough was born on August 29, 1923. He died on August 24, 2014, aged 90

CHENG PEI-PEI

●

Cheng Pei-pei never intended to become a martial arts star. "I knew nothing about kung fu. I was just a dancer," she said. Yet her blade-wielding appearances in a swathe of films led to her becoming known as the Queen of Swords and culminated in her spectacular portrayal of the villainous assassin Jade Fox in Ang Lee's Oscar-winning *Crouching Tiger, Hidden Dragon* (2000).

"It was difficult because I never considered myself a martial arts lady and I had spent six years having ballet lessons," she said. "But I was always a bit of a tomboy and up for a fight. It's exhilarating. So when I got a chance to act out fight scenes, I was happy to oblige."

The enviable dexterity she had acquired as a dancer translated readily to a martial context and the grace, elegance and steely-eyed intensity of her fight scenes made her a compelling presence on the screen.

She first gained prominence almost a quarter of a century before *Crouching Tiger, Hidden Dragon* as the female knight Golden Swallow, who uses her sword to rescue her brother from a gang of eunuch bandits in *Come Drink with Me* (1966).

A classic of the genre known in Mandarin as *wuxia* ("martial arts and chivalry"), Cheng was 20 years old when she was spotted performing in a Chinese opera by the film's director, King Hu. It was her poise as a dancer that led him to cast her, noting that the combat in his pictures was "always keyed to the notion of dance".

All he had to do was to put a sword in her hand and ask her to turn balletic somersaults in mid-air – and she was a natural, dispatching bandits with an icy fury in an epic fight.

Come Drink with Me was the first time a woman had taken the lead role in a martial arts film and she went on to star in another two dozen for the Hong Kong-based Shaw Brothers Studio, sometimes known as Hollywood East. "I thought, 'If a man can do it, so can I'," she said. "I didn't need any special treatment. I'm very proud and competitive to a fault."

Despite her petite stature, she earned a reputation for being a fearless stuntwoman. In one film, the martial arts choreographer misjudged a scene which required her to leap from a second-floor window. "When I jumped I clipped the window, kicked myself in the head and passed out as I hit the ground," she recalled. "I came to and asked, 'Did we get the shot?' When they told me we did, I passed out again."

However, at the height of her success in 1970, she retired after marrying the Taiwanese businessman Yuan Wen-tung. She had been shooting another Shaw Brothers film, *Lover's Rock*, in Taiwan and while there her mother, who had accompanied her, lost a sizeable amount of money playing mahjong at Yuan's family home. Cheng met Yuan when she visited the house to pay off her mother's debt. It was love at first sight but Yuan insisted that if they were to marry and start a family she must give up her acting career.

A year later the couple moved to the United States, where she studied for a business degree. She founded her own television production company, for which she made a series of documentaries about Chinese communities in America.

She returned to acting in the 1990s having divorced her husband and was cast in *Crouching Tiger, Hidden Dragon* after interviewing Lee on her Chinese-language American chat show *Pei-Pei's Time*.

Filmed in Mandarin, *Crouching Tiger, Hidden Dragon* became the first foreign-language film to take $100 million at the US box office and grossed $214 million worldwide. "Love in Chinese and western films are communicated differently," Cheng told *Kung Fu magazine*. "But fights are the same and everyone can understand what they're fighting about."

Nominated for ten Academy awards, at the time the most ever for a film not in the English language, *Crouching Tiger, Hidden Dragon* won four along with four Baftas and two Golden Globe awards. It would exert a considerable influence on Quentin Tarantino's *Kill Bill* films.

She never remarried and is survived by a son, Harry Yuan, a film-maker and television presenter, and three daughters, Jennifer Yuan Martin, Marsha Yuan and Eugenia Yuan, all of whom are actors or dancers.

Cheng Pei-pei was born in 1946, in Shanghai, the eldest of four children to Jiang Xuecheng, a businessman and former policeman who was a supporter of Chiang Kai-shek's nationalist Kuomintang party. When the nationalists were defeated by Mao Zedong's Communists, her father was arrested as a counter-revolutionary and in 1952 was sent to a labour camp in Mongolia. She never saw him again.

After training as a dancer in Shanghai, she moved to Hong Kong where she performed in Chinese opera before being discovered by King Hu, who signed her to an exclusive contract with Shaw Brothers.

In later years she moved beyond the martial arts genre and put in an outstanding performance opposite Ben Whishaw in *Lilting* (2014), the acclaimed debut film by the Cambodian-born British director Hong Khaou. Her final role came as The Matchmaker in Disney's 2020 remake of *Mulan*.

Cheng Pei-pei was born on January 6, 1946. She died of a neuro-degenerative disease on July 17, 2024, aged 78

JOHN HURT

John Hurt typically played life's casualties: the eccentric, disturbed, vulnerable, persecuted or lonely. His most celebrated parts include the outrageous homosexual Quentin Crisp in *The Naked Civil Servant* and the disfigured Joseph Merrick in the biopic *The Elephant Man*. "I have done quite a lot of outsider figures," he conceded in an interview in 2008, "but then drama is all about them. Hamlet isn't exactly one of the crowd, is he?"

Hurt didn't play Hamlet, but he was such a staple of the acting world that he lost track of the number of films he had appeared in – probably more than 150, he thought. With a ravaged face that made him look older than his years and a gravelly voice (he was referred to as the actor with the "most distinctive voice in Britain"), Hurt was not by nature cut out to play romantic leads and he rarely essayed comedy. He preferred modern works to the classics, and one of his few incursions into Shakespeare was as the Fool in *King Lear* opposite Laurence Olivier.

Making misfits, victims and lunatics his speciality, he performed across a range of mediums. He first appeared on television in the early 1960s, yet his big break came when he played Crisp in 1975. It was a courageous move, but one that paid off. Decades later he told The Times about his first reading of the script. "It was an absolutely stunning piece of writing; it screamed off the page," he said. "Many people told me it would be the end of my career."

His portrayal brilliantly captured Crisp's flamboyance. Crisp was so impressed that he called the actor "my representative here on Earth". Hurt reprised the role in 2009 for *An Englishman in New York*.

Another of his most well-known television roles came soon after *The Naked Civil Servant*, in the BBC's production of *I, Claudius*. He played the deranged emperor Caligula (mischievously described by Crisp as "only me in a sheet"). More recently he gave a gripping performance as the War Doctor, an earlier incarnation of the Time Lord, in the *Doctor Who* 50th anniversary special.

On the big screen he appeared as the doomed Winston Smith in an adaptation of George Orwell's *Nineteen Eighty-Four* and as Stephen Ward in *Scandal*, depicting the Profumo affair. He provided one of cinema's most memorable moments in Ridley Scott's *Alien*; his character, Kane, met a grisly end when a slime-dropping monster exploded from his chest. Arguably that was trumped by his drug addict in *Midnight Express*, for which he received an Oscar nomination.

He was somewhat disapproving of the prize-giving rigmarole. "I've always felt, and I think I'm qualified to say so because I've won a few awards, that it's a terrible shame to put something in competition with something else to be able to sell something," he said. Yet he was nominated again in 1981 for *The Elephant Man*, in which his face was obscured by prosthetics as he played a celebrity of Victorian England with severe deformities. The part required seven hours in the make-up chair every morning.

Making bold choices was, in many respects, typical of Hurt. He was often portrayed as a hell-raiser, and before he cut down was a prodigious drinker who once confessed to getting through seven bottles of wine a day and said he was surprised to have reached the age of 30. While he enjoyed carousing with thespians including Peter O'Toole and Richard Harris, he did not let such excesses affect his work – although as recently as 2004 he was thrown out of a Spearmint Rhino bar for boorish behaviour.

One of the best performances he gave in his later years was as the Tory MP Alan Clark in a BBC dramatisation of his politically incorrect diaries. Like Clark, Hurt attracted media attention for his drinking and marital vicissitudes. "When you get into the emotional areas, the animal areas, I think you'll find it's the one area where it doesn't seem to matter what intellect you have. Some of the most highly intelligent people I know have got just the same problems when it comes to sexuality, mistakes and things," he said.

Love was indeed complicated territory for Hurt. "I don't necessarily agree with marriage," he once expostulated, but he was willing to experiment, marrying four times. First to the actress Annette Robertson, although the marriage ended in 1964 after two years – Hurt later described the relationship as "ludicrous". His second wife, Donna Peacock, was also an actress and an old friend; theirs was a more enduring affair, but he said later he had been "on the rebound". He married Peacock in 1984, a year after his girlfriend, the French model Marie-Lise Volpeliere-Pierrot, was killed in a horse-riding accident.

Hurt's marriage to Peacock was dissolved in 1990, and he married again that year. Jo Dalton was a production assistant he met while filming *Scandal* ("I was wildly in love with her"). They had two sons: Sasha, born in 1990, and Nick, born in 1993. Although Hurt came late to fatherhood, he embraced it wholeheartedly. Both his sons became interested in the arts: Sasha is a painter, while Nick shares his father's love of acting. Their parents divorced in 1996 (because of Dalton's exasperation with his drinking) and the boys grew up in Co Waterford. Hurt famously remarked that Ireland, where he lived for many years, was "where he belonged", resulting in a fair amount of wounded English pride.

In 2005 he married Anwen Rees-Myers, a film producer 25 years his junior. It was said, though he rejected the assertion, that his fourth wife "reformed" him, and they settled in Norfolk. Finally he could conclude that "life without love is hideous".

John Vincent Hurt was born in Chesterfield, Derbyshire, in 1940. His father, Arnould, was a talented mathematician before he became a High Anglican clergyman, and his mother, Phyllis, was an amateur actress. His upbringing was strict; the family lived opposite a cinema, but Hurt was forbidden from watching films there.

A small and sensitive boy, he went to an Anglo-Catholic prep school in Kent, then to Lincoln grammar school, where he discovered a talent for acting. He often ended up playing female roles, including Lady Bracknell in a school production of *The Importance of Being Earnest*. "I was pretty, I was small – I thought I was very butch, but there you are." Despite his build, he excelled at sport, captaining the school cricket, rugby and football teams.

In later life he revealed that he, along with others, had been abused by a master at his prep school who would take out his false teeth and stick his tongue in boys' mouths. Hurt spoke phlegmatically of the experience. "I think I just accepted what happened. I kind of knew that it couldn't have been quite right, but it was authority." He described himself as a lazy student and, notwithstanding all the scripts he read, he rarely turned to books. ("I'm not a huge reader, I'd rather live.") He was, however, captivated by Richard Dawkins's *The God Delusion.*

There had been an assumption that he would join the church, but he rejected the notion and chose the life of an agnostic. One of his two brothers also rebelled, converting to Catholicism and becoming a monk at Glenstal Abbey in Co Limerick. "It created a huge rift in the family," Hurt said. "To my father it was as though his son was embracing the Antichrist. I'm sure he used that expression." He also had an adopted sister, Monica, who died of variant CJD in 2005.

He enrolled, aged 17, at the Grimsby School of Art and later Central St Martins College of Art and Design in London – where Crisp was, neatly, one of the naked models he sketched as an art student. Throughout his life Hurt enjoyed the company of artists, counting Lucian Freud and Francis Bacon among his closest drinking pals.

A career as a painter was stillborn, and Hurt instead pursued his other childhood passion, gaining a place at the Royal Academy of Dramatic Art. After he graduated his mother kept, until her death, a scrapbook filled with reviews and articles charting his successes. He was offered a small role in a 1962 film, *The Wild and the Willing,* for which he was paid £75 a week. Soon he started performing on the London stage, and while in a production of *Little Malcolm* was noticed by Fred Zinnemann, who cast him as Richard Rich in *A Man for All Seasons.* Within five years Hurt had been nominated for a Bafta for 10 *Rillington Place,* based on the true story of Timothy Evans (played by Hurt), the semi-literate lorry driver who was wrongly hanged for murder.

Hurt's first foray into the classics came when he played Octavius in George Bernard Shaw's *Man and Superman* at the Gaiety Theatre in Dublin. His theatre appearances became more sporadic, but he made a remarkable return in 2000 in a West End production of

Samuel Beckett's *Krapp's Last Tape*. At the turn of the century he also had parts in film adaptations of two bestselling books, playing Dr Iannis, the kindly Greek sage in *Captain Corelli's Mandolin*, and Mr Ollivander, the wand-seller in three films in the Harry Potter series. He won further acclaim in recent years with roles in the political thriller *V for Vendetta* and the Cold War drama *Tinker Tailor Soldier Spy*.

Hurt grew weary, however, of the endless publicity surrounding each new release – especially *Indiana Jones and the Kingdom of the Crystal Skull*. "I don't suppose we could talk about the lack of enjoyment in making it?" he quipped to one journalist. He was also withering about the film's co-creator George Lucas: "It's all to make Mr Lucas an extra billion, as if he needs it."

Although Hurt had a habit of being moody and mercurial in interviews, beneath the complex veneer he could be amusing and thoughtful. He served as patron of the Proteus Syndrome Foundation, which helps those with the condition that is thought to have afflicted Joseph Merrick, and of Project Harar, a charity that supports children in Ethiopia with facial disfigurements.

As the years rolled by, Hurt retained his sense of style and was a loyal client of the tailor John Pearse, who dressed Jimi Hendrix, Bob Dylan, the Rolling Stones and the like. "He makes superb overcoats," Hurt said.

Even in his seventies he continued working relentlessly not least the role of Father Richard McSorley in *Jackie*, the Oscar-nominated biopic of President Kennedy's wife. He admitted that there had been some "stinkers" along the way, but had no time for regrets. "'If' and 'only' are the two words in the English language that should never be put together," he said.

After his cancer diagnosis he was asked about facing death. He replied, "I hope I shall have the courage to say, 'Vroom! Here we go! Let's become different molecules!'"

Sir John Hurt was born on January 22, 1940. He died of cancer on January 25, 2017, aged 77

ROBIN WILLIAMS

With his fast-flowing, stream-of-consciousness comedy, Robin Williams did for stand-up in the 1970s what James Joyce had done for literature half a century earlier. He became a TV star when a guest appearance as an alien on the sitcom *Happy Days* proved so popular that he was given his own show, *Mork and Mindy*. He went on to become a serious dramatic actor and stalwart of Hollywood.

Whether Williams developed his comic genius as a defence mechanism or an appeal for attention, by any standards his was an extraordinary career. He earned Oscar nominations for his various subversive characters in *Good Morning, Vietnam* (1987), *Dead Poets Society* (1989) and *The Fisher King* (1991), before finally clinching the Oscar for best supporting actor in *Good Will Hunting* (1997). "This might be the one time I'm speechless," he claimed as he accepted his award.

When he was the voice of the genie in *Aladdin* (1992), Disney let Williams improvise in front of a microphone (the studio ended up with 30 hours of voices and impressions covering everyone from Robert De Niro to Carol Channing) and then worked the animation around the recordings. It was a landmark performance, with his witty, intelligent and cine-literate genie appealing to adults as well as children.

Subsequently, however, Williams faced criticism for the sentimentality of his films and the very nature of characters that seemed to be screaming out for the audience to love them. He responded by going to the other extreme with some creepy and disturbing villains, playing a murderous crime writer in *Insomnia* (2002) and a photographic technician who keeps pictures of his customers in *One Hour Photo* (2002).

In spite of the brightness of his glittering career, Williams's personal life was plagued by darkness and occasional despair. He made no secret of his problems with drugs and alcohol. A confessed abuser of cocaine (which he referred to as "Peruvian marching powder" and "the devil's dandruff"), his vices informed his comic material. "Cocaine is God's way of telling you that you are making too much money," he once quipped. He was a close friend of the comedy actor John Belushi and had been with him hours before he died of a drug overdose in 1982; the event deeply affected him. Becoming a father the following year prompted Williams to face his own demons.

Romance also spelt trouble for Williams. One brief liaison resulted in a waitress, Michelle Tish Carter, suing him for giving her herpes. The affair ended his first marriage to Valerie Velardi, a dancer with whom he had a son, Zak, in 1983. Soon after their divorce Williams married his son's nanny, Marsha Garces. Their daughter Zelda was born in 1989, followed by their son Cody. After 20 years of sobriety, Williams's alcohol addiction resurfaced and his family intervened. "I went to rehab in wine country just to keep my options open," he joked. His marriage could still not survive – Garces filed for divorce in 2008. The settlements from his two failed marriages cost him $20 million.

In rare serious moments he spoke of his fatherly devotion, but hinted at unhappiness in his own youth. "They only want to be with you up to a certain point and then they are basically looking at you and going 'Keuch, you're an asshole.' So you have that time of maybe five, maybe seven or eight years, when they really want to know and play with you and share with you ... I don't want to miss it with my children ... because I did miss it with my father."

As a boy his favourite book was *The Lion, the Witch and the Wardrobe*, which he shared with his children: "I would read the whole CS Lewis series out loud to my kids. I was once reading to Zelda, and she said, 'Don't do any voices. Just read it as yourself.' So I did, I just read it straight, and she said, 'That's better'."

Robin McLaurin Williams was born in 1951 in Chicago – not in Edinburgh, as was reported once he rose to fame. He blamed a CIA disinformation campaign. Alternatively, he thought it might have had something to do with an early interview he did in a Scottish accent. The interviewer reportedly asked if he was born in Edinburgh. Williams, in jest, praised the journalist's sharpness and confirmed that he was.

He spent his early years in Bloomfield Hills in Michigan before moving to California in his teens. His father was a wealthy Ford executive and his mother was a former model. At one point they lived in a 40-room house on a vast estate – "It was miles to the next kid". A shy and lonely child, he showed an early aptitude for impersonation, and drama gave him a route for self-expression, although he claimed that his real interest in it was simply "to get laid". When he graduated from high school his classmates voted him "most humorous" and "most likely to succeed".

In the early 1970s he went to Juilliard, the performing arts school in New York, where he demonstrated a prodigious talent for accents and dialects. One of his teachers recommended that he focus on comedy. He developed a manic style as a stand-up; by the time the audience had decided whether a remark was funny, he was already several jokes, voices and impersonations further down the line.

After several appearances on *The Richard Pryor Show* he was given a guest spot on the sitcom *Happy Days*. His alien Mork was a throwback to 1950s B-movies, though he looked more like a spaceman than an extra-terrestrial in his space suit and helmet. However, his funny, high-pitched voice and surreal take on reality – sticking his head on a chair when told to take a seat – seemed suitably otherworldly. Mork was given his own series, *Mork and Mindy*, with Pam Dawber as the eponymous earthling who offers him sanctuary in her attic. It ran for four seasons and brought Williams the first of four Golden Globes. In between seasons he took on the challenge of bringing a cartoon character to life in Robert Altman's *Popeye* (1980), but it disappointed at the box office. "If you watch it backwards, it has a plot," Williams later said of the film. *The World According to Garp* (1982) again did only moderate business, though it provided an early display of the bittersweet qualities – the combination of comedy and pathos – that became Williams's trademark.

It was *Good Morning, Vietnam* that finally allowed him to translate his fast-talking comedy to cinema. He played the real-life disc jockey Adrian Cronauer, who proved popular with troops in Vietnam but not the authorities. In *Dead Poets Society*, Williams appeared as a teacher with the self-consciously literary name of John Keating. At odds with the old-fashioned headmaster in an exclusive private school, he instils in his pupils a passion for literature and life, urging them "Carpe diem". The film struck a chord with audiences and some critics, while others found his character unbearably sanctimonious. It was a matter of debate whether the suicide of one pupil was the fault of the system or a direct result of Keating's subversive influence.

In the early Nineties, Williams starred alongside De Niro in *Awakenings*, based on Dr Oliver Sacks's experiments; the beggar-knight searching for the Holy Grail in Terry Gilliam's *The Fisher King*; and an adult Peter Pan forced to return to Neverland when Captain Hook kidnaps his children in Steven Spielberg's *Hook*.

Other hits followed – dramas, comedies and family films including *Mrs Doubtfire*, *Jumanji* and *The Birdcage*. There were a fair number of misfires too, such as *Jack*, in which he acted as a boy in a man's body – childhood and adults who have never really grown up were recurring threads in his work. His performance in *Patch Adams* was well received by audiences but not by the critics, and his Holocaust comedy-drama *Jakob the Liar* was a box-office disaster.

Yet his popularity remained high. In 1997, the same year that *Good Will Hunting* was released, Williams topped *Entertainment Weekly*'s list of the 50 funniest people alive.

In the past decade he provided voices for the animated films *Robots* and *Happy Feet*, and played a wax model of Theodore Roosevelt that comes to life in *Night at the Museum*. It made $250 million in North America, and he recently reprised the role for *Night at the Museum 3*, due to be released in December. He played another president, Dwight D Eisenhower, last year in *The Butler*.

Not long before he divorced for a second time, his half-brother Robert died of complications following heart surgery. In 2009 he had to curtail a stand-up tour when he himself was admitted to hospital with heart problems. Shortly before an operation (which he said had given him "some great new material") he met Susan Schneider, a graphic designer, whom he married two years later.

Williams's warmth and exuberant personality earned him a wide circle of friends. One of his closest was Christopher Reeve, who had been a peer at Julliard. Williams visited Reeve after the horse-riding accident that left him paralysed. He cheered him up by pretending to be an eccentric Russian doctor and claimed that he was there to perform a colonoscopy. Reeve later wrote: "For the first time since the accident, I laughed. My old friend had helped me know that somehow I was going to be OK." After Reeve's death, his widow Dana described the pair as "closer than brothers"; when she died in 2006, Williams provided financial support for their young son.

Williams's source of happiness was fatherhood. "My children give me a great sense of wonder," he said. His daughter Zelda is also an actress, having first starred alongside him in the film *House of D* when she was 15. His youngest son Cody has dabbled as an assistant film director and is believed to have worked on the set of David Cronenberg's *Maps to the Stars*.

Williams had recently been suffering from severe depression and in June entered a rehabilitation centre. He was a member of the Episcopal Church and his interests included cycling (he owned more than 50 bicycles) and jazz. He was also a video games enthusiast (his daughter was named after the princess in *The Legend of Zelda* series).

Williams's comic genius both on and off screen seemed to touch on every element of the human spirit. As he assures his pupils in *Dead Poets Society*, "No matter what people tell you, words and ideas can change the world."

Robin Williams was born on July 21, 1951. He was found dead on August 11, 2014, aged 63

CHARLIE CHAPLIN

He was the last survivor from among the founding fathers of the American cinema, one of the greatest comic creators in film, and achieved greater, more widespread fame in his own lifetime than perhaps anyone else in the history of mankind. He was the darling of the intellectuals, who loved to theorise on the significance of his comedy, its social responsibility, its relation to the great tradition of *commedia dell'arte* and circus clowning, its anarchic force and vigour. But he also had to a unique degree the common touch – people of virtually any culture were able to respond with laughter to his screen antics, and for generation after generation of children he was the first introduction to the magic world of the cinema.

During the latter part of his long life Chaplin, though loaded with honours and universally regarded as one of the unshakeable monuments of the cinema (whatever controversy his political attitudes might arouse), did begin to suffer from a certain reaction to the excesses of his early admirers. This had something to do with a grudging but progressive disenchantment with his later films, and something to do with the rediscovery and revaluation of the work of his many rivals in silent comedy.

As we moved into the 1950s it became permissible to prefer the refined and unsentimental art of Buster Keaton, who was certainly a far more subtle and imaginative film-maker than Chaplin could ever claim to be, or even the totally unpretentious humour of Laurel and Hardy. The time was coming, in fact, for a thorough reassessment of Chaplin's own work, concentrating on aspects of it which would be more congenial to modern sensibilities: the elements of childlike ruthlessness which had endeared it to the Surrealists, perhaps, rather than the sentimentalising elevation of the "little man" which had made him a hero to liberal humanists.

As with Chaplin's performances, so with his career as a whole, the secret of his success lay in his immaculate timing. His gift was essentially pantomimic, and so ideally suited to the silent cinema. He came into films at a period when the various functions of film-making were undefined, so that anyone with a strong idea of what he wanted to do (which Chaplin certainly had, almost from the outset) was free to go ahead and do it. Having got in on the ground floor, he was able, with the aid of extraordinary business acumen, to build at once on his great success with the public in order to become rich and powerful as well as famous – even in these early days Chaplin off screen, the budding tycoon and central figure in many an over-publicised romantic drama, was sharply differentiated from the somewhat pathetic underdog he played in films, with his cane and baggy pants, his slum-bred cunning, and his understandable tendency to be overlooked by the girl of his dreams. By the beginning of the 1920s he was his own master in films, able to do exactly what he wanted, in exactly the way he wanted – and in his own time.

And with the coming of sound, he alone was able to fight a long rearguard action, making what were in effect silent films with the addition of music and sound effects, and in *The Great Dictator* a little localised speech, until right into the 1940s. He had had the foresight to own outright and control all his mature works and to withhold them from general release for years at a time, so that each reappearance of a Chaplin film had a sense of occasion all its own. And even his later contretemps with the American authorities over his flirtations with Marxism and his staunchly preserved British nationality, which resulted in some years of exile from America, was eventually resolved to the complete satisfaction of both sides.

The central figure of this almost totally satisfactory and successful life, Charles Spencer Chaplin, was born in 1889, at East Lane, Walworth, and his childhood was spent at 3 Parnell Terrace, Kennington Road. His father was of mixed French and Irish descent, and his mother had gypsy blood in her veins. Both were well-known in the music halls of their day.

His childhood was an unhappy one, and when Charles was five his mother, who was never strong, found that the problems of looking after the family in the face of poverty and adversity had become too much for her. Charles and his half-brother Sydney were therefore sent to an orphanage. This was a great shock to the sensitive child and it gave him a sense of insecurity which was to haunt him throughout his life.

He emerged from the orphanage in March 1896, and became a waif of the London slums. His first stage appearance was made soon after at the age of seven, when he performed a clog dance: three years later he was appearing in music halls all over the country as one of The Eight Lancashire Lads. Then for a short time he became a legitimate actor, and played Billy the office boy, in *Sherlock Holmes*, and was also seen as one of the wolves in the first production of *Peter Pan*.

When he was 17 Charles Chaplin joined Fred Karno's pantomime group, and in 1910 was taken as first comedian on the company's tour of the United States. In 1913 he was seen in New York by Mack Sennett, America's foremost producer of comedy films, playing a drunk in a sketch called *A Night in an English Music Hall*, and was taken on as a film comedian to replace Ford Sterling.

Chaplin was reluctant to leave Karno, and his early days in Hollywood only confirmed these doubts. His first film, in which he appeared in a frock coat and top hat, was a failure. Later he adopted the tramp costume of the baggy trousers and ill-fitting suit, but it was not until the making of Tillie's *Punctured Romance* in 1914, with Marie Dressler and Mabel Normand, that he became famous.

Chaplin made about 40 comedies for Sennett, then made 14 for Essanay, and in 1916 he went over to the Mutual Company after signing a contract for what was, in those days, an unheard-of salary. But by now he was world famous, and was writing and directing his own films. More important still was the fact that the character of "the little fellow", as the tramp was always known to his creator, had become firmly established in his mind.

For Mutual, Chaplin made some of his best short comedies, including *The Floorwalker, The Rink*, and *Easy Street*. In 1918 he joined First National, and for them made eight films, including *A Dog's Life* and *Shoulder Arms*. Then he built his own film studios and formed his own company, and in 1919 he joined with the other leading film-makers of the period – DW Griffith, Douglas Fairbanks and Mary Pickford – in forming the United Artists Corporation.

The 1920s were the golden age of the silent cinema, and Chaplin entered this golden age with wealth, power, authority and complete freedom as an independent producer of his own work. To this period belong *The Kid* (1920) with Jackie Coogan, *The Gold Rush* (1925) with Mack Swain, and *The Circus* (1928) with Merna Kennedy. During this period he also startled the film world by writing and directing a picture in which he did not himself appear. This was *A Woman of Paris* (1923), with Adolphe Menjou and Edna Purviance – an interesting and original work, but one that attempted a sophisticated elegance which was not really within Chaplin's province and which Lubitsch was shortly to undertake with much more success in *The Marriage Circle*.

Up to this point in his career there was little room for controversy of any kind: his popularity was unchallenged, and even *A Woman of Paris* enjoyed considerable success, on its own merits rather than as a Chaplin film. It seems likely now that his lasting reputation will rest most securely on the films he made between 1916 and 1928: later reissues of *The Gold Rush, The Kid, Shoulder Arms, Easy Street* and other films of this era in sparkling new prints with musical soundtracks composed by Chaplin himself confirmed their power over new generations of filmgoers, while *The Circus*, which Chaplin had never considered one of his better films, came as a revelation when shown again in this new form. But from the beginning of the sound era things become more arguable. There were many, and are still, who regard *City Lights* (1931) as his finest film. But for others the sentiment in the "little fellow's" love for a blind flower girl becomes cloying and for the first time a deathly self-consciousness about the character's symbolism and message for the world seems to intrude.

In this film Chaplin resolutely turned his back on the talkie, making a silent film with the musical accompaniment on the soundtrack instead of live in the theatre. He used the same approach in *Modern Times* (1936), a would-be satire of the mechanisation of man and, despite funny moments, demonstrated rather clearly that satire and explicit messages were not Chaplin's forte.

It was no doubt inevitable that eventually Chaplin would have to talk on the screen, and he took the plunge at the end of *The Great Dictator* (1940), with a six-minute speech driving home the point of his satire at the expense of Hitler and Mussolini. Most of the film remained speechless, however; it was the swansong of Chaplin's little man character, in the shape of the humble Jewish barber with an uncanny resemblance to a Hitler-like dictator also played by Chaplin.

Monsieur Verdoux (1947) marked a complete break with the past: a talkative "comedy of murders" suggested by the life and career of Landru, it gave us a suave, middle-aged Chaplin very different from anything we had seen before. For the first time it is unavoidable to see the limitations of Chaplin's skill as a film director rather than as a performer – the film is stiff and stagy in the extreme, and not too well written either, in a context where high style is a necessity. *Limelight* (1952) was something of a return to form, however: unashamedly Victorian and sentimental in its tale of an ageing clown's love for a waif-like ballet dancer, it took on an indefinable quality from Chaplin's own nostalgic re-creation of his early days in the London theatre, and at least it did not even try for most of its length to be funny.

Its appearance marked the beginning of an unhappy period in Chaplin's life. When he left America for the European premiere the State Department banned his re-entry (which they could do as he had never become an American citizen), and Chaplin took up residence, at first resentfully, in Switzerland. His next film, *The King in New York* (1957), made in Britain and for long unseen in America, was a bitter but ineffectual satire on America and the American way of life, notable chiefly for Chaplin's succumbing to what is supposed to be the classic comic's temptation, that of playing Hamlet, with an unfortunate rendition of "To be or not to be" during a New York dinner party. But the anger on both sides, product of those witch-hunting days, gradually subsided as Chaplin moved into an honoured old age.

His last film, *A Countess from Hong Kong* (1966), was a light romantic comedy starring Marlon Brando and Sophia Loren, based on a script he had written for himself and his then wife Paulette Goddard in 1938 and showing signs of its age; for the first time since his earliest days he was working for someone else (the film was completely financed by Universal), and for the first time since *A Woman of Paris* he himself made only a token appearance. The film was kindly received, if with many reservations, and was an almost total disaster at the box office.

Nevertheless Chaplin made definite plans to direct yet another film, *The Freak*, starring one of his younger daughters, but the increasingly delicate state of his health precluded him from doing so. In 1973 he was at last received back with open arms into the American film establishment, given a special Oscar in recognition of his lifetime contribution to film art, and commemorated with a statue at the historic corner of Hollywood and Vine. In 1975 he was made KBE in the New Year's Honours.

During the intervals of film-making Chaplin wrote *My Autobiography* (1964), a fascinating if in certain respects disingenuous document which is of particular value for its vivid evocation of the London of his childhood and his early struggles in the theatre; the latter parts become heavy with dropped names and grievances rehearsed. In fact his off-screen life was considerably more eventful than the book gives one to suppose, and his three earliest marriages, to Mildred Harris, Lita Gray and Paulette Goddard (who had starred opposite him in *Modern Times* and *The Great Dictator*) were stormy, plagued by scandal, and ended in divorce. His last marriage, to Oona O'Neill, daughter of Eugene O'Neill, brought him happiness, repose and several children, one of whom, Geraldine, achieved considerable success in her own right acting in films, as had Sydney, the older of his two sons by Lita Gray. His old age was a satisfying crown to a life of activity and creative endeavour, bringing honours and reconciliation and universal reverence for the man and his work. Whatever the ups and downs of taste in the years to come, his greatness as a clown and his crucial role in the history and serious acceptance of the cinema as an art form are certain to stand the tests of time.

Sir Charlie Chaplin was born on April 16, 1889. He died following a stroke on December 25, 1977, aged 88

LAUREN BACALL

———————————•———————————

She was only 19, with little acting experience, but Lauren Bacall's first screen appearance – along with her marriage to her co-star Humphrey Bogart – gave her an early celebrity from which, despite her best efforts, she never escaped.

The extraordinary initial impact of her tumbling blonde hair and heavy-lidded almond eyes as she appeared, cigarette between her lips, in *To Have and Have Not* left an indelible impression on audiences. For her habit of pressing down her chin and glancing up (which, she claimed, was a way of overcoming nerves) she was known simply as "The Look". In her deep, husky voice – cultivated by hours spent reading aloud on her own – she told Bogart's character that if he wanted her, all he had to do was whistle: "You know how to whistle, don't you Steve? You just put your lips together … and blow." As one reviewer wrote: "Lauren Bacall has cinema personality to burn."

And Bogart agreed: she was, he said, "steel with curves". The pair's romantic, wisecracking chemistry and real-life love affair (which ended with Bacall nursing him through cancer) became the stuff of Hollywood legend – although Bacall, who was famously outspoken, was always dismissive of celebrity culture.

A formidable actress, she progressed from precocious femme fatale to Broadway star with two Tony awards and more than 60 films to her name. She remarried, raised three children almost entirely alone and had an affair with Frank Sinatra. But, decades after Bogart's death, she still had to protest that her life and her career had moved on. "Being a widow," she complained, "isn't exactly a profession". Bogart, however, remained the prime topic for newspaper interviewers and television talk show hosts. And Bacall admitted: "Bogie's presence permeated my life ... I'll never get away from it nor should I and don't wish to."

Lauren Bacall was born Betty Jean Perske – her friends always knew her as Betty – into a family of Jewish immigrants from Europe in Brooklyn, New York, in 1924. Shimon Peres, the future prime minister and president of Israel, was a first cousin. "I was a nice Jewish girl," she said. Her father, a salesman, left home when she was six and she was brought up by an ambitious mother, whose maiden name, Bacal, she adopted with the addition of an extra letter. Lauren, which she hated, was a Hollywood invention, bestowed by the director who discovered her, Howard Hawks.

As a girl she used to skip school and sit in the back of the cinema watching her idol Bette Davis on screen. Determined to follow in her heroine's footsteps, she trained as a dancer and attended the American Academy of Dramatic Art (where she briefly dated Kirk Douglas). When small parts in two Broadway plays led nowhere she tried modelling. "I was this flat-chested, big-footed, lanky thing," she said. However, in 1943, she appeared on the cover of Harper's Bazaar where she was spotted by Slim Hawks, the wife of Howard Hawks. The director was hunting for a different kind of star, "a woman with a masculine approach, insolent, someone who could give as good as she got," Bacall reflected. He immediately put her under contract and, in 1944, cast her opposite Bogart's tough fisherman in *To Have and Have Not*, a French Resistance adventure loosely based on a story by Ernest Hemingway.

Hawks encouraged her to develop her already husky voice by practising in quiet places: "Who sat on mountaintops in cars reading books aloud to the canyons?" she wrote. "I did." However, "The Look" she claimed was an accident. As the cameras rolled, she said, "My hand was shaking. My head was shaking. The cigarette was shaking. I was mortified. The harder I tried to stop, the more I shook." She found the only way to hold her trembling head still was to "keep it down, chin low, almost to the chest, and eyes up at Bogart". Promotional posters dubbed her, "Slinky! Sultry! Sensational!" and, although critics were dismayed at the butchering of Hemingway's novel, a new star was born.

Moreover, Bacall and Bogart had fallen in love off screen. Three weeks into filming Bacall was preparing for the final shot of the day: "I was sitting at the dressing table in the portable dressing room combing my hair. Bogie came in to bid me good night. He was standing behind me, we were joking as usual, when suddenly he leaned over, put his hand under my chin, and kissed me." It was her first love affair. (She later said her reaction on hearing she might be cast with Bogart had been: "Humphrey Bogart – yuck.")

The omens were not initially good. Bogart was 45, Bacall was 20 (he nicknamed her "Baby"). Bogart, a habitual womaniser, was on his third marriage and his wife Mayo Methot was famous for her jealous fits of anger. The affair had to be conducted over secret lunches. However, in May 1945, they were married and set up home in the Hollywood Hills. The journalist Alastair Cooke, who became a close friend of the couple, once described their appeal: "So to the curious animal magnetism of Bogart, as of an attractive armadillo, was now added the pleasure of beauty mated with the beast."

It proved to be a warm and close relationship. Bacall gave Bogart much-needed emotional stability after the previous turmoil in his private life. He reduced his drinking and became the proud father of Stephen, named after his character in *To Have and Have Not*, and a daughter, Leslie, a tribute to Leslie Howard who had given Bogart his Hollywood break. For Bacall, still new to the film business, Bogart was an indispensable guide to the Hollywood jungle as well as a shrewd tutor in cinema technique: "He would tell me things and say, 'Long after I've gone, you'll remember this.' He was right."

Meanwhile, on screen, they had further memorable jousts in Hawks's adaptation of the Raymond Chandler thriller, *The Big Sleep* (1946), he as the cynical world-weary private eye, Philip Marlowe, she as a rich divorcee, and in Delmer Daves's *Dark Passage*, in which Bogart was a convicted murderer out to prove his innocence, and John Huston's moody *Key Largo*. They were also both active on the political left and in 1947 led a protest by Hollywood stars in Washington (captured in a celebrated photograph) against an investigation into the alleged communist subversion of the film industry.

However, after its electric start, Bacall's career now faltered. Hawks disliked the influence of her relationship with Bogart, while she increasingly refused parts she thought unsuitable and later got herself suspended on several occasions from Warner Brothers. She came back strongly as one of the trio of gold diggers in *How to Marry a Millionaire* (1953), billed after Marilyn Monroe and Betty Grable but upstaging them both with her incisive comic playing. However, Bogie, she said, wanted a wife, not an actress – and she was happy to play this role. "I would not have had a better life, but a better career," she said later of her choice. When Bogart was sent to Africa for the filming of *The African Queen*, she travelled with him. She helped with the catering on set but also struck up a friendship with Katharine Hepburn.

By the mid-1950s Bogart had developed cancer of the oesophagus. In the last few months of his life when he was in desperate pain and confined to the house, Bacall nursed him devotedly and rarely went out in the evening so as to be at his side. That, Bogart said, is "the way you tell the ladies from the broads in this town". His death in January 1957 was something she never got over: "He was my mentor, my teacher and the love of my life." Decades later she would start a sentence, "Bogie used to say ...".

There followed a much-publicised and brief engagement to Frank Sinatra. The pair had become close in the 1940s when Bacall was known as the "den mother" of the Rat Pack (over which Bogart then presided). After Bogart's death she joined Sinatra cruising on a yacht. It was leaked to the press that he had proposed and when

Bacall let it be known that she had already sold her house in preparation for moving in with the singer, Sinatra called it off. They didn't speak again for years. He was, she said, "a complete shit": "Do me a favour, never mention me in the same breath as Frank Sinatra." Several years later, in 1961, Bacall married the actor Jason Robards. Observers remarked that she fell for him because he seemed to closely resemble Bogart. They had a son, Sam, but the relationship foundered on Robards's alcoholism and ended in divorce in 1969.

Bacall renewed her career with determination and vigour, although with fewer screen successes than before: "I spent my childhood in New York, riding on subways and buses. And you know what you learn if you're a New Yorker? The world doesn't owe you a damn thing." In 1959 she played a Victorian governess opposite Kenneth More in the British film, *North West Frontier*, but it was eight years before she was next on screen, among the all-star cast of suspects in Agatha Christie's *Murder on the Orient Express*.

Meanwhile, she had made a successful return to the Broadway stage, in the comedies *Goodbye Charlie* and *Cactus Flower*, and in *Applause*. Her performance as an ageing Broadway star under threat from a younger rival won her a Tony award. "Miss Bacall is a honey," wrote The Times. She won a second Tony in 1981 for the musical *Woman of the Year* and four years later she was in London in Tennessee Williams's *Sweet Bird of Youth* directed by Harold Pinter.

She received her first Oscar nomination in 1996 as Barbra Streisand's mother in the romantic comedy, *The Mirror Has Two Faces*, but the award went to Juliette Binoche for *The English Patient*. She knew, too, the fear of a bad review and how it felt when the phone ceased ringing with offers for auditions. As she approached her 80th birthday her film career enjoyed an unexpected late revival with a sharp performance in the allegorical *Dogville* (2003), from the Danish director, Lars von Trier, and starring Nicole Kidman.

She supported Kidman again, playing her mother, in the thriller *Birth*, which led to a famous exchange at the Venice Film Festival. A television reporter asked her about "working alongside another screen legend, Nicole Kidman". To which Bacall retorted: "She's not a legend, she's a beginner", adding: "She can't be a legend at whatever age she is, you have to be older." She answered critics: "I figure I'm old enough I can say anything I please and if they don't like it they can take a dive."

Her autobiography, *By Myself,* rose to the top of the US bestsellers in the late 1970s. Typically, she spurned ghost writers and penned it herself. Two decades later she wrote a second memoir, *Now,* tackling her increasing loneliness as her children left home.

Stephen, her son with Bogart, became a television producer and author, publishing an account of his father, while her daughter Leslie became a yoga instructor. Sam, her son with Robards, is an actor. Bacall lived in an apartment in Manhattan and had a much-loved dog, Sophie, who slept on her pillow.

She did not marry again: "There's an acute shortage of real men these days. I don't mean that in a macho sense, but simply men who know where they are going and what they are about." Her tongue remained unfailingly quick. "Remember what Bogie and my mother both used to say," she said in a recent interview: "'Character is the most important thing. All that matters is character!'"

Lauren Bacall was born on September 16, 1924. She died on August 12, 2014, aged 89

PETER O'TOOLE

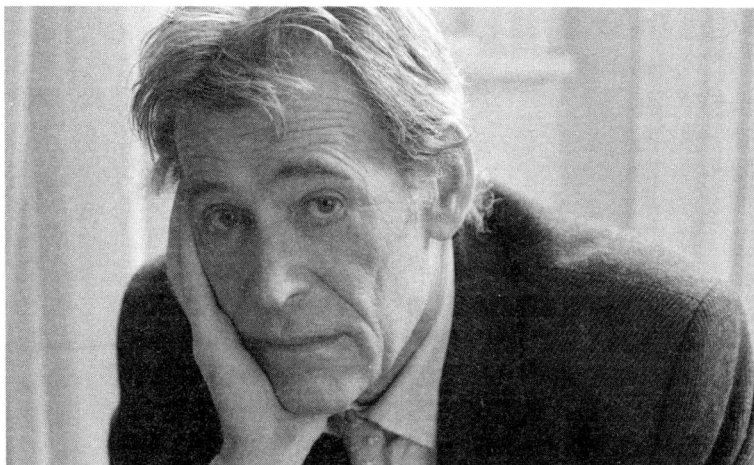

Peter O'Toole was a leader among the roistering generation of British actors. Like Richard Burton, Richard Harris and Nicol Williamson he had immense talent and a rather lesser quantity of self-discipline, especially when it came to drink. All were capable of reaching the heights and indeed did so, but all were also happy to indulge themselves, especially in their younger years when the body was still willing.

When they were around, life would not be quiet and stories would begin to fly, as gossip columnists and showbiz reporters soon recognised. In 1963 the risk was taken of casting O'Toole and Burton together, as king and cleric, in the film of Jean Anouilh's *Becket*. Rumours of heroic drinking in the local pubs began to buzz around the set at Shepperton Studios. However, both men, who at the time were close to their apex in terms of box-office appeal, were greater than their capacity for self-indulgence. The film, to general surprise, was completed on schedule and was a success.

It was not always so. Peter O'Toole had his full share of failures, which he shrugged off as a professional gambler might dismiss a large losing bet. The most notorious was the 1980 *Macbeth* at the Old Vic. O'Toole had been called in to give some glamour back to a house which had become notably short of it after Peter Hall's National Theatre company had left the Waterloo Road. The first night was a calamity as O'Toole crashed into scenery and had the normally decorous Vic audience chortling as he came on covered head to foot in red paint after the murder of Duncan.

This Macbeth was a *succès de rire*, but it looked as though it might be the end of O'Toole's stage career. It was not. He hauled himself back during the 1980s by way of Shaw in the West End. And then, as he was approaching 60, he struck up an unlikely partnership with the director Ned Sherrin and the writer Keith Waterhouse. This led to *Jeffrey Bernard is Unwell* and *Our Song*. The voice, never O'Toole's strongest card, might have been weaker, but the presence was still magical. The body remained slim and the blue eyes retained their ability to mesmerise. There were plenty of hints of the golden boy, whose tall Irish good looks filmed so well. "A beautiful, emaciated secretary bird" was how Burton described him at the time of *Becket*. It was no surprise that a couple of years later the likes of Romy Schneider, Capucine and Ursula Andress were throwing themselves at him in one of the 1960s' wackier screen comedies, *What's New, Pussycat?*

Perhaps Seamus Peter O'Toole's roller-coaster career could have been foretold from his childhood. The place and date of his birth were something of a mystery which even O'Toole himself seemed unable to solve. In his first volume of autobiography, *Loitering with Intent* (1992), he wrote that the family claimed his birth to be in Ireland in June 1932, but that there was a further record of it at "an accident hospital" in England two months later. His *Who's Who* entry gave the date as August 2 and most sources settled for Connemara rather than Leeds, where he grew up in a poor working-class area.

His father was "Capt" Pat O'Toole, who, his son reckoned, never captained anything grander than a football team. He was, like Albert Finney's father, a bookmaker, but of the itinerant kind, setting up his stool, satchel, stand and umbrella on course. Sometimes he did not even bother to do that: he just had a bet. Peter O'Toole spoke and wrote of this man, a serious drinker whose favourite reading was The Racegoer's Annual Form and Handicap Book, with some affection, as he did of his mother, who preferred Dickens and Robert Burns and encouraged a love of literature.

The boy Peter had little schooling and no taste for school discipline and at 15 he joined the *Yorkshire Evening News* as a cub reporter, but he decided quite early on that he would prefer to be written about than do the writing. After National Service in the Royal Navy, which he regarded as a total waste, he got into RADA, with a little flamboyance and the help of a suit borrowed at the YMCA around the corner. Among his fellow students were Alan Bates and Albert Finney. His professional apprenticeship was at the Bristol Old Vic, whose standards were high enough in the late 1950s to merit the occasional London season. In one of these he made his West End debut in *Major Barbara* – Shaw was to remain a favourite playwright.

He did little to diminish his roustabout reputation. On one occasion in Bristol he decided to visit his friend Frank Finlay who was staying in the YMCA. It was the middle of the night and the YMCA was locked. As Michael Freedland wrote in his biography, *Peter O'Toole*: "Peter's solution was to climb through the window – even though it was four storeys up. Fortified by the night's supply of liquor, the long O'Toole legs shinned up the window ledges of the lower floors and found themselves inside Finlay's room. 'Open up,' he called. 'What the hell are you doin' here,' Finlay asked. Peter produced a bottle and all was well."

On another occasion he turned up at the stage door bruised and cut as if he'd been in a fight. His director, Nat Brenner, asked him why he kept courting trouble – "I need it," O'Toole said. "I need to feed on it in order to inform myself about these people."

At Bristol O'Toole played everything from John Osborne's Jimmy Porter to Hamlet, but it was not until 1959 that he gave a performance which caught London's attention. The play was Willis Hall's *The Long and the Short and the Tall* at the Royal Court, directed by Lindsay Anderson. Kenneth Tynan, astutest of talent spotters, picked out O'Toole, playing the foul-mouthed cockney sergeant, from a cast which also included Robert Shaw and Ronald Fraser, sensing "a technical authority that may, given discipline and purpose, presage greatness". Peter Hall agreed and straight away whisked him off to Stratford to play an improbably young but admired Shylock and a rather more appropriately cast Petruchio.

The film career was beginning, with a small part in *Kidnapped* and a better one in *The Day They Robbed the Bank of England*. Sam Spiegel and David Lean were looking for someone to play the title role in *Lawrence of Arabia*. Marlon Brando and Albert Finney had said no. O'Toole was summoned to the Connaught Hotel to meet Spiegel and did not make the best of first impressions when a half-consumed bottle of whisky fell from his overcoat pocket.

However, mainly thanks to Lean's influence, he won the role. The director's confidence was justified. Although at 6ft-plus he was far taller than the 5ft 5in subject, O'Toole probably never surpassed on screen his TE Lawrence and regularly paid tribute to Lean's influence. The performance won him the first of many Oscar nominations, but he must have regretted that the biggest success came so early.

On stage things were different. He was over-flamboyant in *Baal*, an early – and not very good – Brecht at the Phoenix. And his much-publicised *Hamlet*, the opening production of the National Theatre at the Old Vic in 1963, did not win much applause either. By this time he had wed the Welsh actress Sian Phillips, a marriage which was to last some 20 years, often stormy despite the genuine love between them. O'Toole expected her to sacrifice her career for his and she had to endure not only his drinking but the drunken rages which followed. She finally left him for a younger man. However, they did appear together in a number of films as well as on the stage, notably in David Mercer's *Ride a Cock Horse* (1965).

The bulk of his career was being devoted to the cinema, where his striking looks, including that bony face, made him a bankable star. Some of the films were costly failures, such as the dull and un-Conradian *Lord Jim*. He was better in straightforward costume pieces, such as *Becket* and *The Lion in Winter* in which he again played Henry II, this time opposite Katharine Hepburn. Both Henrys made the Oscars shortlist.

His sense of comedy was developing and directors started to cast him as quirky, spiky characters, such as the mad aristo in *The Ruling Class* and, eventually, Don Quixote in the musical *Man of la Mancha*, opposite Sophia Loren. There was, too, a sentimental remake of *Goodbye, Mr Chips*, which in no way measured up to the Robert Donat original.

In the mid-1960s he abandoned the London stage for Dublin, appearing in *Waiting for Godot* at the Abbey. O'Toole was becoming fonder of the land of his fathers, and not just for tax reasons. However, he was also suffering from bad health: stomach and abdominal pains sometimes required hospital attention, which he tried to conceal for fear it would lose him lucrative film offers. Some of O'Toole's heavy drinking at the time has been ascribed to the physical pain he was suffering.

In 1973 he went back to his old alma mater, the Bristol Old Vic, for a generally successful season which took in Chekhov and Ben Travers. He was acquiring a reputation in the cinema for being difficult and at times unreliable, and medical orders to give up drinking did not improve his temper. In 1975 a stomach operation brought him close to death but he recovered to make a rare appearance on television, playing the would-be assassin of Hitler in a polished production of *Rogue Male*.

The Old Vic *Macbeth* came at a low point in his fortunes but his resilience had not deserted him. When reporters staked out his home waving the appalling first night notices O'Toole answered them with reasonable good humour. And at the Old Vic he did at least fill the theatre, as voyeurs came in the hope of seeing a repetition of the opening night calamities.

In the 1980s O'Toole made, amid a lot of dross, films which were critically well received.

His scary movie director in *The Stunt Man* and fading Hollywood star brought down by drink in *My Favourite Year* did much to revive his career. Neil Jordan's comedy *High Spirits* disappointed but he made a big impact in a small part as tutor to the young Chinese ruler in Bernardo Bertolucci's *The Last Emperor*. On stage he clawed his way back to the West End with the help of his trusted Shaw, first with *Man and Superman* (Haymarket, 1982) in which he brought panache to an otherwise insipid production, then with *Pygmalion* and *The Apple Cart*.

Real success returned, however, a little improbably, with what appeared to be a minor play called *Jeffrey Bernard is Unwell* in 1989. Keith Waterhouse fashioned it from the boozy memories of *The Spectator* columnist, a one-time drinking companion of O'Toole's. It looked set for a coterie audience of Soho and Fleet Street habitués. In the hands of O'Toole and his director, Ned Sherrin, however, it acquired wings and filled the house. O'Toole was Jeffrey Bernard: even Bernard thought so. And when he was replaced by another actor the evening scarcely worked.

He was enticed into John Osborne's return to Jimmy Porter, *Déjà Vu*, with his daughter Katherine also in the cast, but argued with the author over the length and loquacity of the text. O'Toole's instincts were right. When *Déjà Vu* eventually arrived in the West End with Peter Egan as Jimmy it had a miserably short run. O'Toole made the right choice again when he joined a second Waterhouse–Sherrin enterprise, *Our Song* (1992), in which, chain-smoking and with almost fluting voice, he played a middle-aged executive besotted with a woman (Tara FitzGerald) less than half his age. Its run was cut short when O'Toole was hauled back for yet another hospital examination.

Apart from a later revival of *Jeffrey Bernard is Unwell* it was the end of a theatrical career which had promised so much. After the disastrous *Macbeth* there was no more Shakespeare and he eschewed the other big classical roles by which the best actors are judged. From now on it was films and television, much of it routine and undistinguished, though he kept busy and retained the knack to surprise.

After seven nominations without a win he was put forward for an honorary life achievement Oscar in 2002. He initially turned it down, telling the Academy of Motion Picture Arts and Sciences that he was "still in the game and might win the lovely bugger outright". He had yet another chance when nominated for his touching portrayal of an elderly actor in lecherous pursuit of the young Jodie Whittaker in *Venus* (2006).

It was his first lead role in years, completed despite breaking his hip midway through shooting, but once more the Oscar went elsewhere. On television he and David Tennant were the older and younger Casanova for the BBC and he played the Pope who excommunicates Henry VIII in *The Tudors*. By then he was in his late seventies and the years of hard living were reflected in a haggard appearance but he showed no sign of wanting to slow down.

His marriage to Sian Phillips was dissolved in 1979. They had two daughters, Katherine and Patricia. In 1983, at the age of 50, he had a son, Lorcan, with an American model, Karen Sommerville, but their relationship ended soon afterwards and the boy became the subject of a long and public custody battle.

Peter O'Toole was born on August 2, 1932. He died of cancer on December 14, 2013, aged 81

MARLON BRANDO

For the generation of cinemagoers which came of age in the 1950s, Marlon Brando was role model, icon and high priest. He had the fortune to arrive in Los Angeles when Hollywood was entering a period of serious moviemaking. He had the talent to embrace the first half-dozen roles offered to him and he put an indelible personal stamp on each of them.

He exuded a new kind of male sexuality, rough and sweating, as Stanley Kowalski in *A Streetcar Named Desire* (1951). The Brando uniform of white T-shirt, often grubby, and jeans, often torn, became de rigeur for males in America and later in Europe. Some have even credited Brando with inventing the combination.

In the title role of *Viva Zapata!* (1952) he fought against injustice and in *The Wild One* (1954), wearing another uniform, this time of black leathers, he took arms against bourgeois values. That low-budget film was effective enough in its rebelliousness to fall foul of the censors, especially in Britain, mainly on the grounds that the gang of bikers, led by Brando's Johnnie, was not seen to be punished sufficiently by the time the final reel came round.

For a time Brando specialised in playing men who broke society's rules. He also spawned a new school of actors, many of them trained in – or imitating – the Stanislavsky-inspired Method. Without Brando there would probably have been no James Dean, perhaps no Al Pacino.

When he was cast as Mark Antony alongside John Gielgud and James Mason in the film of *Julius Caesar* (1953) there was much derision. But Brando proved worthy of the part and silenced a good number of the sneerers. His theatre schooling under the likes of Stella Adler stood him in good stead.

His screen career reached its apex in the role of Terry Malloy in *On the Waterfront* (1954). Again he was a rebel against injustice, but this time the enemy was comprised of the mobsters of New York's dockland.

Surrounded by actors of the calibre of Lee J Cobb, Karl Malden and Rod Steiger, whose style, nurtured by the Group Theater, accorded with Brando's own, he shone as a good man in a dirty world. Most important of all, he had the directorial hand of Elia Kazan, who knew how to handle Brando as few other directors did.

After *On the Waterfront* the Brando reputation slumped for almost 20 years. Films rolled out at regular intervals; some were entertaining and others were outright failures. None truly exploited his talent. Few Hollywood superstars suffered such an eclipse.

The critics who had once vied with one another with superlatives turned against him, and Brando likewise against them. He became "difficult" and reclusive, more likely to appear on the news pages espousing the cause of an ethnic minority or squabbling over alimony than in the showbusiness section. His waistline expanded considerably while his hair thinned. The icon still hung on the wall, but only for the nostalgically inclined.

In 1972, *The Godfather* changed that. Brando fought hard to win the part of Don Corleone – Paramount had wanted Olivier – and once he got it he proved his worth. He was also in a box-office hit after a number of films which had shown little or no return. It was immediately followed by *Last Tango in Paris* (1972), which ran foul of the censors as *The Wild One* had two decades previously. But this time round the aura of sexual explicitness, and sadism in particular, did *Last Tango* no harm at all.

Under Bertolucci's direction Brando towered over the film and certainly eclipsed his now forgotten co-star Maria Schneider. Briefly he was back in favour among the intellectuals.

It did not last long. After the chaotic *Missouri Breaks* (1976) Brando appeared to content himself with cameo parts, often in big-budget productions for either television or the cinema. *Roots* and *Apocalypse Now* (both 1979) were among them. The budgets had to be high because Brando's appearance fees were considerable: he worked when he felt the need to add a few noughts to his bank account. Most notoriously, he was paid $3m for his ten-minute appearance in *Superman* (1978), and he then sued for a share of the gross.

Many explanations have been offered for Brando's slide from eminence. He did not age gracefully in the way of, say, Paul Newman or Britain's clutch of theatrical knights who never gave up or gave in. Richard Schickel, the most perceptive of Brando's several biographers, has suggested that he never felt the true compulsion to go on acting and simply "drifted into self-absorption".

Others have blamed the instability of his early upbringing, as Brando shouldered much of the censure when Christian, his oldest son, was charged with murder (later reduced to manslaughter) in 1990. Brando's mother, Dorothy, was an alcoholic, but she still managed to be one of the pillars of the Omaha Community Playhouse, whose actors at the time included Henry Fonda.

His father, Marlon Sr, was also fond of the bottle and was a serial philanderer when not engaged with the chemical feed business. Communications between Marlon Sr and his son, then known as Bud, were not good and it was no surprise when the latter pushed off to New York and enrolled at acting school.

He joined Erwin Piscator's Dramatic Workshop and before long Piscator was casting Brando in his own productions, notably Gerhard Hauptmann's dream play *Hannele's Way to Heaven* and *Twelfth Night*. Brando's appearance in Shakespeare attracted the critics' attention and won him a juvenile lead in *I Remember Mama*, a popular and sentimental piece by John Van Druten about Norwegian immigrants to San Francisco.

Truckline Cafe, which followed, was much more to Brando's taste. The play, by the old left-winger Maxwell Anderson, was a flop, but it introduced Brando to Harold Clurman – and to the director Elia Kazan, who would go on to draw more from Brando's talents than anyone else.

Brando had a stormy spell with Tallulah Bankhead in Cocteau's *The Eagle has Two Heads*. Then came *Streetcar*, which changed his career. Tennessee Williams invited Elia Kazan to direct his new play and the first intention was to cast John Garfield as Stanley: a somewhat odd choice, as he was no longer the beefy sort. Other baits lured Garfield, and then Kazan remembered the young actor from *Truckline*.

In 1947 Brando was sent to read for Tennessee Williams, and the rest is history. He was at the centre of one of the greatest successes of postwar Broadway and he brought all that he had learned from Stella Adler and the Method school to bear on Stanley Kowalski.

Brando was Williams's "Polack", and when the film came to be made in 1951, with Kazan again directing, there was no challenge to Brando for the screen role. For box-office reasons, however, Vivien Leigh replaced Jessica Tandy.

With *Streetcar*, Broadway had seen the last of Brando as an actor. Fred Zinnemann took him to Hollywood in *The Men* (1950), a serious if reticent film about wounded war veterans, and there, apart from a little summer stock, he was to stay.

Practically everyone got an Oscar for *Streetcar* apart from Brando. For that he was to have to wait until Terry Malloy in *On the Waterfront*. His Mark Antony in Joseph Mankiewicz's slightly eccentric production of *Julius Caesar* was unlikely to win him one: the director had originally wanted the young Paul Scofield for the part, but Brando was selected by one of America's great star-spotters, John Houseman. It was his only classical screen role.

On the Waterfront (1954) reunited him with Kazan. Budd Schulberg's script in some ways looked back to the gritty social dramas of the Thirties, but it gave Brando his greatest screen role as

Terry, a small-time boxer who fights back against the mobsters who once employed him.

The film was unsentimental and at times as grey as the New York docklands in which it was shot, but Brando's performance was passionately physical. The Method school showed that it could offer great rewards to the right actor.

Thereafter Brando became a victim of the studio system. Darryl F Zanuck pushed him into a piece of nonsense called *Desirée* (1954), immediately dubbed "Daisy Ray" by superior British critics, in which he played Napoleon with little conviction. The movie version of *Guys and Dolls* (1955) was considerably better, with Brando both singing (*Luck be a Lady*) and dancing as the gambler Sky Masterson.

Edward Dmytryk got a reasonable performance from him as a German officer in *The Young Lions* (1958) but his return to Tennessee Williams in *The Fugitive Kind* (1959) was disappointing. Williams had written the play on which it was based, *Orpheus Descending*, especially for Brando, who turned it down amid accusations that he had become afraid of the theatre. Perhaps he was right to say no.

In 1960 he tried his hand, quite successfully, at directing. *One-Eyed Jacks* was a spectacular revenge western, which brought back his old screen partner Karl Malden. Brando was dismissive, calling it "Just another product... Movies aren't art".

The rest of the decade included a strange and – in some ways – mesmeric performance in *Mutiny on the Bounty* (1962). Brando argued with a number of directors who worked on the film, including the veteran Lewis Milestone, and he appeared to get on little better with John Huston, whose *Reflections in a Golden Eye* (1967) was one of the worst films to be made by director and star alike.

By the time Paramount started thinking about *The Godfather* Brando's career was in considerable need of rescue. There had been plenty of bad publicity about his marriage to Anna Kashfi, who claimed to be Anglo-Indian but whose father later declared her to be pure Irish.

His public had become disillusioned with Brando in heavy disguises and too often in indifferent films; they yearned for the macho symbol that had brought him stardom. Brando was 47.

He actually auditioned for *The Godfather*. He had lost weight and a spell in the South Seas had made him fitter than he once was: the question was whether he had the capability of putting on 20 years to play Don Corleone. Brando proved that he could, and what had started as a low-budget film became one of Paramount's greatest triumphs, with Francis Ford Coppola at the helm.

When Brando was then teamed with Bernado Bertolucci, another of the rising generation of film directors, for *Last Tango in Paris*, it looked as though his restitution would be complete. In flavour, *Tango* could not have been further from *The Godfather*: it was an art-house film about male menopausal obsession, which drew in a wider public because of its sexual explicitness.

Brando brought back all his old animal power in the improbable setting of a virtually empty Paris apartment and Bertolucci's lens savoured his couplings with Maria Schneider.

But that was virtually the end. He starred with Jack Nicholson in another eccentric western, *Missouri Breaks*, but he thereafter became reclusive, emerging only very occasionally.

One of his rare public outings came in far from happy circumstances in 1991, when he seemed a prematurely old man, all too ready to take on his own shoulders the crimes of his son Christian, which included drink and drug abuse as well as manslaughter.

He confessed that he had not been a good father; all too frequent a shortcoming in the world of showbusiness. Perhaps he was thinking back to his own inadequate upbringing.

The films of his last years were little more than footnotes to his long and impressive career. They included *A Dry White Season* (1989), which won him an Oscar nomination, and *Christopher Columbus: The Discovery* (1992). He turned in a pleasing performance in *Don Juan DeMarco* (1995).

A remake of *The Island of Dr Moreau* the next year was lazily played, with Brando not alone among the cast in sleepwalking through his role. *The Score* (2001) billed him with two successive generations of Method practitioners – Robert De Niro and Edward Norton – but the tawdry thriller plot and the irregular writing meant that the whole failed to add up to the sum of its parts, and anyway Brando seemed aware that all he had to do was turn up.

Brando's personal life was complex. Christian was the only issue of his two-year marriage to Kashfi, whom he divorced in 1959. By his second wife Movita Castenada he had a son and daughter. He had another son and daughter from his third marriage to Tarita Teriipaia; the daughter took her own life in 1995. There were also a son and a daughter by his former housekeeper Christina Ruiz.

Marlon Brando was born on April 3, 1924. He died of idiopathic pulmonary fibrosis on July 1, 2004, aged 80

MAGGIE SMITH

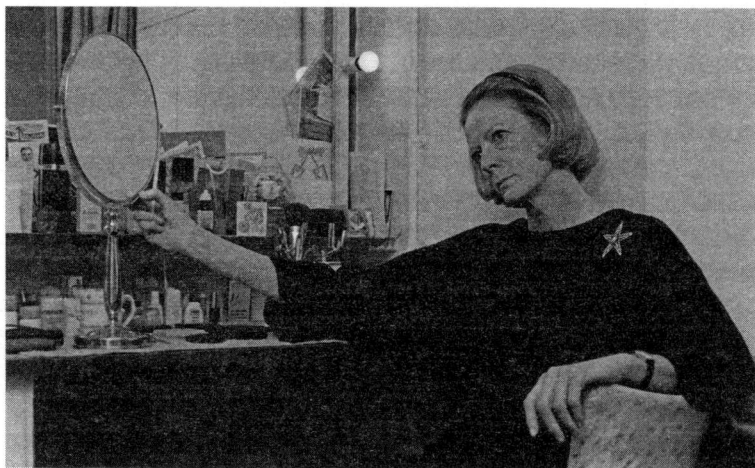

Friends, fellow actors and, of course, the drama critics tried to identify the true source of Maggie Smith's prowess as an actress. They all came up with different answers, even with different parts of her anatomy. "Very tall, very thin ... with all this red hair" was the reaction of the playwright Beverley Cross, later to be her second husband, on first seeing her as Viola in the 1952 Oxford Playhouse's *Twelfth Night*.

Bamber Gascoigne, author of *Share My Lettuce*, which gave Smith her first West End success, lit upon her friskiness, "her limbs all akimbo". Robin Phillips, the director who guided her through the great classical roles with the Stratford, Ontario, company, delighted in "those witty elbows". "Some of the finest fingers in the business," was the Kenneth Tynan verdict.

Then there was the voice, usually a drawl that soon allowed little hint of her lower middle-class background. It was capable of giving an apparently innocuous remark a thousand different meanings. She was a natural mimic, assimilating the Morningside accent of Muriel Spark's Miss Jean Brodie – "My girls are the *crème de la crème*" –

as easily as the soft Dublin tones of Brian Moore's Judith Hearne. The grandes dames of high comedy, from Millamant to Bracknell, were naturals for her. And, as she grew older, the critics began to notice her skill at playing the sad, the repressed and the lonely. She raised anxiety, it was said, to an art form.

The only person, it seemed, not to analyse her acting was Smith herself. Her career, she said, could be summarised in one sentence: "One went to school, one wanted to act, one started to act, and one's still acting." She consistently refused to engage in self-promotional exercises, declining to appear on chat shows and only rarely giving interviews. In the latter she closed the shutters fast when the conversation turned to matters of technique. When Michael Coveney, her highly sympathetic biographer (*Maggie Smith: A Bright Particular Star*) first approached her, he found a blank wall: "There's nothing to write about," was the Smith reaction. "But your art," Coveney persisted. Back came the reply, "I don't know what it is that I do."

Of course she did. But she was not going to share it with the world, which could watch her from a seat in the stalls. She was by nature reclusive and her eyes gradually acquired a look of distrust, partially as a result of the publicity that gathered around her stormy first marriage to Robert Stephens. But the stage, as she once admitted, was the one place where she was never shy. "I like the ephemeral thing about theatre, every performance is like a ghost – it's there and then it's gone," she said.

She made quantities of films – a few forgotten, most of them still watchable, a handful, such as *A Private Function* (1984), *A Room with a View* (1985) and *Gosford Park* (2001), of high quality. But the theatre was her true home, as she decided, with very little family encouragement, when she was a schoolgirl.

Margaret Natalie Smith was born in Ilford, Essex, in 1934. Her mother, Margaret, was a secretary; her father, Nathaniel, is normally described as a pathologist, although he spent most of his life as a modestly paid laboratory assistant, first in suburban Essex and then in Cowley near Oxford. He is said to have taken the strap to his daughter and her two older brothers.

The young Margaret acquired a reputation for little apart from naughtiness and an ability to make people laugh, but she did win an assisted place to Oxford High School. Her mother, a dour Scot, had little influence, although she probably provided a bit of raw material when Jean Brodie came along. Despite its reputation for drama, Oxford High School did not spot the talent in its auburn-haired pupil.

Margaret, though, had read a popular children's novel of the time about the theatre by Pamela Brown, *The Swish of the Curtain*, and with her father's help got into the drama school attached to the Oxford Playhouse. "I was totally obsessed with acting, which confused my parents utterly. Both my brothers were architects and they just didn't know where my ambition to act had come from." The playhouse formed an open door to the world of undergraduate productions and revue, which frequently occupied the playhouse during term time.

It was also home for the Oxford Repertory Players, who gave Smith a job as assistant stage manager, which in turn led to walk-on parts in plays directed by Peter Wood and Peter Hall. During this Oxford period she was more the flame-haired temptress, catching the eye among others of Cross, a Balliol undergraduate. But she was in great demand for Oxbridge revue and it was while appearing on the Edinburgh Festival fringe that she attracted the attention of a New York impresario, Leonard Stillman. He signed her for Broadway in *New Faces* in 1956. Equity already had a Margaret Smith, so she made her American debut as Maggie. And thus she remained.

Michael Codron, who was about to make his name as the sharpest of the young British producers, brought her back to London in 1957 for another revue, *Share My Lettuce*. In this she was teamed with Kenneth Williams, who split the salad of the title with a large white rabbit. The Smith–Williams combination sparkled and the two were close friends until Williams's untimely death.

Critics of Smith's vocal mannerisms reckon that she picked up a number of them from him. Certainly she was not averse to aping Williams's camp and sometimes bitchy sense of humour. Offstage her language could be spicy, although not up to the Coral Browne level. But she was always very careful about her public image. She made her first film, *Nowhere to Go*, now virtually forgotten, in 1958, and appeared in a number of television dramas for ITV in the late 1950s before Michael Benthall invited her to join his Old Vic company.

Those were not exactly glory days in the Waterloo Road, but on stage were actors of the calibre of Judi Dench and Alec McCowen, while Franco Zeffirelli arrived to direct *Romeo and Juliet* – with Dench, not Smith. Smith's major successes were as Lady Plyant in Congreve's *The Double Dealer*, her first excursion into Restoration comedy, and as Maggie Wylie in Barrie's *What Every Woman Knows*, her first "Scottish" part. She was now living with Cross, who had wooed her unceasingly, and she starred in his play *Strip the Willow*. Alas, it never reached the West End.

Theatrical scandal brought her first contact with Laurence Olivier in 1960. He was appearing in Ionesco's *Rhinoceros* opposite Joan Plowright at the Royal Court. The press got wind of an affair between the two leads and when the play transferred to the West End Plowright prudently retired through "illness" and was replaced by Smith. There was later to be a certain rivalry between the two ladies.

Plowright, though, quickly recognised Smith's abilities and was instrumental in persuading Olivier to make her a founder member of his National Theatre company in 1963. Before then Smith had appeared in her first Peter Shaffer play, or rather plays, the double bill *The Private Ear* and *The Public Eye*, a return to high comedy and partnership – in the second and better of the two – with Kenneth Williams. Smith's first reaction to the Olivier offer was to say no: Shaftesbury Avenue and HM Tennent stood waiting with open arms. Cross persuaded her to change her mind.

The National Theatre company drew from Smith some of her greatest performances and at the same time provided the most turbulent period of her life. Her first role, which she took triumphantly, was Silvia in Farquhar's *The Recruiting Officer* – she looked most fetching in drag. Here she played opposite Robert Stephens, with Olivier assigning himself the small and juicy role of

Captain Brazen. When Olivier came to *Othello* he picked Smith as his pale-skinned Desdemona, but he was unwise enough to pass within earshot some disparaging remarks about her suburban vowels.

One evening Smith poked her head around the Olivier dressing room after he had finished applying his black make-up, an operation taking several hours, and mouthed in rounded tones, "How now, brown cow". The oft-told tale not only demonstrated the Smith wit, but proved her to be one of the few people ready to stand up to the ruler.

This she certainly did as Hilde Wangel in Ibsen's *The Master Builder*. Olivier had sacked Michael Redgrave as Solness and taken over the role himself. The fact that Hilde was to be shared by Smith and Plowright made the situation more tense. Smith came out the ultimate victor, allowing Olivier to score no points against her. Simultaneously, another drama was beginning: she had fallen under the spell of her leading man, Robert Stephens. They struck sparks off one another in Zeffirelli's gloriously flashy production of *Much Ado* and again in Peter Shaffer's fizzing one-act, *Black Comedy*, where Stephens took over from Albert Finney. Beverley Cross, her longtime companion, was being eased out of Smith's life.

The secret of the liaison was broken when Smith went to Rome to make a film, *The Honeypot*, with Rex Harrison. Stephens joined her there and Smith was later cited in his divorce papers. They married in 1967, shortly after the birth of their first son, Christopher. For a time it looked as though they were going to be Britain's star theatrical couple, idolised by the public and idealised by the press, but the chemistry was never going to be right: both were too obsessed with their own careers.

Shortly after the marriage Smith won an Oscar for *The Prime of Miss Jean Brodie*, in which she took on screen the title role Vanessa Redgrave had played on stage. It remains among her best films. Stephens was also in it, but the limelight was never his. Another award, the Evening Standard Best Actress, came with *Hedda Gabler* at the Cambridge Theatre, directed by Ingmar Bergman. This particularly icy Hedda, together with the Mrs Sullen in *The Recruiting*

Officer at Chichester under Bill Gaskill's direction, found Smith close to her zenith – in 1970 she was appointed CBE – but Stephens was playing only a supporting role and his own venture into film stardom in *The Private Life of Sherlock Holmes* had not been a success.

The idea of casting husband and wife together in a revival of Noël Coward's *Private Lives*, directed by John Gielgud, might have looked inspired on paper. In reality it was going to be fraught, although some optimistic friends interpreted it as a marriage saver. It turned out to be the reverse and the reference of Amanda (Smith) to "two violent acids bubbling about in a nasty little matrimonial bottle" was all too accurate. They argued constantly. Stephens and Smith parted at the end of the play's run and were not to appear on stage together again.

Stephens, highly volatile and prone to heavy drinking when things went against him, was replaced with John Standing when *Private Lives* went to New York. Smith delivered some of her least satisfactory performances in the mid-1970s. Aunt Augusta, in the film of Greene's *Travels with My Aunt* should have been a ripe plum for the picking but George Cukor's direction turned it into a shrivelled old prune. A return to the West End in a weak comedy about VD, *Snap*, was no better.

It took Robin Phillips, the English director who had just been handed the artistic reins at the Stratford Festival in Ontario, to restore Smith's confidence. He swept her off to his theatre and persuaded her over the next five years, with a break in 1979, to play the great classical roles for him: Cleopatra, Rosalind, Masha in *The Three Sisters*, and Lady Macbeth. Phillips's persuasiveness was London's loss: Britain was denied the prime of Miss Maggie Smith. The only beneficiaries were selected London theatre critics shipped out to Stratford at Canadian expense, who duly reported on the Smith triumphs and those of her regular leading man there, Brian Bedford.

She was tempted back to London in 1979 by Tom Stoppard's play *Night and Day*, in which she took over from Diana Rigg the role of an expat wife dallying with a couple of journalists. It went on to Broadway, where Smith reckoned the audiences understood not a word of it. Phillips returned her to London the following year in a Stratford transfer, *Virginia*, Edna O'Brien's rather undramatic attempt to put Virginia Woolf on stage.

For a time the cinema took a stronger grip. There were character roles in two popular Agatha Christie movies, *Death on the Nile* and *Evil Under the Sun*, and a reasonable comic performance that brought a second Oscar in Neil Simon's *California Suite*. But it was not until 1984 that Smith showed her real skills in front of the camera for the first time since Jean Brodie.

A Private Function, Alan Bennett's social comedy of snobbery and greed in postwar austerity Britain, gave her a chance with the first of a new range of crabbed women. She played the superior wife of a small-town chiropodist, who rears an incontinent pig to fill the stomachs of his "superiors". Betty the pig and Maggie recognised star quality in each other. The performance brought her a Bafta, as did her overbearing Charlotte Bartlett in the Merchant Ivory film *A Room with a View*.

She played another disappointed woman for Alan Bennett – Susan, the vicar's wife, in the Talking Heads monologue, *Bed Among the Lentils*, on BBC television. "The most marvellous thing about Maggie is that she can go from comedy to tragedy in one sentence," Bennett said. "She's very like me in that she thinks things are disastrous and hilarious in equal measure. We are both very lugubrious, but we both like to have a laugh as well."

She captured English poise and eccentricity, and she paired imperiousness or disdain with wide-eyed vulnerability. The most subtle of these anxious creatures was Judith Hearne in Jack Clayton's film of the Brian Moore novel, *The Lonely Passion of Judith Hearne*. Because of distribution problems the film never got the showing, or critical attention, it deserved in Britain. Smith's portrayal of a Dublin spinster who believes (falsely) that love has come along at last is among her finest, not least because her whole box of acting tricks was discarded.

Was she taking on these frustrated, even desiccated, females before her time? Smith's answer was to play Lettice Douffet, custodian of a ninth-rate stately home, with all her old flamboyance in Shaffer's *Lettice and Lovage*. Some of her admirers found her over the top and the play thin; John Dexter, who had directed her so skilfully in *Black Comedy*, was one of them. But audiences disagreed, both on Shaftesbury Avenue and on Broadway, where she won a Tony award. This was Maggie Smith at her most extravagant and in the same year as *Lettice*, 1990, she was appointed DBE.

She made another film, for television, with Jack Clayton, *Memento Mori*, before taking on the role that had long been waiting: Lady Bracknell. *The Importance of Being Earnest* had first been mooted as a London–Broadway venture with Terry Hands directing. In fact Nicholas Hytner did that job and *The Importance of Being Earnest* opened at the Aldwych in March 1993.

There was much speculation over how Dame Maggie would handle the "handbag" line. In the event she did the only possible thing and virtually threw it away. But otherwise she carried the production, which had some weak casting, and filled the theatre at a time when it seemed that only musicals could sell tickets in the West End. When asked whether she wanted to take it to Broadway she said: "I wouldn't take it to Woking." Such was her withering style. Michael Palin once said that "Maggie in a bad mood is clearly a few degrees worse than anyone else in a bad mood". Her moods may have been affected by Graves' disease, a hyperthyroid condition that caused her many health problems including distension of the eyeballs.

Her later theatre work included Bennett's *Talking Heads*, at Chichester and the West End and later on a tour of Australia, and the batty old woman who took root in Bennett's front garden in his *The Lady in the Van* (Queens Theatre), which was later made into a film. There was a West End revival of Edward Albee's *A Delicate Balance* and in 2002 she and Dench, two grandes dames of the British theatre, were on stage together for the first time in David Hare's *The Breath of Life* at the Haymarket.

At the same theatre she took on another Albee, the little-performed *The Lady from Dubuque*, in which she appeared with her older son, Christopher, but in 2008 it emerged that she had been suffering from breast cancer. Although she recovered after chemotherapy, she admitted that the intensive treatment had left her frightened of returning to the stage and it appeared that one of Britain's most glittering theatrical careers might be over.

But she continued in films and on television, where aristocratic, barbed elderly ladies became a speciality. "It's true I don't tolerate fools, but then they don't tolerate me, so I am spiky," she once said. "Maybe that's why I'm quite good at playing spiky elderly ladies." Among them were Lady Hester in Zeffirelli's autobiographical film, *Tea with Mussolini*, Queen Alexandra in a TV movie *All the King's Men*, and the waspish and snobbish Countess of Trentham in Robert Altman's *Gosford Park*. She played Betsey Trotwood in a television *David Copperfield* and enjoyed her turn as Professor Minerva McGonagall, deputy head of Hogwarts, in the Harry Potter films from 2001 to 2011, which became one of the biggest box-office franchises of all time. She was reported to have been the only performer that the author JK Rowling specifically asked for when the books were made into films. "Harry Potter is my pension," she said, speaking slowly, with her distinctive nasal twang.

She and Dench were spinster sisters in *Ladies in Lavender* and from 2010 to 2015 she returned to the aristocracy as the imperious and acid Dowager Countess of Grantham in Julian Fellowes's popular period drama *Downton Abbey*.

Her marriage to Stephens was dissolved in 1974 and he died in 1995. Their sons both became actors, as Chris Larkin and Toby Stephens, both of whom survive her. She was married to Beverley Cross from 1975 until his death in 1998. When asked in 2013 if she was lonely, she replied: "It seems a bit pointless, going on one's own, and not having someone to share it with."

She was appointed Companion of Honour in 2014 and continued to guard her privacy until the end. "If you want to act these days, it seems to be vital that you tell the world everything about your private life and remove every single garment you possess while you are about it," she said. "There's absolutely no mystery any more."

Dame Maggie Smith CH DBE was born on December 28, 1934. She died on September 27, 2024, aged 89

JAMES STEWART

Although James Stewart became an archetype of western heroes and, as a more mature character player, could turn his hand to reprobates, psychopaths and spiky lawyers, the original small-town boy never quite vanished.

He might have put on weight, but there was still the same disarming loose-limbed awkwardness, the hesitation and characteristic gulp in his talk, and the persistent air of slightly hurt bemusement.

He was regarded at the outset of his career as something of a challenge by casting directors. But this very awkwardness was eventually perceived as a tremendous asset, making him unique in acting style among Hollywood's leading men.

His down-home manner and hesitant drawl soon became his hallmarks. Indeed they were so instantly recognisable that he began to ape his screen persona in his private life and it was impossible to detect where the man ended and the actor began. As his wife admonished him at a party one night when he was beginning one of his shaggy dog stories: "Now, dear, don't talk like Jimmy Stewart."

A spindly, bespectacled youngster, James Maitland Stewart grew up in the delightfully cornball ethos of Vinegar Hill, in the town of Indiana, Pennsylvania, where his father owned a hardware store. But he had a good head on his shoulders and got a place at Princeton to study architecture. There, however, he was soon caught up in university amateur dramatics.

On graduation he joined the University Players, established by his contemporary Joshua Logan. Other members of the company were Henry Fonda, who became a lifelong friend despite their political polarity (Stewart remained a committed though unaggressive Republican throughout his life and, like John Wayne, was a staunch supporter of American action in Vietnam) and Margaret Sullavan, with whom there seems to have been a romantic attachment, though it was Fonda who in time became the first of her four husbands.

With Fonda he went to New York, where his first professional appearance was as Constable Gano in *Carrie Nation* at the Biltmore Theatre on October 29, 1932. He landed a run of small parts after this, and was spotted on stage by Hedda Hopper, whose recommendation helped him to get a long-term contract with MGM in 1935.

During the next few years, as he progressed from supporting roles to juvenile leads, he worked with an astonishing roster of the best Hollywood directors of the time: Tim Whelan, WS Van Dyke, Clarence Brown, William Wellman, Henry King and John Cromwell.

His role as Eleanor Powell's leading man in *Born to Dance* (1936) confirmed him as a star. Sullavan, by this time herself established as a star at Universal, asked for him as her leading man in *Next Time We Love* (1936), and they later worked as a charming team in HC Potter's *Shopwork Angel* (1938), Ernst Lubitsch's *The Shop Around the Corner* (1939) and Frank Borzage's *The Mortal Storm* (1940).

Stewart's air of sweet incorruptible small-town boy, personifying the values of an older, kinder, better America, but capable of fighting stubbornly for his principles, was perfect material for Frank Capra's American fables. Before the war Capra directed Stewart in *You Can't Take It with You* (1938) and *Mr Smith Goes to Washington* (1939).

In *Destry Rides Again* (1939), opposite Marlene Dietrich, Stewart played his first classic western role; while George Cukor's *The Philadelphia Story*, in which his co-stars were Katharine Hepburn and Cary Grant, won him an Oscar.

After an anticlimactic run of parts – *Come Live with Me, Pot o' Gold, Ziegfeld Girl* – he joined the US Army Air Corps, rising from private to colonel and receiving the Distinguished Flying Cross for 23 bombing missions over Germany with the Eighth Army Air Force. He became chief of staff of the Eighth Air Force's Second Combat Wing.

After the war he pursued his military duties with the same enthusiasm and rose to the rank of brigadier-general in the Reserve, making him the highest-ranking entertainer in the USAF.

On his return from the war he threw in his lot with Capra's short-lived independent production unit Liberty Films, but the resulting picture *It's a Wonderful Life* (1946) failed to capture the popularity of the prewar Capra films. This setback was followed by William Wellman's *Magic Town* (1947), which proved again that postwar audiences were not in the market for sentiment.

In his mid-thirties, Stewart now had to find maturer roles to offset the persistent boyish charm. He triumphantly revitalised his career with the part of a tough but incorruptible Chicago police reporter in Henry Hathaway's *Call Northside 777* (1948). Adjusting to the new economies of Hollywood, in 1952 Stewart was one of the first stars to enter into a percentage arrangement with his studio, Universal, rather than the traditional employee contract.

Stewart had the reputation among fellow professionals for being a wholly congenial and conscientious worker. He gratefully attributed his capacity for hard work and discipline to his training under the old-time studio system. Directors spoke of his readiness to undertake whatever hardships or special training a role required (for *Winchester 73* he made himself a formidable expert with the weapon of the title).

He first played for Alfred Hitchcock in *Rope* (1948), as the teacher who realises that his own philosophy has led two of his students to motiveless murder. In *Rear Window* (1954) he played a reluctant voyeur – a photographer confined to his room and window by a broken leg; in *The Man Who Knew Too Much* (1956) the role created by Leslie Banks in the 1934 original; in *Vertigo* (1958) a detective beset with personality problems of his own.

His career in westerns was shaped by his association with Anthony Mann, and enabled him to broaden his acting range and techniques. Their first western collaboration *Winchester 73* (1950) was followed by *Bend of the River* (1952), *The Naked Spur* (1953), *The Far Country* (1954) and *The Man from Laramie* (1955).

Later Stewart westerns with John Ford – *Two Rode Together* (1961), *The Man Who Shot Liberty Valance* (1962) and *Cheyenne Autumn* (1964) – seemed to reflect the advancing age of both director and actor, in the more elegiac view of the west they presented. Even after this, however, Stewart frequently returned to western roles – in three films by Andrew V McLaglen: *Shenandoah* (1965), *The Rare Breed* (1966) and *Bandolero!* (1968); in Vincent McEveety's *Firecreek* (1968); in Gene Kelly's *The Cheyenne Social Club* (1970); and for the last time in Don Siegel's memorable epitaph for the west, *The Shootist* (1976).

Stewart was at his dullest in biopics or "institution" stories such as *The Stratton Story* (1949), the phenomenally successful *Glenn Miller Story* (1953), *Strategic Air Command* (1955), *The FBI Story* (1959) and Billy Wilder's *Spirit of St Louis* (1957).

There was always another, offbeat side to Stewart's "nice" image, however. He clearly had a great affection for Elwood P Dowd, the inoffensive alcoholic hero of *Harvey*, which he played repeatedly on stage (the last time with Helen Hayes on Broadway in 1970) as well as in the 1950 film version.

In his later working years he seemed positively to relish less reputable roles: a crook in *Bandolero!* (1968); the heir to a whorehouse in the *Cheyenne Social Club* (1970), which reunited him with Henry Fonda; and in *Fool's Parade* (1971) a righteously vengeful old convict with a companionable glass eye.

His final film appearances seemed whimsical choices: Michael Winner's *The Big Sleep* (1977), the action thriller *Airport 77* (1977) and *The Magic of Lassie* (1978), in which Stewart was an endearing grandad who even sang. He made infrequent appearances in television films.

In 1984 Stewart received a special Academy Award for "fifty years of meaningful performances, for his high skills both on and off the screen, with the respect and affection of his colleagues". His own view of acting was strictly practical, and certainly underestimated his achievement: "The most important thing about acting is to approach it as a craft, not as an art and not as some mysterious kind of religion."

Stewart carried his home-town image into his private life: his long years in the ranks of Hollywood's most eligible bachelors produced no breath of scandal. He was already 41 when he married, in 1949, Gloria McLean, and she came with a ready-made family of two sons. Theirs was regarded as one of the happiest marriages in Hollywood: it endured until her death from lung cancer in 1994. After her death Stewart, devastated by his loss, became a virtual recluse.

He is survived by one of the two stepsons she brought to their marriage, and by their own two daughters. A second stepson was killed while on active service in Vietnam in 1969.

James Stewart was born on May 20, 1908. He died of a heart attack on July 2, 1997, aged 89

BETTE DAVIS

Bette Davis was one of the most durable of all Hollywood film stars and, what does not necessarily follow, one of those most unmistakably gifted with an acting talent.

She was an actress of striking presence, rather than conventional beauty, whose main physical asset was her large eyes. She first made her reputation as the suffering heroine of melodrama, in a genre popularly known as the "woman's picture". Later, as she matured towards middle age, she played a gallery of steely, wilful and scheming women, who knew exactly what they wanted and were usually able to get it. In a third, though less distinguished phase of her career, she became a mistress of the grotesque in a series of horror films.

The resolution and capriciousness Bette Davis displayed on screen was very much part of her private character and during her career she had inevitable battles with studios who tried to curb her independence of spirit. It was a spirit that enabled her to survive an unhappy childhood and three broken marriages and long before feminism became a rallying cry, she was the epitome of the liberated woman.

She was born in 1908, in Lowell, Massachusetts, and christened Ruth Elizabeth. The name Bette (so spelt in tribute to Balzac's *La Cousine Bette*) was adopted in her teens, when her mother became a professional photographer and began to consider some kind of showbusiness career for her.

She early began studying, acting and dancing, and made her professional debut while still at school in a production of *A Midsummer Night's Dream*. In 1928 she entered John Murray Anderson's school in New York, where she studied acting under Anderson and dancing under Martha Graham. A year in repertory led to her first Broadway appearance in a play called *The Earth Between* (1929). Two more Broadway plays later, after her second screen test, she was put under contract to Universal and went out to Hollywood for the first time. From then until the mid-1970s she was rarely away from the studios, and with few intervals she made in regular succession some 90 films, frequently at the rate of three or four a year.

She began, in the traditional fashion, with small roles. In her first film, *Bad Sister*, she played, improbably, the good sister and was apparently regarded as something of a problem: not glamourous enough to be a siren, not conventional enough to play classy, ladylike roles, with a strange nervous intensity which made her difficult to cast.

There her career might have stayed had she not been cast by George Arliss as the female lead in his talkie version of *The Man Who Played God* (1932) at Warner Brothers, her Universal contract having meanwhile expired. In this she was widely noticed, the association with Arliss gave her a new standing in Hollywood, and, perhaps most important, as a result of the film she was put under contract to Warners, the company which controlled her career, and one of whose chief box-office attractions she was, for some 17 years.

Her first great role came in 1934 with her extraordinary creation as Somerset Maugham's unscrupulous Cockney waitress in *Of Human Bondage*, a performance which, despite some obtrusive mannerisms and uncertainties, still holds up remarkably well. It was widely felt that Bette Davis should have won her first Academy

Award for this film, and that the award she got the following year for *Dangerous,* in which she gave a virtuoso performance as an alcoholic ex-actress (at the ripe old age of 27), was something in the nature of a consolation prize.

Immediately after *Dangerous* she made another of her most famous films, *The Petrified Forest,* a rather stagy adaptation of Robert E Sherwood's play in which she starred opposite Leslie Howard, a teaming repeated bizarrely in *It's Love I'm After* (1937), where they were uncharacteristically called upon to play broad comedy.

The teaming was famously not repeated in *Gone with the Wind,* Scarlett O'Hara being a role Bette Davis passionately wanted to play. But, again, she received compensation with a very similar role in the Goldwyn production *Jezebel,* directed by William Wyler, and, again, she was given an Oscar for it.

This inaugurated the 1940s, perhaps the greatest period in her career, with classic following classic. Not that all of them were classics on the same level: some of them were classics, in particular retrospectively, of camp rather than true quality. But among them were films in which Bette Davis was a remarkable part of a remarkable whole, such as William Wyler's *The Letter* and *The Little Foxes,* William Dieterle's historical drama *Juarez,* and John Huston's *In This Our Life.* And the shameless vehicles for a display of big-star fireworks, like *Dark Victory, The Old Maid, Now Voyager, Old Acquaintance, Mr Skeffington* and *Deception* are somehow given a conviction which transcends the nonsense elements in them by the sheer intensity of Bette Davis's involvement in her roles.

The Private Lives of Elizabeth and Essex (1939) was her first film in colour and saw her famous portrayal of Queen Elizabeth I, her favourite role and one she repeated 16 years later in *The Virgin Queen.*

In 1949 her long-lasting contract with Warners, the subject of some famous litigation in the 1930s when Bette Davis spearheaded a revolt of Hollywood stars against the restrictions of the contract system, ended with one of her most peculiar films, King Vidor's *Beyond the Forest,* in which she was called upon to disport herself in a Charles Addams wig as a femme fatale of the Midwest: "Men turned and stared when Rosa Moline passed by" as well they might.

For this film the publicity department coined the immortal slogan "Nobody's as good as Bette when she's bad", a line which nicely if simplistically summed up much of her work during these years.

Strangely enough, this seeming low in her career led, quite by chance (she was the third choice for the role), to what remains perhaps the definitive Bette Davis portrayal, Margo Channing in Joseph Mankiewicz's *All About Eve* (1950) – the temperamental actress, betrayed by her young protégée but finding true love in the process. This used as nearly as any character she played the full range of her talents and an extra something of total instinctive identification between actress and role.

The years that followed brought ups and downs, the most important up being the title role in *What Ever Happened to Baby Jane?*, in which Robert Aldrich brought together two arch-rivals of Hollywood, Bette Davis and Joan Crawford, as rival sisters, both Hollywood has-beens, with vicious designs on each other's health and sanity.

This inaugurated a period of horror and semi-horror films, such as *Dead Ringer; Hush...Hush, Sweet Charlotte;* and *The Nanny*, with Bette Davis, as usual, gallantly trying her hand at anything that offered, absorbed in her craft and the necessity of continuing to exercise it, even in decidedly less than propitious conditions. During this time she also made occasional returns to the stage, notably in a revue, *Two's Company* (1952) with her then husband, Gary Merrill, and in Tennessee Williams's *Night of the Iguana* (1961). She also wrote her autobiography, *The Lonely Life* (1962), one of the franker and more personal of as-told-to Hollywood books.

Though she had lost her looks, and some of her stamina, and had a serious operation for cancer, Bette Davis continued to be busy well into her seventies. Much of her work was now for television, where she enhanced many a routine drama. But there were cinema films as well and when playing an imperious American matron in Agatha Christie's *Death on the Nile* (1978) she showed she could still hold her own in an all-star cast.

Four years before a stage comeback in *Miss Moffat*, a musical version of one of her cinema successes, *The Corn is Green*, proved abortive when she withdrew through illness.

Her last important film role was opposite another veteran actress, Lilian Gish, in Lindsay Anderson's *The Whales of August* which appeared in 1987.

Star quality, the ability to project personality, to just exist interestingly on screen is one thing, and acting talent, the ability to create a variety of different characters, to bury the actor in the role quite another. Bette Davis was the supreme example of their co-existence in one and the same performer: the most star of film actors, the most actor of film stars.

Her unmistakable vocal mannerisms, even her distinctive ways of smoking a cigarette made her the delight of imitators yet, though herself a symbol of Hollywood and the star system, she managed to transcend them both often enough to make the whole thing worthwhile. There never was, and never will be, anyone like her.

Her acting ability appealed to the widest audiences and in the most diverse circumstances. One such testimony of her success was from wartime Britain. "Jock" Colville, Churchill's secretary, in a diary entry of January 1945 wrote: "After dinner there was a film in an Air Ministry room on the ground floor in King Charles St. The PM bid us all cast care aside ... and so all the typists, drivers, servants, etc., saw ... Bette Davis in *Dark Victory*, a brilliantly acted film and one of the few I have seen end as a tragedy".

Of her four marriages, the second ended with the death of her husband and the other three in divorce. Her fourth husband was the actor, Gary Merrill, with whom she appeared in films and on stage. "I have not been very fortunate; I think it is very difficult for a famous woman," was her own comment on married life when talking to reporters in San Sebastian last month.

Bette Davis was born on April 5, 1908. She died of cancer on October 6, 1989, aged 81

DAVID NIVEN

David Niven was a popular star of the traditional type, establishing a screen persona that became instantly recognisable and was repeated, more or less, through film after film. His range as an actor was limited and he was probably at his best in light comedy; but what mattered was that for millions of filmgoers on both sides of the Atlantic he summed up the archetypal English gentleman, witty, debonair, immaculate in dress and behaviour but with mischief lurking not far from the surface.

He came to films almost by accident, and with no previous acting experience, but through a combination of luck, knowing the right people and force of personality he managed not only to break into Hollywood but to survive in a tough and ruthless world. It says much for his staying power that he was still in regular demand after nearly five decades. Surprisingly few of his 90-odd films stay in the memory, however, mainly because he was content to take what was available rather than stick out for good parts. He reckoned that it was enough to be so well paid for doing what he enjoyed.

Niven was born in Kirriemuir, Scotland, in 1910, the son of an army officer who was killed in the First World War. He had an unsettled childhood, being pushed by an unsympathetic stepfather into a succession of barbaric prep schools from which he either absconded or was expelled. Later he went to Stowe and on to Sandhurst to train for the army. He served as an officer with the Highland Light Infantry, mainly on Malta, but resigned his commission after three years and took a succession of casual jobs in Canada and the United States, from selling liquor to promoting pony racing.

In the mid-1930s he arrived in Hollywood to try his luck as a film extra. He registered with Central Casting as "Anglo Saxon Type Number 2008" and though it was an axiom of the film industry that extras rarely graduated into stars, Niven proved an exception. He was fortunate both with his contacts and in being in the right place at the right time. Hollywood was busy filming British subjects and recruiting British actors and Niven fitted happily into an expatriate colony that included Cary Grant, Ronald Colman, Basil Rathbone, Herbert Marshall and the imperious C Aubrey Smith, who ran the Hollywood cricket club.

After abortive screen tests for other producers, Niven was put under contract by Sam Goldwyn and though the relationship was not always harmonious it lasted for 14 years. His first important part came in 1936 in *The Charge of the Light Brigade* (whose star, Errol Flynn, became a close friend and drinking companion); Niven played a gallant young officer who dies trying to get through the enemy lines. He supported Ronald Colman in *The Prisoner of Zenda*, played opposite Flynn in a remake of *The Dawn Patrol* and in formidable competition with Laurence Olivier gave a creditable performance as Edgar Linton in William Wyler's 1939 film of *Wuthering Heights*. His first star billing, and first real chance to show his gift for comedy, came in *Bachelor Mother*, with Ginger Rogers, and he was appropriately cast as Raffles, the gentleman burglar.

By this time the Second World War had started and Niven decided to return to Britain to play his part. He joined the Rifle Brigade, rising to lieutenant colonel and serving in Normandy, Holland, Belgium and Germany. He was twice given leave so that he could appear in films: *The First of the Few*, with Leslie Howard, which told the story of the Spitfire, and *The Way Ahead*, made by Carol Reed as a quasi-propaganda piece for the British Army. Just after the war Niven appeared as the RAF pilot in Powell and Pressburger's elaborate allegorical fantasy, *A Matter of Life and Death*.

In 1946 he returned to Hollywood but found it difficult, after such a long absence, to pick up the threads of his career and there followed a period of undistinguishable parts in mediocre films. This profession trough coincided with a personal tragedy when his wife, at the age of 25, was killed in an accidental fall, leaving two small sons. Niven's second wife, whom he married in 1948, was a leading Swedish model, Hjordis Tersmeden; they had two adopted daughters.

During the 1950s Niven re-established himself as a popular leading man and better parts came his way. He was chosen by Otto Preminger for *The Moon is Blue*, a comedy that gained notoriety by running into censorship problems, and in 1956 he played Phineas Fogg in Mike Todd's lavish spectacular, *Around the World in 80 Days*.

Two years later Niven won the best actor Oscar for his portrayal of the bogus major in the film of Terence Rattigan's play, *Separate Tables*, an honour that brought his career to a critical peak. But still he made a high ratio of indifferent films, interspersed with more worthy vehicles: among the latter were *Ask Any Girl*, a good comedy with Shirley MacLaine; a successful war film, *The Guns of Navarone*; a blockbuster, *55 Days at Peking*; and *The Pink Panther*, in which his suave jewel thief was a perfect foil to Peter Sellers as the accident-prone Inspector Clouseau.

Released in 1964, *The Pink Panther* proved to be one of Niven's last big commercial successes in the cinema. He continued to make one or two films a year but he probably had more impact with a series of television commercials for instant coffee. In 1971, with the publication of an autobiography, *The Moon's a Balloon*, he acquired a new reputation as a bestselling author. Niven was a born raconteur and the book was essentially a succession of funny stories, drawn from his life in the forces and in films and liberally sprinkled with famous names. The formula proved astonishingly successful and led to a second volume of reminiscences, concentrating on Hollywood personalities and called *Bring on the Empty Horses*. Together the two books sold more than ten million copies. In 1981 Niven published a long novel with a Hollywood setting, *Go Slowly, Come Back Quickly*.

In the early 1950s he formed, with Charles Boyer and Dick Powell, a company, Four Star Television, to produce films for the small screen; it made more than 2,000 and helped to launch the careers of several Hollywood stars. Niven had his own series on television and appeared in the popular comedy show, *The Rogues*; later he was much in demand for chat shows, where his gift for anecdote made him an ideal subject.

David Niven was born on March 1, 1910. He died of motor neurone disease on July 29, 1983, aged 73

KATHARINE HEPBURN

Katharine Hepburn was not one of Hollywood's more loveable stars, nor did she ever aim to be. She once observed of the young Maggie Smith: "She has the real star thing, the quality to irritate," and that same quality was very important throughout Hepburn's six decades of screen stardom. There were always those filmgoers who could not stand her at any price, to such an extent that when, in 1938, a leading distributor labelled about a dozen top box-office stars "box-office poison", Hepburn was the only one on the list that anyone afterwards remembered.

This was partly because her reaction was so characteristic: while all the rest shrugged and went on with their careers, she stormed out of Hollywood, vowing vengeance, and promptly achieved it by scoring her biggest success on Broadway in Philip Barry's play *The Philadelphia Story*, to return to Hollywood in triumph in the film version of the play. By the end of her career she had won a record four Oscars for best leading actress – the first for *Morning Glory* and the last for *On Golden Pond*, almost 50 years later. In between she forged a famous alliance with Spencer Tracy, and their partnership in *Guess Who's Coming to Dinner?* led her to an Oscar in 1968.

Where so many other stars were pathetically dependent on feeling that the audience loved them, she was always an awkward customer, determined to do things her own way or not at all. When one of her later films, *Olly, Olly, Oxen Free*, was widely accounted by preview audiences a disaster that could be turned into a hit with some judicious re-editing, she firmly turned down the assistance, freely proffered, of such expert friends as George Cukor and Anthony Harvey, choosing rather to let the film go its own way to oblivion.

On screen she never hesitated to play difficult, aggressive, unloveable characters, though the cynic might observe that she always (or nearly always) made audiences love her before the final fade-out. Certainly it is true, and probably significant, that the two roles of her maturity that she remained unhappy with and did not care to discuss were in *Suddenly, Last Summer* and *Long Day's Journey into Night*, neither of which, in different ways, allowed this final access of audience sympathy.

Many leading traits of her character, personal and professional, must have come from her early background, which was exceptional by Hollywood standards. Katharine Houghton Hepburn's family was socially distinguished and guaranteed her financial independence from the outset. Her father, Thomas Norval Hepburn, was a famous urologist and supported her mother, Katharine Houghton, in her militant campaigns for women's suffrage and birth control; she became the chairwoman in Washington of the National Committee on Federal Legislation for Birth Control. The young Katharine took part in suffrage marches and met prominent feminists such as Margaret Sanger and Emmeline Pankhurst. She was always encouraged to think for herself.

After education at Bryn Mawr, the exclusive women's college near Philadelphia that her mother had attended, she determined that she wanted to become a professional actress, and no one stood in her way. She had previously wanted to be a surgeon, but said that acting seemed to provide unlimited opportunities for both sexes and she was assisted by letters of introduction to leading figures in the theatrical world. Though she paid her dues with a succession of small parts and time in the sticks, she managed to get herself fired from, or walked out of, a number of promising situations before making it to Broadway, playing the Amazon heroine in *The Warrior's Husband* in 1932. Her entrance was a spectacular 15ft leap on to the stage, which she performed each night without breaking a bone.

From there it proved an unexpectedly quick passage to Hollywood stardom in her first film role, the daughter of a veteran who returns unexpectedly to haunt his family after years in a mental institution, in the film of Clemence Dane's controversial play, *A Bill of Divorcement* (1932). Visibly unsure, and already very mannered, the 25-year-old Hepburn at once commanded the screen (which she had always affected to despise), particularly in an early scene in which she crossed the room and lay in front of the fireplace. The director, George Cukor, was to become a lifelong friend and counsellor, and had a house built specially for her lover, Spencer Tracy, on his estate. He went on to direct Hepburn in many of her most successful films, including *Keeper of the Flame* (1942), *Adam's Rib* (1949) and *Pat and Mike* (1952), in all of which Tracy co-starred.

Hepburn was emerging as one of the most effective and individual new stars of the early sound cinema. Less successful was her return to the stage; when she appeared in *The Lake* in 1933, the play closed after only 55 performances and inspired Dorothy Parker's famous line that Hepburn ran "the gamut of emotions from A to B".

But her position on the silver screen was confirmed that same year in *Morning Glory*, for which she won the first of her Oscars in the tailor-made role of a difficult but aspiring young actress.

Until the "box office" slur in 1938 Hepburn's career was an almost uninterrupted succession of triumphs in Hollywood. Her way of dealing with Hollywood was a perfect demonstration of "if you want them to run after you, just walk the other way", though whether this was by design or because she was incapable of behaving differently has remained unclear. She certainly did not do any of the usual things a Hollywood aspirant would do, insisting on striding around in slacks, keeping her private life entirely private and retaining a distant hauteur in her relationships with tycoons unless, like Howard Hughes, they were as eccentric and unpredictable as herself. Her motto could have been "let them hate, provided they fear", and undoubtedly many Hollywood high-ups did both.

But there was no arguing with the success of films such as *Little Women* (1933), *Alice Adams* (1935), *Quality Street* (1937), *Stage Door* (1937) and *Bringing Up Baby* (1938), the archetypal screwball comedy of the 1930s; it could even excuse the occasional misfire such as *Sylvia Scarlett* (1935), which teamed her with Cary Grant and the director George Cukor in an uneasy version of Compton Mackenzie's transvestite comedy.

In all of these films she played variations, pushed towards farce, comedy or occasionally pathos, of her own perceived character: headstrong, independent and at times arrogant, the sort of person people wanted to shake even while they loved her to distraction. This was fair enough as a Hollywood style – what else, after all, did any important star do at the time? – though, remarkably, Hepburn continued to be taken seriously as an actress rather than dismissed as a mere movie star.

She departed from Hollywood after the *succès d'estime* of *Holiday* (1938), also co-starring Cary Grant and directed by Cukor, only to return on her own terms in triumph with the film version of *The Philadelphia Story* (1940), written by the same playwright as *Holiday*, Philip Barry. Howard Hughes offered to finance it even before he had read it and, with a loan from Hughes, she put up a quarter of the costs and bought the screen rights from Barry for $25,000. It was a hit and within a few days of opening, MGM offered her $175,000 for the rights.

This meant that she could dictate that her salary was $75,000, the director was Cukor and that her co-stars would be James Stewart and Cary Grant. Tracy Lord was the definitive Hepburn role and the film version was a hit. It could hardly have done more to confirm everything that everyone had ever thought about her.

For her next film, *Woman of the Year* (1942), her chosen director was George Stevens – with whom she had had a fling when he directed her in *Alice Adams* and *Quality Street*. This film would also change the course of her life since it brought her together for the first time with Spencer Tracy. They starred together in nine films and remained deeply involved for the remaining 27 years of his life.

When they first met she was 33 and he was 42. The story went that she had just come from a meeting with MGM executives, for which she had worn heels which added four inches to her 5ft 7in; Tracy was two inches shorter. "I'm afraid I'm a little tall for you, Mr Tracy," she said. "Don't worry, Miss Hepburn," he replied. "I'll cut you down to my size." And he did. Years later, she said: "I struggled to change all the qualities I felt he didn't like. I was his."

Tracy and Hepburn were together for years, but neither lived together nor went out together; it was said that Tracy and his wife, Louise, could not get divorced on account of being Catholics, but in fact Louise was Episcopalian. Hepburn's relationship with him was an open secret, handled with great dignity by all parties – even, surprisingly, the Hollywood press. She was his secretary, companion and chauffeur – and frequently his nurse.

On screen they were chalk and cheese: he was the roughneck made good, she the society lady able to keep her end up in any amatory and professional tussles through class and gender. But as she grew older – and she did nothing to disguise or hinder the ageing process – her standard characterisation of the difficult but magnetic young woman, relations with whom tended to be a minefield worth traversing, gradually shifted into that of the prickly, cranky old maid whose life might yet be transfigured by affection and romance. A key film in this transition was John Huston's *The African Queen* (1951), in which she was a missionary navigating dangerous waters with Humphrey Bogart as a hard-drinking captain of a disreputable motor launch. The film was shot in the Belgian Congo, from where she wrote long letters to Tracy every day.

The transition was complete when she made *Summertime* (1955), in which she enjoyed a romantic interlude with the deceptively seductive Rossano Brazzi in Venice. In one scene she had to fall backwards into a canal, from which she caught a form of conjunctivitis that led to the teary look that remained with her for the rest of her career.

In 1959 and 1962 came the two effective but aberrant, unsympathetic characterisations: as Tennessee Williams's implacable southern matron in *Suddenly, Last Summer* and Eugene O'Neill's drug-addicted mother in *Long Day's Journey into Night*, both of which, despite her dislike of the roles, won her Oscar nominations.

In the early 1960s Tracy's health deteriorated. Hepburn retired from the cinema to care for him, and by 1966 he was recovering. It was then that the producer Stanley Kramer offered them roles in *Guess Who's Coming to Dinner?* (1967), as an upper-middle-class couple whose only child – eventually played by Hepburn's niece, Katharine Houghton – surprises them with her fiancé, a Black doctor, played by Sidney Poitier. It was completed 17 days before Tracy's death, and Hepburn said that she was never able to watch the film.

It won Hepburn her second Oscar, which was widely felt to be an award for her work with Tracy over the years, and to mark the end of their careers. But with typical perversity she bounced back the very next year with one of the finest of all her performances, as Eleanor of Aquitaine in Anthony Harvey's distinguished version of James Goldman's play *The Lion in Winter* (1968). This time the Oscar was won in earnest, even if it was shared with Barbra Streisand as a result of the only tie in the history of the Academy Awards.

Her subsequent films were mostly more distinguished than popular, including two grand movies for television directed by her old mentor George Cukor, *Love Among the Ruins*, which teamed her for the first time with Laurence Olivier, and a new version of Emlyn Williams's classic *The Corn Is Green*.

But she could still command popularity if she wished it. In 1969 she returned to the Broadway stage, after a long absence, in, of all things, a musical based on the life of Chanel called *Coco*, in which she scored a great personal triumph, making no claims to a singing voice but working out her own form of speech song as effectively as Rex Harrison's in *My Fair Lady*. Six years later she was back on Broadway, with less success, in *A Matter of Gravity*. Even on film she could still reach a considerable audience, and did so in 1975 with John Wayne in a comedy western called *Rooster Cogburn*, which was really a crafty reworking of *The African Queen*, in a different setting.

It must have seemed to everybody that her career, somewhat impeded in its later stages by Parkinson's disease, was coasting to a dignified conclusion, when along came *On Golden Pond* (1981) to confound all expectations. She played the brusque but understanding wife of crabby old Henry Fonda – who throughout the film wore the favourite hat of Tracy's that Hepburn had given him – in a rosy but not too sentimentalised view of old age. It was the first time that they had worked together, and it proved to be one of the great hits of the decade. Both won Oscars, his posthumous, hers an unprecedented fourth.

Subsequently Hepburn made occasional appearances on stage and on television, most notably in *One Christmas*, a television movie based on a short story by Truman Capote. She devoted much of her energy to writing a short book about the making of *The African Queen* and a more ambitious autobiography, *Me*, for which she earned a $4 million advance. It was cranky and teasing in what it revealed and what it glossed over – as both her admirers and her detractors must by then have expected.

Hepburn began by being, and remained throughout her life, totally original and quite unlike anyone else who starred in Hollywood. For six decades she was an inescapable fact of Hollywood life, more durable than any of the companies she battled with, and more honoured than any other star. Unlike many of those whom she met along the way, she did not bow to celebrity; she considered the greatest luxury imaginable to be "nobody telling you to get out of the bathroom".

Nor did she bow to the studios. During the hearings of the House Un-American Activities Committee in 1947, she spoke out publicly against censorship, against the wishes of her studio boss, Louis B Mayer. As a result, J Edgar Hoover wanted to expose her relationship with Tracy to the public. Hoover was advised by Richard Nixon that this would backfire.

Though her private life was kept scrupulously to herself, it is known that Hepburn, who said that marriage was not a natural state, married in 1928 the socialite stockbroker Ludlow Ogden Smith, and that the marriage was quietly dissolved in 1934.

"I married him, spent all his money, broke his heart and discarded him," she said. Though her biographers have hinted at other relationships, notably with Howard Hughes, the central emotional involvement of her life was clearly the 27 years that she spent with Spencer Tracy.

Katharine Hepburn was born on May 12, 1907. She died on June 29, 2003, aged 96

CELIA JOHNSON

————————— • —————————

Among the most gracious and sympathetic players in the English theatre, especially in passages of quiet emotion, Celia Johnson was also a comedienne in the "drawing-room" tradition, marked by her sense of the ridiculous, her close timing, and the eloquent use of her eyes. Though she seldom acted in the classics, she could be a delicate Chekhovian. To thousands she will be remembered for her part in the film *Brief Encounter* starring opposite Trevor Howard.

A doctor's daughter, born in Richmond, Surrey, in 1908, she was educated in London (St Paul's Girls' School) and abroad, and then at the Royal Academy of Dramatic Art. She first reached the London stage at the Lyric, Hammersmith, Nigel Playfair's theatre, in January 1929 when she followed Angela Baddely in the Spanish comedy, *A Hundred Years Old*.

Twelve months later, at the Kingsway, she was in a poor piece, *The Artist and the Shadow*, "a play of Bohemian life in Paris", that lasted only a week. "Celia Johnson, whom I do not remember seeing before," said the critic, "was very good indeed in a difficult part, an artist's model." Many notices echoed this. Within two months, in another short-lived and indifferent West End comedy, *Debonair*, she acted with graceful assurance as a complex heroine given throughout to running away from something or somebody. From this she went straight on to the Playhouse to appear, with Gerald du Maurier and Gladys Cooper, in the best part she had yet had, wholly unlike the others, the shopgirl in *Cynara* who killed herself after a love affair with a married man.

Cynara succeeded, but the next year's parts were mediocre, and in November 1931 she was in New York, on one of her rare Shakespearian adventures, as Ophelia to Raymond Massey's *Hamlet*. Later, though she had a variety of London plays – and was transiently in Anthony Armstrong's long-running *Ten Minute Alibi* – only two parts would occupy her for any length of time: the heroine of

Merton Hodge's student comedy, *The Wind and the Rain* (St Martin's, 1933), an unexacting if protracted task; and, more demanding, Elizabeth Bennet in Helen Jerome's version of *Pride and Prejudice* (St James's, 1936; 316 performances). Her sense of period was sure; the most exigent students of Jane Austen yielded. James Agate observed this Elizabeth's magnanimity, vivacity, and commonsense.

By now, after marriage in 1935 to the author, traveller and critic, Peter Fleming, for many years on the staff of The Times, she was living at Nettlebed in Oxfordshire. Admired in the theatre for her freshness, pathos and the gentle voice that was described as "an unfolding flower", she became nevertheless an actress increasingly hard to find. Indeed, during a decade from 1937 she would have only two major stage parts, Mrs de Winter in Daphne du Maurier's drama, *Rebecca* (Queen's, 1940), and succeeding Vivien Leigh as the Cornish wife in Shaw's *The Doctor's Dilemma* (Haymarket, 1944). Still, she was making a new reputation as a film actress. She had been the captain's wife of Noël Coward's in *In Which We Serve* (1942), the working-class mother in a version of his play, *This Happy Breed* (1943), and, most celebrated, the housewife in *Brief Encounter* (1945; based on *Still Life*), that poignant drama of a chance railway-station meeting. In 1950 she completed her Coward sequence with the doctor's wife of *The Astonished Heart*.

Before then, in the winter of 1947, she had returned to the London stage in *Saint Joan*. It was at the middle of the Old Vic company's exciting tenure of the New Theatre. Celia Johnson split critical opinion; generally it was felt that though she showed only one side of the character, not the girl-warrior whose voice should be "bright, strong, and rough," she was fully in key as the poor "innocent child of God", faith incarnate.

There was another gap before an Italian tour (1950) with the Old Vic company as Viola in *Twelfth Night*; and, after her beautiful Olga in Chekhov's *Three Sisters* (Aldwych, 1951), she again left the stage for three years. With a strong sense of duty to her family, she would often come out of a play before its run closed. During the 1950s her most substantial work was as the mother in *The Reluctant Debutante* (1955) where the author, William Douglas Home, had an ear for nonsense and Miss Johnson the tongue to utter it; and as two very different wives, in Robert Bolt's *Flowering Cherry* (1957) and in Hugh and Margaret Williams's light comedy, *The Grass Is Greener*, where a critic said she could turn the trembling of an eyelid to a packed speech. That year, 1978, she was appointed CBE.

She began the 1960s as a woman named Pamela Puffy-Picq in a lagging two-character play, *Chin-Chin*, adapted from the French, where she could use her gift for comedy on the rim of tears. In NC Hunter's *The Tulip Tree* (Haymarket, 1962) she acted a middle-aged woman who held firmly to the image of the past ("What I fear most is forgetting"); in the autumn of 1963 she enlivened Giles Cooper's comedy, *Out of the Crocodiles*. Later for the National (1965) she took over from Edith Evans's Judith in *Hay Fever*. As Madame Ranevsky in the Chichester Festival's *Cherry Orchard* (1966) she allowed moments of the most genuine feeling to pierce the woman's indolent vagueness. Then, at the Duke of York's (1967), in Alan Ayckbourn's *Relatively Speaking*, her sense of comedy was at its meridian, especially during a final half-hour when she was trying to reconcile her duties as a hostess with a passionate disbelief – expressed by a slight quiver of the eyelid – in practically everything that had happened or could happen. At the same theatre, in the spring of 1968, she returned in histrionic hauteur and surrender to Judith in *Hay Fever* after playing the part in Toronto.

She was seen too rarely on television where her warmth, and expressive features – and sense of humour – were seen to good effect. Television watchers will recall with pleasure her playing in *Mrs Palfrey at the Claremont*, adapted from the novel by Elizabeth Taylor, and her moving performance in Paul Scott's *Staying On* in which she was reunited with Trevor Howard.

Peter Fleming died suddenly in 1971. She is survived by a son and two daughters, one of whom, Lucy, is herself on the stage.

Dame Celia Johnson DBE was born on December 18, 1908. She died following a stroke on April 26, 1982, aged 73

PETER SELLERS

Mr Peter Sellers had a career which took him via the British cinema to an international stardom more spectacular, perhaps, and certainly more meteoric than that of any other British star. Though he began as a comedian, making his way in his profession by the usual stages on radio and television, it was as an actor that he became so rapidly and overwhelmingly popular with the British filmgoing public, afterwards progressing to become internationally acclaimed. He was a comic actor first and foremost, no doubt, but an actor always first and a comedian, incidentally.

His background was theatrical, though more on the management than the performing side. He was born in Southsea in 1925, and descended from the Portuguese-Jewish prizefighter Daniel Mendoza; one of his first jobs was sweeping out the seaside theatre run by his parents and later he began in a small way as a comedian and impressionist with ENSA, followed by a stint, almost obligatory for the budding English comic, at the Windmill.

His extraordinary vocal adaptability soon found him a niche in radio, and in 1951 he met Spike Milligan, whose very personal brand of comedy matched and complemented his own. From this meeting sprang the *Goon Show*, in which Peter Sellers, as one of the team, provided funny voices and off-the-cuff gags week by week to the pleasure of millions – an activity later, though rather less successfully, extended to television with *A Show Called Fred* and *The Idiot Weekly*.

All this time he remained very much one member of a group, popular certainly but hardly known as an individual. And when he first ventured into films it was mainly his gifts as a mimic which were called upon; he was noticed in small roles – as one of the bunch of weird murderers in *The Ladykillers*, as an elderly member of the cinema staff in *The Smallest Show on Earth* – but seemed likely to remain merely one of the large band of capable character-actors the British cinema has always had on call. The film that really changed things, though, the Boulting Brothers' *I'm All Right Jack*, in which his playing of the pompous, pathetic shop-steward Kite, a masterpiece of precise observation, funny because of its truth rather than in spite of it, gathered him enthusiastic notices and made him almost immediately one of the busiest actors of his generation.

His rate of activity after that was positively dizzying. Apart from one brief appearance on the West End stage, in the comedy *Brouhaha*, he devoted almost all his time and energy to film-making, going from one film to another with hardly a break between. The emphasis of nearly all his performances was primarily comic, and his one completely straight role as the sadistic crook in *Never Let Go*, was not a great success, though this might be attributable more to the film than to the performer. But within generally comic terms of definition his variety of characterisation was extraordinary. He said of himself once that he had no marked personality, was in fact virtually unnoticeable, and needed a strongly defined character to play. For this reason he was arguably less at home in farce, where sometimes his thoughtfulness cut against the general grain of the entertainment, but in comedy or tragi-comedy he was unbeatable. His Indian doctor in *The Millionairess*, for instance, stayed just on the right side of caricature and remained always a believable, even if often a very funny, man. The woman-chasing Welsh librarian in *Only Two Can Play*, the pernickety old Scotsman in *The Battle of the Sexes*, the smooth Levantine politician in *Carlton-Brown of the F.O.*, his tour de force as three distinct characters in *The Mouse that Roared*, the ageing general in *The Waltz of the Toreadors*, all these were distinct and believable characterisations, and whatever the varying merits of the films that contained them they at least were almost wholly persuasive.

He branched out once into direction, with his film of Marcel Pagnol's *Mr Topaze*, in which he also played the small French schoolmaster who becomes a big tycoon, and although the film was less popularly successful than most of his it suggested a distinct talent for direction which could have borne further exploration. Subsequent films were *Lolita*, in which he played the mysterious and sinister Quilty; *Heavens Above*, in which he was seen as a cleric who tries to live literally by Christian principles in an unchristian world; *The Pink Panther*, in which he took the part of an eccentric and divertingly inefficient French detective. To this character he returned in 1975 with *The Return of the Pink Panther*, and *The Pink Panther Strikes Again* (1977).

His international reputation had been more firmly secured by films such as *I Love You, Alice B Toklas* (1968), and *What's New Pussycat?* He was made a CBE in 1966.

His last film, *Being There*, in which he gave one of his most accomplished performances, came to London earlier this month.

Though he claimed that he was not funny in himself, he succeeded on the screen amusing audiences the world over; his timing was impeccable, and his insistence on always finding comedy in the truth about the characters he played allowed his brand of humour to transcend barriers of language and nationality. He was one of the very rare British film stars to be almost as popular abroad as at home.

He had one son and one daughter by his first marriage in 1951 to Anne Howe. This marriage was dissolved and in 1964 he married Britt Ekland. They had one daughter. This marriage was dissolved in 1969 and in 1970 he married Miranda, daughter of Richard St John Quarry and Lady Mancroft. This marriage was dissolved in 1974 and he married in February 1977, Lynne Frederick.

Peter Sellers was born September 8, 1925. He died of a heart attack on July 24, 1980, aged 54

JANE RUSSELL

Glamour and Jane Russell were indivisible. Her spectacular physical attributes, statuesque bearing, and the sultry mood she emanated on screen made her a male sexual fantasy during her screen heyday, from the late 1940s to the mid-1950s.

Her sensationally publicised debut in *The Outlaw* has become a part of cinema history. Long before the film was released the public knew her from stills which showed her lying provocatively in a pile of straw, her blouse, slipping off one shoulder, always threatening to reveal her voluptuous assets in their entirety.

Posters made the most of a similar image, whose accompanying legend stridently trumpeted "Mean!... Moody!... Magnificent!", as a taster to any who might be thinking of venturing into the cinema. The tone of all this and the apparently corrupting potential of Russell's display of cleavage proved far too much for the susceptibilities of the US censor. Released briefly in 1943, *The Outlaw* was put on ice for three years and did not gain the Motion Picture Association Seal of Approval for several more years. Interestingly, when the movie was released in the UK the British Board of Film

Censors gave it a "U" certificate – which meant that children could see it without their parents.

One of several screen versions of the Billy the Kid story, which involved Billy the Kid, Pat Garret and Doc Holliday meeting up and quarrelling over a "half-breed" (ie, exemplifying forbidden fruit) girl, *The Outlaw* was the creation of its eccentric millionaire producer Howard Hughes, who also directed it. He had without hesitation cast Russell, then an unknown 19-year-old, as the female lead after pictures of her as a model were sent to him by an agency. Russell always claimed that she never wore the special bra that the characteristically obsessive Hughes designed for her to wear in the role.

The Outlaw might well have proved a mixed blessing for Russell, since it seemed to announce her undeniably as a star, but one of clearly circumscribed capacity who was not likely to progress beyond the self-limiting role of screen siren.

But she could act, as well as sing and dance, and she was able to rise above the apparent drawback inherent in her screen debut (and the stream of double-entendre wisecracks it generated throughout the industry and beyond) to become not just a swooned-over, but actually rather well-liked leading lady during what was to be a relatively brief apogee of her career. She had a gift for comedy on both stage and screen, and in her personal life had a refreshing capacity not to take herself too seriously.

She was born Ernestine Jane Geraldine Russell, in Bemidji, Minnesota, in 1921, the oldest of five children and the only girl. Later the family moved to Southern California and her father worked as office manager in a soap manufacturing plant. Her mother had been a stage actress but, unlike many showbusiness mothers, did not try to push her daughter into the profession. Jane worked as a chiropodist's receptionist and a model, before joining Max Reinhardt's Theatre Workshop and studying under the veteran actress Maria Ouspenskaya.

She began work on *The Outlaw* in 1941 and, as a result of the publicity campaign, was receiving more than 1,000 fan letters a week before the film had even been released. Very soon she was able to join Betty Grable and Rita Hayworth as a favoured pin-up of the

American forces, in her case draped fetchingly amid the straw on top of a rick. Later, in the Korean War, GIs christened a prominent and much fought-over landmark Jane Russell Hill after her.

With something of a hiatus in her movie progress while the *Outlaw* row rumbled on, she tried to launch a musical career, singing on radio with the Kay Kyser Orchestra and recording two singles with him, *As Long as I Live*, and *Boin-n-n-ng*.

Her next film was *The Young Widow* (1946), followed by *The Paleface* (1948), an effective spoof of a wagon train western in which she partnered Bob Hope. It was succeeded by a number of largely run-of-the-mill efforts in which she nevertheless proved herself an effective heroine of melodrama, especially when it was of the tongue-in-cheek kind. These included *Double Dynamite* (1951), a comedy with Frank Sinatra; *His Kind of Woman* (1951) opposite Robert Mitchum; and the western melodrama *Montana Belle* (1952), in which she played Belle Starr, the glamorous real-life outlaw Myra Belle Shirley; before she was teamed up with the emerging Marilyn Monroe in the musical *Gentlemen Prefer Blondes* (1953), directed by Howard Hawks.

The film, in which she played the seasoned showgirl to Monroe's dumb blonde ingénue, the pair of them on a foray to Paris in search of (rich) husbands, demonstrated her gift for comedy and revealed her talent as a singer and dancer, notably in the number *Anyone Here for Love?* which she performed with members of the American Olympic team. Audiences loved it, and Hawks loved directing his spectacular blonde and brunette leading ladies, of whom he said it would have been enough just to have them walking up and down the set to get the audiences in.

In 1955 she returned to the western co-starring with Clark Gable in *The Tall Men*, a tale of the Montana goldfields, for the veteran director Raoul Walsh. Another Walsh film, *The Revolt of Mamie Stover* (1956), in which she played a red-haired prostitute trying to take control of her life, was later (somewhat hopefully) claimed as a feminist statement, though Russell herself was always far from being a flag waver for the movement.

Apart from occasional guest spots and minor roles, her cinema career was effectively over by 1957. But she built up a new career as a singer, appearing on television and in night clubs, and as a recording artist. During the 1960s she brought her act to Britain.

She returned to films after a gap of seven years in *Fate is the Hunter* (1964), made a couple of low-budget westerns and took a supporting part in the private eye thriller, *Darker Than Amber* (1970). Meanwhile she was still receiving $1,000 a week from Howard Hughes under an agreement made in the 1950s.

In 1971 she made her debut on the Broadway stage, replacing Elaine Stritch as the star of the musical, *Company*. In the same year she began a long association with Playtex, advertising their bras with the slogan: "Us big girls have special problems."

She hit the headlines briefly in 1978 when she was sentenced to four days in jail for drunken driving; she had started drinking heavily after the sudden death of her second husband. In 1984 she came out of retirement to join *The Yellow Rose*, a short-lived television soap opera in the *Dallas/Dynasty* genre. *Jane Russell, an Autobiography*, a frank and engaging memoir, was published in 1986.

She married her first husband, Bob Waterfield, a football star, in 1943. Unable to have children, she adopted a boy and two girls and in 1955 founded the World Adoption International Fund (Waif), an adoption charity, and successfully campaigned for a change in the law to allow foreign children to enter the US for adoption before becoming American citizens. When she retired from Waif in 1995, it had placed more than 40,000 children throughout the world.

Divorced from Waterfield in 1968, she married Robert Barrett, an actor and teacher of English; he died of a coronary thrombosis three months after the wedding. She married, thirdly, in 1974, John Calvin Peoples, a Texan property dealer. He died in 1999.

Jane Russell was born on June 21, 1921. She died on February 28, 2011, aged 89

BETTY GRABLE

Betty Grable, the Hollywood song-and-dance star renowned for her "million dollar legs", was for most of the 1940s one of the top box-office attractions in the United States. It was estimated that over a period of ten years her films made a profit of £6m [about £135 million in today's money].

She was well rewarded for this enormous popularity: in 1949 she earned £115,000 and was said to be the highest-paid woman in the world. Yet her talents, as she was the first to admit, were modest and most of her films are now forgotten. She did not dance as well as Ginger Rogers, had an ordinary singing voice and once confessed "I am no actress and I know it". She was a small shapely blonde, who wore a lot of lipstick and her greatest asset was her legs, which were once insured by Lloyd's for £250,000. Perhaps the key to her success was that unlike Dietrich or Garbo she was not some unattainable goddess but an ordinary girl who happened to lead a rather glamorous existence on the screen, the small-town waitress, who in one picture manages to grab herself a millionaire husband. She might have been the GI's favourite pin-up during the Second World

War but she was also someone that millions of girls leading hum-drum lives loved to identify with. She was a likeable actress with a talent for putting over a droll line that not all her directors sensed.

Betty Grable, her real name though curiously enough she began her career as Frances Dean, was born in St Louis, Missouri, in 1916, of a stockbroker father and a mother who was determined to put her into showbusiness. When she was five she was learning to sing and dance and play the piano, at 12 she went with her mother to Los Angeles for further dance tuition and in 1930 made her first film appearance at 14 blacked up in a chorus line.

Her career took a long time, however, to get underway. Sam Goldwyn signed her up and dropped her and RKO did the same, despite her considerable success in *The Gay Divorcee* in 1934. She made a third false start with Paramount, was briefly married to the former child star Jackie Coogan and finally made it with Twentieth Century-Fox. They signed her up in 1940, put her in *Down Argentine Way* when Alice Faye was taken ill and she went on to make nearly 30 films in the next 14 years. They were nearly all musicals, with formula plots and little artistry – and they were unfailingly popular.

Sweet Rosie O'Grady, *Pin Up Girl*, *The Dolly Sisters* (with June Haver), *Diamond Horseshoe* and *Mother Wore Tights* were just a few of them. But towards the end of the Forties, with Grable getting older, busts taking over from legs and musicals slipping out of vogue, Hollywood demanded new stars. In 1951 Betty Grable was suspended by the studio for refusing a part and the same thing was to happen twice more. Finally, in 1953, Fox's leading female star had her contract ended after 13 years and her appearance that year in *How to Marry a Millionaire* with the girl who was to supersede her, Marilyn Monroe, marked the effective end of the Betty Grable era.

She continued in films for a little while more but after the ironically titled *How to be Very Very Popular* in 1955 she decided that the cinema had nothing more to offer and she went into semi-retirement in Las Vegas with her second husband, the band leader Harry James, and their two daughters.

In 1965, to general surprise, her 22-year-old marriage to James ended in divorce and Grable, nearly 50 and soon to be a grandmother, started a comeback on the stage. She did *Guys and Dolls* and *Born Yesterday* and in 1967 turned up as the leading lady in *Hello, Dolly!* on Broadway. Two years later she came to London, her legs and her legend intact, to play Belle Starr in a musical of that name but the show was savaged by the critics and taken off after less than three weeks. At the time of her death she was due to appear in a revival of *No, No, Nanette* in Australia.

Betty Grable was born on December 18, 1916. She died of cancer on July 2, 1973, aged 56

Few stars of Miss Judy Garland's era gained more, or suffered more, from the mercurial quality of their temperament. She had an infectious charm, a buoyant and irresistible vivacity and an unmistakable talent both as a singer and as a film actress; but she was in many ways neurotic, her home life was disturbed by a mother who often tried to drive her too hard, and although Louis B Mayer, the head of MGM, was her mentor, and immensely proud of her, he never really understood her. Her separation from MGM and Mayer in 1950 was a sad affair.

In her last years she was often seen in cabaret in London. There were some rapturous receptions but there were also times of tears and temperament and to those who remembered her in happier days she was now something of a tragic figure.

Judy Garland's real name was Frances Gumm. She was born in Grand Rapids, Minnesota, in 1922. As a child she was part of her mother's vaudeville act, billed as The Gumm Sisters. The mother played the piano, and Frances and her two older sisters sang. The performance was not very good, but in 1935 Louis B Mayer chanced to see them and was taken by this fat little girl of 11 with the buoyant personality. Mayer, at this time, was beginning to concentrate on developing child stars (who enabled him to present his favourite theme of the homely American family), and he had already made a major discovery, in the young Mickey Rooney. Then he found Deanna Durbin, whom he decided to team with Judy Garland in a short musical film called *Every Sunday*. Both girls showed promise, but by some mischance Deanna Durbin's contract was not renewed and MGM lost her to Twentieth Century-Fox. Mayer was so angry that he ceased to take an interest in Judy Garland, who was lent to Twentieth Century-Fox for a college musical called *Pigskin Parade*, in which she sang *It's Love I'm After* in a snowy football stadium.

Little might have come of all this had not Mayer decided some time later to give a birthday party in honour of one of his favourite stars, Clark Gable. MGM's songwriter, Roger Edens, who had great faith in Judy Garland's talents, decided to compose a special number for the occasion, called *Dear Mister Gable*, which Judy sang at the height of the festivities. By the time she had finished it, her reputation was made. She was hurriedly given a part in the current MGM production *Broadway Melody* of 1938, and then partnered with Mickey Rooney in *Thoroughbreds Don't Cry*. They made a good team, and were partnered again – this time in one of the Andy Hardy series which Mayer, with his devotion to American family life, always held to be the best thing which the studios did. In *Love Finds Andy Hardy* Judy Garland played "the girl next door" to Andy, and a delighted Mayer welcomed her into the fold of his special child stars.

But even then luck was to play an important part in her career. When *The Wizard of Oz* was first planned the producer, Mervyn Leroy, wanted Shirley Temple to play the part of Dorothy, the young Kansas farm girl who visits the wonderful land of Oz, and there encounters the Scarecrow, the Tinman and the Cowardly Lion. But Shirley Temple was not available, and so the part was given, on Mayer's advice, to Judy Garland. Jack Haley played the Tinman, Ray Bolgar the Scarecrow, and Bert Lahr the Cowardly Lion. The film did not get off to a good start, but when a new director Victor Fleming was brought in, the elusive mood of fantasy was happily created, Judy Garland sang *Over the Rainbow* enchantingly – a number by which she will always be remembered, and one which was very nearly deleted from the film in its cutting stage.

This was at the beginning of the war. Judy Garland marked its end with another notable musical, *Meet Me in St Louis* in which her singing of *The Trolley Song* was almost as memorable as *Over the Rainbow*. The film was admirably directed by Vincente Minnelli, and the cast included Margaret O'Brien, another child star of remarkable talent.

The Clock, Ziegfeld Follies, The Harvey Girls, Easter Parade (in which she sang *Easter Bonnet* with Fred Astaire), *Words and Music*, and *Summer Stock* followed. Then came the break with Louis B Mayer. The clash had been foreseeable for some time. Judy had suffered a serious breakdown in 1949, and had been forced to retire from *Annie Get*

Your Gun, already half-completed. There had been trouble again during the filming of *Summer Stock*, with Gene Kelly, but the picture was finally finished. After this she was due to make *Royal Wedding* and *Showboat*, but by then she was a mentally sick woman, and she appeared in neither. Mayer had by now lost patience with her, and he even went so far as to quarrel violently with MGM's most promising young producer, Joseph Mankiewicz, when he tried to help Judy. The result was that Mankiewicz left MGM and so did Judy Garland. The father of his studio was not a man who would tolerate being crossed.

This was in 1950, and it was not until nearly five years later that Judy Garland was seen again on the screen. Then Warner Brothers decided to remake an old classic of the 30s, the story of a film star's decline and fall entitled *A Star is Born*, which had originally rescued Janet Gaynor at a moment when her career seemed almost over. Judy Garland played the Gaynor part and James Mason the part originally created by Fredric March, but the film lacked the strength and heart of the original film, and Judy herself showed that she had lost something of her youthful exuberance.

Thereafter her career as a public entertainer, in films and on the stage, was episodic, although she still showed her ability to hold an audience.

In 1961 she was seen again on the screen in Stanley Kramer's dramatic assessment of war guilt entitled *Judgment at Nuremberg*, in which she played the part of a distraught and heartbroken German girl. By now she had come a long way from the mood that had so invigorated *The Wizard of Oz*. Her first British film was *I Could Go on Singing*.

No actress can remain young for ever, but some take to middle age more easily than others. It is most difficult for those who, like Judy Garland, were once a symbol of youthfulness, gaiety, and the zest for life. These were the qualities which were discovered, fostered, and ultimately suppressed in her early and formative years under Louis B Mayer. The burden of stardom proved too much for her.

Judy Garland was born on June 10, 1922. She died of a barbiturate overdose on June 22, 1969, aged 47

JAMES EARL JONES

———•———

Few voices were as instantly recognisable as that of the stage and screen actor James Earl Jones. A seismic rumble of a basso profundo, it could convey both unshakeable authority and chill the very blood with its ominous threat. Not for nothing was Jones one of the most celebrated voice artists in the business.

His line readings as Mufasa in Disney's *The Lion King* (1994) exuded nobility. Of the original cast of the much-loved animation, he was the only one who was invited to reprise his role in the 2019 live-action remake. Earlier he acted alongside Kevin Costner in *Field of Dreams* (1989), which earned three Oscar nominations including best picture. He was, for a time, the voice that announced "This is CNN" on the television channel's identifier, and made those three words electrifying and essential. But most famously, he was the voice of Darth Vader in the Star Wars series.

While the rumbling foreboding of Darth Vader's voice seared itself into the nightmares of generations of children, Jones considered his contribution to be just "a special effect" and asked not to be credited as a cast member. He was paid only $7,000 for his work on the first film, and it was not until the third film in the series, *The Return of the Jedi,* that he finally accepted a named credit.

The voice, then, was a gift. What's all the more remarkable was that, for a considerable portion of his childhood, Jones was essentially mute, shamed into silence by a debilitating stutter.

James Earl Jones was born in 1931, in Arkabutla, Mississippi, to Ruth Jones, a teacher and maid. His father, Robert Earl Jones, absented himself from his son's life from around the time of his birth, pursuing work as a boxer, butler, chauffeur and, later, a stage and screen actor. "I didn't know him, and he didn't raise me, but in high school I would see his picture in national magazines," Jones recalled.

Raised in the uncertainty of Depression-era Mississippi, Jones's early years were spent in the hardscrabble household of his maternal grandparents. His grandmother, who was part Cherokee, part Choctaw Indian and part African American, was "unusual", Jones later said. She taught her children and grandchildren to hate White people and distrust Black people. Her sympathies, during the Second World War, were with the Japanese because they, at least, were people of colour. Jones commented wryly: "We had to keep her inside a lot, in terms of the war effort." If, in later life, Jones preferred not to raise his voice on issues of racial politics, he did acknowledge that his grandmother had at least taught him to make up his own mind on such matters.

When the family was uprooted and moved to rural Michigan, the upheaval unsettled the young Jones to the extent that he developed a stutter. The onset was sudden. "I'll never forget it. I was 12 years old and I was living on a farm with my family. It was the middle of winter and one day my uncle had a seizure. I'd never seen anything like it and it terrified me. I didn't know what to do. My grandmother said, 'Go to the nearest road and find someone to help you get a doctor.' I finally got to a store that had a phone, but I couldn't speak. All I could do was stutter. My uncle's life was in my hands and I couldn't speak. That was the beginning."

Too self-conscious to wrestle with the speech impediment, the young Jones simply stopped speaking altogether. It was a difficult time. He later observed: "One of the hardest things in life is having words in your heart that you can't utter."

When Jones reached high school he found a new means of expression. He started covertly writing poetry, and thanks to an inspiring English teacher who encouraged him to read his verses in class, he began to develop strategies to cope with his stutter, including the precise diction that later became his trademark.

Jones enrolled at the University of Michigan in a pre-med course and joined the Reserve Officer Training Corps. He felt more comfortable with the discipline and camaraderie of the military than he did with his studies in medicine. Working on the assumption that he would soon be called up to serve in the Korean War, he swapped medicine for drama, reasoning that he might as well do something he enjoyed with his time at college. "I figured I'd go into the drama department and at least I'd meet some girls."

He was commissioned in 1953 and attended the officer's basic course and became a second lieutenant. But instead of Korea, his unit was sent to a cold-weather training command in Colorado, near Leadville. Jones was promoted to first lieutenant before his discharge.

Although he had not ruled out a career in the military and had planned to re-enlist if acting did not work out, Jones moved to New York and studied at the American Theatre Wing. He worked as a janitor to support himself and, for a time at least, lived with his father. His main reason was financial expediency rather than rebuilding family bridges. "It was too late to get to know him as a father: if you don't learn that from the beginning, there's no way to catch up. It took us time to accept that if we could be friends, that would be best."

Although he worked steadily in theatre during the 1960s, the point when he fully committed to acting as a career came when he won the lead role in Howard Sackler's play *The Great White Hope*, which moved to Broadway in 1968. It was the kind of work that could support a family, rather than just provide for a hand-to-mouth bachelor existence. Jones played a champion boxer who must deal with the racism from the predominantly White boxing establishment. The role won him a Tony award, and after he reprised it in a film version in 1970, a Golden Globe and an Oscar nomination. Jones cited it as one of his most rewarding roles. "America's relationship with Black boxing champions is strange, isn't it? They like it at first when he wins, but they're even happier when he's destroyed and can't trouble their dreams any more."

Jones went on to become a member of one of the most elite clubs in the world of entertainment: he was one of only 14 performers who could describe themselves as an "Egot", meaning that he had won at least one of all of the four major entertainment awards: an Emmy, a Grammy, an Oscar and a Tony.

The Great White Hope, his first leading film role, came after an auspicious film acting debut, as Lt Lothar Zogg, in Stanley Kubrick's *Dr Strangelove* (1964). Kubrick cast him after seeing him two years earlier in a production of Shakespeare's *The Merchant of Venice* at the Delacorte Theater in New York.

Jones was repeatedly drawn to Shakespeare throughout his career, and was able to transfer the bedrock of classical stage training to elsewhere in his work. There was a composure and gravitas in his demeanour, which could anchor even the flimsiest of fantasies.

Take, for example, the magnetic malice he brought to the role of the villainous Thulsa Doom, in *Conan the Barbarian*. A wordless scene in which Jones, playing Arnold Schwarzenegger's future nemesis, beheads the mother of the young Conan, is a masterclass in quixotic cruelty. The dignity of Jones's performance gives weight to some of the more questionable elements of the film, including his character's ill-advised wig, and the acting of his inexperienced co-star. Jones and Schwarzenegger forged a firm friendship on the set and exchanged acting suggestions and fitness tips.

Theatre was where he honed that voice, a combination of velvet and steel, its measured and precise delivery the result of the concentration required to quell the stutter that never entirely went away.

"Usually it's the voice of authority they hire, ever since Darth Vader. Whether it's Admiral Greer (*The Hunt for Red October*, *Patriot Games* and *Clear and Present Danger*), voiceovers for [the communications company] Bell Atlantic, or Chrysler cars, I don't mind. It's good to have a pigeonhole."

The theatre also played a key role in both of Jones's marriages. He met his first wife, the actress and singer Julienne Marie, while performing the titular role in *Othello* in 1964. They wed in 1968, but the relationship was strained by long periods of separation and because Jones wanted children while Marie did not. They divorced in 1972.

Jones met his second wife, Cecilia Hart, when both were appearing in the television series *Paris*, in which Jones played the Los Angeles police captain Woody Paris and Hart portrayed a young detective, Sergeant Stacey Erickson. In 1982, Hart played a replacement Desdemona opposite Jones's Othello on Broadway, and they were married in March of that year. They were together until Hart's death in 2016 and had one son, Flynn Earl Jones, who worked closely with his father as his personal assistant.

While his voice might have been immediately familiar – for a while, Jones used "Darth Vader" as his handle on CB radio, but had to stop because of the terror his voice was generating within the amateur radio community – he preferred to be anonymous. With typical modesty, he referred to himself as a "journeyman actor" who muddled through his career without a plan. But this approach served him well.

Jones continued to work well into his nineties, and reprised his role as Darth Vader in the most recent film in the Star Wars saga: *The Rise of Skywalker*. In 2022, it was revealed that, despite wanting to step back from the role, his wish to "keep Vader alive" meant that a new AI technology firm, Respeecher, had been engaged to take archival recordings to create new dialogue.

Lucasfilm confirmed that Jones had given his blessing for his voice to be used in all future films, even "those produced after his own passing", which ensures that further generations will be terrorised by Darth Vader long after his death.

James Earl Jones was born on January 17, 1931. He died of undisclosed causes on September 9, 2024, aged 93

MAE WEST

———————•———————

As a star Mae West enjoyed unparalleled longevity: she played her first leading role on Broadway in 1913, and even in what may well have been her 90th year – her exact age was a mystery – was a continuing attraction, well able to command top billing for any appearance she made. As well as being the only important female humourist in films she was, for more than half a century, a universal sex symbol in the proper sense of that much-abused term.

She was born in Brooklyn on August 17 some year between 1885 and 1893, and seems to have taken instantly to greasepaint: she began at the age of five doing imitations at church socials, then went into stock theatre playing child roles such as Little Eva and Little Lord Fauntleroy.

By the age of 15 she was doing her own song-and-dance act in vaudeville, and in 1911 she got married, for the first and only time, to Frank Wallace, with whom she formed a vaudeville team. They soon separated and were divorced in 1943; he died in 1966.

In 1911, too, she achieved her first real public notice in a show called *A la Broadway*, and from then alternated vaudeville tours and appearances in New York musicals and revues. By 1913 and the Rudolf Friml show *Sometime* she was a topliner; in 1926 with the opening (and eventually the legally enforced closing) of her play *Sex*, Mae West definitely became Mae West.

From then on she was the writer and creator of her own material on stage and screen, as well as a prolific author of books and plays and a successful recorded singer. The raw material of all her work was sex; her approach was always comic.

In play after play and film after film she embodied voluptuously proportioned sirens who took a frank sexual interest in the physique of the men in their lives, chose for themselves (the classic invitation "Come up and see me some time" was offered at and for the lady's pleasure only) and found much comic relish in the advantages of being a fallen woman.

By making sex a shared joke, she defused the subject of much of its offensive power – though clearly not enough for many people in the 1920s and 1930s, when she was constantly the target of outraged moralists even while she fortunately remained the darling of the public.

Sex was followed on stage by *The Drag*, a homosexual comedy she wrote but did not appear in, and by two of her most famous vehicles, *Diamond Lil* (1928) and *The Constant Sinner* (1931), both of them also turned into novels and later filmed. It was inevitable that Hollywood, now eagerly on the lookout for talent from the stage that could handle the new talkie medium, and still relatively unrestricted by the self-censorship of the famous Hays Code, should beckon, and in 1932 she heeded the invitation, going out to play a subordinate role in a George Raft vehicle, *Night after Night*.

At least, that was the intention, but from the moment that Mae West entered, about halfway through to deliver the immortal response to a hatcheck girl who says wonderingly "Goodness what beautiful diamonds", "Goodness had nothing to do with it, dearie", no one was in much doubt that this was Mae West's movie.

Though she still had to fight to do things her own way in films, the enormous earning of her films were a powerful persuader, and she turned out in rapid succession *She Done Him Wrong*, *I'm No Angel*, *Belle of the Nineties*, *Goin' to Town* (in which she showed an unsuspected talent by singing for herself a scene from *Samson and*

Delilah) and the less inspired (or more censored) *Klondike Annie* and *Go West Young Man*. In all of them the formula was much the same, the presence, though much imitated, ultimately inimitable.

Her fame became inescapable: she was painted by Dali, parodied by Disney, and a little later entered the dictionary when, during the war, an inflatable lifejacket was named after her.

With the puritanical backlash against her kind of humour on screen she became, paradoxically, one of the biggest stars of that family medium par excellence, radio, and continued to make occasional films, of which the most enjoyable, *My Little Chickadee*, teamed her with another eccentric, self-fuelling *monstre sacré*, WC Fields.

Without actually being sexy (she was, after all, as the camera made obvious, a lady of mature years by this time) she had become the world's shorthand for the idea of sex, a living embodiment of the dangerous truths that sex could be profitable, and sex could be fun.

In the 1940s Mae West returned to the stage with a new vehicle, an historical parody *Catherine was Great* (1944), and revived *Diamond Lil* for a European tour. In 1954 she opened in cabaret in Las Vegas with her famous retinue of loin-clothed musclemen. The 1960s brought her back to the screen, lending her disruptive presence to the film version of Gore Vidal's *Myra Breckinridge* (though not unfortunately, in the title role), and found her singing Beatles songs to heavy rock accompaniment on record.

Her autobiography, *Goodness Had Nothing to Do with It* came out in 1959, and she continued to write novels; plays; advice on life, love and diet; and even a biography of her favourite psychic, right up to the last.

In 1976, when she may quite well have been 90, she was still active and energetic, planning a new starring film, *Sextette*, making a spirited appearance on a Dick Cavett television special, and blandly observing of a projected television remake of *Diamond Lil*: "I could still do it; I still look like Mae West." It was a great part of her charm, and perhaps the main reason for the durability of her legend, that she alone in the world steadfastly refused to be taken in by it.

Mae West was born on or around August 17, 1893. She died following a stroke on November 22, 1980, aged around 87

CARY GRANT

Tall, suave and with dark good looks – though his hair eventually turned snow-white – he had a limited range as an actor. But within the genres that suited him best, the sophisticated comedy and comedy-thriller, he was supreme.

His easy and relaxed playing concealed a magnificent technique, and he was often compared with the English stage actor, Gerald du Maurier, of whom it was said that he excelled at being himself. Grant's basic screen persona was of the romantic charmer and he was teamed successfully with a generation of the screen's leading ladies from Jean Harlow and Katharine Hepburn to Ingrid Bergman, Grace Kelly, Sophia Loren and Leslie Caron.

But in the hands of gifted directors such as George Cukor, Alfred Hitchcock (his own favourite) and Howard Hawks, the Grant character often took on an extra dimension, acquiring a hint of vulnerability and even anarchy.

His voice was unique, with an accent attributable to no country or region. It was neither English nor American, nor even mid-Atlantic. Clipped but with some rather extravagant vowel sounds, it went well with the character of a mysterious loner, whose caustic and cynical manner concealed reserves of passion. Grant's comic gifts were best employed in the series of screwball comedies he made with Hawks. In films such as *Bringing Up Baby, I Was a Male War Bride* and *Monkey Business*, the humour largely stems from placing him in a humiliating situation, whether coping with a baby leopard, being forced to dress up as a woman, or taking a drug which produces a reversion to childhood.

Another constant factor in these films is that Grant is outwitted by the opposite sex – an uncomfortable experience for the screen's great lover. George Cukor helped bring out his talent for comedy in pictures such as *Sylvia Scarlett, Holiday* and *The Philadelphia Story,* while Hitchcock cast him successfully in a number of his lighter thrillers, including *Notorious, To Catch a Thief* and the classic *North by Northwest,* which contains the famous sequence of Grant menaced by a crop-dusting plane in a lonely cornfield.

The ending of another Hitchcock film, *Suspicion,* had to be changed because it was felt that the public would not accept Grant as a murderer.

Even in the slightest of his pictures, he could be relied on for a performance of faultless comic technique, and he carried his years lightly. His riposte to the fan magazine editor who cabled to him, "How old Cary Grant?" is legendary: "Old Cary Grant fine. How you?"

He was born in Bristol in 1904, the son of a clothes presser, but grandson (on his father's side) of an actor. His real name was Alexander Archibald Leach.

As a boy he frequented the Bristol Hippodrome, being initially more interested in the electrical side of stage work than in becoming a performer. But before long, without his parents' permission, he joined a troupe of acrobats as a tumbler and stilt-walker; and while still only 16 he travelled with the troupe to America. He stayed there for three years, for a time selling neckties, and also working as a sandwich man.

He also began to get jobs as an actor, and during the 1920s he alternated between the British and American theatres, mostly in musical comedy and vaudeville. He had a screen test with Paramount but the studio turned him down because of his thick neck and bow legs.

But Paramount later changed its mind and put him under contract. In 1932 he made his screen debut in a musical, *This Is the Night*. In the next few years he averaged half a dozen pictures a year, but it was not until near the end of the decade that he emerged as a major star.

An important influence on his early career was the flamboyant Mae West, who taught him much about the craft of comedy in the course of appearing with him in *She Done Him Wrong* and *I'm No Angel*. Though he had to suffer the inevitable crop of routine pictures to fulfil his contract with the studio, he did manage to appear opposite Marlene Dietrich in *Blonde Venus*, Katharine Hepburn in *Sylvia Scarlett* and Jean Harlow in *Suzy*.

By the late 1930s, with comedies such as *Topper*, *The Awful Truth*, *Bringing Up Baby* (with Hepburn again) and another Hawks picture, *Only Angels Have Wings* (which features a memorable verbal duel between Grant and Jean Arthur), he was indisputably one of Hollywood's big stars.

Further pictures enhanced his position: yet another Hawks comedy, *His Girl Friday*, a remake of the famous newspaper play, *The Front Page*, with Rosalind Russell, *The Philadelphia Story* and *Suspicion*. There was a tailor-made part for him in Frank Capra's version of the celebrated black comedy, *Arsenic and Old Lace*, and an Oscar nomination for his portrayal of the cockney hero of Richard Llewellyn's *None But the Lonely Heart*.

He never, in fact, won an Oscar for an individual performance, but he was given a special award in 1970 for "his unique mastery of the art of screen acting". In making the presentation, Frank Sinatra said: "Cary has so much skill that he makes it all look easy".

The casting of Grant as the songwriter Cole Porter in *Night and Day* was not a success, but he generally managed to choose his pictures shrewdly, and the late 1940s and early 1950s saw him in *Notorious, I Was a Male War Bride* and *Monkey Business*. He also appeared in two pictures with a young actress, Betsy Drake, whom he discovered and later married.

But by 1953, with Hollywood reeling under the first impact of television, Grant (along with some other major stars) came near to being written off by both the industry and the fans, and he was absent from the cinema for two years.

Hitchcock brought him back, opposite Grace Kelly, in *To Catch a Thief*, and it became immediately apparent that his screen obituary was premature. (The film, made on location in Monaco, had important consequences for Miss Kelly, and for the Grimaldi dynasty.) *An Affair to Remember*, *Indiscreet* (a felicitous partnership with Ingrid Bergman), *North by Northwest*, *The Grass Is Greener*, and a polished comedy-thriller, *Charade*, took his career successfully into the 1960s and showed him to be as durable as ever.

By this time Grant had become one of the richest film stars in the world. From 1958 he took no salary for his films but demanded up to 75 per cent of the profits and it was estimated that at least four of his subsequent pictures were successful enough to earn him £1 million each.

His 72nd film, *Walk, Don't Run*, a comedy set against the Tokyo Olympics, appeared in 1966. It proved to be his last. He never formally announced his retirement, but he had reached the point where making films had ceased to interest him, and he decided to fade quietly from the screen. From now on his rare public appearances were in connection with his directorship of the scent company, Fabergé.

In private he was normally as jaunty as in his films, but he suffered periodic bouts of depression. (His mother had a nervous collapse when he was 12.) Though once a chain-smoker, he was cured by hypnosis and then became fanatically opposed to the habit. His political views were strongly right wing.

He was married five times. His first wife was Virginia Cherill, who played the blind flower-girl in Chaplin's *City Lights*. He was next married to Woolworth heiress Barbara Hutton. Betsy Drake followed; and his fourth wife, Dyan Cannon, bore him his only child, a daughter, in 1966. In 1981 he married Barbara Harris, 47 years his junior and, like himself, British-born.

He protested that he did not leave any of his wives, but that they left him. Yet the underlying cause of his domestic instability is clear from his remark: "When I'm married I want to be single, and when I'm single I want to be married."

Cary Grant was born on January 18, 1904. He died following a stroke on November 29, 1986, aged 82

GRACIE FIELDS

Gracie Fields was perhaps the most popular entertainer of the day. She was, moreover, one of those few who are able to step beyond the strict limits of their profession and become a national figure. To many thousands of people who never saw her "Our Gracie" was a beloved character, the very embodiment of that fairy-tale quality in our age which allowed a poor mill girl to rise, by talent, personality and character, above the circumstances of her birth to astonishing heights of success.

Born at Rochdale, Lancashire, on January 9, 1898, her real name was Grace Stansfield, and she was only eight when she first sang in a local cinema. She used also to sing outside the lodgings of music-hall performers in the hope of attracting their attention, but the only engagement she got in this way was one to assist an artiste by singing choruses from the gallery. The child's efforts to do so, were, however, promptly supressed by a woman sitting near her, who did not realise that she was part of the show. Later she danced and sang with Haley's Juveniles – long a famous troupe of children in the music halls – and in 1912 with Cherburn's Young Stars. In 1913 she made her first appearance as a single turn, and the following year, at Oldham, played in her only pantomime. If she could not obtain theatrical engagements she worked, at this period, in a cotton mill, a shop, or a paper-bag factory, and when in 1915 she joined a touring revue her mother told her that if she did not then "make good" she would have to go back to the mill as a permanency – a fate which happily for the world she avoided. Her first revue was *Yes, I think So*, which was produced at Hulme, Manchester, early in 1915, and in July of that year paid a visit to the Middlesex Music Hall, in Drury Lane, where Gracie Fields made her first London appearance.

The principal comedian in the revue was Archie Pitt, with whose productions she was for many years associated and whom later she married. For two years from February 1916, they played together in *It's a Bargain*, and in 1918 began a tour of seven years in *Mr Tower of London*, probably the most successful touring revue ever produced. It several times filled the bill at London music halls, including notably, the Alhambra, and in it the charm, humour, and freshness of Gracie Fields began to attract general notice. After a period in another revue, *By Request*, she appeared again as a single act, and in February 1928, was engaged by the late Sir Gerald du Maurier to act as Lady Weir with him in *SOS*. The fact of one of the most popular "legitimate" actors of his day thus choosing a young music-hall singer for a leading part in one of his productions caused a considerable stir at the time: this was, however, her only "straight" part, and before long she was back again in variety and revue, one of her chief successes being in *The Show's the Thing*, at the Victoria Palace, and subsequently at other London theatres. In 1930 she paid her first visit to America, to perform at the Palace Theatre, New York.

The following year saw the beginning of her screen career, her first film being *Sally in Our Alley*, in which she introduced "Sally", the most popular of all her songs. Her later films included *Looking on the Bright Side*, *Love Life and Laughter*, *Sing As We Go!*, and *Look Up and Laugh*. She signed in 1935 what was then stated to be the biggest contract ever made by a film or stage artist in this country, computed to bring her in about £150,000 in two years. The sale of her gramophone records, too, was vast, four million of them being sold in less than five years. In 1937 she received the freedom of her native town of Rochdale, and in 1938, she was created CBE. A woman of great generosity, she established an orphanage at Peacehaven in Sussex.

Gracie Field's first marriage was dissolved in 1940, and she then married the Italian-born entertainer Monty Banks. It was typical of her lively generosity of spirit that during the Second World War she appeared wherever she could to strengthen morale and enliven servicemen and workers. One almost legendary tour took her, in six weeks, from Scapa Flow to Plymouth, giving three performances a day in army and air force camps and in factories. The performances were themselves unstintedly generous and the last was no less fresh and vigorous than the first.

After the war, and the death of her second husband in 1950, the pace of her career slackened still further. Her third marriage, to Boris Alperovici, in 1952, saw her partial retirement to a home in Capri.

The comparative rarity of her public appearances seemed not to lessen her popularity or her place in the normally fickle memory of the public. She was, in her later days, less a legend than a personal friend of every member of her audiences, a happy, honest, and good-hearted visitor to whose appearances everybody looked forward. Her autobiography *Sing as We Go*, was published in 1960. It conveyed a good deal of the directness, simplicity, and reticence of an artist who never lived or could have tolerated the idea of living her personal life in public. Between the lively, adored entertainer and her private concerns, with their great generosity and secretive kindness, a tactful curtain was always drawn.

She toured Britain, Canada and Australia in 1964 and the United States a year later. She returned to Rochdale in 1978 to open a theatre named after her and was warmly greeted (which warmth she returned in good measure and in characteristic uninhibited style) and subsequently made a surprise appearance at what was to be her last Command Performance. In the New Year Honours List (of 1979) she was advanced to DBE and in February received the insignia at an investiture held by Queen Elizabeth and the Queen Mother.

Undoubtedly Gracie Fields was the outstanding figure of the music hall in the years between the wars. To compare her hold upon the public with that of the great personalities of an earlier generation – say Marie Lloyd or Miss Vesta Tilley – would be pointless, since she worked in such changed circumstances and was able to supplement her music-hall work with the new media of the talking film and the wireless. But though the screen and the radio helped to build up her tremendous reputation, though she made some extremely successful and enjoyable films of an unsophisticated kind and was a tremendous draw also upon the air, she was, first and foremost, a music-hall performer, and those who never saw her in the flesh, singing to an audience actually present, never knew the essential Gracie Fields.

Slender, rather tall, with a slight stoop, thin lips and strongly marked, somewhat pointed features, she caught the attention immediately she appeared. Her face, crowned with a mass of hair rippling back from a broad, high forehead, was intelligent rather than beautiful. As a performer she had two great gifts, a delicious sense of burlesque and genuine, homely fun, and an exceptionally beautiful and flexible voice, with a wide range. Her vocal technique improved steadily throughout her career, and even late in life the beauty of her high notes and the precision and neatness of her phrasing were remarkable. The excellence of her singing, indeed, at one time, seemed a menace to her performance, for the sentimental ditties, on which she lavished so much artistry, were quite unworthy of her talent. Early in her career she had an entrancing trick of indicating her real opinion of these tearful ballads by introducing into the middle of her song some ludicrous trick of voice, or by absentmindedly scratching her back between high notes. Then for a time she became, to the disappointment of her more discerning admirers, more and more a serious sentimental singer, and her charming little buffooneries and her comic songs in her native Lancashire dialect became less and less prominent in her act. Later, however, though she did not return to the burlesque of her sentimental numbers, she restored a proper proportion of comic singing, and would give eight or ten songs on end, alternately sentimental and humorous.

As a comic singer she was delicious. Her fun, which was always good-humoured, inoffensive and full of character, seemed to bubble out of herself, and needed none of the extravagant make-up or costume upon which many comediennes have relied. Gracie Fields could change in a second from the heartbroken night-club frequenter begging for "Music Maestro, Please" to the Lancashire mill girl who owned "The Biggest Aspidestra [sic] in the World" or had been to the christening of "Mrs Binn's Twins" without changing her dress or even altering the set of her hair. Just as quickly and easily she could become the young Welsh girl whose family had "Got to Keep up with the Joneses". Gracie Fields had a very great spontaneous comic talent, a lovely voice and a personality (perhaps the most important asset of all, since the basis of the art of the music hall is personality) which made her, whether she was being funny or sentimental, always unaffectedly good and likeable company.

Dame Gracie Fields DBE was born on January 9, 1898. She died of pneumonia on September 27, 1979, aged 81

JAMES MASON

Mr James Mason was a highly intelligent and creative cinema performer who appeared in more than 100 films. And though many of them were unworthy of his talent he could lift the poorest material just as he could enrich the best. He made a reputation in parts calling for moody and tyrannical introspection, notably as Ann Todd's sadistic guardian in *The Seventh Veil*, before maturing into a versatile and dependable character player.

One of his best performances came under Sir Carol Reed's direction in 1947, when he played a dying gunman on the run in Belfast in *Odd Man Out*. Soon afterwards, expressing his disenchantment with the British cinema, he left for Hollywood where, after a difficult start, he successfully built a new career.

James Mason was born in Huddersfield in 1909, the son of a textile merchant. He was educated at Marlborough College and Peterhouse College, Cambridge where he took a first in architecture and got a taste for acting. His professional debut was at the Theatre Royal Aldershot, in 1931 and two years later he made his first London appearance in *Gallows Glorious* at the Arts Theatre. He joined the

Old Vic company and then the Gate Theatre in Dublin, where he played between 1934 and 1937.

He entered films in 1935, playing a reporter in *Late Extra*, but for several years most of his parts were in low-budget "quota quickies". In 1939, with two friends, Roy and Pamela Kellino, he set up his own film, *I Met a Murderer*, a crime story in which he was the killer of the title. He and Pamela Kellino were married two years later.

During the Second World War, he worked with ENSA and his film career finally took off through a series of costume melodramas which gave him the opportunity to create a memorable gallery of suave and vicious villains. The film that made him into a star was *The Man in Grey*, in which he took a whip to Margaret Lockwood; *Fanny by Gaslight*, *They Were Sisters*, and *The Wicked Lady*, also with Margaret Lockwood, followed in similar vein.

The Seventh Veil proved to be the most successful of all and from 1944 to 1947 Mason was voted Britain's top box-office star. Among those who admired his performance in *The Seventh Veil* was the veteran American director, DW Griffith. But Mason had become increasingly unhappy with the films he was being offered, and with what he saw as a monopolistic stranglehold on the industry by J Arthur Rank; and at the peak of his popularity he departed for Hollywood.

It was to be some time before the move paid off. Mason's outspokenness did not endear him to Hollywood and his choice of parts was not always happy. He appeared in two films for the émigré director, Max Ophuls, *Caught* and *The Reckless Moment*, and made a splendid Rommel in *The Desert Fox*; while his Brutus in the 1953 production of *Julius Caesar* helped to make it one of the best screen versions of Shakespeare.

But it was not until 1954 when he played opposite Judy Garland in George Cukor's remake of *A Star is Born* that he managed a major performance, a harrowing study of a man's tragic decline, for which he gained an Oscar nomination. He brought the same nervous intensity to the part of a drug addict in *Bigger Than Life* (1956), a film which he also produced.

The best of his later roles was Humbert Humbert in Stanley Kubrick's film of the Nabokov novel, *Lolita*, which appeared in 1962.

To his portrayal of a middle-aged man's infatuation with a 12-year-old girl, Mason brought a degree of sympathy, combined with wry humour, that few other actors could have managed. With *Odd Man Out*, it ranks as his outstanding screen achievement.

Three years earlier he had been a memorable villain in Alfred Hitchcock's *North by Northwest* and had given an engagingly tongue-in-cheek performance in an adaptation of the Jules Verne story, *Journey to the Centre of the Earth*. He maintained a prolific output through the 1960s and 1970s, making two and three films a year, though many were routine assignments easily, and perhaps best forgotten.

There was still, however, much to relish. His Timonides in *The Fall of the Roman Empire* was a bright spot in an otherwise dreary epic and he had good supporting parts in *The Pumpkin Eater* and as Gentleman Brown in Conrad's *Lord Jim*. He added to his stock of German officers in *The Blue Max* (1966) and in the same year he was in *Georgy Girl*, a story of the "Swinging Sixties", and a John le Carré thriller, *The Deadly Affair*.

In 1969 he turned producer again for *Age of Consent*, directed in Australia by Michael Powell; but a long-cherished Powell project, *The Tempest*, with Mason as Prospero, proved abortive. The martinet Yorkshire father in *Spring and Port Wine* was a tailor-made part, there were more Germans in *Cross of Iron* and *The Boys from Brazil* and a well-judged Mr Jordan in the fantasy, *Heaven Can Wait*. He was superb as the old tutor recalling his days in India in James Ivory's *Autobiography of a Princess*.

Once he became established in films, Mason returned only occasionally to the stage. He was in an unsuccessful Broadway play, *Bathsheba*, in 1947, and during the 1950s played Angelo in *Measure for Measure* and Oedipus in *Oedipus Rex* at the Shakespeare Festival in Stratford, Ontario.

His marriage to Pamela Kellino, which produced a daughter, Portland, and a son, Morgan, was dissolved in 1964. His second wife was an Australian actress, Clarissa Kaye, whom he married in 1971. His autobiography, *Before I Forget*, appeared in 1981.

James Mason was born on May 15, 1909. He died of a heart attack on July 27, 1984, aged 75

JOAN CRAWFORD

———————●———————

Her most devoted admirers would never have claimed that Joan Crawford was an actress of great range or adaptability: her secret lay rather in doing it superlatively well. She never puzzled her public by appearing in quick succession in a wide variety of parts; at any given period of her career the filmgoer who went to a Joan Crawford film knew just what sort of thing to expect, and knew too that he could expect it to be the best of its kind. Nevertheless, during her long reign as uncrowned queen of Hollywood she showed a remarkable ability to remodel her public personality in accordance with the demands of the public, a quality which betokens, if not necessarily a great actress, at least a great star.

She was born at San Antonio, Texas, at a date variously placed between 1901 and 1908 and her real name was Lucille Le Sueur. She did not take the name of Joan Crawford until after her success in *Sally, Irene and Mary* in 1925. She once wrote of herself that she was convinced from childhood that she possessed talent, but was uncertain what that talent might be. At first it appeared to be for dancing, and she began her professional career as a song-and-dance performer in a small café in Chicago. From there she graduated to the chorus of a JJ Shubert revue in New York called *Innocent Eye*, and then into that of one called *The Passing Show of 1925*. Here she was seen by an MGM talent scout and invited to Hollywood.

She appeared in her first film the same year. This was *Pretty Ladies*, which starred Norma Shearer and Zazu Pitts. During the next three years she appeared in a number of films, among them comedies with Harry Langdon and Charles Ray, but did not make any great mark until *Our Dancing Daughters* (1928), which first established her as one of the most potent and enduring legends of the American screen: indeed, since the death of Gary Cooper, Joan Crawford could claim to be the only major star of silent films still at the top of the acting profession in Hollywood.

After this film her progress was rapid: a number of similar films followed – *Our Modern Maidens* in 1929, *Our Blushing Brides* in 1930 – which all served to strengthen her position as the foremost representative of "flaming youth" on the screen. In the early 1930s, however, she began to broaden her scope with dramatic roles in such films as *Grand Hotel* (with Garbo, Wallace Beery and John and Lionel Barrymore) and the first talking version of *Rain*.

But by 1936 the mood of the times was changing, and in accordance with the new demands of the public a new "mature" Joan Crawford was seen in a series of sophisticated comedies, most notably *The Gorgeous Hussy* (1936), *The Last of Mrs Cheyney* (1937) and *The Women* (1939). It was at this period that an American exhibitor made the much-publicised statement that a number of top stars, among them Katharine Hepburn and Joan Crawford, were "box-office poison" – which, though frequently quoted, did not prevent any of the people concerned from continuing their highly successful careers for, in several cases, another 20 years or so.

During the 1940s, after appearing with notable improbability as a mink-clad heroine of the French resistance in *Reunion in France* (1942), Joan Crawford was absent from the screen for three years through illness. Her return in 1945 with *Mildred Pierce* gave her one of her most spectacular successes and an Academy Award, as well as setting the pattern for her next few films, all of which, with slight variations, recounted the rise of a girl "from the wrong side of the tracks" to fame and fortune though seldom to happiness. Particularly memorable were *Humoresque* (1947), from a screenplay by Clifford Odets about a rich music-lover who becomes too closely involved with her protégé, and *Flamingo Road* (1949) with its intriguing glimpses of Miss Crawford as a dancer in a fifth-rate roadshow. *Sudden Fear* (1952) marked a further development; from now on a new toughness and sometimes even savagery marked the characters she portrayed in such films as *Torch Song, Johnny Guitar* and *Female on the Beach*. In 1957 she came to this country to make her first British film, *The Story of Esther Costello*.

After a year or two away from the screen after the death of her fourth husband Alfred Steele, she returned in a series of strong roles in more or less horrific films, starting with *What Ever Happened to Baby Jane?*, in which she starred for the first time with her one-time greatest rival Bette Davis; after this came *The Caretaker, Straitjacket*, another film with Bette Davis, *Hush, Hush, Sweet Charlotte*, and *Trog* (1971).

Of her performances perhaps the most memorable were those in *Grand Hotel, The Women* (as Crystal Allen the shopgirl vamp), *Sudden Fear, Torch Song* (as a savagely successful stage star who is wooed at last to reason and domesticity) and *Autumn Leaves*, the story of a middle-aged woman who marries a man half her age. Joan Crawford was a personality in the grand manner; Hollywood will never be the same without her.

She was four times married: (1) Douglas Fairbanks, Junior, (2) Franchot Tone, (3) Phil Terry, (4) Alfred Steele. Steele, who died in 1959, was chairman of the Pepsi-Cola Company and after his death Joan Crawford joined the board.

Joan Crawford was born in the first decade of the 20th century. When she died of a heart attack on May 10, 1977, she was thought to have been between the ages of 69 and 76

NOËL COWARD

Playwright, composer, director, actor, singer and dancer, Sir Noël Coward was also on occasion a novelist, short-story writer and autobiographer, as well as a writer of fluent, entertaining light verse. None of the great figures of the English theatre has been more versatile than he. Whatever he had found to do was done with elegantly professional certainty of effect.

During his lifetime, his place in the theatre depended on no single vein of achievement but on his complete mastery of all the stage required for whatever work he had undertaken. One of two of his sentimental songs keep their place among the popular classics of light music; others, wittily mocking, are destined for a longer life. He had little voice, but no singer more naturally gifted could project the wit of these songs with half the effect of his own dry, staccato style. As an actor he carried naturalism to its farthest extremes, but in a number of roles like that of Lewis Dodd, the bohemian composer of Margaret Kennedy's *The Constant Nymph* in the 1920s and Shaw's King Magnus, in *The Apple Cart*, which he played in the Coronation season of 1953, he made every necessary effect with a delightful simplicity and punctuality, adding often to their weight by understatement; he was too disciplined and conscientious an artist to essay what was beyond his capacity for effectiveness.

Posterity may reject his musicals as limited by the tastes and techniques of the 1920s and 1930s. His serious pieces – like *Cavalcade* among his musicals, *The Vortex* and *This Happy Breed* among his plays – may seem too easily sentimental to appeal to later ages, but they reflect their times with startling clarity. Of all his multifarious achievements, it is as master of the comedy of manners that he is irreplaceable; his work in this special field is precisely written, and elegantly economical; it belongs to the classical tradition of Congreve, Sheridan, Wilde and Shaw.

Noël Coward was born in Teddington in 1899, the son of Arthur Coward, who worked for a firm of music publishers. His formal education was limited, for he made his first public appearance when he was ten, in a children's play *The Goldfish*, at the Little Theatre. This brought an offer of a page boy's part, in *The Great Name* from Charles Hawtrey, by whose skills, professionalism and disciplined craftsmanship Coward was permanently and beneficially influenced. Until 1915, when a mild attack of tuberculosis sent him for treatment to a sanatorium, he played a large number of juvenile parts. Because of his illness, when he reached military age in 1918 he was put into a labour battalion, but transferred from that to the Artists Rifles OTC.

After the war he joined Arthur Bourchier's company, but in 1920 he appeared in his own first play, a light and flimsy comedy, *I'll Leave it to You*, at the New Theatre; this was later followed by *The Young Idea*, and in 1923 he acted, sang and danced in *London Calling*, a revue of which he was part-author and part-composer.

Changing his tone, in 1925, he made his first great success with *The Vortex*, a somewhat melodramatic confrontation between a foolish, amorous middle-aged woman and the drug-taking Hamlet who was her son. In it, Coward found an authentic desperation in the self-conscious gaiety of the first postwar period.

Hay Fever, written in a weekend in 1925, is a more dazzling achievement; like *The Importance of Being Earnest*, it is pure comedy with no mission but to delight, and it depends purely on the interplay of characters, not upon elaborate comic machinery. This was followed by a series of musicals produced by C B Cochran which culminated in *Bitter Sweet,* probably the best of Coward's work for the musical stage, in 1929, and *Cavalcade,* a magnificently spectacular pageant of English history, from the death of Queen Victoria to the great slump, as it was seen through the eyes of an upper-middle-class family. *Cavalcade's* sincere, sentimental patriotism converted to Coward's cause many theatregoers who had distrusted the flippancy, the facility and the witty light-heartedness of his earlier work.

Between the two musicals came *Private Lives,* a comedy as beautifully and smoothly made as *Hay Fever,* and no less witty but with a closer relevance to the moral concerns of its day. It exploits with inventive delight its author's gift for the retort discourteous, the comic inflation of the obvious, the urgent pursuit of the wild irrelevancy and his mastery of cleverly economical effect.

In the 1930s he was active in management in England and New York, in partnership with Alfred Lunt and Lynn Fontanne, and he continued to create plays and musicals with no less ease and effect, though for a time with less wit. In 1941, however, *Blithe Spirit* broke new ground admitting the fantastic into his mocking picture of the age; it ran for nearly 2,000 performances.

Present Laughter, written in the following year displays moral perplexities like those of *Private Lives* against a theatrical background; the background is beautifully sketched and the problems are worked out with undiminished wit and hilarity. Between these two uncloudedly sunny plays came *In Which we Serve,* Coward's film in tribute to the Royal Navy, which he wrote and directed himself and in which he played the leading role. *This Happy Breed* achieved a working-class *Cavalcade* of life between the two World Wars.

His later work, with occasional novels and short stories, a war diary to link his prewar autobiography *Present Indicative* to its postwar sequel, *Future Indefinite,* could not always recapture the wit and the tingling contemporaneity of his earlier plays. His musicals remained gracefully made and precise in effect, but they belong to the days before the war, and of his plays, only *Nude with Violin* and *Relative Values* seemed to awaken his sharp revelatory wit.

Never idle, he made Feydeau's *Occupe-toi d'Amelie* into *Look after Lulu*, a typically Coward work even though it seemed unblushingly to allude to earlier effects and to earlier dialogue for effects he knew to be infallible. He appeared in small parts, beautifully observed, magnificently understated and extremely wittily played in a variety of films in the later 1950s and the 1960s.

In 1964, a year in which Granada presented four of his plays on television under the omnibus title *A Choice of Coward*, he had the satisfaction of directing the National Theatre production of *Hay Fever* – the second modern play ever to be directed there by its author. This was followed by a musical version of *Blithe Spirit*, supervised but not written or composed by Coward, and by a revival of *Present Laughter*, with Mr Nigel Patrick playing Coward's old part and directing, which ran for close on 400 performances at the Queen's. Last year Coward attended the first night of *Cowardy Custard* in London – a revue of his revue material. A revival of *Private Lives* with Maggie Smith and Robert Stephens opened in London. He also received an honorary degree from Sussex University.

"If and when," Coward had written in 1958, "she (success) chooses to leave me I shall not repine, nor shall I mourn her any more than I mourn other loved ones who have gone away. I do not approve of mourning, I only approve of remembering, and her I shall always remember gratefully and with pride."

By the time he reached his 70th birthday in 1969, the year in which he was awarded a knighthood, it was possible to see how firmly the best of Coward's work was rooted in the English comic tradition. It is an attack in suitably comic terms on the insincere inflation of emotion, on the dishonesty of meaningless fine manners and unexamined conventions, and on the hypocrisy which masquerades as moral censoriousness; it rejects the easy-going, the undisciplined and the unprofessional. Claiming no more than, in the words of one of his songs, "a talent to amuse", Coward, his public had come to learn, amused them for their own good as well as their delight.

Coward was widely admired and loved in his own profession for his generosity and kindness to those who fell on hard times. Stories are told of the unobtrusive way in which he relieved the needs or paid the debts of old theatrical connexions who had no claim on him.

Sir Noël Coward was born December 16, 1899. He died of a heart attack on March 26, 1973, aged 73

ROBERT MITCHUM

───────●───────

As he showed when he took on the role Dick Powell had created in the 1944 version of *Farewell, My Lovely* for the 1975 remake, Robert Mitchum was one of the great Hollywood stars of the postwar era. Though at 58 he was a good deal too old for the role of Raymond Chandler's world-weary detective, Philip Marlowe, Mitchum's amused cynicism suited the part to perfection. His was the definitive Philip Marlowe in a film which recreated the atmosphere of 1940s Los Angeles with total conviction.

The extraordinary thing about Mitchum was that his achievements were consistently undervalued. The fault was partly his, for he made acting look so effortless and natural that it was easy to conclude that he was not acting at all.

It was a myth he helped to encourage, affecting to hold a low opinion of his craft and once declaring that he had only two acting styles – with and without a horse. His hundred or so films included a high proportion of dross but he could lift the most feeble material and almost never gave a routine performance. And given a sympathetic director and cameraman and a strong script, he could produce performances of unforgettable power of which his murderous preacher in Charles Laughton's *The Night of the Hunter* (1995) was probably the finest. It is quite inexplicable that he never won an Oscar.

A gift for impressionists, Mitchum was a big man with sleepy eyes, a laconic voice and drooping shoulders whose world-weary cynicism was often laced with dry humour. He could be menacing or charming and was sometimes both at once.

Before the cameras he was the complete professional, always word-perfect and generous to his fellow actors. Off screen he gained the reputation, not entirely underserved, of being a difficult and volatile character who was fond of a drink and merciless towards anyone he decided was an idiot.

Over the years he was manna to the gossip columnists. In 1948 he was convicted of smoking marijuana and served 60 days in prison; at the Cannes Film Festival in 1954 he was photographed on the beach with a bare-breasted actress, though the girl had contrived the incident to get herself publicity.

In 1955 Mitchum sued *Confidential* magazine over a story that he had stripped off at a masquerade party, doused himself in ketchup and announced that he was a hamburger. Not unnaturally, he developed a strong suspicion of the media and his interviews were usually terse and unrevealing.

Robert Charles Durman Mitchum was born in Bridgeport, Connecticut, in 1917, and was only 18 months old when his father was killed in a railway accident. He had an unsettled childhood, as the family moved from town to town, trying to scrape a living.

A rebellious youth, he often ran away from home and school, and he was frequently in trouble with the police. At 16 he was arrested for vagrancy and sentenced to a week in jail, which he actually spent in a Georgia chain gang. As a teenager he travelled America, sleeping rough and taking any sort of job that came along. Among them were longshoreman, truck loader, dishwasher and heavyweight boxer. Eventually, at the prompting of his sister, he joined a theatre company in Long Beach, California, where he not only acted but showed creative ability by writing plays and directing them.

He married his childhood sweetheart Dorothy Spence and was working in the Lockheed aircraft factory when, in 1943, he decided to try his luck in Hollywood. He was taken on and made his film debut in a Hopalong Cassidy western. Over the next two years he appeared in more than twenty films, usually as a villain who gets his comeuppance, and showed enough promise for RKO to offer him a long-term contract.

The studio's speciality was the low-budget "black" thriller, the film noir for which Mitchum's intense and moody presence made him an ideal leading man. Although little regarded at the time, films like *The Locket*, with its maze of flashbacks, and *Out of the Past*, in which Mitchum played a private eye ensnared by a no-good woman, are now regarded as classics of the genre. But the first film to gain him wide recognition was made outside RKO, William

Wellman's study of ordinary men at war, *The Story of GI Joe* (1945). Mitchum's portrayal of the battle-scarred infantry officer Lieutenant Walker gained him his only Oscar nomination.

In a different vein he was equally effective as the avenging cowboy of Raoul Walsh's psychological western, *Pursued* (1947), and in Nicholas Ray's rodeo drama, *The Lusty Men* (1952). By the early 1950s he could leave RKO and go freelance. He celebrated by co-starring with Marilyn Monroe in *River of No Return* (1954).

Two contrasting films of the 1950s confirmed Mitchum's quality and range. His psychopathic priest in *The Night of the Hunter* remains one of the most formidable studies of evil that has ever appeared on the screen. In *Heaven Knows, Mr Allison* (1957) he played a tough Marine marooned on a Pacific island with Deborah Kerr's nun, and saved a potentially mawkish picture with his unsentimental acting.

He appeared with Kerr again in Fred Zinnemann's *The Sundowners* (1960), a story of sheep-drovers in Australia, and *The Grass Is Greener* (1960), an untypical venture into drawing-room comedy. In *Cape Fear* (1962) he gave another chilling study of evil, as an ex-convict terrorising the family of the lawyer who sent him to jail. The highlight of his work during the 1960s was the drunken sheriff in the Howard Hawks western *El Dorado* (1967). It was a performance Mitchum could easily have spoilt by overacting, but his playing was a model of subtlety and restraint.

His scenes with another veteran, John Wayne, were deliciously effective. Despite unlikely casting as the hesitant Irish schoolteacher in David Lean's *Ryan's Daughter* (1970), Mitchum came near to stealing the film as he gave yet another demonstration of his ability to dominate the screen with his minimum effort.

Although professing to be in semi-retirement, Mitchum remained active throughout the 1970s and continued to turn in excellent performances. The pick were his ageing gangster in *The Friends of Eddie Coyle* (1973) and, of course, Philip Marlowe in *Farewell, My Lovely*. He returned to *Cape Fear* in the Martin Scorsese remake of 1991, but this time on the side of the terrorised lawyer, in a cameo role as one of his advisers.

Although he never won as Oscar, Mitchum was honoured by the film industry with a Special Lifetime's Achievement Award at the 1992 Golden Globes ceremony. The standing ovation he received at the Beverly Hills Hilton testified to the affection with which he was held in the cinema world.

In the 1980s, with his large-screen career gradually winding down, Mitchum enjoyed a second wind on American television, scoring considerable popular success in several well-crafted series. These included the impressive *The Winds of War* (1983), a saga of the events leading up to the Second World War in which he played a US Navy officer; *North and South* (1985), an American Civil War costume drama, somewhat unkindly described by one critic as "*Dynasty* in fancy dress"; and *War and Remembrance* (1988), in which he returned to his senior naval officer role, adding an impressive dimension of war-weariness to a character who also radiated an unfamiliar kindness. All three series enjoyed great success on this side of the Atlantic as well as in America.

Hard drinking and heavy smoking took their toll of Mitchum's health and in the last ten years of his life he suffered from emphysema and liver damage. When admonished by doctors and concerned friends about his consumption of cigarettes, tequila and gin, he responded with a characteristic verbal shrug of the shoulders: "Well, you gotta die of something." It was entirely of a piece with his persona on and off the screen.

Robert Mitchum was married in 1940 to Dorothy Spence and they enjoyed one of Hollywood's more durable partnerships, in spite of brief separations in 1948 and 1953. They had three children: two sons, James and Christopher, who both followed him into films though with only moderate success, and a daughter, Petrine.

Robert Mitchum was born on August 6, 1917. He died of cancer on July 1, 1997, aged 79

BILL COBBS

Bill Cobbs was 35 years old in 1969 and working as a car salesman when a customer to whom he had just sold a Chevrolet asked him if he'd like to be in a play. "Sure, why not?" he replied in his gratitude for having made the sale.

It was an amateur production and there were only three performances but it changed his life. "I found it so stimulating to go on stage that I then auditioned for another play," he said. "Being up there taught me there were a lot of meaningful things I could say in the theatre about the human condition."

Within a year he had left selling cars behind and moved from Cleveland to New York hoping to make his name as an actor. Supporting himself by driving a cab, his first professional role came off-Broadway with the Negro Ensemble Company in *Ride a Black Horse*.

Further performances followed in small theatres and with a street troupe and at 40 he made his screen debut in the 1974 crime drama *The Taking of Pelham One Two Three*, starring Walter Matthau and Robert Shaw.

He had just one line but he recalled it as the proudest experience of his life and returned to Cleveland to take his parents to see the film so that he could savour the moment with them. "All our friends and neighbours went to see the movie, and everyone was waiting for my appearance," he remembered. "I walk up to a policeman in the subway and say, 'Hey, man. What's goin' on?'"

Over the next five decades he went on to amass almost 200 credits on the screen, many of his most memorable appearances coming in late middle age and beyond.

Martin Scorsese cast him in his 1986 sports drama *The Color of Money*. He played Whitney Houston's manager in 1992's *The Bodyguard* and two years later in the Coen brothers' *The Hudsucker Proxy* he was Moses, the mystical clock man with the ability to stop time. In Rob Reiner's *Ghosts of Mississippi* (1996) he played the older brother of the murdered civil rights activist Medgar Evers. That same year he was a jazz pianist in Tom Hanks's *That Thing You Do!* – a role he particularly enjoyed as his earliest ambition had been to become a musician – and in John Sayles's *Sunshine State* (2002) he was the doctor striving to save his seaside Florida neighbourhood from rapacious developers.

He could do comedy, too, and one of his favourite roles was as a veteran security guard alongside Ben Stiller, Dick Van Dyke and Mickey Rooney in 2006's *Night at the Museum*. He reprised the role in his 80th year in 2014's sequel *Night at the Museum: Secret of the Tomb*.

On television he was seen in such hit shows as *The Sopranos*, *The West Wing* and *Six Feet Under* as well as lighter fare such as *Sesame Street* and *Rugrats*.

Although he was seldom cast in lead roles, he was a familiar and memorable everyman to whom directors and producers kept turning, drawn by his reputation for bringing an eye-catching soulfulness to even the smallest part.

His ability to steal a scene seemed to stem from an almost mystical reverence with which he approached his profession. To be an actor "you have to have a sense of giving", he said. "Art is somewhat of a prayer, isn't it? We respond to what we see around us and what we feel and how things affect us mentally and spiritually."

Wilbert Francisco Cobbs was born in 1934 in Cleveland, Ohio, into a working-class family. His mother, Vera, worked in domestic service and his father, David, in construction. After graduating from high school with little idea of what he wanted to do, he joined the US Air Force, where he served for eight years.

During his time as a serviceman he tried his hand as a stand-up comedian in amateur shows on airbases but on his discharge had no thoughts of a stage career and returned to Cleveland to work for IBM and then a car dealership.

The play in which one of his customers felicitously asked him to appear was the anti-apartheid musical *Lost in the Stars* by Kurt Weill and Maxwell Anderson. Although set in South Africa, the work was conceived as a protest against the lynchings and segregation of the Jim Crow laws in America's Deep South and Cobb was inspired not only by the satisfaction he found in being on stage but by the power of the theatre as social commentary.

"It was 1969 and civil rights were one of the main concerns of the whole country. It was a revelation to me that you could make important points and be entertaining people at the same time," he said.

His move to New York a year later was equally inspired by a desire to act and to be part of a wider struggle. "It was the time when I had the least in my life in terms of material things," he recalled. "But it was the most exciting time of my life because it was hopeful and invigorating as we believed that we could make the world a better place."

The parts he played were not of the kind that tended to win awards but in 2020, half a century after his professional debut, he won an Emmy for his role in *Dino Dana*, a children's educational show. That the citation was for "outstanding limited performance" was an unfortunate choice of words for there was nothing limited about his acting during a career that may have been late in starting but to which he gave his all.

Bill Cobbs was born on June 16, 1934. He died of undisclosed causes on June 25, 2024, aged 90

ORSON WELLES

———————●———————

Physically and intellectually imposing, Orson Welles brought an original and inventive mind to bear on radio, the cinema, the stage and television. His work, though erratic, was never predictable or dull. His career suffered from the enormous critical acclaim for his first film, *Citizen Kane*, made when he was only 26. Its reputation dogged him for the rest of his life, constantly raising expectations that he could not match.

After *Citizen Kane* there was a sense of anticlimax, partly brought on by Welles himself. The freedom granted to him to make that film rarely came his way again. He gained a reputation (which he always refuted) for being extravagant and unreliable. His life was littered with unfinished projects and projects that were announced and never got started.

By the end dozens of cameo parts in other people's bad films, and his voiceovers for sherry and lager commercials, came near to extinguishing the memory of a brilliant artist: an actor of power and charm, a film-maker responsible for some of the finest work in that medium.

With his fine, rich voice and gift for anecdote he was, too, an outstanding raconteur; and he was a more than usually gifted painter. On everything he did from the sublime to the dreadful, he left his mark; a huge talent that too often wasted itself and became frustrated.

George Orson Welles was born at Kenosha, Wisconsin, on the shore of Lake Michigan, in 1915. He was the younger son of Richard Head Welles, a prosperous businessman, and his wife, Beatrice Ives, a concert pianist, and a woman of exceptional beauty and high intelligence. She treated her two sons as her intellectual equals, and as a result both reached intellectual maturity very early in life. At ten Orson was being examined with interest by medical and psychological experts as an infant phenomenon, and by then he had already written a comprehensive thesis on *The Universal History of Drama.*

At 16 he had already travelled extensively, but had an unfulfilled ambition to visit Ireland. Within a few weeks of arriving there, in the autumn of 1931, he made his professional debut as an actor at the Gate Theatre in Dublin, having introduced himself to its directors as "Orson Welles, star of the New York Theatre Guild". He was given the part of the Duke Württemberg in *Jew Süss* after one of the most remarkable auditions ever held in the theatre.

He played at both the Gate and Abbey theatres for a year, and then returned to America where he toured with Katherine Cornell. He made his debut on the New York stage as Chorus and Tybalt in *Romeo and Juliet* in December 1934; in 1936 he became director of the Negro People's Theatre and directed a Black version of *Macbeth*, and in 1937 was appointed a director of the Federal Theatre Project in New York. In the same year he founded and opened the Mercury Theatre with *Julius Caesar*, played in modern dress and without scenery.

By this time he had also made a name for himself on radio, where he earned huge sums in the part of "The Shadow", but it was in October, 1938, that he achieved his radio tour de force by producing HG Wells's *The War of the Worlds*, which he presented with such reality that he terrified half of America into believing that their country was being invaded by Martians.

Inevitably, after this, he was invited to go to Hollywood, where RKO signed a contract which gave him virtual *carte blanche* as producer, director, writer and actor. His first production was to have been *Heart of Darkness*, from the novel by Conrad, but the outbreak of war in Europe caused a change in plan.

Instead he made *Citizen Kane*, a far from flattering biography of a newspaper magnate with obvious similarities to William Randolph Hearst. The Hearst newspapers retaliated by either attacking the film or ignoring it. Kane was played by Welles himself, who described the character as "a great lover, a great American citizen and a dirty dog".

Technically dazzling with its wide-angle and deep-focus photography, intricate flashback structures and such felicities as a devastatingly accurate parody of *The March of Time* newsreel,

Citizen Kane was a critical sensation. It was hailed then as one of the best films ever made and time has not reversed that judgment. For a man in his twenties with no previous cinema experience it was an extraordinary achievement.

His second film, *The Magnificent Ambersons*, from Booth Tarkington's novel about the decline and fall of a late-19th-century aristocratic family, was no less stylish and compelling; but it was severely cut against Welles's wishes and the final sequence, which threw the film out of balance, was shot by another director. Already Welles's disenchantment with Hollywood had started.

For the time being, however, he stayed, portraying a brooding Rochester in *Jane Eyre* and directing himself, as a former Nazi at large in a small American town, in *The Stranger*. He was director and leading man again for *The Lady from Shanghai*, a baroque and at times impenetrable thriller with a famous climax in a hall of mirrors. The female lead was Rita Hayworth, Welles's estranged second wife.

In the same year, 1948, he made a low-budget version of *Macbeth*, shot in only three weeks with himself in the title role. Marred by a poor soundtrack, the film nevertheless had a barbaric splendour. After this Welles came to Europe and played his most popular and enduring role, as the racketeer Harry Lime in Graham Greene's atmospheric thriller set in Vienna, *The Third Man*. Welles himself wrote in the picture's best-remembered line, that 500 years of Swiss democracy had produced only the cuckoo clock.

While *Macbeth* was shot in three weeks, his *Othello*, released in 1955, took three years. His performance, passionate and deeply tragic, was modelled on that of the stage production with which he had made his London debut in 1951. Other notable stage appearances during the 1950s were in his own adaptation of *Moby Dick* and as *King Lear*. Breaking his ankle on the first night, he played the king on the second night from a wheelchair.

In the cinema he directed in two thrillers. One, *Confidential Report*, was taken from his own novel; the other, and more successful, *Touch of Evil*, was a triumph of style over plot with Welles at his most flamboyant as the corrupt police chief. His most striking performance outside of his own films in the 1950s was as the defence attorney in *Compulsion,* based on the Leopold/Loeb murder trial.

In 1963 he directed his own adaption of Kafka's nightmarish novel, *The Trial,* making dramatic use of a disused Paris railway station. But though the film was often visually stunning, it did not quite cohere. *Chimes at Midnight,* a portrait of Shakespeare's Falstaff and his relationship with Prince Hal, was, on the other hand, a film to rank with Welles's best, not only for the central performance but an imaginative use of slender resources.

It was Welles's last completed feature. A film of *Don Quixote,* begun in Spain in the 1950s, came eventually to nothing, though much footage was shot; and a long-cherished *Lear* was also aborted. Welles's final two films as director were *The Immortal Story,* made for French television, and an impish semi-documentary about the art world, *F for Fake.*

Of his acting roles outside his films, the less said, on the whole, the better. Among the exceptions were his Cardinal Wolsey in *A Man for all Seasons.* When he celebrated his 70th birthday in May this year, he was in bullish mood. His *Lear* seemed at last to be getting off the ground; two other films, one started back in 1970 and taking the cinema industry as its theme, were announced as firm commitments. But as so often with Welles, the promise was unfulfilled.

He was married three times: to Virginia Nicholson, whom he divorced in 1940; to Rita Hayworth, from 1943 to 1947; and, 1955, to Paola Mori. Each marriage produced one daughter.

Orson Welles was born on May 6, 1915. He died of a heart attack on October 10, 1985, aged 70

PHILIP SEYMOUR HOFFMAN

Philip Seymour Hoffman was the ultimate actor's actor. An Oscar-winning star of film and stage, he was a committed and dedicated performer who commanded the respect of his colleagues both in front of and behind the camera. Meryl Streep, his co-star in *Doubt*, described him as "fearless ... he's done what we all strive for".

His name on the credits of a film had a cachet rare in a character actor: his involvement in a movie, and the acute, questioning intelligence he brought to each performance, acted like a seal of quality. The director Paul Thomas Anderson, who wrote roles for Hoffman in *Boogie Nights*, *Magnolia*, *Punch Drunk Love* and *The Master*, recalled calling Hoffman after seeing his breakthrough performance opposite Al Pacino in *The Scent of a Woman*, and telling him "You're my favourite actor".

Philip Seymour Hoffman was born in 1967 and, the second youngest of four children, grew up in Fairport, New York. His mother was a lawyer and his father an executive with Xerox. His parents divorced when he was nine and Hoffman dedicated his Oscar win for his performance as Truman Capote to his mother, saying, "She brought up four kids alone, and she deserves a congratulations for that."

Although Hoffman's interests and talents initially veered towards sport, a wrestling injury put paid to any further sporting ambitions.

At around the age of 12, he fell in love with the theatre. The light bulb moment came at a production of *All My Sons* that he attended near his hometown in upstate New York. He was, he said, permanently changed by the experience of watching the play, which he described as being "like a miracle".

In high school, Hoffman started to audition for roles in plays. He joked later that the impetus for his interest in acting was a beautiful girl on the drama course, but there is no doubt that from the outset, Hoffman took it very seriously.

The first love of theatre remained throughout his career. He was the co-artistic director of the LAByrinth Theater Company in New York. In addition to numerous stage performances – he was three times nominated for the Tony award for Best Actor – he directed many plays, including *Our Lady of 121st Street*; *In Arabia, We'd All Be Kings*; and *Jesus Hopped the A Train*.

Hoffman attended drama school at New York University, working to contribute towards the expensive tuition fees. He was fired from numerous jobs, including as a restaurant waiter and as a lifeguard at a spa. Despite the deep connection he felt for New York's theatre world and for the city, after graduation Hoffman moved to Los Angeles to try his luck in cinema.

A small role in the television series *Law and Order* followed but the opportunity that Hoffman credited with launching his career was as the cruelly manipulative prep school student George Willis Jr in *The Scent of a Woman* (1992). It was, he said, "like winning the lottery", the first push which started a career domino effect.

It was a characteristically eye-catching performance. He managed to combine a distinctive physical presence – he was frequently described as "chunky" – and a characteristic laconic drawling delivery with the ability to transform himself and meld into each new character.

Hoffman soon proved himself with a string of memorable supporting roles. He was sweatily uncomfortable in his own skin as the love-sick porn cameraman in Paul Thomas Anderson's *Boogie Nights* (1997), combined self-loathing and self-abuse in Todd Solondz's bleak *Happiness* (1998), and was wonderfully abrasive as the playboy hedonist Freddie Miles in *The Talented Mr Ripley* (1999).

As his career developed, he was courted by both the elite of the arthouse directors, working with the Coen brothers, Paul Thomas Anderson, Anthony Minghella and Charlie Kaufman among others, and by mainstream Hollywood. He was equally at home – and equally impressive – playing an arch-villain in JJ Abrams's *Mission Impossible III* (2006) as he was playing a gas-huffing widower in the low-budget indie drama *Love Liza* (2002).

His graduation to leading roles was inevitable, given the plaudits that garlanded his work. Perhaps his most remarkable achievement was the fact that, despite his height and heft, Hoffman transformed himself into the diminutive, waspish writer Truman Capote in Bennett Miller's *Capote* (2005).

It was for this performance that Hoffman won his only Oscar, although he was nominated on three other occasions, for *Doubt* (2008), *Charlie Wilson's War* (2007) and most recently for his barnstorming performance as the leader of a cult-like religion in Paul Thomas Anderson's *The Master* (2012).

But it is perhaps another lead role, in Charlie Kaufman's *Synecdoche, New York* (2008) that had most resonance for Hoffman as a man and as an artist. In it, he played Caden Cotard, a theatre director who wins a grant and uses it to stage a hugely complex play of his own life within a giant warehouse.

It is a profoundly melancholy film which deals with missed chances, mortality, lost love and thwarted dreams. Hoffman is the emotional anchor to which the audience is linked throughout the baffling, buffeting plot. He clearly identified with Cotard – Hoffman was not a man who embraced levity. For all his passion for acting, it was a vocation that constantly troubled and tested him, something that he frequently described as a "struggle".

He had a history of problems linked to substance abuse. He gave up drinking at the age of 22, saying later that he was not able to exercise willpower around drink or drugs. Having been clean for 23 years, it was reported that Hoffman relapsed last year and entered a detox facility for heroin abuse.

His death leaves a question mark over the final instalment of the *Hunger Games* series, which is currently filming and which starred Hoffman as Plutarch Heavensby.

Hoffman had been in a long-term relationship with Mimi O'Donnell, a costume designer whom he met while directing *In Arabia, We'd All be Kings*. She survives him, together with their three children, a son Cooper, 9, and two daughters Tallulah, 7, and Willa, 5.

Philip Seymour Hoffman was born on July 23, 1967. He died of a suspected drug overdose on February 2, 2014, aged 46

RICHARD BURTON

———•———

Mr Richard Burton was an actor who began his career as a performer of fine promise on the classical stage and progressed to become an international star, the details of whose private life came, alas, to command almost more attention than his very great gifts.

Richard Burton was born in Pontrhydfen, a mining village in South Wales in 1925. He was educated at Port Talbot Secondary School and at Exeter College, Oxford, but he spent a year between the end of his school life and the beginning of his brief university career on the stage.

He first acted in public in November 1943, as Glan, in Emlyn Williams's *The Druid's Rest*, at the Royal Court Theatre, Liverpool and then, in January 1944, at the St Martin's Theatre, in London. After three months of the play's London run, he relinquished his part to go up to Oxford, where his stay was cut short by National Service, which occupied him until 1947. He found time while at university to achieve an impressive performance as Angelo in *Measure for Measure*, the OUDS production of 1944.

In less than ten years after his return to the stage he had built up not only a great reputation but also a power and authority which made it seem that he was destined for the commanding heights of his profession in spite of occasional forays into the cinema. In February 1948, he appeared as Mr Hicks in *Castle Anna*, but moved from theatre into his first film, *The Last Days of Dolwen*. During 1949 and 1950 he was seen in the then excitingly original plays of Christopher Fry, as Richard, in *The Lady's not for Burning*, Cuthmen, in *Boy with a Cart* and Tegeus, in *A Phoenix too Frequent*.

The Lady's not for Burning took him to his first appearance in New York, and when its run ended he stayed there to play in *Legend of Lovers*. Back in London in 1952, he played the title role in *Montserrat* at the Lyric, Hammersmith, and then joined the Old Vic company for the seasons of 1953 and 1954 in what can perhaps justly be remembered as the last of the creation of the National Theatre company.

With John Neville, an actor of equal force and intelligence but entirely different in temperament, he alternated the roles of Othello and Iago. In London and at the Edinburgh Festival he was seen as Hamlet, incisively intelligent, richly emotional though hardly irresolute. The bastard Philip Faulconbridge, in *King John*, was a role which he fitted exactly, and his Coriolanus was acting of violence and authority if hardly of patrician disdain. Sir Toby Belch offered him a rare opportunity to show his gift of humour, and his Caliban was both ferocious and pathetic. His acting compared to John Neville's as a sabre to a rapier; the two exactly complemented each other and won the devotion of Old Vic audiences, particularly of a vociferously appreciative gallery audience of young enthusiasts.

Tempted to Hollywood to be the Antony to Elizabeth Taylor's Cleopatra in the spectacular film epic *Cleopatra* (it seemed to his admirers that Shakespeare's Antony could give him far more than a very luscious film had to offer), he began to concentrate on film roles, working in the theatre only intermittently. In New York he was the King Arthur of the original production of Lerner and Loewe's *Camelot* in 1960, and in 1964 he played Hamlet in Sir John Gielgud's controversial production of the play. The production and Burton's acting both received a great deal of attention, commentary and analysis; both were, the commentators suggest, tensely exciting and moving, but both, apparently, were visibly flawed.

Two years later, as an act of homage to Oxford and the OUDS, both Burton and Elizabeth Taylor, his second wife, played there in Marlowe's *Doctor Faustus*. His subsequent film of the play, based on the Oxford production, fails altogether to do him justice, sacrificing both his own performance and the play itself to visual clichés of almost ineffable bad taste.

The breakdown of Burton's first marriage, to Sybil Williams, and his subsequent marriage to Elizabeth Taylor, had given the press of Great Britain and the United States a modern romance of which it made as much as it could, and the luxury of their later life – the fruits of their success in the cinema – was widely reported; they never for long managed to escape the public eye.

For all that, Burton kept a certain natural simplicity, an obvious love of his native country and the people of the mining village in which he had grown up. The partnership with Miss Taylor, however, bore fruit in several films in which he discovered how to project the force of his stage personality through the lens of a camera, and if *Doctor Faustus* was a disaster and *The Taming of the Shrew*, directed by Franco Zeffirelli, a colourful romp in which neither Burton nor his wife was ideally cast, so that the best was not made of Shakespeare's play, in the film of Edward Albee's *Who's Afraid of Virginia Woolf?* the Burton–Taylor duet was powerful in purely cinematic terms, sourly-comic in a way new to Burton's acting, finely drawn and moving.

Without Taylor, Burton played the title role in *Becket* opposite Peter O'Toole, was an unfrocked priest in *The Night of the Iguana* and an intelligence agent in John le Carre's *The Spy Who Came in from the Cold*. There were also film records of his by now rare stage appearances, such as *Hamlet*, directed by John Gielgud.

During the 1970s Burton seemed, professionally, to lose his way. He was no longer able to hold out for huge salaries in the cinema and his work was less distinguished. He settled for mainly routine adventure films with, now and then, something more challenging, such as playing Trotsky for Joseph Losey or repeating his stage role as the psychiatrist in Peter Shaffer's *Equus*. There was sadness that his talent was being under-used, not only in films but in the theatre, where apart from *Equus* his only venture in more than ten years was the musical, *Camelot*. Plans to play *King Lear* came to nothing. In 1977 he narrated a 26-part BBC radio series about British monarchs, produced to mark the Queen's Silver Jubilee.

His private life continued to fill the gossip columns. His marriage to Elizabeth Taylor ended in separation and divorce; they briefly remarried and divorced finally in 1976. In the same year he married his fourth wife, Mrs Susan Hunt, former wife of the racing driver James Hunt, a marriage which also ended in divorce. From the mid-1970s, his career was threatened by a serious – and admitted – drinking problem. He married fifthly in 1983, Sally Hay.

For all that, and for his appearance in many films where, without Miss Taylor, he played no less effectively than he did in the duet which seems to be the high point of his art as a film actor, it is not possible to think of Richard Burton except as a bitter loss which the theatre sustained when it could ill-afford to lose an actor of presence, personality and controlled energy. At a time when he was still developing unusual natural gifts, he all but abandoned the stage. Like Olivier an extrovert actor, brilliant in technique and with an apparently infallible instinct for theatrical effect, he never reached the summit of what promised to be a great stage career.

Like many highly intelligent actors, he had a rooted distrust as well as a love of the stage, and by the 1950s he was ready from time to time to discuss in public the possibility of a future career in which acting played no part; in 1969, for example, he talked of settling for some time to teach in Oxford with a temporary fellowship. But for all that he will be remembered as a stage actor physically and temperamentally built for great heroic and tragic roles, with the vocal range and colour (as a number of gramophone records testify) such roles demand. Together with these went a swift stage intelligence. What he achieved was both moving and powerful; it promised an unachieved greatness which must always be lamented.

Richard Burton was born on November 10, 1925. He died following a stroke on August 5, 1984, aged 58

GRETA GARBO

It seemed that nobody, in the ordinary sense of the words, knew Greta Garbo. Hers was a career of remoteness and splendour. It was half of her extraordinary quality; the other half was a beauty which exceeded the physical.

It was in the days of the silent cinema, in the 1920s, the true beginning of the adoration of stars, that her name was first heard. Her earliest films came from Sweden, and in the mid-Twenties nobody bothered much about Swedish cinema. But she had a director. Mauritz Stiller recognised something out of the ordinary in the girl who played for him in *The Atonement of Gösta Berling*, where she was pursued by wolves; and when Hollywood made advances he accepted and took her with him.

Their story becomes a version of Pygmalion. The girl bewitched the public and her first creator, overshadowed, was forgotten; he died within a few years. Garbo became a star in a way nobody is a star any longer.

"Garbo Talks!" they announced when *Anna Christie* appeared in 1930 and the fabulous husky voice was first heard. After that the famous films succeeded one another – *Queen Christina, Anna*

Karenina – and they were liked by women as much as, probably more than, by men.

Born in 1905, her real name was Greta Lovisa Gustafsson and she came of a long line of Swedish farmers. Her father died when she was 14, and she took her first job as a "soap lather girl" in a barber's shop, a common enough occupation for a young woman of the period. It was at this time that she first began dreaming of a stage career. In the summer of 1920 she went to work as an assistant at "Pub", one of Stockholm's largest department stores, and it was there, a year later, that her photogenic qualities were first discovered. She modelled hats for the store's spring catalogue of 1921. When the store decided to make a short advertising feature about women's clothes, Garbo was invited, as an afterthought, to appear in a small, semi-comic sequence to demonstrate what *not* to wear.

She appeared in several more small commercial films, and then was given a part as a bathing beauty in a cheap picture called *Peter the Tramp*, but her performance aroused little interest; so she gave up her work and became a student at the Royal Dramatic Theatre Academy. When, in 1923, Mauritz Stiller, the leading Swedish film director, asked the academy to recommend a promising young actress to him, her name was at once put forward.

The Svengali-like influence which the flamboyant Stiller is said to have had over the young girl may well have been exaggerated, but his was a dominating character. He bullied her, praised her and cajoled her. He also told her she was too fat. Shortly after his first interview with her, he chose her for a leading part in his film *The Atonement of Gösta Berling*; and made her change her name from Gustafsson to Garbo.

At this time Berlin was the centre of European film production, and Stiller took his picture and his leading lady there, where he allowed her to make *The Joyless Street*, directed by GW Pabst. Garbo played the part of a prostitute.

Her performance was far from perfect. Yet of it, James Agate wrote: "To the critical eye the hardly begun symphony of Garbo's acting is more worthwhile than any other score complete to its last double bar."

About this time, Louis B Mayer, the head of the newly formed Metro-Goldwyn-Mayer company, was in Paris, and asked to meet Stiller and see one of his films. The two sat down together to watch *The Atonement of Gösta Berling*. Opinions differ as to what happened, but the outcome was that Stiller and Garbo set out for Hollywood in July 1925. Their arrival passed almost unnoticed.

Her first film for MGM was *The Torrent*, directed by Monta Bell. Stiller was chosen to direct her second picture for MGM, *The Temptress*, but proved so difficult that he was replaced by Fred Niblo. *The Temptress* proved to be an indifferent film, but Garbo's talent was apparent and it was generally well received.

A turning point in her film career had now arrived. For her third American film, *Flesh and the Devil*, Garbo was given a new director, Clarence Brown, and a new leading man, John Gilbert. Both were destined to play an important part in her future success.

Gilbert was then a famous star, colourful and tempestuous. The two fell in love, and this undoubtedly influenced the performances which they gave in *Flesh and the Devil*. The studio publicity experts joyfully exploited the romantic aspects of the production. From then on Greta Garbo was an established star.

The coming of sound only served to enhance Garbo's career. Her first talking picture was an adaptation of the O'Neill play *Anna Christie*. Mayer, and his right-hand man, Irving Thalberg, were apprehensive and pessimistic; and they delayed Garbo's debut as a talking star for as long as possible.

Anna Christie had its New York premiere on March 14, 1930, and was immediately successful. Her first appearance in the film was in drab clothes in a dingy waterfront saloon, and her first words were "Gimme a visky" – spoken in the husky, slightly guttural voice that was to become so typical of her in the years to come. Garbo made 14 sound pictures for MGM. She never worked for any other studio in Hollywood.

She retired in 1941 after making *Two-Faced Woman*, a sad finale to her career. She was still in her prime, and yet she probably felt that she had already enriched the cinema with all she had to give. Perhaps she also felt that change was in the air, and that a harsh and realistic postwar world would produce in the cinema an era that was out of sympathy with her majestic style of acting. Asked by a reporter in 1946 what she planned to do with her life, she replied: "I have no plans. I am drifting."

For more than 40 years after her retirement she lived in a seventh-floor apartment overlooking the East River in New York, occasionally venturing out but doing her best to go unrecognised. She also kept a summer residence in Switzerland. Of her private life little emerged.

Whatever else it may or may not have been, Greta Garbo's career in Hollywood was almost perfectly managed; largely, it seems, because it was hardly managed at all. It was a sublime accident that she arrived in Hollywood just when she did, in 1926, at the psychological moment when the tango-Twenties were turning into the Charleston-Twenties. Garbo was something different: neither a vamp nor a flapper, but a pure flame of passion, enthralling in her directness and simplicity on screen.

She seemed completely unmanipulated. Of course this was not literally so: on arrival in America, she was slimmed, groomed, and had her teeth capped. But it was more than quality of personality which was at issue. Her acting was so open and uncluttered in its effects, that one seemed to be seeing a real person, without veils and equivocations, just *being* in front of the camera. The following year Gary Cooper produced exactly the same effect in *Wings*: as soon as either of them walked across the screen, everyone else in sight suddenly looked stilted and old-fashioned.

The result in Garbo's case was instant, overwhelming popularity. She was the kind of woman that other women wanted to be like, that men wanted to be passionately involved with. No doubt Garbo's studio, MGM, had its hopes, but the reality seems to have taken the studio completely by surprise. Her initially humble contract could be renegotiated; she could do more or less what she liked. She had her own ideas about that. But she really seems not to have had any overriding ambition, so it was easy for her to be strong and silent.

Laurence Olivier recalled that the only remark Garbo volunteered to him in the brief period before he was fired from playing opposite her in *Queen Christina* was: "Life's a pain anyway." A good attitude for a new star in Hollywood: like Rhett Butler, she really didn't give a damn. This meant that she assumed early on a position of unparalleled independence among Hollywood stars. By the arrival of the talkies, Garbo was recognised as the reigning goddess.

There were, perhaps, some drawbacks to being a goddess. As her career advanced through the Thirties, there were fans who remembered her in silents, and preferred her like that. She had a strong erotic dimension, as a woman capable of loving and being loved, rather than a deity to be enshrined. Those who felt a slight cooling in their attitudes to her often related it to the vexed questions of whether Garbo could *act*. The obvious answer to that is that she could act at least as well as her films ever required her to do. She or her producers had the sense to tailor the roles to her talents.

With her disappearance from the screen, her wanting to be even more alone, came the creation of a different kind of legend. As a private person she had always been mysterious: despite various rumoured love affairs she had always walked alone, and now she was to make a career of doing just that. But was that what she wanted, or were the frequent demands for privacy accidentally counterproductive? At least they brought her back in a way to where she had started in America: as a new, independent, wholly unconventional sort of woman. This time, no doubt, far fewer wished to take her exactly as a role model, but the women's movement could still respect her as an exemplar of feminine resolution and independence.

This might suggest that her example has been important to the new breed of female star which has come to prominence since the Sixties. But that would be to discount the essential uniqueness of any real star, and surely Garbo, above all.

In New York in the last days she clung to her secrecy, yet after 60 years she was still a great name. On the screen there was something elusive about her. There were deplorable performances (*Mata Hari*, for instance); yet the name is indestructible. Just by the look and the voice she could wring hearts; the cinema shrinks without her.

Greta Garbo was born on September 18, 1905. She died of pneumonia on April 15, 1990, aged 84

PAUL NEWMAN

———————•———————

Paul Newman and glamour were indivisible. It was sometimes said of him, even by those who purported to admire him, that his good looks carried him effortlessly through his screen career, without any tangible application of talent. "Handsome", and therefore "limited", were the epithets often waspishly applied to diminish his achievement when measuring it against that of other "serious" actors.

A preternaturally modest man despite his star status – "I had the privilege of doing the worst motion picture filmed during the Fifties," he recalled of his 1955 screen debut in *The Silver Chalice* – Newman was quick to agree with his critics that he was often typecast. And he springs to mind most readily through such stylishly genial romps as *Butch Cassidy and the Sundance Kid* (1969) and *The Sting* (1973) – both with Robert Redford – which nevertheless remain enduring classics of their genre.

But he was an actor of far greater variety and range than this might suggest. A New York Actors Studio-trained player, he had afterwards cut his teeth on the Broadway stage and won acclaim there. And he carried this ability to create truth to character to the 1958 screen version of Tennessee Williams's *Cat on a Hot Tin Roof*. His performance in the pool table drama *The Hustler* (1961), in which his would-be tough but youthful rookie is brilliantly cast against the icy assurance of the mature George C Scott, is remarkable in its depiction of a brittle character gradually collapsing under the unrelenting pressures of his chosen *modus vivendi*.

The sheer tour de force of his depiction of an indomitable convict in a southern country jail in *Cool Hand Luke* (1967) is a simply indelible one and as good as anything he did. In a penal establishment where he has been committed for trivial crimes, the convict Luke sustains the spirits of those who serve unending terms in a prison whose regime is one of unrelieved brutality – an injustice against which there is no appeal. None of these performances suggests a character freewheeling through the Hollywood landscape, and of them all *Cool Hand Lake* is perhaps the most memorable in the power of its protagonist to create in his fellow inmates a belief in justice for the human condition where we know that there will be none.

Newman came on the scene after the demise of the studio system that had created and supported the star system, and he was one of the few screen actors to emerge as unmistakable superstars in the grand Hollywood style. But he was well able to shape his own career. An actor who happily graduated to mature roles as he grew older, he was also a successful producer and a gifted director, able in this to build on the talents of his gifted second wife, the actress Joanna Woodward, whom he directed in a number of films. Both were political activists in the Democratic interest, and campaigned for a wide range of liberal causes.

Paul Newman was born in 1925 in Shaker Heights, Ohio, a suburb of Cleveland, where his father ran a sporting goods store. His father was Jewish and his mother came from a Roman Catholic family in what is now Slovakia, though she later converted to Christian Science.

After graduation he began his university career at Kenyon College in Ohio, but enlisted in the Navy in 1943 and did not complete his degree, in economics, until after the Second World War.

He had hoped to be a pilot but tests proved that he was colour-blind and he trained as a radioman and gunner. He served in torpedo squadrons in the Pacific and took part in the battle for Okinawa. While at university he got bitten by the acting bug, and immediately upon graduation he went straight into repertory theatre. From here he went into daytime television, and by 1953 into his first Broadway production, William Inge's *Picnic*. Playing a lesser role and understudying the lead, he was noticed and offered a Hollywood contract.

He had meanwhile married Jackie Witte and had three children, and had in his spare time enrolled as a student at the Actors Studio, then in its most famous phases as the home of the Method school. But while understudying in *Picnic* he had met another understudy,

Joanne Woodward, and after his divorce they married in 1958. This second marriage was to prove extremely important to him, professionally as well as personally. Although Newman's and Woodward's careers took off separately, they managed to play opposite each other in a succession of films, while Newman directed her in some of her best independent roles. As late as 2005 they appeared though not together, in the two-part TV spectacular *Empire Falls*.

Newman's first film role was the lead in a disastrous Roman epic called *The Silver Chalice* (1954), which brought forth misleading comparisons with Marlon Brando and nearly ended his film career at a stroke. Fortunately he was almost immediately cast in the leading role of *The Desperate Hours* on Broadway, renewed his studies at the Actors Studio, and when his next approach from Hollywood came it was far more suited to his talents. This was to play the tough street tearaway turned world middleweight boxing champion Rocky Graziano in Robert Wise's 1956 biographical film *Somebody Up There Likes Me*.

It at once established his star image, tough yet sensitive, and established him as one of the cinema's finest physical actors, superb at conveying the reality of process, in this case the fabric of a prizefighter's life. From this time on he was continuously in work, either filming in Hollywood or, especially in the early days, appearing in a number of prestigious television dramas during what in retrospect was seen as a Golden Age for the medium in America. They included Thornton Wilder's *Our Town*, with Eva Marie Saint and Frank Sinatra. He also, on occasion, returned to his first love, the stage.

In the cinema he was a startling Billy the Kid in *The Left Handed Gun* (1958), the first film directed by Arthur Penn, with whom he had worked in television. Newman's Billy was a psychological study which owed much to the Method. In that same busy year he was in *The Long Hot Summer*, a Faulkner subject in which he co-starred for the first time with Joanne Woodward, Tennessee Williams's *Cat on a Hot Tin Roof*, with Elizabeth Taylor, which brought his first Oscar nomination, and an eccentric but intermittently hilarious Leo McCarey comedy, *Rally Round the Flag, Boys*, again with Woodward.

In 1959 he was back on Broadway in the premiere of another Tennessee Williams play, *Sweet Bird of Youth* – a role he subsequently re-created, less successfully, on film.

In 1961 he played one of the key roles in his career, Fast Eddie Felson, the rebel pool-player hero of Robert Rossen's *The Hustler*. The character had all the characteristics of Newman's star persona – the irreverence, the obtrusive cool, the sheer gall that made him an idol for a disaffected younger generation, but also embodying its vulnerability, in spite of its apparent freedom of action. Two years later in *Hud*, he played the ne'er-do-well son of the new cattle country baron who gets his way with his family mainly on his insolent charm, and wins the sympathy of audiences even while kicking everyone else in the teeth.

In the mid-1960s he had another big success, as the eponymous sub-Chandler private eye in *Harper*, but in Alfred Hitchcock's patchy spy thriller *Torn Curtain* (1966) his search for psychological truth seemed to sit ill with Hitchcock's primarily mechanistic view of the world his characters inhabit.

Then came *Cool Hand Luke* and the decade ended in fine style with one of the most commercially and critically successful of all his films, George Roy Hill's *Butch Cassidy and the Sundance Kid* (1969), which created a great new double act with Robert Redford in a nicely irreverent half-comic western.

He had already made his directing debut with *Rachel, Rachel* (1968), starring Joanne Woodward in an unexpectedly gentle study of a spinster schoolteacher nearing desperation. Although hardly the sort of film audiences associated with Newman the actor (he did not appear in it himself), it was carried off with great skill and conviction.

The 1970s brought a change of image for Newman, taking him away from his insolent rebel roles and – at his own choice – more in the direction of character acting. Two of his most interesting films at this time, both directed by John Huston, *The Life and Times of Judge Roy Bean* (1972) and *The Mackintosh Man* (1973), failed to achieve the popularity they deserved. But a new teaming with Robert Redford as Chicago conmen in *The Sting* (1973) brought them both a big hit, with the likeable exuberance of its two irrepressible protagonists.

His third film as a director, *The Effect of Gamma Rays on Man-in-the-Moon Marigolds* (the second, *Sometimes a Great Notion*, was taken over from another director, and did not satisfy him) contained another superb performance from Woodward and demonstrated if anything an increase in Newman's finesse and directorial control.

Unfortunately, perhaps, Newman chose not to develop this talent much further. He directed three more films, all of them starring Woodward, but in only one of them, *Harry and Son* (1984), did he appear himself. All were praised for their direction of actors and their straightforwardly convincing realism; none received much public notice, though the last of them, the third screen adaptation of Tennessee Williams's *The Glass Menagerie* (1987), was generally accounted the best version, with Woodward particularly impressive in the role previously played by Gertrude Lawrence and Katharine Hepburn.

After *The Sting* and his next film, *The Towering Inferno* (1974), a superior disaster movie which saw nearly a dozen stars variously involved in a flaming skyscraper (and being killed off in reverse billing order), Newman was at the peak of his career. As he progressed through his fifties, he continued to develop as a character player. While he continued to make relatively uncomplicated star vehicles such as *The Drowning Pool* and *Slap Shot*, where he played such traditional iconic roles as a detective or a sportsman, he also, always a knowing selector of directorial potential, began to work with such emergent talents as Robert Altman, in *Buffalo Bill and the Indians* (1976) and *Quintet* (1979), and the Merchant Ivory team, in *Mr and Mrs Bridge*. But among the best of his later performances was the alcoholic lawyer in Sidney Lumet's *The Verdict* (1982).

As time went on he had the good sense to work with, and sometimes play second fiddle to, the new generation of stars. In Martin Scorsese's *The Color of Money* (1986), supporting Tom Cruise, he reprised his character Fast Eddie Felson from *The Hustler* and after several near misses he finally won an Oscar.

In Sam Mendes's gangster drama, *Road to Perdition* (2002), he played a Chicago gang boss to Tom Hanks's hitman and was Oscar-nominated yet again. He was then 77 and it was his final film role. Few Hollywood superstars coped with advancing years so gracefully, and perhaps none managed to remain, according to his female fans at least, so irresistibly sexy.

In 2003 he was back on the Broadway stage in a revival of Wilder's *Our Town*, this time in Frank Sinatra's role of the stage manager, but he announced his retirement from acting four years later.

Away from screen and stage Newman launched a range of food products, Newman's Own, including salad dressing, pasta sauce, lemonade and popcorn, donating all the profits to charity. One of his pet projects was a summer camp for seriously ill children. He was also a motorsport enthusiast who successfully competed in races until he was well past 70. A liberal in politics, he was a prominent supporter of the Democratic Party, and in 1978 was appointed by President Jimmy Carter as a US delegate to the UN Conference on Nuclear Disarmament.

Paul Newman's career was symptomatic of an important change of emphasis in Hollywood during the later 1950s and 1960s. He developed from a star on a traditional model – though a particularly compelling one – into an actor of stature, an astute businessman and a director of considerable talent – an all-round creator in a cinema which required its idols to fend for themselves, create and control their own image without the assistance of a paternalistic studio. That he managed this so well was a tribute to his force of personality, but also to qualities which marked him as a specifically modern figure in an American film industry otherwise living too much, too blindly, on the relics of a vanished past.

He is survived by Joanne Woodward, and their three daughters, as well as by two children of his first marriage to Jackie Witte (1949–58). His son with Witte, Scott Newman, an actor, died from an accidental drug overdose in 1978.

Paul Newman was born on January 26, 1925. He died of cancer on September 26, 2008, aged 83

Paul Newman

INDEX

Peck, Gregory 118, 120, 140, 180, 208–213
Pei-pei, Cheng 251–253
Poitier, Sidney 48, 56–60, 321

Reed, Oliver 12, 102–106, 124, 125
Reynolds, Burt 10, 30–37
Robinson, Edward G 8, 176, 200–202, 246
Russell, Jane 8, 331–334

Sellers, Peter 26, 314, 328–330
Seymour Hoffman, Philip 384–387
Sharif, Omar 178–182
Smith, Maggie 293–301, 316, 369
Stewart, James 8, 10, 11, 35, 118, 119, 302–306, 319
Sutherland, Donald 86–90

Taylor, Elizabeth 8, 10, 95, 164–173, 326, 389, 390, 391, 399
Temple, Shirley 24, 108, 165, 183–188, 339
Tracy, Spencer 108, 137, 144–147, 167, 316, 318, 319, 323

Wayne, John 11, 12, 80–82, 133, 137, 174, 186, 303, 321, 373
Welles, Orson 10, 104, 119, 150, 201, 379–383
West, Mae 347–349, 352
Wilder, Gene 59, 64–69, 115
Williams, Robin 241, 260–265
Windsor, Barbara 10, 38–43

PHOTO CREDITS

Front cover (Marilyn Monroe): Moviestore Collection Ltd / Alamy Stock Photo

Back cover, left **(Sidney Poitier):** Keystone Press / Alamy Stock Photo

Back cover, middle **(Ingrid Bergman):** Getty Archive Photos / Stringer

Back cover, right **(Philip Seymour Hoffman):** J. Vespa / Getty Images

Page 23 (Sean Connery): Julian Herbert / Times Newspapers Ltd

Page 24 (Gina Lollobrigida): E Webb / Times Newspapers Ltd

Page 30 (Burt Reynolds): Associated Press / Alamy Stock Photo

Page 38 (Barbara Windsor): Pictorial Press Ltd / Alamy Stock Photo

Page 44 (Tony Curtis): Trinity Mirror / Mirrorpix / Alamy Stock Photo

Page 50 (Gene Hackman): Vera Anderson / Getty Images

Page 56 (Sidney Poitier): Keystone Press / Alamy Stock Photo

Page 61 (Marilyn Monroe): Pictorial Press Ltd / Alamy Stock Photo

Page 64 (Gene Wilder): R. Diamond / Getty Images

Page 70 (Rex Harrison): Julian Herbert / Times Newspapers Ltd

Page 74 (Jerry Lewis): Keystone Press / Alamy Stock Photo

Page 80 (John Wayne): Pictorial Press Ltd / Alamy Stock Photo

Page 83 (Grace Kelly): Allstar Picture Library Ltd / Alamy Stock Photo

Page 86 (Donald Sutherland): Simon Walker / Times Newspapers Ltd

Page 91 (Errol Flynn): Everett Collection Inc / Alamy Stock Photo

Page 94 (Carrie Fisher): Francis Specker / Alamy Stock Photo

Page 101 (Humphrey Bogart): Masheter Movie Archive / Alamy Stock Photo

Page 102 (Oliver Reed): Chris Ware / Stringer

Page 107 (Doris Day): PictureLux / The Hollywood Archive / Alamy Stock Photo

Page 114 (Marty Feldman): Rolf Adlercreutz / Alamy Stock Photo

Page 116 (Charlton Heston): Tom Dixon / Times Newspapers Ltd

Page 122 (Glenda Jackson): Independent / Alamy Stock Photo

Page 129 (Kirk Douglas): Graham Wood / Times Newspapers Ltd

Page 136 (Lee Marvin): Associated Press / Alamy Stock Photo

Page 139 (Ingrid Bergman): Archive Photos / Stringer

Page 144 (Spencer Tracy): Glasshouse Images / Alamy Stock Photo

Page 148 (Rita Hayworth): Alfred Harris

Page 151 (Stan Laurel): Everett Collection Inc / Alamy Stock Photo

Page 153 (Irrfan Khan): ZUMA Press, Inc. / Alamy Stock Photo

Page 157 (Jean Harlow): Allstar Picture Library Ltd / Alamy Stock Photo

Page 159 (Dennis Hopper): Chris Harris / Times Newspapers Ltd

Page 173 (Elizabeth Taylor): Daily Sketch / Times Newspapers Ltd

Page 177 (Steve McQueen): James Drake / Getty Images

Page 178 (Omar Sharif): Harry Kerr / Times Newspapers Ltd

Page 183 (Shirley Temple): Victor Blackman / Stringer

Page 189 (Danny Kaye): Chris Sanderson / Times Newspapers Ltd

Page 199 (Alec Guinness): Allan Ballard / Times Newspapers Ltd

Page 200 (Edward G Robinson): Allstar Picture Library Limited /
Alamy Stock Photo

Page 207 (Audrey Hepburn): ScreenProd / Photononstop /
Alamy Stock Photo

Page 213 (Gregory Peck): Allstar Picture Library Ltd /
Alamy Stock Photo

Page 214 (Gene Kelly): Horace Tonge / Times Newspaper Ltd

Page 219 (Vivien Leigh): RGR Collection / Alamy Stock Photo

Page 223 (Clark Gable): RBM Vintage Images / Alamy Stock Photo

Page 229 (Fred Astaire): Allstar Picture Library Limited /
Alamy Stock Photo

Page 230 (Leslie Nielsen): Paul Harris / Getty Images

Page 234 (Ava Gardner): Pictorial Press Ltd / Alamy Stock Photo

Page 237 (William Hurt): UPI / Alamy Stock Photo

Page 242 (Richard Attenborough): Jon Voos / Times Newspapers Ltd

Page 251 (Cheng Pei-pei): Associated Press / Alamy Stock Photo

Page 259 (John Hurt): Crispin Rodwell / Times Newspapers Ltd

Page 265 (Robin Williams): Associated Press / Alamy Stock Photo

Page 266 (Charlie Chaplin): GL Archive / Alamy Stock Photo

Page 273 (Lauren Bacall): Everett Collection Inc / Alamy Stock Photo

Page 279 (Peter O'Toole): Steven Markeson / Times Newspapers Ltd

Page 286 (Marlon Brando): Kelvin Brodie / Times Newspapers Ltd

Page 293 (Maggie Smith): Roy Cuckow / Times Newspapers Ltd

Page 302 (James Stewart): Associated Press / Alamy Stock Photo

Page 307 (Bette Davis): Everett Collection Inc / Alamy Stock Photo

Page 312 (David Niven): United Archives GmbH / Alamy Stock Photo

Page 316 (Katharine Hepburn): Michael Gough / Times Newspapers Ltd

Page 327 (Celia Johnson): Daily Herald Archive / Getty Images

Page 328 (Peter Sellers): Times Newspapers Ltd

Page 331 (Jane Russell): J.H.Smith / Times Newspapers Ltd

Page 335 (Betty Grable): Album / Alamy Stock Photo

Page 341 (Judy Garland): IanDagnall Computing /
Alamy Stock Photo

Page 342 (James Earl Jones): The Washington Post / Getty Images

Page 347 (Mae West): Pictorial Press Ltd / Alamy Stock Photo

Page 350 (Cary Grant): Times Newspapers Ltd

Page 355 (Gracie Fields): Chris Davies / Times Newspapers Ltd

Page 360 (James Mason): Kelvin Brodie / Times Newspapers Ltd

Page 363 (Joan Crawford): Everett Collection Inc / Alamy Stock Photo

Page 366 (Noël Coward): Pictorial Press Ltd / Alamy Stock Photo

Page 375 (Robert Mitchum): Pictorial Press Ltd / Alamy Stock Photo

Page 376 (Bill Cobbs): UPI / Alamy Stock Photo

Page 383 (Orson Welles): Archive PL / Alamy Stock Photo

Page 384 (Philip Seymour Hoffman): J. Vespa / Getty Images

Page 388 (Richard Burton): Allstar Picture Library Ltd /
Alamy Stock Photo

Page 392 (Greta Garbo): cineclassico / Alamy Stock Photo

Page 403 (Paul Newman): Harry Kerr / Times Newspapers Ltd